ork Times.

THE WEATHER.

Unsettled Tuesday; Wednesday, fair, cooler; moderate southerly winds, becoming variable.

[For the weather report see Page 23

1912—TWENTY-FOUR PAGES,

ONE CENT   In Greater New York, Jersey City, and Newark.   Elsewhere, TWO CENTS

AFTER HITTING ICEBERG;
A, PROBABLY 1250 PERISH;
YBE, NOTED NAMES MISSING

Biggest Liner Plunge to the Bottom at 2:20 A. M.

RESCUERS THERE TOO LAT

Except to Pick Up the Few Hundreds Who Took to the Lifeboats.

WOMEN AND CHILDREN FIRS

Cunarder Carpathia Rushing New York with the Survivors.

SEA SEARCH FOR OTHER

The Californie Stands By on Chance of Picking Up Other Boats or Rafts.

OLYMPIC SENDS THE NEW

Only Ship to Flash Wireless Messages to Shore After the Disaster.

ed Out of Belfast Harbor.

LATER REPORT SAVES 866.

BOSTON, April 15.—A wireless message picked up late to-night, relayed from the Olympic, says that the Carpathia is on her way to New York with 866 passengers from the steamer Titanic aboard.

TITANIC LIVES

Also by Richard Davenport-Hines

Dudley Docker
Sex, Death and Punishment
The Macmillans
Glaxo
Vice
Auden
Gothic
The Pursuit of Oblivion
A Night at the Majestic
Ettie
(Edited) *Hugh Trevor-Roper's Letters From Oxford*
(Edited) *Hugh Trevor-Roper's War Journals*

RICHARD
DAVENPORT-HINES

Titanic Lives

Migrants and Millionaires,
Conmen and Crew

Harper
Press

HarperPress
An imprint of HarperCollins*Publishers*
77–85 Fulham Palace Road,
Hammersmith, London W6 8JB
www.harpercollins.co.uk

Published by HarperPress in 2012

2

Hardback endpapers image:
New York Times reports loss of Titanic © Bettmann/CORBIS

A catalogue record for this book is available from the British Library

ISBN 978-0-00-7 32164-3 (HB)
ISBN 978-0-00-7 43122-9 (TPB)

Set in Minion by Palimpsest Book Production Limited,
Falkirk, Stirlingshire

Printed and bound in Great Britain by Clays Ltd, St Ives plc

*For Patric Dickinson and David Kynaston
and for the gentle memory of Cosmo Davenport-Hines*

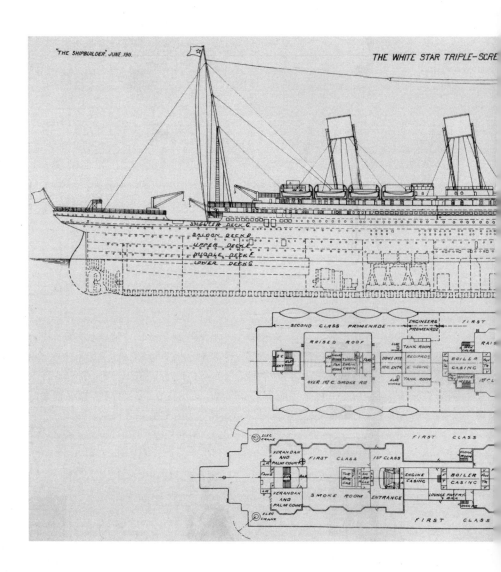

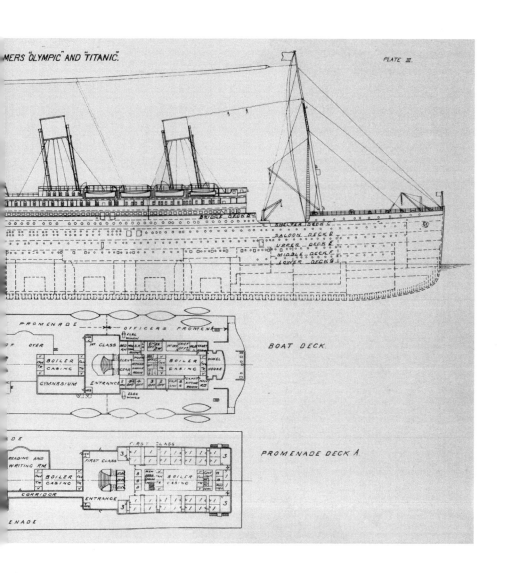

BOAT DECK.

PROMENADE DECK A.

CONTENTS

LIST OF ILLUSTRATIONS

Plan of *Olympic* and *Titanic*, reproduced on pp. vi–vii. © *SSPL via Getty Images*

Harland & Wolff hull-drawing office. © *National Museums Northern Ireland / Collection Harland & Wolff, Ulster Folk & Transport Museum*

Gantry over the building berth for *Titanic* and *Olympic*. © *National Museums Northern Ireland / Collection Harland & Wolff, Ulster Folk & Transport Museum*

Shipyard workers disembarking from *Olympic*. © *National Museums Northern Ireland / Collection Harland & Wolff, Ulster Folk & Transport Museum*

Captain Smith and Lord Pirrie on *Olympic*, 1911. © *Southampton City Council, Arts & Heritage*

Lord Pirrie and Bruce Ismay inspecting the hull. © *National Museums Northern Ireland / Collection Harland & Wolff, Ulster Folk & Transport Museum*

Titanic being escorted by tugs through Belfast Lough. © *National Museums Northern Ireland / Collection Harland & Wolff, Ulster Folk & Transport Museum*

Titanic pulling away from White Star dock, Southampton. © *National Museums Northern Ireland / Collection Ulster Folk & Transport Museum*

First-class Café Parisien on B Deck, March 1912. © *National Museums Northern Ireland / Collection Harland & Wolff, Ulster Folk & Transport Museum*

First class parlour suite 'B59', March 1912. © *National Museums Northern Ireland / Collection Harland & Wolff, Ulster Folk & Transport Museum*

Crowds waiting to embark at White Star Wharf, Queenstown. © *The Irish Picture Library/Father FM Browne SJ Collection*

Murdoch and Lightoller seen from the tender at Queenstown, 11 April 1912. *Courtesy Southampton City Council, Arts & Heritage*

Looking up from the tender, with Captain Smith and passengers gazing down. © *The Irish Picture Library / Father FM Browne SJ Collection*

Titanic's first-class gymnasium. © *The Irish Picture Library / Father FM Browne SJ Collection*

The promenade deck. © *The Irish Picture Library / Father FM Browne SJ Collection*

Second-class passengers on the boat deck. © *Irish Examiner*

Lifeboat 14 under Lowe towing Collapsible D. *Courtesy Southampton City Council, Arts & Heritage*

Crowds outside White Star offices. © *Southampton City Council, Arts & Heritage*

Survivor Samuel Rule talking to his brother at Plymouth. © *Southampton City Council, Arts & Heritage*

Able seaman Horswill, possibly with a cheque for Lifeboat 1. © *Southampton City Council, Arts & Heritage*

Crew arrive at Southampton, April 29. © *Southampton City Council, Arts & Heritage*

White Star company men enter St Mary's Church. © *Southampton City Council, Arts & Heritage*

Corpse of a *Titanic* victim onboard rescue vessel *Minia*. *Courtesy Nova Scotia Archives*

From Greenland's Icy Mountains

Its most striking feature was the stillness – and deadness – and impassability of this new world: ice, and rock, and water surrounded us; not a sound of any kind interrupted the silence; the sea did not break upon the shore; no bird or any living thing was visible; the midnight sun – by this time muffled in a transparent mist – shed an awful, mysterious lustre on glacier and mountain; no atom of vegetation gave token of the earth's vitality; a universal numbness and dumbness seemed to pervade the solitude.

Marquess of Dufferin and Ava, *Letters from High Latitudes*

There were no witnesses. It didn't look like a moment from history. A great block of ice broke off the end of a glacier, and crashed down into a fjord with a rumbling roar. Probably it was the Jakobshavn glacier, the source of most of the world's largest icebergs. A hundred years ago Jakobshavn was the fastest-moving glacier in the world, pushing down from the ice cap at the rate of 65 feet a day, until it reached the west coast of Greenland. About 10 per cent of all Greenland icebergs have split – or 'calved' – from the end of Jakobshavn. After they have wrenched away from the glacier, itself made of densely compacted snow which fell on the Arctic ice cap thousands of years earlier, icebergs rock and tilt on the water until finally they settle into balance.

Although there is a human settlement at Jakobshavn, Greenland is an inhuman landscape of neverending wastes. One cannot hope for mercy from the elements in this savage land of lifeless gloom.

Long, dark, freezing winters are followed by brief, colourful summers – so bright that Matthew Henson, the black American who accompanied Robert Peary to the North Pole in 1909, found summer midnight in Greenland's ice-bound wilderness as bright as dusk in New York on the 4th of July. The land belongs to polar bears, reindeer, musk oxen, wolves, arctic foxes and mountain hares. White-tailed eagles rule the skies, especially near Cape Farewell; black ravens are ubiquitous with their croaking; guillemots and ptarmigans are hunted as food; stiff-winged gliding petrels, snow buntings and peregrine falcons abound. There are fish, and walruses, but until recently no pleasure-seekers in the fjord. In such a wilderness of primeval rocks and eternal ice was launched the iceberg that made history.

Since 2000 the tongue of Jakobshavn glacier has retreated at an alarming rate from the coast, and the ice flow behind has sped up. Jakobshavn, indeed, is one of the great loci of global crisis. Nowadays 35 billion tonnes of iceberg calve from the glacier each year and float oceanwards down the fjord. Only about one-eighth of an iceberg is visible above water: the submerged seven-eighths can be so deep that icebergs get wedged on the floor of the fjord, and remain jammed there until broken by the weight of other icebergs smashing onto them from the glacier. As they are largely submerged, the drift of icebergs is governed by current and little affected by wind.

Some icebergs from Iceland are carried by the east Greenland current round Cape Farewell, where they join thousands of other icebergs from the western glaciers and together sweep into Baffin Bay. There they are taken by the Labrador Current, which carries them southwards towards the Grand Banks of Newfoundland. Many icebergs run aground on the coast of Labrador or on the northern part of the Banks and there disintegrate. The first appear near the Grand Banks about the beginning of March – 'cold monsters that are so beautiful to look at and so dangerous to touch', in the words of a Cunard captain on the North Atlantic run.[1] By the end of June they have ceased. During a normal year some 300 to 350 icebergs drift south of Newfoundland, and about fifty are borne south of the

Grand Banks. Short of bombardment there is no means to destroy an iceberg except by waiting for it to melt. The largest of them drift 2,500 miles before they dwindle away in the sun around Latitude 40. From the bridge of a liner on a clear day a large iceberg can be seen at 16 to 20 miles distance. In bright sunshine it appears as a luminous white mass. In dense fog its sombre bulk is undetectable at more than a hundred yards. On a fogless night without a moon an iceberg would be visible at a quarter of a mile, but in moonlight it might be seen at a distance of several miles.

Field ice – great sheets of ice piled on one another by wind and currents – is formed on salt water. It is practically impassable, and a ship caught by it will have difficulty getting free without damage. Field ice drifts out of the Arctic all year long, is carried south by the Labrador Current and supplemented by coastal ice. Often it runs ashore in bays along its route. It is susceptible to wind, unlike icebergs, and by early February of each year covers much of the Grand Banks of Newfoundland. There it drifts at the mercy of winds and currents until it melts. It is hard to detect at much distance, especially by night; but can be spotted by a flickering luminosity in the sky called 'ice blink'.

The Arctic winter of 1911–12 was exceptionally mild. This accelerated the calving of icebergs from glaciers jutting over Greenland's west coast. The icebergs were larger than usual, which meant that they took longer to melt as they drifted southwards. In April 1912 there was therefore more ice than usual floating in the Atlantic, and it was further south than usual, too. During the previous months of February and March, violent storms had pounded the Newfoundland side of the north Atlantic. The 3,000-ton sealing ship *Erna* vanished with thirty-seven souls; a schooner, *Maggie*, struggled for two months to cross from Portugal to Newfoundland until – battered, leaking, and with one crewman dead – it was crushed in the ice pack. By early April the tempests had abated, but the North Atlantic was strewn with spars, planks, and lost cargo. Over a thousand icebergs had drifted to the eastern edge of the Grand Banks off Newfoundland where for years at a time it had been rare to see an iceberg. As the

Labrador Current sent these icebergs southwards, a sheet of pack ice, a hundred miles square, went with them. In mild weather, icebergs may split apart, with sharp reports, creating large lumps of ice called 'growlers'. But in April 1912 the biggest bergs did not split into growlers. Instead, these hard, implacable masses headed at the rate of 25 miles a day towards the shipping lanes of the North Atlantic.

PART ONE

Embarkation

One of the most difficult – strictly speaking, impossible – things for historians to recapture is a sense of what people did not *know at the time.*

Timothy Garton Ash, *Facts are Subversive*

ONE

Boarding

'A seaport without the sea's terrors, an ocean approach within the threshold of land' . . . Enemies or tourists, missionaries or immigrants, they all entered or left land here, and in some other age their phantoms are still processing along Southampton Water.

Philip Hoare, *Spike Island*

In 1901, H. G. Wells likened the urban poor to an iceberg with much of its rock-hard bulk lurking under the surface: 'the "submerged" portion of the social body, a leaderless, aimless multitude of people drifting down towards the abyss'.[1] This submerged mass of the poor had accumulated from across the world: their recruitment accelerating as spreading railway and steamship routes more easily carried migrants from remote fastnesses to great cities. If the iceberg was a metaphor, the great modern liner was a paradigm of Western society – 'a monstrous floating Babylon', wrote one of the *Titanic* passengers during its maiden voyage.[2] G. K. Chesterton made a similar analogy between modern liners and the society that built them. 'Our whole civilization is indeed very like the *Titanic*; alike in its power and its impotence, its security and its insecurity,' he wrote after the ship's loss. 'There was no sort of sane proportion between the extent of the provision for luxury and levity, and the extent of the provision for need and desperation. The scheme did far too much for prosperity and far too little for distress – just like the modern State.'[3]

Over eighty years later the paradigm was sharpened into class war. James Cameron's film *Titanic* diabolized rich Americans and educated

English, anathematizing their emotional restraint, good tailoring, punctilious manners and grammatical training, while it made romantic heroes of the poor Irish and the unlettered. If Cameron's film had caricatured the poor as it did the rich there would have been an outcry. Instead Jiang Zemin, the President of China, hailed the film as a parable of class warfare, in which 'the third-class passengers (the proletariat) struggle valiantly against the ship's crew (craven capitalist lapdogs and stooges)'. He urged fellow Marxists to see the film and study its depiction of money and class. Similarly, Serge July, editor of *Libération*, told his fellow French *Marxisants* that the film represented the suicide in mid-Atlantic of a society divided by class rather than a sinking ship.[4]

Class demarcations on ocean steamers were based on hard money rather than notions of social justice. The German-American Edward Steiner described how, after a mid-ocean storm in 1906, seasick third-class Atlantic passengers sidled from the hold looking shaken, pale and unkempt. On deck they made a diverting spectacle for richer voyagers who, from their spacious upper deck, looked down on them 'in pity and dismay, getting some sport from throwing sweetmeats and pennies among the hopeless-looking mass' of emigrants who wanted to be accepted as Americans. 'This practice of looking down into the steerage holds all the pleasures of a slumming expedition with none of its hazards of contamination,' Steiner continued, 'for the barriers which keep the classes apart on a modern ocean liner are as rigid as in the most stratified society, and nowhere else are they more artificial or more obtrusive. A matter of twenty dollars lifts a man into a cabin passenger or condemns him to the steerage; gives him the chance to be clean, to breathe pure air, to sleep on spotless linen and to be served courteously; or to be pushed into a dark hold where soap and water are luxuries, where bread is heavy and soggy, meat without savour and service without courtesy. The matter of twenty dollars makes one man a menace to be examined every day, driven up and down slippery stairs and exposed to the winds and waves; but makes of the other man a pet, to be coddled, fed on delicacies, guarded against draughts, lifted from deck to deck, and nursed with gentle care.'[5]

For the millionaires on board, but also for surprising numbers of the poorest passengers, an Atlantic crossing was a regular round-trip which they made twice or more a year. For many others, though, it was momentous. An ocean voyage separates and estranges. People are parted, sorrowfully or cheerily, as it may be, with hope, regret or relief. At departure some think only of their next reunion, and others are set on a lifelong repudiation. There are times when leave-takings open chasms. US immigration laws stipulated that passengers of different classes must be separated on liners by locked metal barriers to limit their supposed power to spread contagion, but some obstacles between the classes were more insurmountable even than barred gates. Money made the difference. Contrast the contents of the pockets of two *Titanic* corpses recovered from the ocean: John Jacob Astor IV ('Colonel Jack'), the richest man on board, had $4,000 in sodden notes in his pockets; but the jacket of Vassilios Katavelas, a nineteen-year-old Greek farm worker, had more meagre treasures: a pocket mirror, a comb, a purse containing 10 cents and a train ticket to Milwaukee.

The White Star Line, which operated the liner, promoted its leviathans as expressions of racial supremacy, for this was an epoch when Africans and Asians were customarily described as 'subject races'. 'The *Olympic* and *Titanic*,' declared the owners, 'are not only the largest vessels in the World; they represent the highest attainments in Naval Architecture and Marine Engineering; they stand for the pre-eminence of the Anglo-Saxon race on the Ocean.' Both liners 'will rank high in the achievements of the twentieth century'.[6] Such clamorous confidence was soon to seem like deadly hubris.

Southampton, on England's south coast, was White Star Line's new port for its New York service. When Alfred the Great was king of the Anglo-Saxons in the ninth century, Southampton was his harbour. After the Norman Conquest in 1066, Southampton became a vital port between the duchy of Normandy and the kingdom of England. Roman barges, plague ships, merchant vessels, troop ships, Sir Francis Drake's *Golden Hind* bringing Spanish gold to Queen Elizabeth – they all used Southampton harbour. After 1750,

Southampton was developed as a smart spa town: spacious Georgian stucco terraces were built, and pretty villas studded the surrounding countryside. In 1815 the first steamship came to Southampton, and in 1839 the railway to London was opened.

It was not until 1892, when the London & South Western Railway (L&SWR) bought the Southampton Dock Company for £1,360,000, that the port mounted its challenge on Liverpool. Southampton held an advantage with which Liverpool could not vie: a double tide caused by the way that the Isle of Wight juts into the English Channel and diverts ebb tides. Norddeutscher-Lloyd and Hamburg-Amerika steamships already stopped at Southampton, as they plied the emigrant traffic between Germany and the United States, but it was an auspicious day when, in 1893, the liner *New York*, owned by the American financier John Pierpont Morgan, docked at Southampton, where its passengers were carried away on the South Western Railway. By 1895 the railway company had invested £2 million in the port, through which passenger traffic had risen by 71 per cent. Norddeutscher-Lloyd then built three ocean greyhounds, *Kaiser Wilhelm der Grosse* (1897), *Kronprinz Wilhelm* (1901) and *Kaiser Wilhelm II* (1903), while Hamburg-Amerika's *Deutschland* (1900) held the Blue Riband, for the swiftest North Atlantic crossings in three consecutive years (at an average speed exceeding 23 knots). First-class passengers, especially rich Americans, became disinclined to make the railway journey to Liverpool, for embarkation on Cunard or White Star liners, when from London they could reach more readily the swift German steamships halting at Southampton.

In 1907 White Star withdrew its Atlantic liner service from Liverpool and inaugurated a new outward service from Southampton to New York, via Cherbourg in Normandy and Queenstown, Ireland, with a return service calling at Plymouth rather than Queenstown. A director of White Star, Lord Pirrie, became a director of L&SWR to ensure that relations between the two companies were lubricated by trusty cooperation. To meet White Star's needs, the railwaymen erected a passenger and cargo shed at Southampton, 700 feet long, with passenger gantries for passengers to embark on *Olympic* and

Titanic. It was said that 'what Brighton is to London for pleasure, Southampton will be to London for business'. Other railwaymen called it 'London-super-Mare'.[7]

But by 1911–12, Southampton's prosperity was faltering. Seamen and ships' firemen had long been pitied by trade unionists as the most downtrodden of workers. In 1911 they struck for higher wages, and after tense weeks in which money was short in Southampton, the shipowners yielded to the strikers' demands. This outcome encouraged dockers to strike several weeks later, and in August two men were shot dead when the army was used to quell riots in Liverpool docks. Later that month, during the first ever national railway strike, two further men were shot dead by soldiers during rioting. On 1 March 1912, continuing the unrest, 850,000 coal miners struck for a minimum wage. Once the mines shut, another 1,300,000 iron and steel workers, seamen and others were thrown out of work. Despite the government introducing minimum-wage legislation, the strike had its own stubborn impetus and was not settled until 6 April. This left insufficient time for newly mined coal to reach Southampton and be loaded into *Titanic*'s bunkers, and 4,427 tons of coal had to be transferred from other liners lying at the quayside.

The gross tonnage of the *Titanic* was 46,328 tons. It measured 882 feet long and 92 feet wide. Its eight decks reached the height of eleven storeys. The top of the captain's quarters was 105 feet above the bottom of the keel. Three million rivets held its hull together. The ship's three propellers were each the size of windmills. Its steel rudder, weighing 101 tons, was 78¾ feet high. Its three anchors weighed a total of 31 tons. Its four funnels (one of them a dummy, added for aesthetic balance) were 22 feet in diameter and rose 81 feet above the boat deck. With such proportions a high crane, movable along the side of the liner on rails set into the concrete quay, was needed to lower cargo into the ship's hold long before passengers arrived.

The freight laden into *Titanic*'s holds resembled the twentieth-century equivalent of the luxuries pictured in John Masefield's poem

'Cargoes', with its Spanish galleon carrying rare gems and tropical spices and its quinquireme from Nineveh rowing across the Mediterranean bearing its treasure of ivory and peacocks. Precious stones sent from Antwerp alone were insured for nearly £50,000. One diamond merchant lost stock insured for £18,000 when the ship went down: 'a North Atlantic liner, freighted with millionaires and their wives, is a little diamond mine in itself'.[8] A consignment of ostrich plumes valued at £10,000 was also carried.[9] There was a red 25-horsepower Renault motor car, and high-class package freight such as velvet, cognac and other liqueurs, cartons of books, as well as fine foods such as shelled walnuts, olive oil, anchovies, cheese, vinegar, jam, mushrooms, and goods like goat skins and jute bagging. Some 3,435 bags of mail were loaded at Southampton: business letters, of course, but equally precious to the recipients, letters going to migrants' homes and boarding houses, from Finland, Sweden, Italy, Greece, Lebanon and the rest, bringing their treasures of memory and love from the old country. There were thousands of registered packets. Joseph Conrad has posted the manuscript of his story 'Karain' to his New York admirer John Quinn, one of those American collectors who rifled Europe for rarities to hoard in their private troves. 'Karain' was lost in the sinking, together with a seal ring belonging to the Irish dramatist Lady Gregory. Fortunately, Conrad had sent the manuscript of 'The Secret Agent' to Quinn by an earlier ship. *Titanic* was also carrying a rare copy of the *Rubáiyát of Omar Khayyám* in a unique jewel-studded binding by the English binders Sangorski and Sutcliffe. A Colorado mining millionairess, Margaret Brown, who made a late booking on *Titanic*, travelled with three crates containing architectural models of the ruins of ancient Rome, which she intended to give to Denver Art Museum.

It was providential that there were not more grievous, irreplaceable losses. When *Titanic* sailed, many European art rarities were in packing cases awaiting their final far migration to a New York millionaire's show place on Madison Avenue. The US Revenue Act of 1897 had imposed a 20 per cent tariff on imported works of art destined for private homes. As a result, collectors like Pierpont Morgan had for fifteen years kept their acquisitions in London or Paris. But the balance of tax advantages had recently shifted. In the United States, partly at Quinn's instigation, the Payne-Aldrich tariff act of 1909 repealed the import duty on art works; while in Britain, Lloyd George's 'People's Budget' raised the level of death duties. Morgan's aversion to paying tax spurred him to order the transfer of his London collection to New York – despite Lloyd George issuing an official statement in January 1912: 'Mr Pierpont Morgan's art treasures would not be liable to death duties in England unless they were to be sold.'[10] That January, to the consternation of English cognoscenti, Morgan's paintings, furniture, miniatures, silver, sculpture, bronzes, ivories, majolica, enamels, porcelain and jewellery began to be packed for transatlantic shipment. The princely house in Kensington which served as a show case for his collection – 'it looks like a pawnbroker's shop for Croesuses',[11] the connoisseur Bernard Berenson observed – was given over to packers, hammerers and carters. Pierpont Morgan felt that the ships of the White Star Line, which he owned, had an inviolable safety record, and insisted that his precious rarities were carried on its vessels. White Star liners conveyed Morgan's first packing cases across the Atlantic in February, but in March shipments had to be suspended for lack of an official who was required by pettifogging US customs regulations to monitor the packing. By this chance not a particle of Morgan's collection was shipped on *Titanic*.

Most *Titanic* passengers reached Southampton from Waterloo station in London. Cart-horses were still used for haulage in the capital, and society women maintained carriages for the fashionable throng in Hyde Park, but a whirligig of motor cars, taxis, vans and buses had set about exterminating the old, slow horse-drawn traffic. The stench of exhaust fumes stifled passers-by, reverberations from motors cracked ceilings in the best districts, the sound of engines quelled conversation, chauffeurs with goggles and peaked caps were superseding liveried coachmen in cockades. There had been many types of horse-drawn vehicles – the brougham, cabriolet, landau and phaeton among others – and now there were new brand names to be mouthed by votaries of the cult of speed: De Dion-Bouton,

Panhard-Levassor, Delaunay-Belleville, Lozier, Winton Bullet, Stoddard-Dayton, Pierce-Arrow, Pope-Toledo, Hispano-Suiza, Siddeley-Deasy. Such were the steeds carrying *Titanic* passengers to Waterloo.

E. M. Forster wrote in 1910 of 'the poised chaos of Waterloo'.[12] The station was being rebuilt so as to provide one of the world's largest passenger concourses. A wide roof of glass and steel – soaring high so that the smoke from the engines might disperse – would protect passengers from rain, wind and cold. From the concourse, which would provide twenty-three gated platforms, strange new-fangled moving stairways called escalators were to take travellers down to the infernal tunnels of the underground railway system. The rebuilding was incomplete in 1912, and the new glazed roof stopped short: high girders jutted into mid-air; a jumble of smutty old office buildings awaited demolition; travellers could see timber roof beams and blackened smoke troughs in the remains of the old Victorian station. The station buffet still disappointed famished travellers with its dusty cakes and fossilized sandwiches. The ticket office remained a place where during busy rushes one could lose precious minutes as well as shillings. Porters' trolleys piled with trunks weaved between the crowds. The station, recalled a railway historian, had a pervasive odour compounded of 'empty loose-lid milk-churns, horses, Welsh coal and oil lamps, the London and South-Western smell'.[13] It was a distinctive sooty smell which stretched halfway to Southampton, said Sinclair Lewis.[14] Before the departure of the *Titanic* train, there was an extra ingredient in the Waterloo medley: 'camera fiends', as one of the first-class passengers had called them, *paparazzi* as they are called now, edging up the platform to take 'snapshots' of eminent men like John Jacob Astor.[15]

The design, compartmentalization and pricing of British railways were permeated by class demarcations. Class-feeling was innate and inexorable, as an Anglican clergyman demonstrated in 1912 when he protested at the Great Western Railway's proposal to abolish first-class carriages on short runs: 'this forcing [of] passengers accustomed to live in sweet and wholesome surroundings to herd with the unwashed and, very often, strongly malodorous things that one meets in a third-class compartment, is nothing less than an outrage'.[16] Carriages were divided into small compartments, and classed as first, second or third class. Amenities varied between companies. The South Eastern Railway, which had bought Folkestone harbour as early as 1842 and served the cross-Channel ferries, followed the European mainland practice of providing pleasant second-class carriages and rough, rackety third-class. South Eastern was thought to be working well when its rolling stock left Victoria Station with third-class passengers packed as tight as anchovies in a tin, crushed in sweaty promiscuity, with everybody trying to read a crumpled copy of *Pearson's Weekly* with someone else's elbow in their face.

London & South Western provided less brutalizing third-class carriages, sombrely decorated in red, black and chocolate, while their second-class carriages had golden-brown plush seats, well stuffed and sprung, edged with Grecian frets in black and gold lace. There was a folding elbow rest in the middle of each row of second-class seats, thus providing four seats as against five in third-class. London & South Western carriages allotted a yard-wide seat to each first-class passenger: two seats (covered in blue cloth with gold lacing) faced one another in each compartment, and the luggage racks were gilded. Passengers could lounge, if they wished, as if they were in a club. Americans were accustomed to undivided railway carriages, where they could gaze down long aisles studying their fellow passengers, and found it odd of the privacy-conscious English to seclude them-selves in separate compartments. The black and white photographs, with coloured-in details, of picturesque scenery like Bedruthan Steps or Boscastle harbour, which were framed above the seats, seemed quaint to travellers from the great republic.

On the morning of 10 April 1912 the Southampton boat-train left Waterloo station with a roar at 7.30, jolted over Vauxhall points and clanked towards Southampton docks. Just as the carriages were divided by class, so were the houses and towns on the journey. At first the train rolled along the lines on which weary, resigned commuters paid their daily tax of time as they travelled to and from London. The tight terraced houses of inner London with cindery sunless backyards yielded to tidy red-bricked suburban villas with ripening spring gardens. Then the boat-train reached the countryside. At a prudent distance from the rattle and smoke of the railway, the country houses of Surrey stood in pleasances and parklands. One of them, Polesden Lacey, had been bought by Sir Clinton Dawkins, the financier who had clinched the deal whereby Pierpont Morgan's Wall Street firm won control of the White Star Line. After Dawkins had been worked to death by Morgan, a new owner employed the architects of the Ritz Hotel, Charles-Frédéric Mewès and Arthur Davis, to refit the interior. Polesden Lacey became a sumptuous display of Edwardian opulence and the material expression of the Edwardian spirit. Mewès and Davis were specialists, too, in designing first-class accommodation for Atlantic liners.

One can conjure the different walks of the embarking passengers at Southampton. The measured, steady treads; the hasty, bustling steps; the erect high-stepping of the proud or confident; the mournful plod; the skipping gait; the insolent slouch; a whistling saunter; the ruffled and huffy; the furtive types who sidled, the men who walked like panthers, the others who shambled like defeated men. The hats, too: Colonel Astor's immaculately balanced bowler, trilbies worn cavalierly askew, sporting ulsters with black and white checks, flat caps jammed down on poor men's heads. Women's headwear, too, was an always precise indication of their social status. There were gradations down from women with the latest Paris hats on their head, and the freshest New York scandal on their tongues, to peasant women in shawls whose knowledge of the world was hardly longer than the shadow of their village steeple.

Four hundred and twenty-seven first- and second-class passengers boarded at Southampton with eager unclouded anticipation of the pleasures of White Star's newest and finest equipage. They foresaw feasts, games and indiscretions ahead; they had presentiments of shipboard friendships, but none of death. There were 495 third-class passengers – many of them creased and dishevelled migrants with their bundles – boarding by a different walkway. Nikola Lulic, who boarded in Southampton, had crossed the Atlantic at least twice before. A Croat villager, he had deserted from the Austrian army in 1902, or else had absconded to avoid military conscription, and went to work as a miner in Chisholm, Minnesota. On *Titanic* he acted as interpreter and chaperone to a dozen other Croats who boarded with him at Southampton, and to others who embarked at Cherbourg: few had crossed the Atlantic before.

On the morning of departure, many of the 'black gang' – *Titanic*'s stokers and trimmers – went ashore for a last crawl through the dock pubs in Canute Road and Platform Road. A fireman called John Podesta later described how he and William Nutbean started drinking in the Newcastle Hotel before proceeding to a pub called the Grapes, where they met three of their shipmates – brothers called Bertram, Tom and Alfred Slade. At 11.50 they left the Grapes for the docks, and were walking towards *Titanic* when a passenger train trundled along the lines towards them. Podesta and Nutbean darted in front, and reached the vessel in good time by noon. But the Slades hung back, as did stokers Shaw and Holden, and trimmer Brewer. It proved a long train, and though they sprinted towards *Titanic*, the gangway was already being swung aside. They called to be let on board, gesticulated and argued, but Sixth Officer Moody, in charge of the gangway, decided that they were unreliable, and summoned a standby crew: Richard Hosgood, Alfred Geer, Harry Witt, Leonard Kinsella, and men called Lloyd and Black. The six stand-ins all died five days later. Podesta and Nutbean survived.

Ships' names signify. In 1913 King George V vetoed the suggestion of the First Lord of the Admiralty, Winston Churchill, that a newly commissioned battleship should be named in commemoration of an English statesman, *Pitt*. 'The name *Pitt* is neither euphonious nor dignified,' the King thought. 'There is moreover always the danger of the men giving the Ship nicknames of ill-conditioned words rhyming with it.'[17] No-one could make rude rhymes out of *Titanic*. It was, however, a word that resounded for Churchill – a word, he thought, that encapsulated the Edwardian epoch. 'The wonderful century which followed the battle of Waterloo and the downfall of the Napoleonic domination, which secured to this small island so long and so resplendent a reign, has come to an end,' Churchill declared in 1909. 'We have arrived at a new time. Let us realize it. And with that new time strange methods, huge forces, larger combinations – a Titanic world – have sprung up around us.'[18]

The words 'Titanic grandeur' seemed synonyms to Edith Wharton in 1910.[19] Everyone felt the impregnable modernity of the White Star liner's name. 'The *Titanic* was indeed a Titan,' a Cunard officer reflected when White Star launched its new liner. 'The very name of this gigantic new ship had a fascination. It was a masterstroke of nomenclature . . . She would be the superb, the supreme liner. Her name, like that of HMS *Dreadnought*, was an inspiration expressing the confidence of a seafaring folk at the zenith of power.'[20] To the French, too, 'this *Titanic* seemed invulnerable, the most formidable affirmation of modern power. It was the most gigantic liner that had been seen afloat since the beginning of the world. It belonged to the world's most admired maritime nation. It was equipped with the latest refinements of science and civilisation.'[21]

In 1914, Hugo Hirst, chief of the General Electrical Company in Britain, addressed a meeting of Cambridge undergraduates. 'You cannot think of the greatness of America without at once bringing to your mind the names of Morgan, Rockefeller, Vanderbilt, Carnegie,' he declared. 'You cannot think of Germany without conjuring up the titanic figures of Krupp or Ballin, Rathenau or Henkel-Donnersmark; and it is these men, these captains of industry, men who turn hundreds of thousands of unskilled labourers into skilled workmen for the benefit of their country, who add to the strength and power, the prosperity and dignity, of the modern State.'[22]

This book is about the ship that Pierpont Morgan owned and 'the titanic figures', as Hirst called them, who were the industrial and financial rulers of the great republic; but it is also about the hundreds of thousands of labourers who were needed in the mines, factories, work gangs, sweat shops and street trades of Europe and America – and the thousands of craftsmen, mechanics, engineers and people with skilled trades, too.

A white marble monument stands in Áyos Sóstis, the village in Messinia province from which young farm worker Vassilios Katavelas and another man, Panagiotis Lymperopoulus, originated. It is inscribed in both Greek and English:

IN MEMORY OF THE FOUR HELLENES VICTIMS OF THE 1912 TITANIC TRAGERTY [sic] WHO WERE SEEKING ECONOMIC OPPORTUNITY IN THE USA FOR THEMSELVES AND FOR THEIR FAMILIES.*

The Áyos Sóstis monument also bears four words of Pittakos, from 650 BC: 'Reliable land, treacherous sea.' Men's control, as Byron wrote, stops with the shore; but on board the largest ship in the world, named *Titanic*, it was easy to forget the primitive, witless, impersonal, annihilating power of the ocean. A man going to sea in a small boat may make mistakes and drown, Chesterton moralized after *Titanic* sank, 'but, cautious or reckless, drunk or sober, he cannot forget that he is in a boat and that a boat is as dangerous a beast as a wild horse'. But a ship so large that it resembles a spa hotel can make its passengers oblivious of the ocean's dangers. 'An aristocrat on board ship who travels with a garage for his motor almost feels as if he was travelling with the trees of his park. People living in open-air cafés sprinkled with liqueurs and ices get as far from the thought of any revolt of the elements as they are from that of an earthquake under the Hotel Cecil.'[23]

---

*The two other Greek victims were brothers, Apostolos and Dimitrios Chronopoulus, labourers in their twenties.

TWO

Speed

God of Speed, who makes the fire –
God of Peace, who lulls the same –
God who gives the fierce desire,
Lust for blood as fierce as flame.
Julian Grenfell, 'To a black greyhound'

Titanic cast off at noon on Wednesday 10 April. Eager sightseers lined the vantage points, and cheered or waved handkerchiefs as in spring sunshine the stately vessel was guided seawards by six tugs.[1] Because of a coal strike, a small armada lay in Southampton docks in enforced idleness – tied side by side as there were insufficient berths for them all. As tugs guided *Titanic* through a narrow channel, the huge backwash of water churned by its starboard propeller sucked the American liner *New York* from its moorings. *New York*'s ropes tautened, then snapped one by one, making a noise like a series of gunshots, and the ship's stern swung adrift towards *Titanic*. By the quick action of a tug which threw a line to *New York*'s stern, a collision was averted.

Titanic continued at half-speed down Southampton Water, with its low, swampy western shore, edged into the Solent, the waterway separating Hampshire from the Isle of Wight, then increased speed and walloped its way through the waves eastwards towards France. In the previous summer, when *Olympic* left on its maiden voyage, a throng of holidaymakers had lined the rails of Cowes promenade to watch it pass, but this was a blustery April morning, better suited to flying kites than lazing in the sun, and there were scant bystanders as the great ship passed Cowes. The summer resort looked bedraggled and desolate in April: it was weeks before the summer season when Punch would thwack Judy on the beach, and cocky young clerks in blazers would strut along the front. As *Titanic* passed the Isle of Wight, a second-class passenger, widower Lawrence Beesley, sat down to write a letter to his young son. 'The ship is like a palace. There is an uninterrupted deck-run of 165 yards for exercise and a ripping swimming-bath, gymnasium and squash racket court & huge lounge & surrounding verandas. My cabin is ripping, hot & cold water and a very comfy looking bed & plenty of room.'[2]

Titanic steamed past Ryde, the Isle of Wight resort with its half-mile long pier, where the military fort had been converted into a park for holidaymakers, with tennis lawns and bowling greens laid out among ramparts, bastions and gun emplacements. At Ryde, white-walled houses rose in tiers up the steep hillside embowered with lilacs and laburnums sporting their spring buds. Many of these squat semi-detached boxes bore signs in their front windows announcing rooms to let for summer visitors. As Henry James noted when he visited nearby Ventnor, the boxes stood in serried rows with the resplendent surnames of noble families painted upon their gate posts: Plantagenet, Percival, Montgomery, Montmorency made fine names for boarding houses. Even on seaside holidays it was impossible to escape from class-consciousness and pretension.

As *Titanic* passed along the Isle of Wight, a few hardy families playing on the sands interrupted their games and swivelled their eyes; cottagers craned their heads out of upstairs windows; coastguards trained their telescopes from cliff-tops – and all of them, a few days later, and to the end of the lives, remembered that they had once, briefly, glimpsed the doomed leviathan. 'The *Titanic*,' a county historian recorded, 'was a palace of light and life and wonder. She was the greatest ship that ever sailed the seas. She was the greatest thing that was ever made by the hands of men. 60,000 tons moved away when the *Titanic* floated upon the sea . . . her engines had the power of 46,000 horses. Every two minutes her fires consumed a ton of coal. She was the last-made wonder of the world.'[3]

It was about 80 miles – taking four hours – to the roadstead off Cherbourg, where *Titanic* dropped anchor around 6.30 p.m. As dusk fell, embarking passengers were ferried out to *Titanic* on two tenders, *Traffic* for steerage passengers and *Nomadic* for the others. Thirteen first-class and seven second-class passengers left *Titanic* on *Nomadic*. Cargo went ashore, too, including two bicycles belonging to an army major, and a canary consigned by a Lincolnshire man named Meanwell, who had paid five shillings as its fare.

At Cherbourg, 142 first-class, 30 second-class and 102 third-class passengers came aboard – most of them having travelled on the special *Train transatlantique*, which had left Paris earlier that morning. In Zola's railway novel *La bête humaine* (1890) there is an American businessman whose job takes him from New York to Paris, via Le Havre, every three weeks, based no doubt on a real-life commuter whose journey was thought extreme but feasible;[4] and there were businessmen who traversed the ocean several times a year. Some first-class passengers embarking at Cherbourg were returning from Egypt: the Jack Astors of New York, Margaret Brown, and Emil Brandeis, who ran the men's goods department in the great store founded by his father in Omaha, Nebraska. Other first-class ticket holders came from Paris. The couturier Lady Duff Gordon had a shop there, and was hastening across the Atlantic because of a summons from her New York branch. Martin Rothschild, a New York clothes manufacturer (and uncle of the satirist Dorothy Parker), had been inspecting Paris fashion houses. Charlotte Drake Cardeza, a textile and insurance heiress from Germantown, Pennsylvania, came aboard with her adult son, his valet, her maid, fourteen trunks, four suitcases and three crates, which suggests that she had splurged in the Paris dress shops.

Third-class passengers embarking at Cherbourg doubtless recognized from each other's bearing that they shared similar hopes and had survived similar deprivations. Many of them were economic migrants, aspiring to prosperity, who recognized the kinship of each other's experiences and ambitions even if they had never met before. Boarding an Atlantic liner was only the middle phase of a longer journey. Vassilios Katavelas, for instance, had travelled from Áyos Sóstis in the Peloponnese to the port of Piraeus, and thence by ship across the Mediterranean to Marseille, and finally by train via Paris to Cherbourg. *Titanic*, he expected, would carry him from Cherbourg towards New York and then Milwaukee. He and Panagiotis Lymperopoulus met two fellow Greeks on their journey. They had taken the first available transatlantic steerage berths, which turned out to be (doubtless to their agreeable surprise) on *Titanic*. Katavelas's *Titanic* ticket cost £7 4s 6d (half the price of Lawrence Beesley's second-class ticket and a tiny fraction of £512, which was what Charlotte Cardeza and her son had each paid for their tickets). None of the Greeks survived. Other voyagers were as much political or religious refugees as economic migrants. Eighty-one third-class passengers and two second-class passengers were listed as 'Syrians' in *Titanic*'s rosters. Almost all were Lebanese Christians, who had embarked at Cherbourg. Syria had been an exploited province of the Ottoman Turkish Empire since 1516, but grew increasingly restive after the Turkish revolution of 1908 overthrew the Sultan. The ancient kingdom of Armenia had also been tyrannized for centuries by the Turkish sultans, and its population intermittently massacred. Over a dozen Armenians, who like the Lebanese were seeking safe asylum as much as economic advantages, had also embarked at Cherbourg.

The ship raised its great anchor around 8 o'clock in the evening, but its outline remained clear to those on land, for lights gleamed from its portholes like a galaxy of stars, and lamps shone from its masthead. A first-class passenger recorded his first days at sea:

> This, indeed, is the one great impression I received on my first trip on the *Titanic* – and everyone with whom I spoke shared it – her wonderful steadiness. Were it not for the brisk breeze blowing along the decks, one would scarcely have imagined that every hour found us some 20 knots further upon our course . . . The lordly contempt

of the *Titanic* for anything less than a hurricane seemed most marvellous and comforting. But other things besides her steadiness filled us with wonder. Deck over deck and apartment after apartment lent their deceitful aid to persuade us that instead of being on the sea we were still on *terra firma*. It is useless for me to attempt a description of the wonders of the saloon – the smoking-room with its inlaid mother-of-pearl – the lounge with its green velvet and dull polished oak – the reading room with its marble fireplace and deep soft chairs and rich carpet of old rose hue – all these things have been told over and over again, and lose in the telling. So vast was it all that, after several hours on board, some of us were still uncertain of our way about – though with commendable alacrity some 325 found their way to the great dining saloon at 7.30 when the bugle sounded the call to dinner. After dinner, as we sat in the beautiful lounge listening to the White Star orchestra playing 'The Tales of Hoffman' and 'Cavalleria Rusticana' selections, more than once we heard the remark, 'You would never imagine you were on board a ship.' Still harder was it to believe that on the top deck it was blowing a gale, but we had to go to bed. Then the morning plunge in the great swimming bath, where the ceaseless ripple of the tepid sea-water was almost the only indication that somewhere in the distance 72,000 horses in the guise of steam engines fretted and strained under the skilled guidance of the engineers, and after the plunge, a half-hour in the gymnasium helped to send one's blood coursing freely, and created a big appetite for the morning meal.[5]

Big appetites were satisfied on *Titanic*. Here is the first-class breakfast menu for the morning of Thursday 11 April:

Baked Apples	Fresh fruit	Stewed Prunes
Quaker Oats	Boiled Hominy	Puffed Rice
Fresh Herrings	Finnan Haddock	Smoked Salmon
Grilled Mutton, Kidneys and Bacon	Grilled Sausage Grilled Ham	Lamb Collops Vegetable Stew

Fried, Shirred, Plain and Tomato Sirloin Steak &		
Poached	Omelettes to Order	Mutton Chops to
& Boiled Eggs	Cold Meat	Order
Mashed, Sauté	Vienna & Graham Rolls	Soda & Sultana
and Jacket Potatoes	Corn Bread	Scones
Buckwheat Cakes	Blackcurrant Jam	Narbonne Honey
Oxford Marmalade	Watercress	

This was an age, evidently, that cherished luxury, but it admired spartan values, too. Western culture in 1912 provided an emotional environment where taking risks, to the edge of physical extinction, was a point of honour. Men were always on the dare: they admired military bravado and its civilian equivalent, imprudence. In retrospect, it seems an age of warmongers. Frederick Scott Oliver was a draper, a business partner in the great Oxford Street store of Debenham & Freebody, providing soft silks, pretty textiles, mantles and millinery to home-makers and beauties. To him, England seemed enervated, flabby and doomed: he was roaring for a fight. '*Nothing* will save us except the sight of red blood running pretty freely,' he had written to his friend Lord Milner at the time of *Titanic*'s launch. 'Whether British *and* German blood, or only British, I don't know – nor do I think it much matters. "Blood" is the only necessity.'[6]

Shipyards have never been soft places, like draperies, but *Titanic* had been built in the most violent shipyard in the world. An MP in the House of Commons claimed months after *Titanic*'s maiden voyage that a Catholic workman at Harland & Wolff had been stripped naked and roasted over a furnace until rescued by co-religionists brandishing sledge hammers and threatening to smash the skulls of his Protestant attackers. This story was denied, which did nothing to undermine its currency among those who wished to believe it. A few years earlier, when a Harland & Wolff worker was elected to the Commons, his supporters sang 'Derry Walls', a militant Protestant song celebrating the defeat of a Catholic king in a long, fearful siege of 1689:

The blood it did flow in crimson streams
Through many a winter's night
They knew the Lord was on their side
To help them in the fight.

This was an age when violence was considered by many to be virtuous.

'The world's splendour has been enriched by a new beauty: the beauty of speed,' declared Marinetti's Futurist Manifesto published three years before *Titanic* was launched. Speed was hailed as the chief weapon that modern civilization had added to the armoury of human pleasures. 'We will sing of the fervid night-time vibrations of armaments factories, and shipyards blazing with violent electric moons; gluttonous railway stations devouring smoke-plumed serpents; factories hung from the clouds by their crooked trailing smoke; bridges that leap rivers like giant gymnasts, and blind the watcher with reflective flashes of harsh sunlight; bold steamers sniffing the horizon; broad-chested locomotives whose wheels paw the tracks like the hooves of vast steel horses bridled by tubing; and the sleek flight of aircraft whose propellers turn like banners in the wind.'[7] In the seven days after *Titanic* left Southampton, the American Harriet Quimby became the first woman to pilot an aircraft across the English Channel, Prince Scipione Borghese, who had already raced across Mongolia in a fast car, gave a press interview on his projected Peking to Paris air flight, and two aeronauts who flew out of Hendon in a race to Dublin both crashed and died.[8]

Moneyed men and women expected that their conveniences would be fast. The rich confirmed or cancelled their *Titanic* cabin reservations in the final days before the voyage if not at the last minute. Headlong changes of travel plans were signs of wealth; it proved one's power to have sudden impulses as suddenly fulfilled. Instantaneous satisfaction of needs or whims became a measure of value if not the hallmark of quality. Immediacy was a keynote of the Edwardian mood. There was an impatience that had been unknown twenty years earlier. Undoubtedly the helter-skelter of the times was accentuated by the telephone. 'The mistress of the house has all her local tradesmen, all the great London shops, the circulating library, the theatre box-office, the post-office and cab-rank, the nurses' institute and the doctor, within reach of her hand,' wrote H. G. Wells. 'The businessman may sit at home in his library and bargain, discuss, promise, hint, threaten, tell such lies as he dare not write, and, in fact, do everything that once demanded a personal encounter.'[9] There were telephones in all first-class cabins on *Titanic*: several liners had arrangements whereby as soon as they docked, the on-board telephones were connected to the land system so that millionaires could begin ringing their brokers, lawyers and butlers.

It was apt that American millionaires loved speed: the word had once been a synonym for success and good fortune. Henry Clay Frick, Pittsburgh's Coke King, who cancelled his reservations on *Titanic's* maiden voyage, was eulogized in terms that stand for his class: 'His real hobby was speed, terrific speed, which came as a reaction from years of patient drudgery and as the revival of the impatience of an inherently eager disposition. Motoring he found delightfully exhilarating unless hampered by road regulation, to which ultimately, after securing the most expertly daring chauffeur to be found in France, he paid little heed. Nevertheless, with the multiplication of cars, came more and more "jams" and hateful "crawling along" until finally automobiling, as a pastime, was perforce abandoned.'[10] In 1910 Frick sent his chauffeur for aviation lessons, and ordered him to buy a good flying-machine, as he was 'sick' of motoring between New York City and the Myopia country club at South Hamilton, Massachusetts.[11] This was the sort of speeding millionaire for whom *Titanic* was built.

John Jacob Astor IV was one of the first Americans to buy a motor car, had eighteen vehicles in his garage and, like Frick, felt more real and alive when bucketing along the roads with dauntless celerity. Once, bedecked in train-driver's overalls, he drove a steam engine at full tilt drawing a coach filled with millionaires. He was avid to hear the latest exploits of dashing young William K. Vanderbilt II, nephew of a man initially booked on *Titanic*, who in quick succession, with the wild hurry of the aimless, was thrown from his Renault when it crashed at 60 mph; scattered a hundred hapless spectators perched on wooden crates with one nonchalant twist of his steering-wheel at the start of the Madrid to Paris motor race; fired his revolver at Provençal *paysans* who tried to lash him with whips when he almost smashed their cart by reckless speeding; and drove one mile in 39 seconds at Ormond Beach, Florida. Several *Titanic* passengers were car-mad or speed-crazed. Algernon Barkworth, heir to a Hull shipping fortune, was proclaiming the need for better English roads at the moment when *Titanic* met its iceberg. Another passenger who boarded *Titanic* at Southampton was Washington Roebling II, heir to a New Jersey engineering fortune. The designer of the Roebling-Planché racing car, in which he finished second in the Vanderbilt Cup Race in 1910, he had just completed a motoring tour of Europe, no doubt at breakneck speed, in his new Fiat. The Michigan industrialist Dickinson Bishop, who boarded at Cherbourg with his nineteen-year-old bride, was to be met in New York by his newly bought Lozier, the most expensive line of cars then made in the United States, with new models priced at $7,750. In 1914, speeding after a dance at the Bishops' country club, his car slammed into a tree, catapulting Helen Dickinson onto a sidewalk, fracturing her skull, and inducing epilepsy which killed her two years later.

Contempt, too, was basic to this world – not just the contempt of a Vanderbilt for peasants on their cart or gawpers on upturned boxes. Everywhere it seemed people were loftily insistent on their superiority while disdaining others' inferiority. Few people bothered to notice the true value of others and behave accordingly. In Belfast a touchy group of bank clerks moved out of their boarding house when another lodger wearing workman's clothes used the front door. They valued their dignity so highly because they paid so little for their rooms: they had little else to value except appearances. The low mechanic whom they despised eventually took control of the shipyard that built *Titanic*: he became Viscount Pirrie, Knight of St Patrick, Privy Counsellor, but remained so gnawed by false appearances that he lost a fortune living in a showy style which he could not afford. Several dozen Cornish miners travelling second-class on *Titanic* were heading for the Houghton County copper belt in Michigan. At sea or on land, above ground or hundreds of feet below, they would never think of talking or eating with the trammers – lowly Finns and Swedes who, once the miners had broken the rock face, loaded the minerals onto mining-cars, hauled them to the shaft, lugged back timber and rails for new levels. Insecurity, scorn and subordination were the psychological mainsprings of the *Titanic* era. People flinched from one another as upstarts, pretenders and failures. Andrew Carnegie, the Steel King, derided Pierpont Morgan, whose company owned *Titanic*, because he left only $68,300,000: 'to think he was not a rich man'.[12]

'A wonderfully quick trip,' wrote Edith Wharton after crossing first-class on a liner from New York to Cherbourg with over a thousand other souls: 'Literally not a human being on board with whom to exchange a word.'[13] An American patrician, drawing her money from inherited landholdings, Wharton deplored 'the innumerable army of American businessmen – the sallow, undersized, lack-lustre drudges who have never lifted their heads from the ledger'.[14] A salaried pen-pusher of undiluted Yankee stock deprecated Peter Widener, the richest man in Philadelphia, whose son and grandson died with *Titanic*, because his grandparents were German emigrants. This fight for rank was humanity's version of the farmyard pecking order: the merchant despised the pence-pinching shopkeeper, who frowned on the sordid publican, who looked down on the crafty farmer, who exploited the labourer tied to his toil. Most of them, in their way, were mad about the main chance, but could not afford to recognize what they shared.

Titanic, after it sank, was the cynosure of envious eyes: its doom aroused malicious satisfaction as well as horror. It was packed with millionaires, who provoked envy and awe, and migrants who aroused envy and contempt. The Atlantic people traffic was one long story of human denigration. In the turn-of-the-century prairie town of Galesburg, Illinois a Jewish immigrant was called a 'sheeny', a Swede a 'snorky', a Yankee a 'skinflint', Italians were 'dagoes', Germans were 'Dutch', Irish were 'micks', and Blacks were 'niggers' or 'smokes'. 'When you hated or wanted to be mean you said, "goddam mick" or "goddam nigger",' recalled the writer Carl Sandburg, 'but if they called us "goddam snorkies" . . . then we would look for bricks to heave'.[15] A university professor wrote in 1914 that 'Steerage passengers from a Naples boat show a distressing frequency of low foreheads, open mouths, weak chins, poor features, skew faces, small or knobby crania, and backless heads'.[16] He dismissed 'the lower class' of east European Jewish migrants as 'moral cripples' who 'smirk and cringe and trick' once they reach America: 'they rapidly push up into a position of prosperous parasitism, leaving scorn and curses in their wake'.[17]

This was a merciless, bloodthirsty and speed-crazed epoch; but in Edwardian England people were enjoined by their churches to be unselfish, and taught that the mere raw fact of being alive was less important than being seen to behave well. A month before *Titanic* sank, an episode during Robert Scott's expedition to the South Pole encapsulated the prevalent morality of masculine self-denial. Young Lawrence Oates, who was incapable of further marching because of frostbite and gangrene in his feet, left the other men in their tent and crawled into an Antarctic blizzard of −40° Centigrade. 'We knew that poor Oates was walking to his death,' Scott confided to his diary, 'we knew it was the act of a brave man and an English gentleman.' Rather than denounce Oates as a suicide, clergymen preached sermons lauding his courage in choosing death in the pitiless white blizzard in the hope of saving his companions. 'Captain Oates,' declaimed Lord Curzon of Kedleston, 'the Eton boy, the cavalry officer, the South African hero, the English gentleman. Does history contain a finer picture than this young fellow, only thirty-two years old – exactly the same age as Sir Philip Sidney at Zutphen – walking out of the tent in the shrieking snowstorm to give up his life for his friends?'[18] Oates's sacrifice saved no-one: Scott and his men starved and froze to death.[19]

J. M. Barrie's play *Peter Pan*, from its opening night at Christmas 1904, and his subsequent novel, *Peter and Wendy* (1911), proved an enduring tale of Edwardian desires, fears and ideals. Its gentle heroes contrast with the pirate crew commanded by Captain Hook, a debonair Old Etonian who is mortified by dirty ruffs and never more dangerous than when being silkily polite. 'There is a touch of the feminine in Hook, as in all the greatest pirates,' says Barrie's stage direction. Hook agonizes over 'good form', which he fetishizes, and 'bad form', which he abominates. In the duel scene of the novel, flagging in his sword-fight with Peter Pan, Hook craves one last satisfaction: to see Peter Pan betray himself with 'bad form'. As Peter Pan closes on him, Hook springs onto the bulwarks, and looking over his shoulder at Peter, gestures at him to use his foot and not his sword. Peter kicks instead of stabbing: Hook gets the boon for which he yearned. 'Bad form!' he jeers as he goes content to the open-jawed crocodile.[20] Another resonant line closes the scene in which Peter goes to Tiger Lily's rescue. 'To die,' Peter says in a shaky voice, 'will be an awfully big adventure.' Barrie's friend, the American impresario Charles Frohman, was so permeated by the *Peter Pan* spirit that he too, like Hook, was thinking of good form – manly nonchalance – in the moments before he died. 'To die will be an awfully big adventure,' Frohman murmured just before he plunged to his death when *Lusitania* sank in the Atlantic in 1915.

In another scene, Hook ordains that the children must walk the plank, and calls for silence so that Wendy ('with noble calmness') can steady them. 'I have a message to you from your real mothers,' says Wendy, 'and it is this, "We hope our sons will die like English gentlemen".' The boys avow in quavering voices that they will do what their mothers hope. National stereotypes are powerfully enforcing. Thomas Andrews, designer of *Titanic*, helping to launch its lifeboats, was a real-man's Wendy as he steadied scurrying passengers on deck, 'Now, men, remember you are Englishmen: women and children first.'[21]

Whether one behaves in a crisis like a calm hero or a frantic coward often depends on how much time one has to think. If the danger is sudden and intense, people often lose all self-mastery. This was demonstrated in the swift blazing horror at a La Charité Maternelle bazaar held in a wooden hall by the Champs Elysées in Paris on 4 May 1897. A spirit lamp kindled to light a cinema projector set the gimcrack edifice afire. All was of flimsy, flammable materials, with draperies and canvas covering the woodwork, and the stalls heaped with dresses, millinery and pretty combustible toys. Within a few minutes the roof was blazing, and its flaming fragments falling on the *beau monde*. 'It all came upon them so suddenly, and passed so quickly, for the crowded hundreds of people gasping and struggling or fainting beneath a roof of flame, enclosed between flaming walls, pelted with a shower of flaming scraps and tatters, encountering their fellow creatures whose burning dresses carried the same danger to every neighbour in the shrieking, screaming mob of women.'[22] The best-known fatality was the Duchesse d'Alençon, a Bavarian princess, and sister of both the Empress of Austria and the Queen of Naples. Of 130 people burnt to death, 123 were women (mostly of the upper classes), although about 200 men had been present, including the Papal Nuncio, the Duc d'Alençon, the Marquis de Lubersac, and the fashionable clubman Henry Blount. Loyal to their false conventions, newspapers lauded male heroism, but the truth is that most men fled, pushing, kicking and punching their way through the crowd, flailing out with their sticks rather than selflessly standing back.

Equally, if one has too long to brood on one's desperate situation, selfless restraints collapse. On 1 March 1942, after the surrender of British Malaya, the Dutch steamer *Rooseboom*, carrying 500 mainly British evacuees to safety in Ceylon, was torpedoed by a Japanese submarine off the coast of Sumatra. The sequel made the awkwardness in *Titanic*'s lifeboats seem regulated and considerate. Walter Gibson, a soldier in the Argyll and Sutherland Highlanders, recorded that eighty survivors were crammed in one lifeboat, where five soldiers (led by a Liverpudlian) banded together – cutting the throat of one young soldier with a jagged bully-beef tin so as to slake their thirst by drinking his blood, killing and jettisoning twenty weak survivors – until themselves hurled overboard by the majority. 'Three, as they came to the surface, got their hands to the gunwale and tried to drag themselves back. It was a confusion of pleadings and curses and choking half-smothered obscenities. Relentlessly we battered at their fingers with the rowlocks. We were down to the elemental now.' Others in the lifeboat were driven by hunger and thirst to end their suffering by jumping overboard, though they hated the thought that others might survive conditions which had broken them. 'That was a strange feature of every suicide,' Gibson wrote. 'As people decided to jump overboard, they seemed to resent the fact that others were being left with a chance of safety. They would try to seize the rations and fling them overboard. They would try to make their last action in the boat the pulling of the bung which would let in the water. Their madness always seemed to take the form that they must not go alone, but must take everyone with them.'[23]

This violence was the product of tropical heat and thirst, but also of war's destruction of accepted rules, and of the cruel prolongation of the calamity, which induced the wild brooding that destroys restraint and self-respect. It was not only the *Rooseboom* suicides who had different codes of life from Lawrence Oates: everywhere there were men who would never see dying as an art, a Christian virtue, an act of class affirmation or a gesture of self-respect. Not everyone wished to die like English gentlemen or treat death as an awfully big adventure. Eddie Ryan, a young labourer travelling to his sister in Troy, New York, with the hope of finding work as a chauffeur, wrote to his parents in Tipperary describing how he had inveigled his way into a lifeboat by throwing a towel over his head so as to pass as a woman, and his parents gave the letter to the *Cork Examiner* to publish.[24] When an officer ordered the men out of Lifeboat 13, Daniel Buckley from Kingwilliamstown in County Cork kept his place when a female first-class passenger threw her shawl over him and later gladly told of the woman's resourceful subterfuge.

Ryan and Buckley were among 113 third-class passengers who boarded *Titanic* in Ireland. The liner dropped its anchor off Queenstown, the great sheltered harbour on the south coast of County Cork, at 11.30 p.m. on Thursday 11 April. 'The coast of Ireland looked very beautiful as we approached Queenstown Harbour, the brilliant morning sun showing up the green hillsides and picking out groups of dwellings dotted here and there above the rugged grey cliffs that fringed the coast,' recalled schoolmaster Lawrence Beesley. 'We took on board our pilot, ran slowly towards the harbour with the sounding-line dropping all the time, and came to a stop well out to sea, with our screws churning up the bottom, and turning the sea all brown with sand from below.'[25] Queenstown had been a port of call for White Star's Atlantic steamers since the 1870s. For over a century it was a great staging-post for emigrants: 30,000 Irish people emigrated to America in 1912 alone. Two paddle steamers, *America* and *Ireland*, brought out 1,385 mail bags to *Titanic*, and 120 passengers, including three first-class and four second-class. Seven passengers disembarked, including a Jesuit priest, Francis Browne, who took the last photographs of *Titanic* as it steamed away.

Later, when the liner was at the bottom of the Atlantic and over a thousand people had perished, many saw its collision as emblematic of the coming cultural crash. John Thayer junior ('Jack'), a teenage *Titanic* survivor who was traumatized by his ordeal, wrote in 1940 that until the catastrophe, 'the world had an even tenor to its ways. True enough, from time to time, there were catastrophes like the Johnstown Flood, the San Francisco earthquake, or floods in China – which stirred the sleeping world, but not enough to keep it from resuming its slumber.' The *Titanic* disaster shocked the world awake, 'keeping it moving at a rapidly accelerating pace ever since, with less and less peace, satisfaction and happiness . . . To my mind, the world of today awoke April 15, 1912.'[26] Sir Osbert Sitwell, too, recalling the Edwardian swansong before the Great War, saw the sinking as 'a symbol of the approaching fate of Western Civilization'.[27]

At 1.30 *Titanic* cast off from its Queenstown moorings, and steamed out into the Atlantic carrying 1,320 passengers, a total of 2,235 souls including crew; 3,435 bags of mail, 6,000 tons of coal, 900 tons of baggage and freight. 'In our wake soared and screamed hundreds of gulls, which had quarrelled and fought over the remnants of lunch pouring out of the waste pipes as we lay-to in the harbour entrance; and now they followed us in the expectation of further spoil,' Beesley noted. 'The gulls were still behind us when night fell, and still they screamed and dipped down into the broad wake of foam which we left behind.'[28] Fishermen were out in small boats that afternoon, and fish slithered in the nets, floundering and entangled, as the great ship sailed past. Later, some of the Irish emigrants gathered at the stern for their final glimpse before Ireland disappeared beneath the horizon. Eugene Daly, a twenty-nine-year-old farm labourer from Athlone, played 'Erin's Lament' on his uilleann pipes. The most terrible wreck in the history of shipping was four days off. Thousands of miles to the west a shape of ice drifted southwards from Greenland's icy mountains.

THREE

Shipowners

Middle-class people these, bankers very likely, not wholly
Pure of the taint of the shop; will at table d'hôte and
    restaurant
Have their shilling's worth, their penny's pennyworth
    even:
Neither man's aristocracy this, nor God's, God knoweth!
                    Arthur Hugh Clough, 'Amours de Voyage'

'There is no mistake about it, the ocean is simply disgusting,' a first-class passenger wrote to his wife as he crossed the Atlantic on the White Star liner *Teutonic* in 1905. 'We are nearing New York, in a fierce snowstorm which makes the ship roll atrociously . . . We have had what is considered a good winter passage, but oh, Lord, it's been abject misery almost all the while for me. I've not been actually sick, but I have never been actually without the feeling that I might be . . . It seems seven weeks, seven months, seven years since I left you – one never sleeps properly. It's like a feverish nightmare the whole way. Then if it approaches a calm there's sure to be a fog, and then you have the hooter blown every two minutes and everyone gets as jumpy as fish.'[1]

This was the sort of experience that a new generation of super-liners was meant to stop. Cunard enlisted government subsidy to build its famous trio of ships – variously described as leviathans and ocean-greyhounds – *Lusitania*, *Mauretania* and *Aquitania*: the first two of these had their maiden voyages in the autumn of 1907. It was a pre-emptive move, to mitigate the challenge posed by these new ships, that White Star transferred its Atlantic traffic from Liverpool to Southampton in June 1907 shortly before the Cunarders entered service. Soon afterwards Bruce Ismay, chairman of White Star, proposed building three liners, surpassing all others in size and luxury, in order that his company might supplant Cunard as the dominant power on the North Atlantic run. Three ships were a logistic necessity for a company intending to provide a high-speed transatlantic service departing on set days of the week: that was why Cunard built *Lusitania*, *Mauretania* and *Aquitania* in 1907–14 and Hamburg-Amerika their formidable triumvir *Imperator*, *Vaterland* and *Bismarck* in 1912–14. Ismay's proposal was the origin of the so-called Olympic class, comprising liners named *Olympic*, *Titanic* and *Britannic* (which was sunk by a German mine in 1916). He mooted his idea at a dinner with Lord Pirrie, head of the Belfast shipyard of Harland & Wolff. He envisaged *Titanic*, so he later said, as 'the latest thing in the art of shipbuilding; absolutely no money was spared in her construction'.[2] Pirrie enjoyed a reputation for infallibility, and was as much a mover of the big idea as Ismay. Both men knew from the outset that there was not a berth, dry dock or pier in the world that could handle ships of the size they envisaged. The challenges ahead incited them.

Long before *Titanic* put to sea, men were at work on land creating the greatest ship on earth. Lord Pirrie, whose shipyard built it, Bruce Ismay, whose company operated it, and Pierpont Morgan, who owned it, were chief amongst these men. Pirrie, Ismay and Morgan, with their political influence and monetary power, stood at the apex; beneath them lay the brute force of the shipyards and vaunting pride of the shipping lines.

Lord Pirrie was a small, masterful man with intrepid nerves and unshakeable self-confidence: he thought nothing of removing grit from one of his shipyard worker's eyes with the blade of a knife. He measured situations swiftly, made up his mind in minutes, pounced on the weak points of other people's arguments, rejected advice, and was 'so independent he never agrees with anybody or in anything'.[3]

He was steely in enforcing compliance with his wishes: 'Correct me if I am wrong, but did not I tell you to . . .' he would ask an underling – sometimes as a prelude to sacking him. Pirrie seldom read anything but business papers, technical journals and newspapers. Occasionally, with pensive care, he studied books about masterful leaders who bent other men to their will, and impressed their characters on their age. Pirrie worked long hours, but his vitality was never slaked: he took ten-minute power naps, and woke invigorated. He was a master salesman, who made a point of being seen smiling and spoke with an unabashed Belfast accent which convinced other businessmen that he was sincere and trustworthy. It was said of him while *Titanic* was being built, 'Lord Pirrie has a sort of magic by which he charms orders for ships out of customers.'[4]

Pirrie's father had died in New York in 1849 when his only son was two. The fatherless boy was intensely close to his mother, who instilled in him the precepts that made him industrious, persevering and forceful. When he turned fifteen, in 1862, she paid for him to be apprenticed to a young Belfast shipbuilder, Edward Harland. Harland's shipyard covered part of a manmade island created by the soil and rubble when a new channel was cut to straighten the river Lagan as it meandered through Belfast, and was only a few miles from the Irish Sea. Harland was an innovative shipbuilder who installed iron instead of wooden upper decks in his steamers, thus strengthening hulls by creating a box of metal girders; and he increased the capacity of his ships by having flat bottoms and square bilges. He dispensed with bowsprits and figureheads, though his steamships still carried masts and sails until the late nineteenth century. Belfast technical expertise was melded with Hamburg Jewish financial skills when in 1862 Harland took Gustav Wolff as his business partner.

Pirrie achieved a partnership in Harland & Wolff at the age of twenty-seven, travelled abroad seeking orders from foreign shipowners, studied the amenities in top European hotels, and adapted them for the public saloons of Belfast-built liners. He became chairman of the shipyards following Harland's death in 1895, and after 1906, when he bought Wolff's shareholding, turned them into his personal fiefdom. He kept control by hugging all crucial information jealously to himself. His fellow directors were marginalized: when he was away from Belfast, meetings were chaired by his wife. Copies of all letters sent from the shipyards were submitted to his scrutiny. His managers were never privy to the shipyard's finances or contractual details with shipowners. A ship's architect who discussed finance with a shipowner was fired by Pirrie, who ordered that the man's locked desk be broken open to find what further indiscretions had been committed. He was so secretive that when he died, no-one else in the company knew the state of negotiations with its potential customers, which threw the business into crisis.

Ships were built to Harland & Wolff designs: Pirrie consulted shipowners only as to general specifications, sketching rough designs for every vessel personally in consultation with the owners, and charging building costs plus 4 per cent profit.* Under Pirrie's propulsion Harland & Wolff was by 1900 the biggest shipbuilder in the world (employing 9,000 workers and producing 100,000 tons of shipping a year). The English newspaper editor W. T. Stead, who perished in the *Titanic* disaster, profiled Pirrie shortly before the liner's maiden voyage: 'He is the greatest shipbuilder the world has ever seen. He has built more ships and bigger ships than any man since the days of Noah. Not only he builds them; but he owns them; directs them; controls them on all the seas of the world.'[5]

Pirrie's control of the seas was enforced by his involvement with Pierpont Morgan's International Mercantile Marine Company of New Jersey, which in 1902 bought the White Star Line. As a result of this deal, IMM contracted that all orders for new vessels, and for repairs undertaken in Britain, were to be placed with the Belfast shipyard if its prices were competitive with those of US shipyards. Harland & Wolff was thus practically constituted as IMM's

---

*When Harland & Wolff agreed in the 1950s to build the liner *Canberra* for P&O on a fixed-price contract, it took a certain step towards insolvency. The shipyard survived on British government subsidies from the 1960s until 1977, when it was nationalized and incorporated into British Shipbuilders; it was privatized in 1989.

shipbuilders, and secured most of the repair work for IMM's great fleet: repairs were reckoned to be more profitable than building, and kept the yards busy when new orders were scarce. An American associate wrote of Pirrie: 'Born to command, he had larger ideas than others and a greater insight into men.' The American likened him to the railwayman Jay Gould, the oilman Rockefeller, the steelman Carnegie: 'like these Pirrie stands out conspicuously – giants all of them among dwarfs'. He seemed 'easily the biggest man in Ireland'.[6]

Pirrie had a full measure of vanity, and his appetite for public recognition was hard to appease. He was Lord Mayor of Belfast in Queen Victoria's diamond jubilee year of 1897: Lord Cadogan, the Irish Viceroy based at Dublin Castle, recommended him to the Prime Minister for a baronetcy in the jubilee honours, but was told 'Lord Salisbury is very sorry but he fears it is not possible to do anything now for Mr Pirrie'.[7] Instead Pirrie was nominated as a Privy Councillor of Ireland. During his mayoralty Belfast's mellow old Linen Hall was demolished to provide the site for a bombastic new City Hall, completed in 1906, with a baroque exterior, marble staircases and inlaid floors, garnished with statues and portraits of lord mayors, freemen and councillors. Pirrie was elected a Freeman of Belfast in 1898, his wife became the city's first honorary freeman and first woman magistrate, but they wanted higher prestige. 'You know what an excellent and ambitious little body Mrs Pirrie is,' Lord Dufferin, the former Viceroy of India on whose Clandeboye estate Pirrie had grown up, wrote to Cadogan in 1898. 'She wishes me to submit to you that her husband should be made Lieutenant of the County and City of Belfast . . . I can back Mrs Pirrie's request with a clear conscience, for undoubtedly her husband is a very sensible, able man, and during his Mayoralty became extremely popular.'[8] Cadogan responded by offering the Lieutenancy to Dufferin, whose refusal letter conceded that Pirrie 'has many merits, but he has also many enemies, and perhaps his elevation would excite considerable jealousy amongst the magnates who would consider themselves as good as he'.[9] Belfast businessmen were too envious to let one of their number be singled out for this honour, which went to the drunken magnifico Lord Londonderry. Mrs Pirrie can hardly have been satisfied that her husband was instead picked as High Sheriff of Antrim in 1898.

Pirrie wanted to become Unionist MP for South Belfast, but was rejected by the party hierarchy in Ulster – one of several snubs that he received from less successful men who felt he presumed too much. It proved an unforgivable slight that he was not knighted in 1903 when King Edward VII opened Belfast's Royal Victoria Hospital, which was built with money given by Pirrie and donations solicited by his wife. As a result, he subscribed to Liberal Party funds before the 1905 general election, and in 1906 was rewarded with a barony by the new Liberal government. King Edward protested at being asked to grant a peerage to Pirrie – indeed he asked for another nominee to be substituted for him – and presciently doubted that the shipbuilder would prove useful in the House of Lords. Further recognition came from the Liberals: Pirrie was appointed Lord Comptroller of the Household at Dublin Castle in 1907, and was installed as a Knight of St Patrick in 1909. The other knights of St Patrick, members of the Irish hereditary nobility, resented the appointment of a Belfast businessman to their order, and boycotted his investiture. King Edward felt that he had been misled into agreeing to Pirrie's new honour when none of the other knights would meet him: the investiture, ignominiously, took place in private at Dublin Castle.[10] The Pirries, however, were unabashed about being commercial people. At the next St Patrick's ball held at Dublin Castle, Lady Pirrie wore a sea-blue linen dress sporting a train decorated with fish and White Star ships, while in her hair she wore a ship's bow and bowsprit made in silver. Pirrie enjoyed pageantry, and liked to be photographed in the uniform of an Irish Privy Councillor, with its white-plumed hat, bedizened with the star of St Patrick.

The Pirries were ostentatious householders. First, he bought Edward Harland's Belfast house, Ormiston, an austere neo-baronial house surrounded by swathes of lawn and rows of gaunt fir trees but with no flower beds, and added a banqueting hall during his mayoralty. In 1898, when Harland & Wolff moved its headquarters to London, he bought a showpiece house in Belgrave Square belonging to an Irish nobleman, the Marquess of Downshire: it is now the Spanish Embassy. Later, in 1909, he bought a big neo-Tudor house, Witley Park, near Godalming, for over £200,000. Witley had belonged to a City swindler called Whitaker Wright, who had taken cyanide after being sentenced to seven years' penal servitude for fraud a few years earlier. The house had an astronomical observatory, velodrome, theatre, palm court, ballroom, rose gardens, Italian statuary, a bathing pavilion and boathouse designed by Lutyens, three lakes (under one of the lakes there was a circular billiard room with a glass dome through which fish could be watched: the point of the glazed dome supported a giant statue of Neptune which seemed to stride across the lake's surface). Like a White Star liner, the house's interior was a hodgepodge of styles: Ionic, Jacobean, Louis XIV, William and Mary, Georgian, Indian and Arabian motifs made a visual flurry that was scarcely calming. As another show of *parvenu* ostentation, Pirrie in 1911 paid £16,000 for the steam yacht *Valiant*, which had been built for a Vanderbilt.

The Pirries were speckled with snobbery, if the essence of that vice is the wish to impress other people. Their imaginations were vivid with tinkling coronets and a highborn throng in their rooms. But their social ambitions were repeatedly chastened. Neither smothering of compromising ancestors nor spanking new accessories could make the Pirries acceptable. Despite the opulence of Downshire House and Witley, their parties were neither smart nor envied. Pirrie had received his peerage on the understanding that he would support the Liberal government in the House of Lords, where the majority of peers were Conservatives. On this basis, he was further rewarded with the Lord Lieutenancy of Belfast in 1911 – a long-delayed satisfaction for his wife. But he had too strong a sense of the reverence due to him to accept party discipline, or perhaps his wife felt their rebuffs too keenly. The Marchioness of Londonderry, who protested to King George V at Pirrie's eventual appointment to the Belfast lieutenancy, delivered a resounding snub to Lady Pirrie on the House of Commons terrace. As Lady Craigavon recorded in her diary, 'Lady Pirrie, whose husband had ratted to the other side, rushed up to her, and . . . said: "What very changeable weather we are having"; Lady L sniffed loudly and replied: "I dislike change of any sort", and turned her back.'[11]

This mortifying incident occurred in January 1913, shortly before a crucial vote on the Irish Home Rule Bill, in the week that Pirrie wrote from his yacht *Valiant*, off Malta, to the Leader of the Liberals in the Lords, Lord Crewe, explaining that he was visiting 'Mediterranean ports in which the White Star and other Lines in which I am interested are concerned,' and therefore could not attend the Home Rule Bill vote. 'You will understand my feeling that I must attend to the requirements of my business, and also I promised my doctor,' he continued lamely, 'that I would take a little holiday from my London office at the beginning of the New Year, although I am glad to say I am perfectly well, and indeed never felt better.'[12] The list compiled by Lord Colebrooke, the Liberal whip, of holidaying peers who had failed to support the bill was headed by 'Pirrie, who is yachting in the Mediterranean.'[13] The matter was referred to the Prime Minister, Asquith, from whom Pirrie received a letter which he would 'not . . . soon forget.'[14]

Pirrie seldom rested: the first long break of his working life was in 1912, and saved his reputation as well as his life, for he cancelled his booking on *Titanic*'s maiden voyage because he was recuperating from a prostate operation. If he had travelled on the ship and died, he would have been the most notable British fatality; and if he had survived in a lifeboat, he would have been an international scapegoat. Pirrie liked to reach Harland & Wolff's London office by nine in the morning, and sometimes stayed for ten or twelve hours. His wife would arrive at six in the evening in a chauffeured Rolls-Royce and help her husband to finish his day's work. The only man he trusted unreservedly was Sir Owen Philipps, chairman of the Royal Mail Steam Packet shipping group, described in 1913 as 'a man who fights for his own hand and looks to commercial success.'[15] The two men were wizards of financial improvisation with astounding memories for the details of debts and credits. They implemented their ideas with a fixed stealth; they hated to relax their control of financial data; and they relished intricate schemes of borrowing. Lady Pirrie, the only other person whom Pirrie trusted, resented Philipps as if he was a love rival. Phillips, too, received a peerage, and became Lord Kylsant.

At the end of the war, as Pirrie told the Prime Minister, Lloyd George, he intended to donate his Witley estate as the official country residence of British Prime Ministers, but another millionaire pre-empted him by bestowing Chequers on the nation. He was described in 1923 by the banker Lord Swaythling as England's 'second richest man with perhaps £3,000,000 annual income', and by his fellow shipowner, Lord Inverforth, in June 1924, as 'probably the richest man in England'.[16] Two days later Pirrie died on board a ship approaching Cuba. His imposing façade and opulent habits were swiftly revealed as flimsy impostures. Kylsant, who was installed as next chairman of Harland & Wolff, was startled to find that his predecessor was destitute. Pirrie left an overdraft of £325,000 at the Midland Bank (of which he had been a director since 1906), and was personally committed to buy £473,260 worth of preference shares in his shipyard. There was little prospect of dividends from his shareholdings, and Kylsant advised the trustees to declare Pirrie's estate bankrupt. Inverforth, and another shipping man, Lord Inchcape, wished to hide from Lady Pirrie the fact that she was penniless, and induced companies with which Pirrie had been involved to pay for her maintenance. In the years that followed, Harland & Wolff proved a fatal drain on Royal Mail finances.

Pirrie cultivated close relations between Harland & Wolff and many shipping lines, but none was bound more tightly to the Belfast yards than White Star. In 1867 a Liverpool shipowner called Thomas Ismay bought for £1,000 an insolvent shipping firm specializing in transporting emigrants to the Australian goldfields. A bantering conversation during a billiard game two years later determined Ismay to divert White Star ships from their Australian routes, which never paid well, to the North Atlantic. It was a good moment to change tactics. The expansion of the United States since the end of the American Civil War was attracting thousands of European immigrants, who needed berths on transatlantic steamships. From the outset, in 1869, Harland & Wolff arranged the finance for Ismay's expanded building programme on condition that their Belfast yard got the orders.

The first Harland & Wolff ship for White Star, *Oceanic*, was launched at Belfast in 1870 and set new standards for size and comfort. At 3,078 tons it was the largest ship on the ocean: capable of 14 knots it crossed the Atlantic in eight to ten days carrying up to 200 cabin and 1,000 steerage passengers, with 130 crew. First-class cabins were larger than was customary, and boasted electric bells for stewards and baths with running water. The most conspicuous novelty in *Oceanic* arose from the decision to abandon the Royal Navy's quarterdeck tradition. Traditionally, passengers' quarters had been near the stern, where the ship heaved in most weathers. In steamships, the juddering from the propeller was constant in the stern, while in rough conditions the propeller lashed through the air rather than the sea causing a nasty 'racing' effect. Harland & Wolff shifted the first-class cabins amidships, where there was reduced heaving and racing, as well as less pungent galley smells: cheaper steerage berths remained in the stern. 'The change to midships was so universally appreciated that the White Star Line at once leaped to a foremost place in Atlantic enterprise,' recorded the *Liverpool Daily Post* in 1899. Competitors had to match White Star standards of comfort: 'Mr Ismay was, in truth, the inventor of luxurious ocean travel.'[17]

After *Oceanic*, Harland built *Adriatic*, *Britannic*, *Germanic*, *Arabic*, *Coptic*, *Ionic* and *Doric* for White Star. In all there was an emphasis on the convenience of passengers. The intention was to make Atlantic crossings potentially enjoyable rather than certainly dreadful. In 1887 the keels were laid in Harland & Wolff's shipyard of two important new White Star liners, *Teutonic* and *Majestic*. These were the first vessels built for White Star that relied solely on steam power and dispensed with square-rigged sails as back-up. They had another innovation, twin propellers, which meant that they could achieve a speed of 20 knots. Their displacement was just under 10,000 tons. Until *Teutonic* and *Majestic*, White Star liner accommodation had been divided between cabin class and steerage; but these new ships inaugurated the era of three classes. They had accommodation for 300 first-class passengers, 190 second-class and 1,000 third-class. *Teutonic* took the Blue Riband for a westward Atlantic crossing in 5 days, 16 hours and 31 minutes in 1891. This was the last time that a White Star liner held the Blue Riband, for their ships were built to be pleasurable rather than gustily high-speed.

H. G. Wells pictured the primary symbol of the nineteenth century as a steam engine running along a railway, but it could as well have been a steam-powered ship churning through waves, for the world-wide transport revolution happened at sea as well as on land, as he knew. 'The Malay nowadays,' he wrote in 1902, 'sets out upon his pilgrimage to Mecca in an excursion steamship of iron, and the immemorial Hindoo goes a-shopping in a train.'[18] The sea-transport revolution had begun when the American ship *Savannah* (using its steam engines as auxiliary power) first crossed the Atlantic in 1819. As *Savannah* steamed eastwards, other sea-going vessels offered help, thinking that the smoke from its chimney was caused by fire on board, and the crew of an English revenue cutter were puzzled to see it skimming along with furled sails. *Sirius* was the first vessel to cross the Atlantic under total steam power in 1838. Soon afterwards, the British government awarded a contract worth £55,000 a month to carry post between Liverpool and North America to a Canadian, Samuel Cunard. His first paddle steamer, with 1,150 tonnage, took a fortnight to reach Boston from Liverpool. Charles Dickens, who crossed in 1842, said that he, his wife and their two trunks had a cabin in which they could no more fit than a giraffe could be forced into a flower pot.

Thomas Ismay – backed by Harland & Wolff – was challenging Cunard for North Atlantic business by the 1870s. In business he was prone to tyrannize. At home he was a martinet. Every self-made

Victorian ogre had a domestic citadel built for him: Ismay's was an ornate mock-Elizabethan house south of Liverpool. Each morning at eight he began his daily walk to Thurstaston station. If he saw a fallen leaf on his carriage-drive, he would put a stone on top of it; and woe betide his ten gardeners if the stone and leaf were still there when he returned in the evening. This was the sort of attention to detail, slyness and intimidation in which Victorian businessmen took pride. Ismay cut a great figure in the world. The naval review at Spithead of 1897, a display of imperial might to mark Queen Victoria's diamond jubilee, was attended by all the Home Fleet, many overseas squadrons and the Prince of Wales on the royal yacht, plus Thomas Ismay with his son Bruce on their liner, *Teutonic*, sporting its eight guns as an armed merchantman. A few years later, in 1899–1900, both *Teutonic* and *Majestic* carried thousands of troops to the war in South Africa.

At the age of twenty-nine, in 1892, Bruce Ismay became managing director of White Star, after a spell as its New York agent, and he took charge after his father's death in 1899. He was described (at the time of *Titanic*'s disaster) as 'a quietly dressed, rather youthful man of unassuming mien . . . speaking in a low, well-modulated voice that carried well . . . He looks and speaks so unlike the commonly accepted type of commercial monarchs as could well be conceived. A cultured cosmopolitan, if you like, but not a strong ruler of strong men.'[19] He is often presented as a typical English upper-middle-class public schoolboy, because he had good manners and *Who's Who* recorded that he had been educated at Harrow school. But this is misleading, for Ismay spent less than eighteen months at Harrow, which he left at the age of fifteen; he was, moreover, there in an undistinguished generation, for none of his classmates achieved distinction, and few of them enjoyed even middling hereditary privileges. Ismay was inescapably the son of a northern millionaire, who was trained in commerce after his interlude at Harrow and then sent to New York to be toughened in the transatlantic rate wars. He stood 6 feet 4 inches tall, and was a robust sportsman, though not in the class of the shipping tycoon Hermann Oelrichs, who was ostracized in the New York Athletic Club because he was an insufferably successful all-rounder who thought nothing of swimming out alone several miles into the Atlantic.

Like many self-made millionaires, old Ismay was stormy, egotistical and showy; and like many sons of such men, Bruce Ismay disliked brouhaha, was guarded in his reactions, only relaxing when in the company of those he trusted. Bruce Ismay, though, commanded high prestige, for shipowners stood at the apex of British business. It was only in the 1880s that Prime Ministers began recommending to Queen Victoria that she bestow peerages on men who were company directors. Bankers and brewers secured the earliest peerages, but in 1897 Sir John Burns of Cunard became the first shipowner with a coronet, Lord Inverclyde. In the next quarter-century – Britain's shipping apogee with *Titanic*'s maiden voyage about halfway through – another eight peerages went to shipping directors. As well as Pirrie's barony (resisted by King Edward VII), Charles Wilson of the Wilson Line became Lord Nunburnholme in 1906;[20] Christopher Furness of Furness, Withy received his barony in 1910; Sir James Mackay of the Peninsula & Oriental Company became Lord Inchcape in 1911; Andrew Weir became Lord Inverforth in 1921; Sir William Vestey of the Blue Star line and Sir Joseph Maclay received baronies in 1922; and Sir Owen Philipps was transmuted into Lord Kylsant in 1923. It is likely that, but for the *Titanic* disaster, a peerage would have gone to Bruce Ismay, as it eventually did to his shipping son-in-law Basil Sanderson.

Ismay came to power at White Star at a time of keen competition from the two leading German shipping lines. Until the 1890s, Hamburg-Amerika and Norddeutscher-Lloyd had specialized in emigrant traffic, and left first-class passengers to Cunard and White Star. By 1903 German lines owned the four fastest ships in the world: their speed ensured that they attracted first-class travellers; and their patriotic names proved how much this was a matter of national pride as well as profit. Norddeutscher-Lloyd made so much money that Hermann Oelrichs, its head in the USA, had the millions to build a summer palace at Newport, Rhode Island – although he grew disgusted by the pomp, and preferred to eat in a chop house. While Germans built their ships for speed, White Star targeted travellers who preferred a seven-day transatlantic journey in comfort, even luxury, to a five-day journey under conditions of relentless Teutonic propulsion. American, British, Dutch and German shipowners had run cartels – known as shipping conferences – to regulate services and fix the rates of the lucrative North Atlantic passenger trade since the 1870s; but in 1898 the British withdrew from the cartels complaining that their allotment of emigrant passenger traffic was unfair.

In 1886, Thomas Ismay failed to convince other English ship-owners to form a consortium to acquire the Inman Steamship Company (originally called the Liverpool & Philadelphia Steamship Company), which was pushed towards bankruptcy by the cost of renewing its fleet. Ismay's compatriots thought it would be good business to let Inman fail, but instead the line was bought by Pierpont Morgan. An American railway financier, with a war chest containing millions of dollars, thus acquired a shipping company flying the British flag. The reconstituted Inman & International Steamship Company won the lucrative US mail contract in 1892 on condition that all their ships flew the US flag.

Pierpont Morgan was the most powerful personal force in the United States.[21] He had the self-absorption of a pampered invalid. As a child he had suffered fits which frightened his parents. As a teenager he complained of eczema, lethargy and rheumatic fever. Anxiety surrounded but also cushioned him. He came to expect all the consideration due to a confirmed valetudinarian. His lifelong habit of transatlantic journeys began when he was a boy: he finished his schooling at Vevey in Switzerland and attended Göttingen university; he spoke fluent French and German, loved Rome above all cities, had London tailors and an air of patrician entitlement.

The only touch of frivolity in Pierpont Morgan's upbringing came from a feckless uncle who wrote that timeless ditty, 'Jingle Bells'. At the age of twenty-four, in 1861, Morgan had a love match with a bride who died of galloping consumption four months after their marriage. In the years that followed he was smitten by recurrent collapses into melancholy, crippling headaches, bouts of helpless lassitude, and convinced himself (and others) that to forestall collapses, which took him away from the office, he had an imperative duty to coddle himself. Luxury thus became for him a moral necessity. To be incommoded or thwarted made him ill. Morgan often felt worthless, and slumped into despondency unless he could achieve something big which restored his sense of worth. 'If you could pierce him through,' E. M. Forster wrote in 1910, 'you'd find panic and emptiness in the middle.'[22] For half a century he raked in the dollars yet seemed to one English diplomat, who met him in Egypt, 'the saddest of millionaires'.[23] It was in Egypt that he spent hours gazing at the temples of Karnak, fell into a depressed stupor in which he scarcely ate, became unresponsive and, in 1913, died away in Rome.

Pierpont Morgan was an inarticulate, rough-mannered man who took his measure on the spot. He was incapable of small talk and expressed himself in grunts. He reached his unassailable position as ruler of Wall Street after intervening to save the US Treasury from defaulting on the gold convertibility of the dollar in 1895. He consolidated his position as the banker who had only inferiors twelve years later. An outbreak of jitters on Wall Street in 1907 caused the collapse of a bank, a trust and a brokerage firm. Individuals could not obtain money for daily use; businesses went bankrupt; railroad building was suspended; industrial output fell; unemployment rose. Wall Street floundered until Morgan rallied other dismayed bankers, and shored up the tottering fabric of American finance by raising $50 million to support troubled banks and trusts. 'Morgan,' declared an observer, 'has saved the country from a terrible catastrophe, and all America is ringing with his praises.'[24]

The 1907 crisis intensified American suspicions that bankers were fraudulent, inept, overweening and reckless. However, until the Federal Reserve Act of 1913, which passed shortly after Morgan's death, the United States had no central bank: he instead acted for nearly twenty years as the nation's central banker, upholding the

ormation of a chiefly agrarian nation into the world's most powerful
industrial state and in the vast transfer of wealth from Europe to
the United States. He ruled a paper kingdom, bristling with interim
prospectuses, listed stocks, paper securities, collateral trusts, cumulative dividends, uncomputed millions; there was money for him in
manufacturing, but more money in mergers.

Morgan was the sort of patriot who felt sure that his own aggran-
dizement served the good of his country. He saw no distinction
between national interest and his personal interest. Although adept
in handling people whose interests coincided with his own, he was
obtuse in dealings with people who felt their interests diverged from
his. He did not believe in laissez faire or the invigorating power of
a competitive market. Trusts, pools, syndicates and market-rigging
seemed to him rational and orderly, and he therefore made himself
their master. He provided resolute leadership which enforced stability
by taming the prowling, mauling lions of market forces and caging
the frisky, destructive monkeys of speculative profiteering. With
similar resolve he forced economic adversaries – whether chiefs of
rival corporations or representatives of clashing employers and
strikers – to open negotiations and agree truces. He seldom repined
over the past, but lived in the present, and was indifferent to what
would come after he was gone.

Sir Clinton Dawkins, who ran his London office, described the
Napoleon of Wall Street at his apogee in 1901. 'Old Pierpont Morgan
and the house in the US occupy a position immensely more
predominant than Rothschilds in Europe . . . Taken together the
Morgan combination of the US & London probably do not fall very
far short of the Rothschilds in capital, are immensely more expansive
and active, and . . . the US is going to dominate in most ways.'[25]
Visiting New York a few months later, and installed in Morgan's
offices at 23 Wall Street, Dawkins was tired but exhilarated. 'This is
the place where things "hum", and they have been humming a great

51

deal and not always agreeably since I have been over here. But it is extremely interesting to find oneself in the very heart of the Wall Street excitement and combinations, and to note the prodigious amount of nervous excitement and energy the Americans throw into their work. Part of the buoyancy and excitement is also due, I suppose, to the comparative youth of the vast majority of them. Few of them live through it to advanced years except physical and intellectual giants like Morgan who has something Titanic about him when he really gets to work. Most of them drop out suddenly. Total collapse very often . . . all this stress & excitement is carried on in a climate like Alexandria at its worst, aggravated by asphalt streets, tall houses and elevated railways.'[26] Dawkins proved to be one of several directors who died in his forties because of the crushing over-work and nerve-wracking pressure created by Morgan business methods.

After 1900, Morgan became one of the great collectors of the world. High noblemen disposing of exquisite rarities knew him as one of the few men able to afford their prices. Dilapidated gentry realized with inward sobs of relief that his acquisitive mania would save them. Gibbering, importunate touts thronged the halls of his hotels to the exasperation of other guests, and thrust every sort of rubbish at him. More suave dealers called by appointment at his houses, and waited civilly in antechambers when he was late. The thought of what he owned was a comfort to him, but the thought of what he might buy next week enlivened him. Morgan and similar American collectors were a different species from the collector-dukes and bachelor-connoisseurs known for centuries in Europe. They staked higher claims as they amassed their collections. Morgan ranked himself with the pharaohs and popes, the ruling houses of Medici, Hapsburg and Bonaparte, the princes and dukes whose collections he dismembered and acquired. His monarchical aura was noticed by the English art critic Roger Fry, who once travelled to Washington DC in Morgan's private railway carriage. 'He behaves not as a host but exactly as a crowned head . . . the whole thing regal and yet somehow infinitely provincial,' Fry described. 'I felt, as I sat next to him, like a courtier who has at last got an audience, and as though, for a few minutes, I wielded absolute power.' Morgan's circle seemed oddly malleable, 'for they've not got anything but money to intimidate you with. There's precious little distinction or cachet about the whole lot.'[27]

At the start of the twentieth century, Morgan engineered not only his most successful set of mergers, which culminated in the creation of US Steel, but his worst failure, the amalgamations that produced International Mercantile Marine. The tale of IMM began in Blackfriars railway station in London in 1892, when a middle-aged English shipowner called Frederick Leyland startled the porters by collapsing and dying. Leyland's shipping interests came under the control of John Ellerman, an accountant not yet thirty years old, but a man with the Midas touch who was to become, within fifteen years, the richest man in England. Ellerman took charge of the Leyland Line, and led bold expansion into the North Atlantic trade. With a modernized fleet, Leyland paid an average dividend of 11 per cent over the eight years that it was headed by Ellerman. He was a reclusive man, fixated on the beauty of numbers, for whom money-making seems to have been an incidental satisfaction. His fortune was not based on Stock Exchange ramps and plunder. He had no interest in becoming an English version of Pierpont Morgan, controlling banks, factories and human destinies, and indeed he is notable for his lack of annihilating ego. He had no public life, no enemies and was described by the *Daily Mail* as 'the Silent Ford – the invisible Rockefeller'.[28]

Morgan had a millionaire amateur's interest in seamanship. He owned a series of fast, luxurious yachts named *Corsair*, and was a Commodore of the New York Yacht Club. During 1900 he agreed to finance a merger involving Atlantic Transport Company of Baltimore, to advance the money to build six new ships and to arrange the sale of preferred stock. In 1901 his London office offered $3.5 million for Leyland, but Ellerman pushed them up to $11 million in cash. White Star was the Morgan combine's next target. Pirrie sat on White Star's board, controlled the second largest block of White Star shares after Ismay, recognized that Harland & Wolff could win a great deal of work from the new combine of shipping companies and considered that if White Star was caught in a rate war with IMM, the amount available for Harland & Wolff orders would fall. He wanted to defend Harland & Wolff's tied market by cooperating with the combine, and travelled to New York to agree tactics with Morgan. Then, using Pirrie as their intermediary, Morgan's men approached Bruce Ismay about the inclusion of White Star in IMM. Ismay's first reaction was that the proposal was 'a swindle and a humbug',[29] but he was ultimately coaxed into an agreement to sell White Star. Pirrie was keen to tighten his shipyard's connection with Hamburg-Amerika, and insisted that Albert Ballin's company be involved in the scheme. With Morgan's support, he arranged for the purchase of 51 per cent of the German company by Harland & Wolff. Both the German and the White Star arrangements were finalized in February 1902. Pirrie's patriotism in promoting the mergers was challenged: 'Mr Pirrie has about as much sentiment as a Muscovy duck,' complained a shipping journal.[30]

Pierpont Morgan wanted to include Cunard in the combine, but found that its stock was too dispersed to be easily bought up. His interests offered to buy Cunard at up to 80 per cent above its market value, but Cunard declined this offer, whilst indicating that they might later accept a higher price. Subsequently, its young chairman, the second Lord Inverclyde, convinced the British government that Cunard could compete with neither government-subsidized German lines nor the American-financed IMM without government aid. He dangled before the British government the possibility that Cunard shareholders would sell to IMM if a high enough price was tabled. This convinced the government to loan £2.4 million to Cunard to build two fast liners for the North Atlantic, and to grant an annual operating subsidy of £150,000. In return, Cunard undertook that it would not sell to IMM or anyone else for twenty years. The two new liners were launched in 1907 as *Lusitania* and *Mauretania*. It was in response to them that Ismay and Pirrie determined to build *Olympic*, *Titanic* and *Britannic*.

After failing to involve Cunard, the new combine was unveiled on

19 April 1902 in both New York and London. The new company (holding the majority stock in the Leyland, White Star, Atlantic Transport and other shipping lines) was named International Mercantile Marine: Pirrie as well as Ismay joined its directorate. Morgan assembled a $50 million underwriting syndicate to support the bonds issues needed to raise the initial cash requirements; $36 million was raised in New York, and $14 million in London, with Harland & Wolff subscribing £615,438, which constituted a massive short-term commitment. However, the failure to include Cunard in the trust damaged the issue of IMM ordinary stock, much of which was left in the hands of the promoting syndicate. Although owned by a New Jersey company, the vessels of the English companies were kept on the British register. 'The irrepressible and insatiable Morgan Syndicate' has bought White Star, the *Economist* reported in April 1902. The arrangement might have pleased shareholders in costly but modestly remunerative steamships, but to traders and travellers the prospect of higher freights and fares was unwelcome, 'and to the patriotic Briton it is not a pleasant thought that the great transatlantic trade is in future to be "bossed" by a syndicate of American capitalists'. The *Economist* opined that White Star submitted 'too readily to the schemes of the American capitalists who, with all their bounce, were really powerless to hurt them'.[31]

It was soon clear that the Americans had prodigally overpaid for the English companies. Ismay remained as White Star's chairman, and accepted the presidency of IMM in 1904 when Morgan relented in his stipulation that he must move to New York. When Ismay's appointment as president was announced, the *Economist* recalled the flamboyance with which IMM had been launched. 'We were assured at the time that the "Morganization" of the North Atlantic would shortly become an accomplished fact, that the British flag on the ocean highway between England and the United States was doomed to be overshadowed by the Stars and Stripes, and that . . . substantial benefits would accrue to the companies which threw in their lot with the great Morgan combine.' Within two years the disillusion was absolute: IMM had bond capital of £14,000,000, share capital exceeding £20,000,000, but its net profit, after interest charges, was a measly £71,059. Ismay, declared the *Economist*, faced 'a gigantic task'.[32]

The British government's subsidy of Cunard forced IMM to build competitive new ships costing huge sums which the combine was not earning. Moreover, IMM was a holding company which permitted its constituent companies to retain their previous national registrations, house flags and identities. It was the Humpty Dumpty of Morgan's combines in which the component pieces were never put together. There was neither integration of its subsidiaries nor rationalization of its operations. As a result IMM never achieved the economies that a tight, streamlined organization would have yielded. Harland & Wolff held £250,000 worth of bonds in IMM, but after these had yielded no dividends, Pirrie undertook in 1907 to buy them personally over the course of the next five years. This left him with a large, unprofitable stake in the company. English shipowners, a financial journalist reported in 1907, 'all know that the American Combine does not pay, and that it never will pay on the immense capital recklessly sunk in it'.[33] IMM defaulted on its bonds, and a year after Morgan's death in 1913, his Humpty-Dumpty combine went into receivership. In 1927 Lord Kylsant, Pirrie's successor at Harland & Wolff, paid £7 million to buy White Star back from IMM.[34] The singular means by which Kylsant financed this deal resulted in him serving a year in prison for issuing a false company prospectus.

'He's a brigand like all these great businessmen,' Roger Fry decided of Morgan. '"Business is warfare" is their acknowledged motto.'[35] *Titanic* was a ship that super-brigands owned and fighting Irishmen built.

FOUR

Shipbuilders

The land of scholars and saints:
Scholars and saints my eye, the land of ambush,
Purblind manifestoes, never-ending complaints,
The born martyr and the gallant ninny;
The grocer drunk with the drum,
The land-owner shot in his bed, the angry voices
Piercing the broken fanlight in the slum,
The shawled woman weeping at the garish altar.

Louis MacNeice, 'Autumn Journal'

Titanic was an Irish ship, built by Harland & Wolff, in the years when Belfast boomed. The story of Ireland in the years of Belfast's apogee is a compound of crime, conspiracy, threats and murder. Whenever the 'Irish Question' arose, English politics was jerked from its sedate course of political jobbing and somnolent debates into a flurry of sensational or lurid surprises. Sometimes the incidents were reported in headlines that sounded like chapter headings from Sherlock Holmes' casebook: the Pigott Forgeries, the Parnell Divorce, the Phoenix Park Murders, the Dublin Castle Crime (when a miscreant herald stole the Irish Crown Jewels). Sometimes they were the stuff of suspense novels: army officers breaking oaths and plotting mutiny; Sir Roger Casement being rowed ashore one dark night from a German submarine in a cockleshell dingy, through the booming rollers pounding the strand at Tralee Bay, and caught next day by the police lurking amidst the stones of a ruined Viking fort. Often they were a cut-throat horror: the Earl of Leitrim ambushed and riddled with shot, and a howling rabble trying to drag his coffin from the hearse; Lord Mountmorres found lying in a lane with six bullet wounds – his widow and children so menaced that they took refuge in Hampton Court Palace, where Queen Victoria gave them apartments; Lord Lismore driven from Shanbally Castle by death threats; Lord Ardilaun's bailiff beaten to death and his corpse thrown in a lake; Lord Erne's agent boycotted; Lord Bandon kidnapped. A few years after *Titanic* came the climactic enormities of civil war: gun-running, pitched battles, martial law, internment camps, hunger strikes, prison escapes, derailed troop trains, arson attacks on castles and manor houses, reprisal burnings.

Ireland was becoming a land of landless noblemen. By the time that *Titanic* was launched, Ireland's premier duke, the epileptic Duke of Leinster, owned not an acre, and was living in a bungalow in an Edinburgh suburb. Young Lord Mountmorres, who took refuge in England after his father's murder, became a car salesman and went bankrupt in 1909 with assets of £296. The Marquess of Donegall, whose family built Belfast Castle, left an estate valued at £27 when he died. Lord Wallscourt also died destitute, of alcoholism, aged forty-five; his widow, her tobacconist's shop in Putney having failed, took poison the next year. As one commentator wrote after the Land Purchase Act of 1905, which enabled landowners to sell their estates, often at handsome prices, for division among their tenants, 'Aristocracies come and go like the waves of the sea; and some fall nobly and others ignobly. As I write, this Protestant Anglo-Irish aristocracy, which once owned all Ireland from the centre to the sea, is rotting from the land in the most dismal farce-tragedy of all time, without one brave deed.'[1] What was to replace them as the first-class of Ireland? Self-made industrialists with brimming coffers, Lady Pirrie hoped, eyeing her husband. Harland & Wolff's shipyards vied with the Guinness brewery as the most famous manufactory in Ireland. How did the shipyards stand to the rest of Ireland? What of the Belfast men who built *Titanic*?

Pirrie, as we have seen, was shunned because he was singular among Belfast Protestant money men in supporting the Liberal government's commitment to grant Home Rule to Ireland. Home Rule could only be achieved by ignoring the protests of implacable Protestant firebrands in the north-east province of Ireland, Ulster. Four of the nine counties of Ulster had been populated since the seventeenth century by ill-assimilated Protestants, of English or Scottish ancestry, many of whom abominated the Pope, Catholic priests and papist dominion. The other counties had a penurious Catholic majority with a richer Protestant minority. To supplement the terse, grim monosyllables of the Protestant catchphrase 'Home Rule is Rome Rule', Lord Randolph Churchill coined the pugnacious slogan, 'Ulster will fight and Ulster will be right'.[2] In the year that Pirrie and Ismay agreed to build *Olympic* and *Titanic*, an onlooker described how every Sunday outside the Customs House in Belfast, thousands of bystanders with florid, angry faces were bellowed at by Protestant rabble-rousers. 'The Pope is dethroned, scalped, roasted and consigned to eternal perdition every Sunday afternoon during busy times from this platform. Popery with its works and pomp is denounced, menaced, and torn to pieces. Orange demagogues expatiate on the creed and politics of Papists and call forth thunders of applause.'[3]

Many Harland & Wolff workers were Orangemen – that is, members of Orange lodges, named after Prince William of Orange, 'King Billy', the Protestant who dethroned the Catholic king, James II, and expelled him from Ireland after the Battle of the Boyne in 1690. Each 12 July, on the anniversary of the Battle of the Boyne, Orangemen paraded in purple, orange or black sashes. Their sectarian animosity crushed incipient working-class unity by setting Protestant and Catholic workers at violent odds. The Orange demonstration on 12 July 1902 was disrupted by a Harland & Wolff workman, Thomas Sloan, who mounted the platform and started a shouting match about Catholic convent laundries. Sloan was a cementer who led evangelical meetings in a shipyard shed during lunch breaks; he was also a temperance agitator and street-corner haranguer. Five days later the MP for South Belfast died. Pirrie expected to be adopted as Unionist candidate in his stead, and was affronted when the by-election candidature was allotted to a Cornish-born Etonian named Charles Dunbar-Buller. The Belfast Protestant Association thought Dunbar-Buller was too well bred, and nominated the workman Sloan as an independent candidate. Pirrie's brother-in-law and business partner Alexander Carlisle, who boasted that he had read only one book in his life, *The History of Elmwood Presbyterian Church, Belfast*, but that he read every page of the *Daily Mail*, backed Sloan. When rowdies shouted down speakers and smashed furniture at Dunbar-Buller's meetings, Pirrie was blamed by Dunbar-Buller's supporters: 'the money that was creating the mob of the unwashed to beat down free speech, was not supplied by Mr Sloan, but by the cloven foot behind him, who wanted to sit in Parliament'.[4] Sloan won the by-election, and defeated another gentlemanly official Unionist at the next general election. In Parliament he championed the Orange Orders and teetotalism, voted for improved housing and trade union rights, and promised to make his enemies tremble to do the will of Protestant Belfast. His puritanical supporters however grew disgusted when he was seen wearing an overcoat with a fur collar and was rumoured to imbibe alcohol in the House of Commons bar: he was defeated in 1910.

By the time that *Titanic* was fitted up after its launch in 1911, political and sectarian tension had turned Ulster into a tinder-box. Orange lodges began to practise military drills in preparation for an armed fight against a Catholic parliament in Dublin. In response to this militancy, Pirrie booked the Ulster Hall in Belfast for a meeting on 8 February 1912 at which Winston Churchill (then a Liberal Cabinet Minister) was to address Home Rule supporters. Protestant Unionists, led by Pirrie's enemy Lord Londonderry, retaliated by promising to stop the Ulster Hall meeting 'at all hazards', even riot.[5] Pirrie transferred his meeting to a marquee at Celtic Park football ground in a Catholic district, and decried his opponents for their mindless loyalty to inherited sectarian slogans.[6] Churchill on his way to Celtic Park faced a crowd of scowling Orangemen yelling their resentment and brandishing their fists in Protestant districts, while in the Catholic Falls Road he was cheered by black-shawled mill girls. It was a day of true Belfast weather with relentless rain, which seeped through the canvas of the marquee in a continuous stream. 'Churchill,' wrote his Cabinet colleague Lord Lincolnshire, 'triumphed over the forces of disorder and intolerance and delivered yesterday at Belfast unmolested a speech which was a magnificent and unanswerable plea for Home Rule. 7,000 people listened to him for seventy-five minutes as he spoke in a huge tent: and cheered him to the echo. It poured in torrents all day, and the people were deep to their ankles in slush and mud.'[7]

Churchill's presence aroused little violence: at worst, the motor car carrying him to Celtic Park was rushed by rowdy shipyard workers in the hope of overturning it. Nevertheless, when Pirrie boarded his steamer at Larne on 11 February to return to England, a mob of 600 people pelted him with rotten eggs, flour and herrings amidst shouts of 'traitor'. His clothes were spoilt, and he only got on board under police protection.[8] Two days later, he attended a full dress dinner of Liberal peers hosted by Lord Lincolnshire, where he was congratulated for his courage in defying the ire of his rampaging workforce.[9] Then, as the Ulster crisis reached a high pitch of excitement, Pirrie fell ill with an enlarged prostate gland. He underwent surgery on 20 February – a serious operation for a man over sixty – and was advised to rest. He took a long cruise on his ex-Vanderbilt yacht, *Valiant*, missed *Titanic*'s maiden voyage, but attended Kiel regatta, where he entertained Albert Ballin of the Hamburg-Amerika line.

A demonstration attended by 100,000 Home Rulers in Belfast in March 1912 was followed by a counter-demonstration of 300,000 Unionists in April. On the day before *Titanic* left Southampton, the Conservative Party leader Bonar Law, supported by Lord Londonderry, reviewed Protestant paramilitaries marching in file through a Belfast suburb. Law told them that they were being deprived of their birthright and were justified in violent resistance. As Lincolnshire noted in disgust, 'The Primate of All Ireland prayed, and the gathering sang the 90th Psalm'.[10] On 11 April, the day *Titanic* left Queenstown,

Asquith's government introduced its Home Rule Bill. 'The Belfast men,' declared a Tory whip, 'want a row at once.'[11]

These convulsions occurred just before *Titanic*'s maiden voyage; and the political storms thundered ominously in the months after the sinking, with Harland & Wolff's shipyards at the centre of the maelstrom. On 29 June 1912, at Castledawson, a Presbyterian Sunday School party numbering about 500 – mainly women and children – met bandsmen of the Ancient Orders of Hibernians, the Catholic equivalent of the Orange Orders. The bandsmen harassed the school-party, and assailed them with pikes and bludgeons. A Protestant rescue party appeared, armed with forks, shovels and sticks, each mob pelted the other with stones, and they dispersed only after the police levelled their rifles and fixed their bayonets. Some of the Castledawson children came from shipyard families, and on 2 July riots started in the Belfast shipyards. In the yards and streets outside, Catholics, Protestant Liberals and Home Rulers were beaten and terrorized by apprentices and riveters' assistants called heater boys. Assaults and intimidation forced 2,000 Catholics to leave their ship-yard jobs: by 12 July, there were under a hundred Catholics left at Harland & Wolff. This disruption was intolerable to Pirrie's managers, who threatened to lay off their entire 17,000 workforce unless Catholics were re-admitted.[12] The Belfast Commissioner of Police reported after the 1912 expulsions that ordinarily his men 'did not do duty in the shipyards and their presence there was regarded as an intrusion and an insult. Even in ordinary times, a policeman in uniform has missiles frequently thrown at him if he has to go down the Queen's Road. Missiles were thrown at the police marching to and fro from duty by men working on the ships.'[13] The disturbances of 1912 chastened Pirrie: 'I keep out of Irish politics,' he said a few years later.[14]

Sandy Row was the Orange quarter of Belfast as Falls Road was the Catholic; and it took no time to get a broken head if you forgot which quarter you were in. 'Belfast hums with industry and calls itself progressive,' wrote a bemused visitor in 1907, 'and yet, under-lying all this commercialism, all this thrift, and all this cult of the main chance, there is a cast-iron bigotry – a cruel, corroding, unfathomable, ferocious sectarian rancour.'[15] Preachers in their pulpit sent the male congregation out onto the streets, furious with zeal, like drunks fighting-mad from a pub, primed to knock down the first man they did not like. Boys of seventeen were flogged by their fathers for being fifteen minutes late returning from no greater orgy than tea with neighbours.[16] Some outsiders admired the brutal raucous philistinism of the city. 'The roar and rush of Belfast' delighted Rudyard Kipling on his visit in 1911. 'Those grim-faced businessmen met without any of the graces, and none of the airs of the South, put away enormous slugs of whiskey quite unemotionally at 10 a.m.; did their job, and marched out into the wet and black of the streets.'[17]

The clang of trams as much as the hooting of shipyard sirens made Belfast a noisy city – its population was approaching 400,000 in 1912. The noise was what outsiders noticed. 'Belfast, with its industrial clamour, its new red brick that screams at you and its electric trams that fly faster than the trams anywhere else,' wrote a visitor in 1909, 'has made itself hastily, too hastily, and when it lies silent through the fear of God on the morning of the seventh day, you see that it is as yet an industrial camp and not a city.'[18] It made a similar impression on another Edwardian tourist, who hailed from southern Ireland. 'Belfast impresses you as being a very rich and a very busy city . . . I saw churches of all denominations, Freemason and Orange lodges, wide streets, towering smokestacks, huge factories, crowded traffic. And out of the water, beyond the Custom House, dimly seen through smoke and mist, rose some huge, shapeless thing which I found to be a shipbuilding yard wherein 10,000 men were hammering iron and steel into great ocean liners. I saw palatial banks and insurance houses and counting houses and vast emporiums. I saw thousands of well-dressed people hurrying to and fro with no flash of humour in their glances and no bloom of health in their set and earnest faces. The noise of wheels and hoofs and cranks and spindles and steam hammers filled my ears and made my head ache.'[19]

Ballymacarrett, south-east of Belfast, with its rows of identical workmen's cottages, was Harland & Wolff's township. Pirrie might have made Ballymacarrett into a model suburb, well designed and salubrious, like the second-class accommodation on his liners, but the idea seems never to have struck him. It remained steerage quality while he revelled in the ostentation of his millionaire's model estate, Witley. Ballymacarrett remained a mean, hard place where grim, rasping, monotonous lives were endured in homes smeared by factory smut and ruled by snarls, cuffs and blows; where the women stood outside their front doors talking loudly to one another and shouting rebukes at their children playing noisily in the street. The differentials in pay and housing between skilled Harland & Wolff workers, and the unskilled labourers, known as spellsmen, were more pronounced than anywhere else in Britain. Spellsmen received £2 for working a forty-nine-hour week in the shipyard.

A visitor to Harland & Wolff in 1912 was awed by a tour which felt like a marathon. 'In and out, up and down we went, through heat and rain, over cobble stones and tram lines; now stepping on planks right down the double bottom, three hundred yards long, from which was soon to rise the *Titanic*'s successor; now crouching amongst the shores sustaining the huge bulk of another half-plated giant; now passing in silent wonder along the huge cradles and ways above which another monster stood ready for launching.' The work-shops seemed all full of wonders. 'Boilers as tall as houses, shafts a boy's height in diameter, enormous propellers hanging like some monstrous sea animal in chains, turbine motors on which workmen clambered as on a cliff, huge lathes, pneumatic hammers, and quiet slow-moving machines that dealt with cold steel, shearing it, punching it, planning it, as if it had been so much dinner cheese. Then up into the Moulding loft, large enough for a football ground, and its floor a beautiful maze of frame lines; on through the Joiners' shops, with their tools that can do everything but speak; through the Smiths' shops, with their long rows of helmet-capped hearths, and on into the great airy building where an army of Cabinetmakers are fashioning all kinds of ship's furniture.' He was shown the ship-yard's Power Plant, which daily generated enough electricity to light

Belfast, and the high-arched Drawing Hall where the plans were made, before going 'out to a wharf and over a great ship, full of whir and clamour, and as thronged with workmen as soon it would be with passengers'.[20]

Another Harland & Wolff visitor recorded the shattering noise during the building of the White Star liner *Baltic* in 1903. 'The thunder of riveting was flung across the river, against the quayside sheds and the ranks of cross-Channel steamers with their white-painted upper-works and gaily painted funnels; the gantries stood like towers against the sunset; red-hot rivets glowed like lamps in the interior of a cathedral where no sooner than one act of creation was finished then another was shatteringly begun – creation only momentarily interrupted when, lifting her stern towards the stars, *Titanic* slid down with a thunderous roar into the ice-cold Atlantic, abruptly extinguishing the plush-and-gilt Edwardian dream.'[21]

The building of *Baltic* had been supervised by Thomas Andrews, later the designer of *Titanic*. His mother was Pirrie's sister, and at the age of sixteen, in 1889, he was apprenticed for five years to the shipyard. He trained in the joiner's shop, the main store, the moulding loft, with the cabinet-makers, shipwrights, painters, fitters, pattern-makers and smiths. Eighteen months in the drawing office completed his apprenticeship. 'His job, first and last and always' was what drove him: 'that was the man's way.'[22] Andrews was appointed in 1905, aged thirty-two, as Chief of the Design Department, and in 1907 as Managing Director. Though his uncle never trusted him with finan-cial confidences, he was an omnipresent force at Harland & Wolff, controlling his unruly workmen. His biographer pictured him 'big and strong, a paint-smeared bowler hat on his crown, grease on his boots and the pockets of his blue jacket stuffed with plans, now making his daily rounds of the Yards, now consulting his Chief, now conferring with a foreman, now interviewing an owner, now pouring over intricate calculations in the Drawing office, now superintending the hoisting of a boiler by the 200-ton crane into some newly launched ship by a wharf.' There were other images of him at work: running amok among a gang of workmen whom he surprised heating their tea-cans before horn-blow; lambasting men whom he found stealing a crafty smoke below a tunnel-shaft; kicking aside a red hot rivet, that had fallen 50 feet and missed his head by inches, and striding on with a laugh. Another tale had him standing by a ship's precarious gangway down which 4,000 hungry workmen were jostling homewards for their evening meal. When the gangway's guard-rope snapped, and his workers were at risk of a 90-foot plunge, his commanding voice rang out, 'Stand back, men!' and singly he held the thousands back until the rope was repaired. Andrews would often intervene in fights or sectarian violence amongst his workforce. 'Once he found a great fellow ill-treating a small foreman who had docked his wages; whereupon Andrews took off his coat and hammered the bully. During labour and party troubles, he several times, at risk of his life, saved men from the mob.'[23]

The Hamburg-Amerika liner *Amerika* (22,225 tons), which was built under Andrews's aegis and launched at Belfast in 1905, broke moulds – and not just because it had the first electric lift in an Atlantic liner. Until *Amerika*, the first-class interiors of liners were a muddled pastiche of styles: Tudor, Jacobean, Olde English, Louis XIV, Italian Renaissance. This sterile fakery appeared even in innovative ships like *Mauretania* which, having copied *Amerika* by having a brace of lifts, enclosed them in sham Renaissance grillework made of aluminium. But in 1903 Albert Ballin hired Charles-Frédéric Mewès and his partner Arthur Davis (designers of the Carlton and Ritz hotels in London) to work on the first-class interiors of *Amerika*: at the same time he enlisted César Ritz to train the catering staff to Ritz-Carlton standards. Mewès and Davis produced striking designs for *Amerika*, and later worked on the ritzy interiors of Hamburg-Amerika's *Kaiserin Auguste Victoria*, and the Cunarder *Aquitania*. Davis was told by his employers that their passengers were mostly seasick Americans who wanted to forget that they were on a ship when they went to sea. They sent him across the Atlantic to watch passengers in mid-ocean. Voyagers on these Atlantic leviathans were not amateur yachtsmen out to enjoy the ocean waves, he saw, but squeamish types who expected Ritz-Carlton or Waldorf-Astoria standards on land and sea.

At 10,650 tons the Inman Line's *City of Paris* had been the world's largest ship when it was launched in 1889; by 1907, within twenty years, Cunard's *Mauretania* – 'the monstrous nine-decked city' with 'seventy thousand horses', as Kipling called it – was triple that size.[24] *Lusitania* and *Mauretania* were larger than any ships yet built, and had the first steam turbine engines to be installed on a passenger line, which guaranteed a speed of 24½ knots and provided more. They immediately took the Blue Riband for the fastest Atlantic crossings. Speed not only satisfied the impatience of rich Americans, but shortened their sufferings in rough weather. 'By night-fall,' wrote a first-class American heading for Paris in 1907, 'turbid waves were upon us, & they shook & harried & hunted us from one continent to the other. We really had a brutal crossing, but it was a very short one, luckily, as we were on a fast boat.'[25]

White Star commissioned *Olympic*, *Titanic* and then *Britannic* to compete with *Mauretania*, *Lusitania* and ultimately *Aquitania*. A new double slipway was erected at Pirrie's shipyard: on 16 December 1908 work began on Keel 400 – later *Olympic*; and on 31 March 1909, on Keel 401 – later *Titanic*. By the end of 1910, the shipyard had 11,389 employees, double the number working there a year earlier and a fillip to the prosperity of all Belfast. White Star did not try to compete with Cunarders on speed, but chose to build slower, larger, more luxurious ships which were lean and elegant in design – far removed from the lumbering bulk of Hamburg-Amerika's *Imperator*. Whereas *Mauretania* (31,938 tons) was designed to carry 563 first-, 464 second- and 1,138 third-class passengers, and *Imperator* (51,969 tons) 700 first-, 600 second- and 1,000 third-class and 1,800 steerage, *Olympic* (45,324 tons) was the first and only vessel to carry about the same number of first-class and third-class passengers (about 1,000 each) and 500 second-class. It was launched in October 1910 (sales of spectators' tickets raised £486 for the Pirries' pet charity, the Royal Victoria Hospital, Belfast), and made its maiden voyage in June 1911.

The arrival of *Olympic* in New York was a major event. The ship steamed up the Hudson, as the stewardess Violet Jessop described, 'flag-bedecked and gay, fussily escorted by all manner of official and unofficial small craft, up past the huge buildings in Battery Park, the wharves and ships, all of which appeared to shimmer with the moving, cheering mass of people. Not a window, however small, but had a little flag or handkerchief waving from it, as we slowly passed to the accompaniment of shrill tootings from everything afloat that had a whistle to blow.' Thousands of inquisitive sightseers crowded on board during the next forty-eight hours with strident and sometimes inane questions. On the second night, White Star invited its 600 agents drawn from across the United States to inspect the liner and enjoy a boozy dinner. 'As the hours wore on, both they and their steward escorts – by now more or less on a brotherly footing – began to show signs of wear,' Jessop recalled. 'At 3 a.m., there was a lull in the convivial din, after which men were found sprawling asleep in the most out-of-the-way places: inside baths and half under beds, where they had seemingly dropped in their tracks . . . Others wandered aimlessly about, apparently lost and muttering for some guiding soul to rescue them. It took many hours to reunite coats, hats and shoes with their rightful owners but everyone voted the *Olympic* and its crew "swell". The surprise was that she was not burnt to the water's edge, seeing the masses of cigarette and cigar ends swept up next day, and the burnt patches that could not be swept up.'[26]

Olympic replicated the amenities which the rich expected of their luxury hotels in New York or the European capitals and watering places. Lord Winterton, who crossed from New York on her in 1912, recorded his pleasure in his diary. 'She really is a fine ship. Exceeds one's imagination. Racquet Court, Gymnasium, Swimming Bath, Restaurant, & Public Rooms are splendid. Decorations all over in real and not (as generally at sea) in tawdry taste. Food in Restaurant quite excellent. No "shippy" smell.' His cabin was larger than the bedroom of his bachelor chambers in Mayfair, and his first day on board delighted him: 'one really feels as if one was in a Sea-Side Hotel'. The other first-class passengers included the Duke and Duchess of Sutherland, their daughter Lady Rosemary Leveson-Gower, Lord

Alistair Kerr, and several American youths going up to Oxford or Cambridge. Life on land seemed drab to Winterton after *Olympic*. 'A glorious blue sky & warm sun in the Solent, and we were able to sit out on deck and listen to the band. Got to Southampton at 2 p.m. & found a dirty old train, with no Sunday papers on sale, labelled as the "White Star" Express. This was our welcome to England!! Before reaching London, we ran into dense grey sooty fog.'[27]

Ismay and Andrews travelled on *Olympic*'s maiden voyage, and made close observations which resulted in changes to the plans for *Titanic*. The second ship, which was three inches longer, thus came nearer to White Star's ideal of perfection. Ismay decided that some of the deck space on *Olympic* was superfluous and should be allotted for passenger cabins on *Titanic*, which was able to accommodate 163 more passengers than its sister ship – mostly in first-class. On both the top deck, known as the boat deck, and the upper promenade deck, known as A Deck, more cabins were added. Moreover, on the promenade deck, known as B, two specially spacious first-class suites were installed comprising a sitting room, two bedrooms, a bathroom and servant's quarters – for which £870 a trip would be charged at the height of the season. Each of these suites had a private promenade deck, protected from the sea winds by steel screens pierced by large windows, and ornamented by mock-Elizabethan half-timbered walls and bogus oak beams on the ceiling. One of these princely suites was allocated for Pierpont Morgan's use whenever he crossed the Atlantic. Ismay also fussed about the potato peeler in the crew's galley, wanted cigar holders to be fitted in first-class lavatories, found the beds too springy and stipulated that sliding glass windows should be installed on the A Deck promenade to protect strollers from sea winds and spray. These windows, which were fitted on *Titanic*, became known as the Ismay screens.

Harland & Wolff identified three hazards that might make a liner sink. It might run aground; it might collide with another ship or obstacle; or another ship might run into it. To meet the first danger, they provided *Titanic* with a double bottom, though not a double hull, as Cunard had specified for *Lusitania* and *Mauretania*. Seven feet above the lower steel plates they inserted a second set of steel plates so that if the keel was holed by the sea bed, the ship would not be flooded by water. To meet the second and third dangers, *Titanic* was fitted with fifteen bulkheads, which divided the hull into sixteen watertight compartments. The bulkheads required apertures, so that crew and passengers could move about the ship, but these were fitted with watertight doors which could be shut with the flick of a switch by the ship's officers. Each bulkhead door automatically shut if the compartment became flooded with more than six inches of water. If *Titanic's* bow was smashed by a collision, it would stay afloat even if the first four of these compartments were flooded. If another ship stove in its side, *Titanic* could float with any two of its central compartments flooded. This seemed impressive, even indefeasible, for most ships had only one or two bulkheads in the bow as a defence against collision – not sixteen watertight compartments. However, the bulkheads added to the ship's cost, and Harland & Wolff's designers concluded that it was unnecessary for them to reach higher than D Deck fore and aft, and E Deck amidships. In places, therefore, the bulkheads were no more than 15 feet above the waterline. Although *Titanic* would not sink if the first four compartments were holed in a head-on collision, or if two compartments were breached by another ship hitting broadside, it was a different matter if the front six compartments were somehow damaged. Then the bow would sink so low that water would flood over the top of the bulkhead separating the sixth from the seventh compartment, and from the seventh to the eighth – a process that would continue until the ship sank. This seemed unthinkable.

Alexander Carlisle, Harland & Wolff's general manager, who was in charge of the equipment and decoration of *Olympic* and *Titanic*, anticipated that the Board of Trade, the government department regulating British-registered ships, would introduce regulations requiring a greater provision of lifeboats on super-liners. His brother-in-law Pirrie told him to make plans on that assumption, and he brought proposals for forty-eight or even sixty-four lifeboats to conferences with White Star. At these conferences Pirrie and Ismay did all the talking: Carlisle recalled that he and Ismay's deputy, Harold Sanderson, 'were more or less dummies'.[28] At one day-long meeting, they talked for a total of five or ten minutes about lifeboat provision; and despite Carlisle's misgivings, which he dared not express before Pirrie, the provision of lifeboats was cut from forty-eight to twenty once it became clear that the Board of Trade were not going to alter its regulations. This reduced clutter on the deck as well as costs, but meant that the liner would have lifeboat capacity for a maximum of one-third of its passengers and crew. The risk seemed minimal when the consensus held that the liner was invulnerable.

It is notorious that *Titanic* was certified to carry 3,547 passengers and crew, but had lifeboat capacity for 1,178 souls. Indeed, the ship was certified to carry 1,134 steerage passengers, and would have required nineteen lifeboats if each of them were to have a place. Instead it carried fourteen wooden lifeboats (30 feet long) with an official capacity of sixty-five each; four Engelhardt boats with collapsible canvas sides which could take forty-seven passengers apiece; and two cutters for rescuing people who had fallen overboard, which were both capable of taking forty people (a total deficiency on *Titanic* of 2,369 places). This was not markedly worse than the figures for other liners of all nationalities and sizes. The French vessel *La Provence* was best in providing for 82 per cent of passengers and crew; but the Cunarder *Carmania* could only account for 29 per cent. Cunard's *Mauretania* and *Lusitania* both had capacity for 2,350 passengers and 900 crew, but with twenty lifeboats, had a deficiency of 2,150. Hamburg-Amerika's two liners *Kaiserin Auguste Victoria* and *Amerika* could each carry 2,770 passengers with 550 crew, and had twenty-four boats, leaving a deficiency of 2,000 people. Norddeutscher-Lloyd's *George Washington* could carry 3,262 passengers, 590 crew, and had twenty lifeboats, making a deficiency of 2,752. The figures for the Holland-Amerika line's *Rotterdam* were 3,585 passengers, 475 crew, eighteen lifeboats, leaving a deficiency of 3,070.

The Board of Trade's lifeboat regulations, framed under the Merchant Shipping Act of 1894, had a scale requiring two lifeboats for ships up to 200 tons, and ending with a minimum of sixteen lifeboats for ships exceeding 10,000 tons. The Board's scale was futile: there was no reason to stop at 10,000 tons, and super-liners had nearly five times that displacement. Sir Alfred Chambers, Nautical Advisor to the Marine Department of the Board of Trade 1896–1911, was however a past master of the school of government regulators that disbelieved in regulations. 'It was the safest mode of travel in the world, and I thought it neither right nor the duty of a State Department to impose regulations . . . as long as the record was a clean one,' he testified. Asked after the *Titanic* sinking why lifeboat regulations had not been updated despite the increase in size of vessels, he replied that he preferred the provision of lifeboats to depend on shipowners' voluntary action rather than imposing inflexible rules. He even claimed that if there had been fewer lifeboats, more people would have been saved: passengers would have rushed the boats and filled them to capacity.[29] There was also an official feeling that it would be 'unfair' if older ships afloat were obliged to increase their lifeboat provision because of *Olympic* and *Titanic*.[30]

There were other unimaginative safety procedures. Captain Maurice Clarke, the inspector who approved *Titanic* for sailing, oversaw a boat drill which comprised lowering and raising two lifeboats, manned by a special crew, while the ship was docked at Southampton. Questioned by Lord Mersey – who headed the Board of Trade enquiry into the loss of *Titanic* – he conceded that this was a cursory, unexacting routine which he followed because it was 'the custom'. Asked by Mersey if he followed 'custom although it was bad', Clarke replied, 'Well, you will remember I am a civil servant. Custom guides us a good bit.'[31]

Why were White Star and Harland & Wolff content with lifeboat provision that barely sufficed for a ship less than a quarter of its size? Ship designers and shipowners reckoned that lifeboat accommodation encroached on bedroom suites, promenade decks, public rooms and other amenities; and that lifeboat seats for every passenger and crewman were superfluous. When Arthur Rostron, captain of the small liner *Carpathia*, which steamed to the rescue of *Titanic* survivors, was subsequently interrogated by the US Senate enquiry, he explained why his ship and the biggest super-liners, carrying different numbers of passengers and crew, were required by Board of Trade regulations to carry the same number of lifeboats. 'The ships are built nowadays to be practically unsinkable, and each ship is supposed to be a lifeboat in itself,' Rostron testified. He regarded actual lifeboats 'merely . . . as a standby'.[32]

Titanic's first-class passenger accommodation was placed amidships, and extended over five decks: the Promenade Deck (A); Bridge Deck (B); Shelter Deck (C); Saloon Deck (D); and Upper Deck (E). Two grand staircases, three electric lifts and sundry stairways provided access to the different decks. The expanse of decks amidships ran for almost two-thirds of the total length of the ship. With the exception of the officers' quarters on the boat deck, the second-class smoking-room at the after end of B Deck, and the second-class library and third-class lounge and smoking-room on C Deck, most of this superstructure was dedicated to the needs of first-class passengers. In first-class everything seemed spacious: the public rooms were vast, the corridors were wide and high, the stairs and landings were broad; nothing was cramped or mean. 'She has everything but taxi-cabs and theatres, Table d'Hôte, Restaurant à la Carte, Gymnasium, Turkish Baths, Squash Court, Palm Gardens, smoking-rooms for "Ladies and Gents", intended I fancy to keep the women out of the men's smoking-room which they infest in the German and French steamers' – so wrote an American on the maiden voyage, Frank Millet, who was reminded of the Jacobean interior of the Duke of Rutland's seat, Haddon Hall. 'As for the rooms they are larger than the ordinary hotel room, and much more luxurious with wooden bedsteads, dressing-tables, hot and cold water, etc., electric fans, electric heater. The suites with their damask hangings and mahogany oak furniture are really very sumptuous.'[33]

In addition to the first-class public rooms listed by Millet there was a dining saloon, lounge, reading and writing room, lending library, veranda café, barber shop, photographers' dark room, and clothes-pressing room. There was a lounge for the first-class ladies' maids and gentlemen's valets. There were quarters for first-class dogs.

Titanic included the first swimming pool to be installed on board a ship. Instead of a crude sick bay, its medical facilities included an operating theatre. White Star had been to the forefront since the 1890s in raising standards for second- and third-class Atlantic passengers. On *Titanic* the public saloons on the lower decks were spacious, welcoming and spic and span, creating a festive holiday mood, while the berths were as airy, hygienic and agreeable as Andrews's team of designers could devise. The ship's power plant supplied electricity for evaporation and refrigeration, four passenger lifts, a telephone system, the Marconi wireless station, hundreds of heaters, eight electric cargo cranes, electric pumps, motors and winches.

The interiors were a medley of styles which were intended to give an eclectic rather than bastardized effect. 'You may sleep in a bed depicting one ruler's fancy, breakfast under another dynasty altogether, lunch under a different flag and furniture scheme, play cards, smoke or indulge in music under three other monarchs, have your afternoon tea in a veranda which is modern and cosmopolitan, . . . [and dinner] in imperial style,' one publicist wrote approvingly.[34] The first-class suites had beds rather than berths, telephones, and (instead of round portholes) panoramic windows that looked out over the blue sea like the windows of a cliff-top castle. Instead of stoves or radiators, there were open grates in which coal fires burnt brightly. The suites had varied styles: Second Empire; Louis XIV, Louis XV and Louis XVI; Tudor; Early Dutch; Adams; Hepplewhite; Regency; Italian Renaissance, Georgian, Old Dutch, Colonial, Georgian, Jacobean, the Regency, and Queen Anne.

The 60-foot high main staircase was supposedly in William and Mary style, but Frenchified *à la* Louis XIV, with ironwork relieved by bronze flowers and foliage. Atop the staircase was a large dome of iron and glass, beneath which, on the uppermost landing, there was a carved panel containing a clock, flanked by bronze female figures, representing Honour and Glory crowning Time. The first-class dining saloon was the largest room afloat, seating 532 diners, running the full 92 feet of the ship's width and 114 feet in length. Its style was Jacobean, but instead of the sombre oak panels found in great English houses, the walls and ceilings were painted a shiny, hygienic white. Oak furniture was meant to heighten the Jacobean air, but the effect was marred by patterned linoleum floor tiles. The separate restaurant on B Deck was equally commodious, measuring 60 by 45 feet, but in a fake Louis XVI style, with fawn-coloured walnut panelling, gilded mouldings, brass and gilt light brackets, a long buffet table with a marble *fleur de pêche* top, and fawn silk curtains across the bay windows, with flowered borders and embroidered pelmets. The plaster ceiling was patterned with trellises and garlands, the Axminster carpet was of Louis XVI design, the walnut chairs upholstered by tapestry of a *treillage* of roses; and there was an inevitable bandstand.

The reception room extended the width of the ship. It, too, had white panelling in Jacobean style, hung with Aubusson tapestry work. The first-class lounge situated on Promenade Deck A was derived from the style of the Palace of Versailles. The reading and writing room was in the Georgian style of the 1780s. The smoking room, where convivial men foregathered in sprawling apathy, was mahogany panelled, supposedly in the Georgian style of the 1720s. There was a French café with little tables, cane settees and wicker easy chairs, climbing plants trained on green trellis to create the illusion of being ashore. The Turkish baths were designed in seventeenth-century Moorish style, tiled in blue and green. It was 'all very marvellous', declared a Philadelphia journalist, 'the luxurious hotel transferred to the ocean; the glittering lobster palace afloat.'[35]

FIVE

Sailors

*It is a blessing, no doubt, to be rid, at least for a time, of
All one's friends and relations.*

Arthur Hugh Clough, 'Amours de Voyage'

Titanic was the greatest steamship in the world, but its officers were
called sailors for a reason: they were all men who had been trained
at sea under sail. Herbert Pitman, its Third Officer, who had sixteen
years' experience as a mariner before joining *Titanic*, had four years
as an apprentice under sail followed by three years on sailing ships,
before serving on Blue Anchor Line steamships running to Australia.
The Fifth Officer, twenty-eight-year-old Harold Lowe, had been
seafaring half his life, having run away from his apprentice-master
at the age of fourteen, and served on seven schooners and several
square-rigged vessels before graduating to West African steamships.
William Murdoch, *Titanic*'s First Officer, had left school at fifteen to
become an apprentice seaman on a barque plying between Liverpool
and the Pacific coast of America. Neither their pride nor their sentiment let White Star officers forget that they had learnt seamanship
in the days of rigging, not funnels. The components of the rigging,
with such names as buntlines, gooseneck, halyard, parrel beads and
stay mouse, and the varieties of sail, including crab claw, laleen,
moonsail, spanker and topgallant, already seemed picturesque in the
age of *Titanic*. The dangers and hardships of sailing ships were
extreme: the men who had served on them were not prone to idealize
or prettify past conditions; but most regretted the obsolescence of

sail and hankered for the old days. With little prompting, they shared hair-raising memories of typhoons, accidents and privations, as incontrovertible proof of the masculine hardiness which they had shown when young.

Arthur Rostron, born in 1869, was apprenticed in 1887 to the full-rigged ship *Cedric the Saxon*, spent eight winters in the South Atlantic and ten years under sail. He recalled with pride, not loathing, being 'up aloft for hours on end, very often all through the raging night; six or eight hours on a foreyard trying to furl the foresail, the canvas soaked with rain and sea spray, hard as sheet-iron, until the finger-nails were torn off, leaving raw bleeding wounds; drenched to the skin, oilskins blown to ribbons and sea-boots full of water'. It was a memory that no-one could take from him, 'the eternal rolling and pitching and the almost constant hurricanes . . . down below the Horn'.[1] Charles Herbert Lightoller, Second Officer on *Titanic*, recalled his first voyage on a steamship from New York in the 1890s: 'Frankly, I didn't like it. Good times; good food. Always sure of your watch below. Yet I loathed the smoke and the smell, and longed for the towering tiers of bellying canvas, the sound of water rushing past the scupper holes, in place of the monotonous clank and bang of machinery. I sadly missed the feel of something living under my feet.'[2] It was consolation, though, that his steamer took only a fortnight to reach Glasgow.

James Bisset, a future Cunard captain, recalled that when he passed his exams as First Mate in 1905, aged twenty-one, he had served as an apprentice and Second Mate on four round-the-world voyages (on a 1,098-ton barque and full-rigged ship of 1,323 tons carrying coal and guano) but never in a steamship. 'My commonsense told me that windjammers were doomed to extinction by the competition of steam; yet, in 1905, there were still many hundreds of sailing vessels under the British flag, and hundreds more under the American, French, German, Scandinavian and other national flags. They were owned and manned by diehards, of an ageing generation, and were kept going, with increasing financial difficulties, by the force of habit inherited from centuries of tradition.'[3] Officers of Bisset's

generation – he was born in 1883 – recognized that steamers promised better pay and conditions, swifter voyages and better chances
of promotion, but he felt devalued when he moved over from sail
to steam in 1905: 'No more hounding men aloft, at risk of life and
limb, to take in or make sail in a howling hurricane; no more tedious
pully-hauly, sweltering in the doldrums; no more starvation on the
bare whack of putrid pork and hard biscuits! But . . . no more of
the peace and quiet of a sailing ship, snoring along in the trades
with all sails set and everything drawing; no more exhilaration of
running the easting down; no more thrills of gazing aloft at graceful
curving sails . . . For the rest of my nautical life, I would be going
to sea in oblong steel boxes with smoking funnels, thumping engines,
vibrating propellers, rattling derricks and clattering winches; I would
be dolled up like a gilded popinjay in my brassbound uniform, to
impress the passengers; and perhaps there would be little real sail-
orizing to be done.'[4]

The contempt of the hard men for the new softness is caught in
a poem written by Kipling during the transitional 1890s:

> cabins with marble and maple and all,
> And Brussels an' Utrecht velvet, and baths and a Social Hall,
> And pipes for closets all over, and cutting the frames too light.[5]

But for passengers the supersession of sail by steam seemed wholly
beneficial. In 1872 the average crossing from Liverpool to New York
by sailing vessel took forty-four days: by steamship, under a fortnight. Deaths during Atlantic passages were put at 1 per 184
passengers on sailing ships compared with 1 per 2,195 passengers
on steamers. Young children were especially vulnerable. Corpses
were wrapped in sailcloth weighted with a sandbag, and tipped
overboard from a tilting plank while the captain read a snatch of
the funeral service. *Umbria* (1884; 7,718 tons) was the last Cunarder
on the Atlantic run to be fitted with auxiliary sails in addition to
two funnels.

Lightoller, a crucial witness in *Titanic* history, had been born in the Lancashire mill town of Chorley. His mother died a month after he was born. His father left for New Zealand when his business failed, leaving Herbert and his sisters in the care of an uncle and aunt. They sent him to Chorley Grammar School, where his reports were unsatisfactory; he had religion drilled into him, was thrashed with the strap, stinted of pocket money. When he decided to escape this deprivation by going to sea, his uncle was pleased to be shot of the expense. In 1888, just short of fourteen, he signed on as an apprentice on a steel-hulled, four-masted barque of 2,500 tons, *Primrose Hill*. He paid £40 surety as an apprentice; signed 'articles of Agreement' in which he pledged to stay out of taverns and keep his master's secrets; and was bound to his employers for four years without pay at the end of which he would be well trained in seamanship. He was outfitted with pilot coat, heavy trousers, two pairs of overalls, heavy underwear, sea boots and sea stockings, oilskins with storm cap, two shore-going uniforms, a knife, spike and straw mattress – all packed in a sea chest. He was quartered in the half deck, in a cramped, smelly den, lined with bunks for the boys, reached by a steep ladder from the poop deck above.

The life was brutalizing, though it gave discipline, cohesive loyalty and proud resilience to boys who had often felt adrift, squashed or unwanted at home. Bertram Hayes, an officer on White Star Atlantic steamships, recalled his food as an apprentice seaman: 'The biscuits, commonly called "Liverpool pantiles", were so hard you could only break them with a hammer or on the corner of a chest, and they became full of weevils after a short time at sea. The salt beef and pork I could never eat and envied those who could. The beef was called "salt horse", and . . . was so hard that the sailors used to cut models of ships out of it.'[6] Bad grub was not the only unpleasantness, as Lightoller recalled of his first voyage on *Primrose Hill*. 'It grew hotter and hotter, until the pitch boiled up out of the seams in the deck, to stick to and blister our still tender feet. It brought other things also; not exactly out of the deck, but from below deck, in the shape of rats and cockroaches.' Lightoller and his shipmates used to kill the rats with belaying pins, or by stamping on them with their bare feet. At night, as the men lay in their bunks, rats would chew their toenails, and the calloused flesh on the soles of their feet, without waking the exhausted men. Cockroaches nearly two inches long had 'the same happy habit of browsing on our feet', Lightoller recalled. 'For their benefit we kept a tin of very strong caustic soda and a small brush with a handle two feet long, and when they started to make themselves objectionable a dab with the brush settled their hash.'[7]

There were eye-opening wonders and outlandish beauty for a boy going to sea. In Bisset's sailing-ship days, it was customary for young seamen passing through the Sargasso Sea to collect choice seaweeds and preserve them in large bottles. The bottles were decorated with twine plaiting, daubed with cheery red and green paint and taken home to impress landlubbers. If filled with sea water and sealed, they kept bright and clear for years. Bisset returned from his first sea voyage with (he hoped) the most profusely decorated bottle of weed ever landed at Liverpool. His other curios included a shark's jawbone that had been bleached by the sun, a tobacco pouch made from the webbed foot of an albatross (complete with claws), a walking stick carved from a shark's backbone, a flying fish with outspread wings mounted on a wooden stand, and best of all, a ship in a bottle. All these treasures were secreted in a gaily painted sea chest with rope grummets for handles, and a painting inside the lid of a four-mast barque bowling along under a good wind. For years Bisset gloated over his collection.[8]

The time would come when a young sailor completed his apprenticeship and was qualified, so far as sea service went, to sit the examination for his Second Mate's certificate – known as a 'ticket'. This required him to have swotted up enough mathematics, navigation, nautical astronomy and seamanship to meet the standards set by the sleepy, stultified Board of Trade. For the youngsters, life on land often seemed more threatening and insalubrious than at sea. Lightoller recalled touring New York when he was a young sailor in the 1890s. At one dive he saw a 'butting match' between a billy goat and a black man, crouching on all fours. When the goat was released, it bounded forward and the two collided head-on: the goat broke its neck, and the man was knocked out to thunderous cheers. Lightoller was sickened too by seeing knuckle-dusters used in New York brawls. 'After the clean breath of the sea, where everything is open and above board, where men settle their differences in their bare feet, on a white deck, with a perfectly good pair of fists, all this gouging, twisting, and bone-breaking left me thoroughly disgusted with the so-called "high spots" of New York.'[9] The perils on land revolted Arthur Rostron too. 'Harpies and sharks are waiting in every port. With friendly word and false smiles they meet these sailors, who, maybe, have been long out of sight of land . . . with his pay in his pocket and eyes dazed a bit by the almost-forgotten glitter of port life, he easily falls prey to these emissaries of Satan. He is lured into their parlours, sometimes to die, always to be robbed, often to be beaten, filled with loathsome liquor and, alas, not infrequently with disease.'[10]

Storms were an unforgettable experience for the youngsters. A sailing ship caught in a heavy gale, which, through lack of speed or bad steering, fell into the trough of the sea, was said to have 'broached to'. A ship that 'broached to' in heavy seas would wallow in the troughs of the waves, with sails ripped to shreds, and probably her masts crashing about under her lee side, pounding the hull, and threatening to sink the ship. The crew would make furious efforts to cut away this lethal tangle of wire, ropes, canvas, chain, wood and iron, as Bisset pictured: 'A handful of men with knives and axes, cold, tired, soaked and saddened, daring and desperate, one minute up to their necks in icy water, clutching for dear life to the shattered bulwarks, and the next hacking and slashing furiously as the water leaves them to go sweeping across the deck on the roll, and all the time glancing fearfully to windward where the great towering seas, rearing their foaming phosphorescent crests, come terrifyingly down out of the darkness.'[11] Many battered sailing-ships resembled the vessel described in Masefield's poem 'The Wanderer':

So, as though stepping to a funeral march,
She passed defeated homewards whence she came
Ragged with tattered canvas white as starch,
A wild bird that misfortune had made tame.

There was constant anxiety about a night-time collision with an iceberg. The only way to detect them on a moonless night was by the white foam at their base: with moonlight it was easier to spot a glint of what is called 'ice blink'. Lightoller recounted an occasion in the South Atlantic when the cold became piercing, the wind fell away and suddenly the crew were confronted by the threatening, spectral outline of a monstrous berg which had been taking the wind out of their sails. With difficulty the ship drew off from the menacing ice walls – all the crew worrying whether there were protruding under-water ledges which might hole the ship beneath the water line and sink it. 'With the first streak of dawn it was easy to see what a narrow shave it had been,' Lightoller recalled. 'With the full day there was revealed an impenetrable wall of ice for close on fifteen miles astern, and more than double that distance ahead.' The ship had to sail for two days before it left that mass of ice. 'Pinnacles, bays, chasms and cathedral-like structures, huge ravines and bridges, bridges of ice, looking for all the world as if they had been built by some clever engineers, and would have done credit to them at that.'[12]

A worse danger than icebergs were the derelicts drifting about the seas: often dismasted, waterlogged Nova Scotia schooners, carrying timber and hard to sink. The hull of a schooner might float for months, entombing a starving crew without control of its navigation or means of contact with other ships, and could hole an unwary liner. Infectious diseases were another common hazard. Lightoller was once on a sailing ship a fortnight out of Rio de Janeiro when the crew began to fall sick. 'The first chap we said was loafing, until he died. That's nearly always the verdict on a sailing ship, anyway. A man is invariably "mouching" until he dies, and then we say, "Oh, he must have been bad after all".' In this case, it was smallpox, there was of course no ship's doctor, and the only medicine on board, a half cup of castor oil, was drunk by a patient in mistake for water. 'We just had to rely upon our cast-iron constitutions and stick it out,' Lightoller averred. 'Twice I read the burial service, or such parts as I could find, in a gale of wind when the Mate couldn't leave the poop. Sometimes we couldn't get the body over the rail: then it was beastly.'[13]

On 16 March 1912, just a month before *Titanic* sank, another liner built by Harland & Wolff, P&O's *Oceana*, outward bound from the Port of London to Bombay, was lost in the English Channel after a collision with a German steel barque. *Oceana* stayed afloat for six hours after the collision, and 241 passengers and crew were rescued. Nine however drowned when the first lifeboat capsized after its launch – a memory which surely contributed to the initial reluctance of *Titanic* passengers to board their lifeboats. Another *Oceana* lifeboat was so leaky that, despite constant bailing of water, it was foundering by the time its scared occupants were finally saved by the Eastbourne lifeboat. There were claims of panicking Asiatic seamen, whose reliability was questioned in Parliament. The *Spectator* felt that insufficient precautions were taken to 'police' passengers and crew in a crisis. 'The crew, as in the case of the P&O Company, may contain Asiatics and Africans, who may or may not behave well. In P&O ships the Lascars are generally to be trusted, but one cannot speak so certainly of the Hindu firemen.'[14]

When, in 1907, James Bisset joined the Cunarder *Caronia*, he was awed by the profusion of instruments on the bridge: aside from the steering wheel and compass, there were two engine-room telegraphs for port and starboard, anchoring and docking telegraphs, speaking tubes, fire-alarm boxes and telephones.[15] Elsewhere on the ship there was a Marconi wireless operator capable of tapping out coded messages to other ships and the mainland Marconi receivers. In addition, since 1866, the Atlantic telegraph cable had functioned fully and reliably. It increased the sense of busy men that the ocean between Europe and America should be instantaneously bridgeable. The deep-sea cables in Kipling's poem about the Atlantic telegraph are vaunting about their brave technology yet apprehensive of the crushing, inanimate, deadly power of the deep ocean on whose bottom they lie:

> The wrecks dissolve above us; their dust drops down from afar –
> Down to the dark, to the utter dark, where the blind white sea-snakes are.
> There is no sound, no echo of sound, in the deserts of the deep,
> Or the great grey level plains of ooze where the shell-burred cables creep.
> Here in the womb of the world – here on the tie-ribs of earth
> Words, and the words of men, flicker and flutter and beat –
> Warning, sorrow, and gain, salutation and mirth –
> For a Power troubles the Still that has neither voice nor feet.[16]

After the *Titanic* calamity, there was a general reaction that liners had been steaming ahead too dangerously fast. Even so, there were those who mitigated the risks of speed. The shipping publicist who wrote *Travelling Palaces* in 1913 declared that for businessmen competing against keen competitors every wasted hour was money lost. 'How, too,' he asked, 'can the American tourist, taking a month's holiday, cross the Atlantic twice and "do" the United Kingdom and Ireland and most of Europe to his own satisfaction in the rest of the month if hours, minutes and seconds be not saved?' The Pittsburgh banker Thomas Mellon, for example, took longer to cross the Atlantic both ways than he allowed for his entire European holiday. The hastening American divorcée in Edith Wharton's story 'Autres Temps' (1911) chafed because her liner *Utopia* took eight days to cross from Cherbourg to New York. The steamship companies profited from rich passengers in a hurry. In the publicist's words, 'the hustler and rusher help fill the most expensive cabins, and to pay for the luxuries in speed and surroundings they require. If it were not for the comforts and luxuries, and the enforced rest, and the recuperative effect of a sea voyage . . . some American tourists would die of exhaustion, and many of the commercial men who rush from one side of the Atlantic to the other . . . would collapse under the strain.'[17]

There was an unnecessary cost to this thoughtless haste. Rostron recalled his first winter crossing of the Atlantic on a Cunarder, *Umbria*. 'We bore into the heavy seas and I was staggered at the speed that was maintained in spite of the damage the weather was causing to the ship. But in those days speed was the be-all and end-all of the crack ships.'[18] Damage costing thousands of pounds to repair would be sustained in a few minutes because captains would not lose a few hours. Lightoller, who joined White Star in 1900 and spent twenty years on the Atlantic service, also deplored the relentless driving of ships through gales. Liners lurching through heavy seas, with the propeller coming out of the water, were more stomach-turning than a passenger lift plunging from an upper floor of a skyscraper; but junior officers dared not even murmur their objections. 'Time and again,' declared Lightoller, 'I have seen the ship driven into a huge green wall of water, crowned with that wicked, curling breaker, which it seemed utterly impossible for anything to withstand. An immediate dash is made for an iron stanchion, and, gripping this with might and main, one awaits the crash. Not infrequently the steel-fronted bridge, stanchions and rail are driven back, and nearly flattened to the deck.' As liners grew bigger and faster, their captains were urged by their companies to reduce speed when necessary, but seldom did so.[19]

Crashing into storm waves was not the heaviest jeopardy. Cocksure attitudes by Atlantic passengers, and unimaginative complacency by Board of Trade regulators, were worse. Crewmen and officers who had begun their working lives on vulnerable little ships of sails and rigging – blown hither and thither by winds, creeping slowly across the water's surface as the natural elements ordained – felt impervious on these great, steel liners that sped across the ocean so swiftly that they were called Atlantic greyhounds. 'Everyone starts for India, America, Africa or Australia with the assumption that there will not be a wreck,' the *Spectator* objected after *Oceana* sank. 'It would surely be better to assume that there *might* be a wreck, and to have the passengers as well as the whole ship's company informed of what they are expected to do, and knowing what penalties they will be exposed to if they indulge in any irregular act, dictated by either panic or selfishness.'[20]

The elation of a working life under sail was lost to most seamen by 1912, and the sense of perils at sea had diminished too. Yet on Atlantic steamships, sailors continued to work as look-outs, scanning for icebergs, derelicts, schooners or the perilous little skiffs of Newfoundland cod fishermen. For the look-outs a great Atlantic liner deep in the night seemed vast, uncanny, deserted: they felt alone with the steady onward drive of the screws,

the beat of the off-shore wind,
And the thresh of the deep-sea rain.[21]

SIX

American Millionaires

*There is almost as much dishonesty about what is called snobbishness
as about sex. By giving a deep and universal passion a ridiculous name,
Thackeray provided the English with yet another device for concealing
from themselves the passions by which human beings are impelled.
Snobbishness is the assertion of the will in social relations, as lust is in
the sexual. It is the desire for what divides men and the inability to
value what unites them. What Thackeray called snobbishness is the
theme of* Macbeth, *the discord which Christ tried to resolve in the
Sermon on the Mount, the mainspring of the careers of dictators and
millionaires.*

Hugh Kingsmill, *D. H. Lawrence*

A German butcher's boy books a winter passage from England to
Baltimore. His ship takes a southerly route to avoid pack ice, but the
winter of 1783–84 is so harsh that his ship spends four months at
sea, and becomes trapped in the frozen waters of Chesapeake Bay.
Eventually, in March, when the ship is still immovable, the boy
disembarks, and slithers across the ice to the American shore. He is
carrying a box of flutes, which he intends to sell in New York. A year
later he traverses the Atlantic again. This time he has a larger consignment with him – pianos, spinets, guitars, violins, flutes, clarinets and
musical scores – which he sells at high prices. Soon he realizes that
he can make a fortune buying furs from Indian trappers and selling
them in Europe. Every summer he leaves New York, driving his
wagon through swamps and forests, northwards up the Hudson

valley and along the shores of Lake Champlain. At each halt he bargains for pelts, then beats and bales the foul-smelling skins, lugging them back in heavy bags to his wagon, which waits on a trail miles off. In 1800 he organizes a shipment of furs, textiles, cochineal and ginseng to Canton. A year later his ship returns with Chinese silks, satins, nankeens, taffetas, Souchong teas, fans, porcelain, nutmeg and other rare commodities. He founds the American Fur Company, buys parcels of land near Bowery Lane, accumulates property in Manhattan until he is the biggest landlord in New York. Long before his death in 1848 he is America's richest man – worth perhaps $40,000,000. His name is John Jacob Astor.

In the year before Astor's death a twenty-year-old pedlar leaves the Jewish ghetto at Lengnau in Switzerland. His family have been oppressed and abused for generations; but the final provocation has been that his tailor father, a widower, has been forbidden by the Swiss authorities from marrying a Jewish widow on the pretext that they are too poor. The couple with their combined dozen children board a Rhine riverboat for Hamburg, where they take a ship to Philadelphia. Their Atlantic crossing takes two months, in cramped conditions, sustained by hardtack biscuits, dried fish, rationed wine and water. During their voyage the pedlar falls for his future step-mother's adolescent daughter, later marries her, and fathers seven sons. He peddles in the Pennsylvania anthracite towns. He sells shoestrings, lace, ribbon, pins, needles, spices, stove and furniture polish to the wives of miners and Pennsylvania Dutch farmers. He devises a stove polish that does not blacken hands, which his father makes at home with a sausage machine. He starts selling coffee essence, opens a grocery store, makes money as a supplier during the American Civil War, shifts commodities so as to maximize his profits. He is prospering as a lace and embroidery merchant when he gets a tip to buy stock in the Hannibal & St Joseph Railroad, a freight line serving Kansas City. Soon the financier Jay Gould, who wants to incorporate the Hannibal line into his Missouri Pacific system, needs the man's 2,000 shares. The ex-pedlar holds out until he is sure of a profit of $300,000. In 1879 he gives a small loan to help run two mines in Leadville, Colorado, the Rocky Mountains boom-town. The mines flood, he takes control of operations, his overseers strike the highest silver content of any mine in Leadville. Leadville becomes part of the American West's dream of easy money. Soon his mines produce silver and lead worth $750,000 a year, and are valued at $14 million. He builds himself a smelter. Within a few years he and his sons are the copper kings of America – later still of the world. His name is Meyer Guggenheim.

These are two stories of the United States: of emigrants forsaking hard, painful, ugly lives and prospering under American enterprise. They are also part of *Titanic* history, for an Astor and a Guggenheim died when the ship sank. The surname Astor carried connotations that were what people meant when they used the word 'America'. By the time of 'Colonel Jack's' birth in 1864, the Astors had been an American legend for three generations: their obscure origins, their fierce enterprise, their relentless accumulation of capital, were components in creating notions of the American Way. Similarly, the Guggenheims' family historian never doubted the meaning of the lives of his heroes: stupendous money-making, dynastic pride and triumphant retaliation for centuries of insult. 'Once in America, the Guggenheims, like thousands of other European immigrants from oppressed classes, would take their unconscious revenge against the ruling class of their native land,' he wrote in *The Guggenheims: an American Epic*. 'They would show the *Landvogt* of Baden, the Diet of the Swiss Confederation, the stuffy, moralistic Christians of the valley of the Surb what kind of people they had prevented from marrying, from owning land, from freely choosing a profession, from accumulating capital . . . They would live in grander and more magnificent palaces than the *Landvogt*'s. They would own properties larger than the entire valley of the Surb. They would not have to plead for their lives before diets; they would serve in the Senate of their new country's confederation. They would not only mine and smelt the metals used in coins, they would own and operate the largest and richest silver, copper and gold mines in the world. And as they progressed in their adopted country, they would acquire riches and honors and splendours so vast as to make the self-satisfied Christians of Lengnau look like beggars.'[1]

The Astors and Guggenheims differed in origins, race, religion, temperament and personal history, but some convictions they shared: they believed in their superiority, and that others should be made to feel abject. Many Americans cherished the illusions that their nation was not class-bound, that opportunities were open to all, that equality made the basis of citizenship. Yet the United States was supremely a competitive society: there was equality neither in its starts nor finishes; and the winners then as now needed the losers to know that they had lost. Lithe, garlanded, spotless champions look down their noses from the victor's podium on the maimed, besmirched, sapless runners-up. Although a distinctive brand of snobbery was rampant in the United States, there seemed to be less envy than in Europe. Perhaps the explanation is that American millionaires were super-rich. The hungry beggar who glimpses a sumptuous feast feels more marvel than hatred. Envy occurs when people become capable of mutual, and invidious, comparison; but, as Helmut Schoeck noted, 'overwhelming and astounding inequality, especially when it has an element of the unattainable, arouses far less envy than minimal inequality, which causes the envious to think: "I might almost be in his place".'[2]

In France the Jacobin republic, Napoleon Bonaparte's coronation as Emperor, the Bourbon restoration, the revolutionary convulsions which brought about the Citizen King's monarchy, the Second Republic, the Second Empire – these tumults pulled down some families and pitched up others. The novels of Balzac and Zola show the class ferment of nineteenth-century France. New terms were coined, such as *arriviste*, *nouveau riche* and *parvenu*, to describe the varieties of brash, pushy, touchy men with their newly minted wealth. It was different in the United States, a nation dating only from 1776, with states that were still rudimentary a hundred years later. There, as Joseph Epstein has written, 'almost all riches had to be *nouveaux*, everyone was an *arriviste*, and everybody counted himself *parvenu*. In its early decades, nearly the entire United States was engaged in one vast social climb.'[3] Snobbery in America involved devising, imposing, honouring, exulting in distinctions, demarcations and divisions that set people apart.

The Guggenheims' feeling of superiority at the expense of other people was praised by their devout family chronicler, but it was an Astor wife who honed, rigidified and enforced snobbery as nineteenth-century New York knew it. Class-consciousness, class discrimination, class rivalry are central to *Titanic* history.

John Jacob Astor I's grandson William Astor fathered four daughters before the birth in 1864 of his only son, John Jacob Astor IV, the 'Colonel Jack' of *Titanic*. After accomplishing a male heir, he and his wife Caroline lived somewhat apart. He withdrew to the Florida sunshine while in New York she made her redoubtable mark. At the outbreak of the American Civil War in 1861, there were supposedly only three millionaires in the United States; but after 1865, the figure soared and by the close of the century there were nearly 4,000. New York's social leaders were richer, more upstart and ephemeral than their counterparts in Boston's Back Bay or Philadelphia's Rittenhouse district. Riled by the promiscuity of new fortunes, Caroline Astor determined that the upper reaches of New York society must be protected from the ostentatious money-bags, corrupt hustlers and shameless philistines that swarmed over its best addresses.

In 1879 Henry James assessed his native land: 'the United States – a country without a sovereign, without a court, without a nobility, without an army, without a church or a clergy, without a diplomatic service, without a picturesque peasantry, without palaces or castles, or country seats, or ruins, without a literature, without novels, without an Oxford or a Cambridge, without cathedrals or ivied churches, without latticed cottages or village ale-houses, without political society, without sport, without fox-hunting or country gentlemen.'[4] But the United States had its Gilded Age and Caroline Astor. 'There was gold everywhere,' a banker's daughter recalled of the era. 'It adorned the houses of the men who had become millionaires overnight, and were trying to forget with all possible speed the days when they had been poor and unknown . . . They cultivated the Midas touch to such good purpose that truth to tell they were often bewildered by their own magnificence.'[5]

Caroline Astor was determined to keep every upstart Midas of the Gilded Age in place. Discarded by her husband, who was frolicking on his yacht with actresses, she imposed her social will like a czarina backed by the Divine Right of Kings and regiments of cuirassiers with swords drawn. She divided New Yorkers into the 'Four Hundred', the families who were acceptable in her house, and eliminated the other millions of city dwellers from any claim to be good society (New York City's population was 1.5 million in 1890 and 3.4 million by 1900). Mrs Astor enlisted Ward McAllister as her master of protocol. McAllister was a drawling dandy who had made money as an attorney during the California gold rush, learnt to ape the manners of European nobility during a tour of spas, distinguished himself as an organizer of impromptu Newport picnics. As a woman member of the Four Hundred described him, 'He read books on heraldry and precedence, studied the customs of every Court in Europe. He revelled in forms and ceremonies, his cult of snobbishness was so ardent, so sincere, that it acquired dignity; it became almost a religion. No devout parish priest ever visited his flock with more loyal devotion to duty than did Ward McAllister make his round of the opera-boxes on Monday evenings. He would listen to plans for forthcoming parties with the utmost gravity, offer his advice as to who should be invited . . . and all the while his watchful eyes would be observing the neighbouring boxes, noting newcomers, whom they were talking to, who was taking them up.'[6] McAllister remained Mrs Astor's vizier until he published a laughably silly volume of memoirs, which led to his speedy, pitiless derogation.

The acme of Mrs Astor's heroics of hospitality was her January ball. This was the origin of the phrase 'Four Hundred', for her ballroom could hold 400 people, and she and McAllister pronounced that only 400 people could be worth inviting to the ball. Her guests qualified by virtue of ancestry and uniformity of manners: to them any breach of custom was an affront; any outbreak of originality seemed a presumption; they preferred to have their thinking and taste decided by the collective sense of their caste. Their personal code was a set of turgid, inflexible rules that took the place of loving kindness. Caroline Astor sat on a red velvet divan on a raised platform overlooking the ballroom. Cards inscribed with the names of half a dozen ladies privileged to sit with her were arrayed on the divan. The ballroom was lit by massive candelabra, long rows of chairs were tied in pairs by ribbon, and the band in the musicians' gallery wore the blue Astor livery. Caroline Astor acquired pretentious imitators in other American cities: Louise Hill, wife of a smelter millionaire, said that there were only sixty-eight Denver residents whom she would have in her house, and later tried to seem more exclusive by reducing her list to the 'Sacred Thirty-Six'. When a journalist wrote that the Four Hundred 'devoted themselves to pleasure regardless of expense', one of them retorted that they 'devoted themselves to expense regardless of pleasure'.[7] In its exclusivity, décor, self-reverence and sham, Mrs Astor's New York was the inspiration and incitement of first-class life on *Titanic*.

Did Caroline Astor's Four Hundred temper New York society's competitiveness or instil any enduring standards? It seems unlikely. 'New York is not,' Lord Dufferin wrote in 1874 during the early years of the Four Hundred, 'a place I should care to return to. Individually the people are nice enough, and wonderfully kind and civil, but their jealousy and abuse of each other is stupendous. Every American Lady seems ashamed of her best friend.'[8] In 1906, shortly before Caroline Astor's death, Roger Fry described New York society in terms that showed that little improvement had occurred in thirty years. 'Intrigues and jealousies here make society almost chaotic. Moreover, everyone seems very nervous about public opinion and very few seem to have any courage . . . The trouble is that no-one . . . has any true standard. They are as credulous as they are suspicious and are wanting in any intellectual ballast so that fashion and passing emotions drift them anywhither.'[9]

As Joseph Epstein notes, there are no snobs in the Bible, Dante and Shakespeare. Three or four centuries ago people might swoon in the company of dukes, but snobbery – an insistence on one's superiority as a way of bolstering one's sense of worth and of diminishing others; or a cold, insolent insistence on the exclusivity of one's caste – was first aroused by the spread of democracy. Until then, there was ready acceptance of a stratified world of rank and privileges with the expectation that almost everyone would be everlastingly locked in their place. Snobbery flourishes in societies where people can vault from being a door-to-door pedlar of stove varnish to the richest man in town, or from being a consigner of flutes to the richest man in the country. 'The snob,' writes Epstein, 'fears contamination from those he deems beneath him . . . What the snob wants is deference, inevitably quite a bit more than he deserves.'[10]

Caroline Astor wanted more deference than she deserved. Her social despotism relied on controlled publicity to lull her inferiors into admiring submission. News was filtered and sanitized, and then given in stirrup cups to the society columnists. In his Newport cottage McAllister was available to journalists between nine and ten each morning. He thrived on publicity, was always primed with catchy quotes and proved a reliable tipster as to who was ascendant or sinking. Millionaires used their social secretaries to ensure that the chronicling of their comings-and-goings was prominent but innocuous. 'What is Doing in Society', a regular column in the *New York Times*, provided this anodyne commentary on 8 May 1900: 'It is difficult to locate people just at present, as they are coming and going, stopping in town for a few days as they flit from one house party to another. Servants are being sent from the town house to the country seat to arrange for the Summer, and everyone is more or less picnicking. Plans are changed so frequently that it is impossible to tell at present what the arrangements will be for the warm months . . . Col. John Jacob Astor is booked to-day to sail for Europe . . . Mrs Stuyvesant Fish will not go to Garrisons-on-the-Hudson until about the 20th. Her visit will be very short and from there she goes to Newport . . . Mr William K. Vanderbilt, who is now in Paris, will set sail quite shortly for America . . . In the *New York*, sailing for Liverpool tomorrow, there are booked, among others, Mr

& Mrs Henry Phipps, Mrs Perry Tiffany, the Duke of Newcastle, Mrs Cardeza of Germanstown.'

High-minded savants stoutly defended this flaunted wealth. 'What matters it then that some millionaires are idle, or silly, or vulgar, that their ideas are sometimes futile, and their plans grotesque?' asked a Yale professor. 'The millionaires are a product of natural selection, acting on the whole body of men to pick out those who can meet the requirements of certain work to be done . . . They live in luxury, but the bargain is a good one for society.'[11] Yet overall American attitudes to their millionaires commingled envy, aspiration, contempt and repudiation. 'Having been born in Virginia, I cannot admit that either the Vanderbilts or the Astors were ever born at all,' Nancy Langhorne Shaw told dinner guests in Boston before marrying an Astor in 1906. 'But if people insist that they were, I will acknowledge that the Astors stopped skinning skunk a few years before the Vanderbilts began taking tolls on the ferry.' At a sumptuous dinner given by the Fricks in 1910 for US President Taft and Back Bay Bostonians, the White House aide Archie Butt asked if Adelaide Frick was 'a well-born woman'. 'Yes,' he was told, 'as well-born as it is possible for anyone to be who is born in Pittsburgh.'[12] These discriminations were part of the carefully graded world of Emily Post's *Etiquette* handbook published in 1922, with its social stereotypes bearing Bunyanesque names: the Worldlys, the Gildings, the Oldnames, the Eminents, the Snobshifts, Jim Smartlington, Mrs Toplofty, Mr and Mrs Spendeasy Western, Mrs Oncewere, the Upstarts.

In an outspoken republic, the Four Hundred's coquetting with publicity was dangerous. 'One sketches one's age but imperfectly,' Henry James declared, 'if one doesn't touch on . . . the invasion, the impudence and shamelessness of the newspaper and the inter-viewer, the devouring *publicity* of life, the extinction of all sense between public and private. It is the highest expression of the note of "familiarity", the sinking of *manners*, in so many ways, which the democratization of the world brings with it.'[13] The Astors, Morgans and Vanderbilts, and in Britain men like Lord Pirrie, lived – if not in a storm of publicity – at least under a pelting rain of newspaper paragraphs. Their social secretaries – people like Mrs Gilding's Miss Brisk – fed digestible gobbets to the press. Eric Homberger argues in *Mrs Astor's New York* that 'in the 1880s the "society page" invented "society" and that the uneasy relations – the Faustian bargain – between New York's upper class and its journalists produced a dramatic change in the nature of upper-class life – an acceptance of the idea that aristocracy was "conspicuous", that of necessity it existed in the full glare of press publicity'.[14]

Henry James in 1888 published a novel entitled *The Reverberator*. It was named after a newspaper providing society news furnished by the millionaires' social secretaries. Gossip 'served up at every breakfast table in the United States – that's what the American people want and that's what the American people are going to have', a hustling young *Reverberator* journalist declares. 'I'm going for the secrets, the *chronique intime* . . . what the people want is just what isn't told, and I'm going to tell it. Oh, they're bound to have the plums! That's about played out, anyway, the idea of sticking up a sign of "private", and thinking you can keep the place to yourself. You can't do it – you can't keep out the light of the Press. Now what I'm going to do is set up the biggest lamp yet made and to shine it all over the place. We'll see who's private then!'[15] Privacy was a luxury, but there were no iron-clad sureties that it could be bought. Always there was the nagging fear that one's relations would be named in a 'spicy paragraph'. When in 1908 the railway heir Howard Gould sought to divorce his wife, who had taken 'Buffalo Bill' Cody as her lover, newspapers blazoned such headlines as 'SORDID TROUBLES OF THE MARRIED RICH: ONE DAY'S DISPATCHES REVEAL MANY SKELETONED CLOSETS', and opened its lip-smacking paragraphs: 'That portion of the public that has been waiting so patiently for the oft-delayed washing of the family linen of the Howard Goulds is about to have its reward.'[16] The revelations were blared so loud that they impacted on Nebraska's Swedish and Bohemian farmers in Willa Cather's *O Pioneers!* (1913).

Journalists ladle out butter when it suits them, but their sickly adulation can turn almost overnight to envenomed harassment. This was demonstrated in 1880 when Caroline Astor's nephew William Waldorf Astor stood as Republican candidate for a congressional district of New York, which contained many slum tenements owned by him. The deference of his tenants coupled with lavish expenditure on torch-lit parades was expected to secure an easy win; but he was trounced in two electoral campaigns because the New York yellow press vilified him as a spoilt creature toying with politics. He blamed his failure on the insults and travesties of American pressmen.

For a century the Astors had been inveterate Atlantic voyagers, discounting storms, sickness and smells because there was so much that they wanted on both continents. In the aftermath of his newspaper drubbing, W. W. Astor quit America. In Rome, he enjoyed the sumptuous comforts of the Grand Hotel; in Paris, he stayed at the Ritz; and in London, the Savoy. Their style and amenities contrasted with the leading hotels in great American cities, with their piled-up luggage, spittoons, elbowing loungers, truculent porters, and shaggy men writing letters at tables inlaid with advertisements.[17] Astor preferred the Grand, the Ritz and the Savoy, with their calm discretion mixed with assured luxury, and resolved to introduce similar top-class effects in New York. In 1892 he demolished his father's mansion on the corner of Fifth Avenue and 33rd Street, and a year later opened the thirteen-storey Waldorf Hotel on its site. The site abutted the house owned by his haughty aunt Caroline Astor; and the fact that demolition, construction and hotel bustle were obnoxious to her added piquancy to his project.[18] She soon moved, her old home was razed to the ground and on its site her son John Jacob IV built the Astoria Hotel – four storeys taller than the Waldorf. The two enterprises were combined in 1897: the Waldorf-Astoria, with 1,500 bedrooms, was the *Titanic* of hotels.

Next Jack Astor built the St Regis hotel on the corner of Fifth Avenue and 55th Street. 'The new Hotel St. Regis, Jack Astor's pride,' opened in 1904 having cost $5.5 million.[19] It was the first hotel with air-conditioning, telephones in every bedroom, and mail-chutes. There was a ballroom on the top floor, a dining room that could seat 150 guests at one table, and every luxury. The St Regis set the standard to which White Star aspired when they designed the pampering first-class accommodation on *Titanic*, just as Jack Astor's next hotel, the Knickerbocker, promising Fifth Avenue comforts at Broadway prices, set the bar for White Star's second-class amenities.

The Waldorf-Astoria and St Regis were showcases of marble, velvet, gilt – and people. They soared towards the New York skyline and stretched down their blocks.* Their rooms had tens of thousands of windows which at night shone with electric lights – casting a bright glow such as *Titanic* passengers saw as their lifeboats pulled away from the sinking ship. The two hotels provided a public space for New Yorkers who wanted publicity rather than privacy. Hostesses held dinners in the private dining rooms, but their parties contrived to be detectable, tantalizingly visible to open-eyed bystanders, described in the social columns of the *New York Times* as well as lower papers, rather than absolutely secreted. First-class life on *Titanic* was a microcosm of the New York that Caroline Astor devised, and which the Astors' hotels turned into a rich, sumptuous spectacle. Their denizens feared solitude, and plunged into parties, noise, activity – any distraction to numb awareness. New York de luxe hotels were not restful, as the English hostess Lady Desborough described during her first visit to the city: 'We are in a simply giant hotel, like a huge town – they all scream & shriek & rush up & down in lifts & yell down telephones & nearly give one brain-fever even to look at!!!'[20]

Lady Desborough's friend Edith Wharton wrote drily in 1911, three years after Caroline Astor's death, 'it would take an arbitration commission a great many sittings to define the boundaries of society nowadays'.[21] During the preceding fifteen years, American capitalism, and American moneyed society, had been transformed.

---

*The US Senate enquiry into the *Titanic* accident held its first meetings in 1912 in a Waldorf-Astoria conference room. The building was demolished in 1929 to make way for the Empire State Building. A newly built Waldorf-Astoria hotel opened on Park Avenue in 1931.

1896 was the beginning for Western industrialized economies of an inflationary cycle which exhausted itself in the worldwide recession of 1913. Gross National Product in the USA grew twice as fast in the period 1896–1913 as in the preceding or succeeding periods. The transport and construction sectors had an average annual growth rate exceeding 10 per cent. In 1898 the United States fought its first overseas war – against Spain – and acquired its first colonies, the Philippines, Guam and Puerto Rico, as well as privileges in Cuba. After the close of the 1898 war, the United States boomed its way to become the world's most powerful economy. This spurt startled politicians and intimidated capitalists in Europe's richest business nations: hence the defensiveness of some English Cabinet ministers when Pierpont Morgan bought White Star. A surge of acquisitions, mergers and consolidations culminated with the creation in 1901 of the United States Steel Corporation and of a comparable railway trust, the Northern Securities Company. Corporate America was born, and spawned the mass production factories, brutalizing urban environments, managerial hierarchies, marketing systems and political culture associated with it.

The Astors with their social exclusiveness, cult of newspaper publicity, sybaritic hotels and century-long habit of transatlantic dashes provided the mental outlook, customs, expectations and amenities that governed *Titanic*'s building and *Titanic*'s post mortem. They had no direct part in the eruption of corporate prosperity that burst over the United States after 1896 and began the relative decline of Europe. That role was taken by families like the Guggenheims.

Benjamin Guggenheim was one of the last to buy *Titanic* tickets: he had been booked on *Lusitania*, but transferred his entourage to *Titanic*. After his father's AY and Minnie mines in Leadville, Colorado had struck silver in the 1880s, Ben had been sent as his father's agent to Leadville at a time when his elder brothers were occupied by lace and embroideries. Leadville, 'The Greatest Mining Camp in the World' as publicists called it, was perched high on a mountainside of the Mosquito Range, with freezing winters and unimaginably muddy springs. Ben Guggenheim sat in a shack near the shaft, with a revolver

on his belt, keeping the books and paying a hundred miners. The life
suited his robust, expansive, skittish spirit. At night he danced in Tiger
Alley with whores at fifty cents a dance, played cards with miners and
mule-skinners at Crazy Jim's, or drank corn whisky in a saloon. In
1888 the Guggenheims opened a copper smelter at Pueblo, Colorado,
built at a cost of $500,000, to reduce the costs of refining ore. Ben
superintended Pueblo smelting operations, and took charge of his
family's Perth Amboy refinery after it opened in New Jersey in 1894.

While at Perth Amboy, he married Florette Seligman, who came
from an established New York Jewish dynasty which disparaged the
Philadelphia *arrivistes* as 'the Googs'. Ben left the family business in
1901, ostensibly because he mistrusted his elder brother Dan's
strategy for wresting control from William Rockefeller of the
American Smelting & Refining Company. The truth is that Ben was
at odds with the self-engrossed seriousness of Dan and his brothers
who thought him a scamp. Whereas he preferred to avoid unpleasant
contingencies, it was the grim joy of his brothers to provoke
confrontations in which they could prove their mastery. When the
Guggenheims won control of Rockefeller's trust, it was without Ben.

After his resignation, Benjamin Guggenheim installed himself with
his wife and three daughters in a tall, commodious house on the corner
on Fifth Avenue. 'A trifle overdone – typically Guggenheim', the
historian of the Guggenheims says of this *ménage*. The marble entrance
hall was adorned by a fountain and a stuffed American golden eagle
with outspread wings shot by Ben, illegally, in the Adirondacks. A
marble stairway led to the palatial dining room, hung with seventeenth-
century Flemish tapestries, the conservatory filled with tender plants
and the opulent Louis XVI salon with gilt-framed mirrors from floor
to ceiling, and furniture imported from Loire chateaux. A gilded grand
piano and bearskin rug were jarring features of the room. Elsewhere,
there were galleries hung with heavy-framed Corots and Watteaus,
and a library with red damask walls and glass-fronted bookcases
enclosing unread leather-bound editions. The fourth storey was the
nursery floor. Up dark stairs, the fifth storey, with its low ceilings and
jail windows, accommodated the servants.[22]

As part of Meyer Guggenheim's dynastic strategy, the entire family left Philadelphia for New York in 1888. Several Guggenheim sons built palaces at Elberon on the New Jersey coast – a resort which gained a reputation as a Newport, Rhode Island for Jews and theatre people. They were too successful to be bothered with good taste: good taste was the consolation of people who had little else to be proud about. Daniel built an Italianate *palazzo*, Solomon commissioned a pseudo-Moorish mansion, Simon paid for a reproduction Southern colonial manor house and Murry raised a marble version of Le Petit Trianon. The family also built a white marble mausoleum fit for a Roman emperor in a cemetery on Long Island. The Vanderbilts had led the fashion for mausoleums of imperial dimensions to awe passers-by: Carl Sandburg's poem 'Graceland' contrasts one such pompous repository of dead men's bones with the rented room of a shop girl earning $6 a week, and turning tricks for extra nickels: when she tugs up her stockings as she dresses she is reckless about 'the newspapers and the police, the talk of her home town or the name people call her'.

The Guggenheims' family solidarity was a source of strength, but entailed ruthless collective egoism. Whatever suited their interests, stood. Whatever obstructed their interests was trampled. When their copper mines were disrupted by strikes, the family recruited violent strike-breakers. When great opportunities were identified in Mexico, the government there was suborned. Large bribes were paid to ensure the election to the US Senate of Simon Guggenheim in 1907. Collaborating with Pierpont Morgan, the Guggenheims exploited the Kennecott copper mine in Alaska, and acquired the world's two most productive copper mines, Bingham Canyon in Utah and Chuquicamata in Chile. To service the Kennecott mine they built a railroad costing $25 million on glaciers. At Chuquicamata they invested another $25 million in a project 9,500 feet high in the Andes. Daniel Guggenheim was the corporate Napoleon of the second generation, though Arnold Bennett, on seeing him, felt he 'looked like a little grocer'.[23] He was a puritanical automaton who wanted no lull in the tension of his life. Even holidaying in Paris he never relaxed from his business, but in his Ritz suite kept a long wooden table fixed with pegs showing the location and depth of every mine he controlled.

In addition to an Astor and a Guggenheim, two Wideners went down on *Titanic*. Indeed, *Titanic* killed three Wideners, for old Peter Widener, the founder of the dynasty and Traction King of the United States, was flattened by the loss of his son and grandson. Thereafter, when he went outdoors, he looked as frail as a dead leaf being blown by the wind. Increasingly, he lay sequestered in his marble mansion, Lynnewood Hall, surrounded by some of the world's most valuable paintings and the finest ceiling in the United States, for a Tiepolo transported from an Italian palace covered the Lynnewood library ceiling. The firm endurance of his possessions seemed almost a mockery of his growing infirmity. It was at Lynnewood that he died three years later – his domestic pomp still shining as his vision dimmed.

Under the headline 'P.A.B. Widener, Capitalist, Dies', the *New York Times* gave him an obituary fit for the ruler of a Balkan state. 'His ancestry was German; in character and disposition thoroughly American. Born in Philadelphia on Nov 13 1834 . . . his father was a brick-maker, and was not burdened with the goods of this world. Peter A. B. Widener saw no future in making bricks without straw, and turned his attention to supplying something which he was sure that the world would need – that was meat. At first he was a butcher boy, and then, by saving money and borrowing a little, he was able to start a mutton shop. It was said of him that he handled the cleaver with celerity and that he could trim chops in a way which was the admiration of skilled bench-men.'[24] As first proof of Widener's enterprise, he built up one of the earliest chains of butcher shops in America. As he stood at his chopping block, he reflected that Philadelphia would expand if its people had reliable transport from new suburbs to their workplaces, with efficient traction lines replacing antiquated horse cars.

Widener entered politics as a way of obtaining traction franchises. He joined the Republican Party, rose to be City Treasurer, bought holdings of street railway stocks, used his dividends to buy yet more stocks, and amassed his earnings. As City Treasurer, he knew where Philadelphia's new blocks of streets and nascent suburbs, requiring transit systems, would be built. Widener joined his political influence to the money of William L. Elkins. Buying secretively, they gained control of many streetcar lines. Horse cars, then cable cars, and finally swift electric trolleys: from Philadelphia to Chicago and New York, then Baltimore, Washington and Ohio, his traction interests spread. At the start of the twentieth century most of Widener's fortune was in traction stocks, but by his death in 1915 he held about $15 million in American Tobacco, and was a large holder of US Steel, Standard Oil, Land Title & Trust Company as well as of Union & Philadelphia Traction and Philadelphia Rapid Transport. And whereas the old man had entered Philadelphia politics in order to make money, his son George was president of the township board of Cheltenham, Pennsylvania as 'a hobby'.[25]

Peter Widener was involved in Pierpont Morgan's great trusts, United States Steel and International Mercantile Marine. The episode of the steel trust, indeed, is an epic of the *Titanic* age. US steel output rose 520-fold from 22,000 tons in 1867 to 11.4 million tons by 1900. Judge Gary, an expert in corporate law who never visited a steelworks, was chairman of Pierpont Morgan's combine, Federal Steel. Gary organized fourteen companies capitalized at $80 million to combine in National Tube, and twenty-five companies capitalized at $60 million to combine in American Bridge, and increased Federal Steel's supply to these new trusts, which therefore bought less from Carnegie Steel. Morgan sat up talking until 3 a.m. at his Madison Avenue mansion with Charles Schwab of Carnegie Steel, and agreed to create a huge combine with Carnegie Steel at its centre. Schwab took Andrew Carnegie, who owned 50 per cent of the company bearing his name, for a round of golf, let him win and over a good lunch announced Morgan's proposition: to buy Carnegie Steel at a price named by Carnegie. Carnegie brooded overnight, and next day gave Schwab a sheet of paper on which he had pencilled his terms: $480 million – representing about twelve times Carnegie Steel's annual earnings.

Schwab went straight to Morgan, who read the paper, grunted with approval and did the deal. Carnegie netted $240 million by the signature of the agreement, and Morgan motored across New York to congratulate him on becoming the richest man in the world.

The formation of United States Steel, with capitalization of $1.4 billion, was announced in March 1901. United States Steel – the Billion Dollar Trust – owned steel mills, blast furnaces, coke ovens, ore lands, coal mines, railways, steamships. It produced 7 million tons of steel a year. United States Steel issued $304 million worth of 5 per cent gold bonds, $550 million in 7 per cent convertible preferred shares, and $550 million in common stock. A syndicate of rich investors, including Peter Widener, took over the preliminary financing, and was rewarded with $50 million in preferred and common stock. US Steel's earnings eventually justified the high value of its paper, although its promoters were much decried. 'The frantic rush of everybody to beg or steal or plunder is appalling,' Henry Adams wrote after the US Steel deal had been signed. 'Pierpont Morgan is apparently trying to swallow the sun.'[26] Morgan travelled to Europe on White Star's *Teutonic* shortly afterwards. In Paris, he paid 2 million francs ($400,000) for an altar-piece painted by Raphael – he bought it on the first day he saw it – and spent another million francs on works by Rubens and Titian.

Peter Widener was by then amassing an art collection for his newly built house. Lynnewood Hall in Elkins Park – finished for him in 1900 – was built in the style of an eighteenth-century English country house, with clean, symmetrical lines and a long imposing front broken by a six-pillared portico. It was a place where old objects were introduced to new money. Inside were arrayed pictures, sculptures, furniture, glass-fronted cabinets, all demanding recognition and applause, and declaring their owner's entitlement. 'To combine many periods in one and to commit no anachronism, to put something French, something Spanish, something Italian, and something English into an American house and have the result the perfection of American taste – is a feat of legerdemain that has been accomplished time and again,' wrote Emily Post, who might have had Lynnewood in mind.[27]

Widener paid $700,000 to Lady Desborough for Raphael's Cowper Madonna, $500,000 to Lord Lansdowne for Rembrandt's 'The Mill', and $1,000,000 to Lord Wimborne for three Rembrandts. At Lynnewood there hung three Van Dyke portraits; Titian's portrait of Emilia and Irene of Spilimberg; Botticelli's 'Madonna of the Thorns' bought from Prince Chigi in 1900 and smuggled out of Italy; paintings by Corot, Constable, Turner, Gainsborough, El Greco, Velasquez, Murillo, Rubens and Veronese. The great ballroom had four crystal chandeliers, Chinese vases, Louis XV furniture. The centrepiece of the formal gardens was an eye-catching fountain with water spouting from tritons and nereids.

To Henry Adams, who glimpsed Widener in Paris on an art-buying foray in 1908, he seemed 'an odious old American'.[28] The art connoisseurs Bernard and Mary Berenson, in the same year, enjoyed his deference in showing them his collection. As she reported, 'When you forget how he had made his money, it was rather touching to have old Mr Widener (he is very broken) trotting round and saying meekly "Mr Berenson, is this a gallery picture, or a furniture picture, or must it go to the cellar?" (this is their formula, and about 160 pictures *are* already in the cellar!). He was very much pleased whenever we would allow a picture to stay in the gallery, even if shorn of its great name. But we had to banish several. Then the prices!! Jo Widener told us all. They have paid on an average for their Italians from $10,000 to $40,000 for pictures worth at the outside $500!'[29] *Tout passe*, but everything passes at greater speed in the environment of multimillionaires. Twenty-five years after Peter Widener's death, his family vacated Lynnewood, which served as a training centre for military dogs in the Second World War, was sold in 1952 for $192,000 and has fallen into heartbreaking dereliction since its purchase by the First Korean Church of New York.

There were two ways for a Midas in America to spend his fortune: in philanthropy, or in ostentation (the two forms of spending were not exclusive, but one usually prevailed over the other). Philanthropy was good taste, and ostentation – by definition – bad taste. The Guggenheims, Wideners, Morgan, Carnegie, and others did not love their fellow men, but they gave away tens of millions of dollars voluntarily, without even the sugaring of tax write-offs, and thus transformed the prospects of US universities, museums and hospitals. A foremost example of a capitalist monster redeeming himself by the good taste of his philanthropy was Henry Clay Frick, the Coke King, steelmaker and railway investor, *Titanic*'s greatest non-show after Pierpont Morgan. Frick's company towns were as dark and barren as the cinder tracks of his railways; but his art collection (chosen by himself) was abundant in colour, fertility and joy. He did not buy nudes of either sex, or (with the exception of a Goya) paintings portraying the labouring poor – an example of what Edith Wharton called 'the *nouveau riche* prudery which classes poverty with the nude in art, and is not sure how to behave in the presence of either'.[30]

In 1916, three years before Frick's death, 2 per cent of the US population owned 33 per cent of the wealth while the poorest 65 per cent of Americans owned 5 per cent. Two million people owned 20 per cent more of national wealth than the remaining 90 million. Between 66 per cent and 75 per cent of women workers in factories, stores and laundries earned under $8 a week; 20 per cent earned under $4 a week. Six dollars was the price of three theatre tickets, three pairs of gloves, a pair of shoes or dinner for two. In retrospect the defiant ostentation of the age of titans seemed as provocative as the hubristic speed of *Titanic*. The rise of the great trusts, the power of money, the ruthless brutality, the glaring social injustice, defined the age of *Titanic*, and was the unread evidence that foretold the coming doom.

SEVEN

Atlantic Migrants

*Poor peasants, who make the soil productive and suffer from hunger
– fellaheen, coolies, peons, mujiks, cafoni – are alike all over the world:
they form a nation, a race, a church of their own, but two poor men
identical in every respect have never yet been seen.*

Ignazio Silone, *Fontamara*

'Our third-class passengers streamed on board with much hullabaloo,'
wrote an officer on the Cunarder *Caronia*, which lay at the Liverpool
quayside shortly before the Great War. They looked 'picturesque in
their variety of garb and racial features, as they plodded up the
gangway in seemingly endless procession, carrying bundles which
perhaps contained all their possessions. Their accommodation down
below, though certainly not luxurious, was fair enough at the price,
with meals included. A week's discomfort was endurable for the
benefit . . . of becoming Americans. Some would be millionaires
there, and some hoboes, but the magic word "America" lured them
all.'[1]

What did the magic word mean to immigrants? Nothing sensible,
in some cases. For Lebanese 'Amerka' meant Australia and West Africa
as well as the Americas: 'I am emigrating to that part of Amerka that
is under French rule: it is very hot there and the people are black,'
one said of Senegal. 'Nayurk' meant the United States: 'it is just like
Lebanon, consisting of a capital and villages, and I am going to join
my brother in one of the villages,' declared a Lebanese destined for
Chicago.[2] A young Swede, receiving letters from her fiancé

postmarked 'Soperville', a windswept crossroads with a coal mine and a post office on an empty Illinois plain, conceived it as the most exciting marvel in America. When she disembarked in New York, and saw the busy streets and high buildings, she said in wonder, 'If this is New York, what will Soperville be like?'[3] Fifty years later her son wrote the greatest biography of Abraham Lincoln.

The bounty of 'America' was as vague as its location. Three verses of Hans Christian Andersen's 'The America Song', popular across Scandinavia, ran:

> Trees which on the ground do stand
> Sugar – oh, so sweet!
> And everywhere about the land
> Girls there are to meet.
>
> If you wish for one that's real,
> Soon you will have four or more,
> Meadows and fields
> Grow money by the score.
>
> Ducks and chickens raining down,
> Geese land on the table,
> Forks are out and birds done brown,
> Eat now if you are able.[4]

Within the Jewish Pale of Settlement in Russia during the 1890s, '"America" was in everybody's mouth. Businessmen talked of it over their accounts; the market women made up their quarrels that they might discuss it from stall to stall; people who had relatives in the famous land went around reading their letters for the enlightenment of less fortunate folk.' Children devised emigration games; old folks shook their heads over the evening fire and predicted calamity for those so rash as to cross the seas; 'all talked of it, but scarcely anyone knew one true fact about this magic land'.[5] This was the memory of fifteen-year-old Mary Antin, whose father had preceded his wife and children to Boston. The family quivered with excitement when he raised enough money to pay for tickets and bribes. 'At last I was going to America! Really, really, going at last! The boundaries burst! The arch of heaven soared. A million suns shone out for every star. The winds rushed in from outer space, roaring in my ears, "America! America!"'[6]

Louis Adamic recalled how, around 1907, a man returned to his native village of Blato, in Carniola, then a Slovenian duchy of Austria-Hungary: 'the man had left the village for the United States, a poor peasant clad in homespun, with a moustache under his nose and a bundle on his back; now, a clean-shaven *Amerikanec*, he sported a blue-serge suit, buttoned shoes very large in the toes and with India-rubber heels, a black derby, a shiny celluloid collar, and a loud necktie made even louder by a dazzling horseshoe pin, which, rumour had it, was made of gold, while his two suitcases of imitation leather, tied with straps, bulged with gifts from America for his relatives and friends in the village'.[7] Adamic sidled within earshot of this nabob as he sat under the linden tree in front of the wine house, 'ordering wine and *klobase* – Carniolan sausages – for all comers, paying for accordion players, indulging in tall talk about America, its wealth and vastness, and his own experiences as a worker in the West Virginia or Kansas coal mines or Pennsylvania rolling mills'. As a result of the nabob's boasting, Adamic pictured the USA as 'huge beyond conception, thousands of miles across the ocean, untellably exciting, explosive, incomparable to the tiny, quiet, lovely Carniola; a place full of movement and turmoil'. There, he decided, 'one could make pots of money in a short time, acquire immense holdings, wear a white collar, and have polish on one's shoes like a *gospod* – one of the gentry – and eat white bread, soup, and meat on weekdays as well as Sunday'.[8]

Adamic's mother warned that calamities had befallen men from Blato's hinterland in America. One *Amerikanec* had perished in a mining accident. Others had returned without an arm or leg. A man who had been a coalminer for seven years returned to die: 'a gaunt, bent and broken man, hollow-eyed, bald, mostly skin and bone, with a bitter expression on his face'. When a respiratory spasm seized him, his face became empurpled, his eyes bulged frantically and he clutched his chest as he fought to breathe.[9] Speakers at nationalist meetings denounced Austria for driving honest Slovenian parents to America, and America for ruining good Slovenian peasants. The United States broke the health of emigrants, mangled their bodies, defiled their morals, obliterated their dialects and sapped their self-respect. Nationalists sponsored a popular novel recounting the misfortunes of a group of simple Slovenians lured to the bogus Land of Promise, where they were humiliated by immigration officials, swindled by sharpers, exploited by landlords, brutalized by mine managers and sweatshop owners, and condemned to hunger and squalor.

The *Caronia* officer said that his passengers were hellbent on becoming Americans; but what did it mean to be called an American? A few years after the hopefuls boarded *Caronia*, Somerset Maugham spent ten days travelling on the trans-Siberian railway from Vladivostok to Petrograd with a bagman from Philadelphia. 'He was proud of his English ancestry, but proud too of his American birth, though to him America was a little strip of land along the Atlantic coast and Americans were a small number of persons of English or Dutch origin whose blood had never been sullied by foreign admixture. He looked upon the Germans, Swedes, Irish and other inhabitants of Central and Eastern Europe who for the last hundred years have descended upon the United States as interlopers. He turned his attention away from them as a maiden lady who lived in a secluded manner might avert her eyes from the factory chimneys that had trespassed upon her retirement.' When the Englishman mentioned a millionaire of German descent who owned some of the finest pictures in America – doubtless Peter Widener of Philadelphia – the New Englander replied that the millionaire's grandmother had been an excellent cook. 'My great-aunt Maria was terribly sorry when she left to get married. She said she never knew anyone who could make an apple pancake as she could.'[10] A man might be the Traction King of America, with a Tiepolo ceiling transplanted into his new mansion, and yet only be acknowledged for the distinction of his grandmother's pancakes.

In America, the high iron railings of class distinction bristled with spikes to exclude mongrel stock.

Official statistics listed people as Russians, Italians, Germans or Austro-Hungarians, but provinces mattered more than nationalities. 'Russians' included Finns as well as Ruthenians (Ukrainians) and Ashkenazy Jews from the Czar's western provinces. The outlook and experiences of Sicilians and Neapolitans were irreconcilable with those of Tuscans, Piedmontese or Lombards. 'Germans' included people from the Black Forest of Württemberg as well as Prussians. Austro-Hungarian immigrants (338,452 in the peak year of 1907) included Croatians, Slovenians, Germans, Magyars, Poles, Slovaks and Jews. Emigrants from the derelict mining districts of Cornwall had dialect, kinship groups and patterns of immigration that were distinct from other English, let alone Scots or Welsh.

Some idealists hoped that these multifarious peoples – escapees from plodding destitution or political harassment – would shed their differences and meld as Americans. 'America is God's Crucible, the great Melting-Pot where all the races of Europe are melting and reforming,' declared the protagonist of Israel Zangwill's play *The Melting Pot* (1908). 'Here you stand, good folk, think I, when I see them at Ellis Island . . . with your fifty languages and histories, and your fifty blood hatreds and rivalries . . . Germans and Frenchmen, Irishmen and Englishmen, Jews and Russians – into the crucible with you all! God is making the American!'[11]

Was assimilation easy? Was it even desirable? At the entrance to New York harbour stands the green-grey Statue of Liberty which a Russian steerage passenger of 1913 assured his companion was the tombstone of Columbus. Every American schoolchild knows Emma Lazarus's secular hymn 'The New Colossus' (1883) with its famous lines carved into the Statue of Liberty,

> Give me your tired, your poor,
> Your huddled masses yearning to breathe free
> The wretched refuse of your teeming shore . . .

But many Americans – like the Yankee on the train to Petrograd – did not want the old American stock to be diluted or given toxic foreign flavours. The Pittsburgh banker Thomas Mellon, who had been born in an Irish hovel and went steerage to America as a boy, deplored later incomers. 'This country has lately served as an asylum for the spendthrifts, the desperadoes, and other criminal classes of the Old World,' he warned in 1885. 'Every thief, or crank, or cut-throat, for whom it is made too hot at home, makes his escape, if he can, to America. He knows that ours is not a strong government, and that his chances for impunity are better here . . . the dispropor-tion of the depraved and dangerous classes bodes no good to our future peace.'[12] Even more striking was the opinion of Louis Adamic, who in 1913 reached New York, via Le Havre, on the steamship *Niagara* with Poles, Slovaks, Czechs, Croatians, Slovenians, Bosnians, Jews, Greeks, Turks, Germans, Austrian-Italians. 'Immigration,' Adamic wrote twenty years later, 'is in no small way to blame for the fact that the United States today is more a jungle than a civiliza-tion – a land of deep economic, social, spiritual and intellectual chaos and distress.'[13]

Migrants were people who saw the improvident, luckless and useless beneath them; and did not want to sink. Their motives were negative: they knew what they feared, despised and rejected more clearly than what they wanted. It was easy for them to know whom they disparaged, for they saw them at close quarters. They were vaguer about those whom they admired, for they glimpsed them at a distance dimly. Immigrants were trying to avoid slipping backwards into failure; they were not from the lowest economic or social strata, but people trying to protect their self-respect, or what historians call status.

Gyula Illyés in his classic *People of the Puszta* discussed the changes on the great agglomerated farmsteads of the Hungarian plains. The relics of serfdom had survived there until the 1880s, and a quarter of a century later, in the age of *Titanic*, there was nostalgia for the comforts and secure boundaries of those times. 'When grandfather from Néband got married he had in his chest six pairs of ordinary wide trousers, six pairs with fringed edges and six round-necked shirts. In addition, he had two pairs of top-boots, a real silver cane and a sheepskin coat.' How many shirts, they asked, does a hired lad own nowadays? What, indeed, do the people now eat? In grandfather's time, wives carried lunch to the farm-workers in enormous wooden bowls: 'the sheep-dogs would raise their heads a good mile away as they sniffed the paprika stew whose scent floated like a glimmering ribbon through the thousand smells of the fields'. In those days there were no poor folk: 'the beggars rode in carts'. This restful age ended with the coming of the railway. Engines and wagons shook asunder the self-sufficient, insular, arrested settlements of the country districts. Urban markets became accessible, wheat as well as cattle could be transported, pastures were ploughed, and peasants who had always reaped and threshed were superseded by machines. Peasants' plots were divided into ever smaller strips, their children forced from the land to become farm servants and landless labourers. As these classes grew in numbers, Illyés described, 'the more the earth beneath them groaned and cracked like ice beneath the weight of a crowd'. This plunge in status was doubly disturbing because the *puszta* was ruled by a caste system of an inflexibility that would have been the envy of Caroline Astor's New York 'Four Hundred'. The steward's son was sure of becoming steward too; the foreman's son, though he might toil as a carter, would become a foreman if he lived long enough. A labourer's children would keep this status for perpetuity. 'As for putting a horse-driver among the ox-drivers, it would be like trying to make a Negro out of a white Yankee. Even the very rare marriages between these families are regarded as a mild race-degradation.'[14]

After the land reforms in the Hapsburg empire in 1848, peasants became free proprietors. They saw themselves as part of a proud line of inheritance and tradition running back for centuries, and upheld their duty to both ancestral reputation and posterity. The masters, *Herrschaften,* were their superiors, but farm hands, cottagers and labourers their inferiors. These land-holders prospered in Austro-Hungarian provinces where land was bequeathed to one heir, but foundered in areas where land was subdivided among the heirs on a man's death. Subdivisions in every generation meant that many landholdings were too small to support a family. Emily Balch in 1910 'counted thirty men ploughing at the same time, each working his share of the same big, unbroken field – open, for each man's share is marked, not by hedge, fence or wall, but only by a burrow some thirty centimetres (about a foot) wide, which must not be planted'.[15] Some strips were so narrow that men had to walk on their neighbours' land to lead the plough horse. When land was divided among the sons of a dead man, strips were split lengthwise: otherwise one son would get the sunny slope or rich hollow, while another was saddled with a chill slope and poor, sandy soil. In some districts, the petty landholder who could not support his family from his own plot might amass debts which put him at the mercy of creditors: a peasant failing to meet mortgage payments, or saddled with children whom he could not give an adequate patrimony, was destined to suffer a humiliating plunge in status for himself and his children to the low state of a landless labourer. It was this smarting humiliation which drove Slovaks, Poles, Ruthenians to fare overseas or to send their sons to the new land from which men returned with savings.[16] As Illyés wrote, 'Emigrants will undertake any work in the distant parts of the world because it is only at home that they count themselves to be real people.'[17]

The Spartans who came to the USA from the 1870s were the Greek equivalent of the Pilgrim Fathers. An estimated 75 per cent of men aged between 18 and 35 left Sparta between 1870 and 1910, mainly for the United States. They were seldom the poorest, but travelled with money gained from selling livestock or land. Farm labourers, indeed, were unknown as an indigenous class: if labourers were needed in Greece they were recruited from Albania, Bulgaria and Montenegro. Peasants resented heavy levels of taxation, which until 1913 was collected by private tax collectors, who stipulated on which days crops should be harvested, regardless of whether crops were ripe. It was also hard to borrow money to invest in land or equipment except at usurious rates. Emigration from the province of Arcadia increased after 1892, and eventually overtook Sparta: the peasants there had grubbed up their olive groves to plant vines and supply currants, only for the price of currants to collapse. In parts of the province of Corinth, it was said that priests and schoolmasters were the only adult males left. Districts with the largest number of immigrants were notably prosperous, owing to the money remitted home from the United States.[18]

Emigrants left their villages as solitary individuals, in groups of relations and neighbours, and as part of a chain of migration. As Josef Barton described, Sicilians trekked down from their mountain villages to the port of Sant'Agata, where they entrained for Palermo or Messina, or were ferried to Naples, and there waited until a ship steamed into port, already half-filled with Galician Poles, Montenegrins and Slovenes who had boarded at Trieste. Romanian villagers walked to a railway station, took a train to the central junction at Sibiu, and then made the long journey to Bremen or Hanover, or (after 1910) the nearer trip to Trieste. 'As the train moved northwest through the Alföld and onto the Tisza plain, Hungarian peasants from the great heath farmsteads (*pusztas*) crowded the stops along the way. At Košice, on the margin of the great Hungarian plains and the Slovak hills, a big crowd of Slovaks waited to entrain – bound, like the rest, for Bremen or Hanover.'[19] There would be a few German-speakers among them who might mollify the officials of the Hapsburg and Hohenzollern empires who halted the emigrants' progress.

Isabel Kaprielian-Churchill, the historian of the Armenian diaspora, writes that the men from Keghi who were represented on *Titanic*, 'moved about not only as individuals, making solitary decisions, and as members of kinship or clan groups, but also as parts of a regional or migratory caravan. Sometimes they blazed new trails; sometimes, they retraced the steps of fathers, uncles and older brothers.' Extensive international networks of brothers, uncles and cousins 'exchanged money and information about the obstacles and pitfalls ahead, government regulations and shipping agents, jobs and accommodation. Impelled into an unknown and intimi- dating world, far from customs and social controls of home, men considered it a matter of family and village honour to take care of each other. They *expected* help from each other. Across land and sea the migration chain would clamour and reverberate with the shameful news of a man who had refused to aid a brother in need.' These networks of mutual aid, based on love, respect and pragmatism, preserved the cohesion of migrating Keghetsis. 'The "caravans" they created spanned half the world: from Keghi to Constantinople, Alexandria, Varna, Sophia, Batum, Tiflis, Baku, Marseille, Liverpool, Boston, East St Louis, Detroit, Troy/Watervliet, New York, Brantford and back again.'[20]

Shipping companies and their agents incited emigration. There was, for example, negligible emigration from Iceland – despite sheep epidemics and diminishing fish catches – until after 1873, when an immigration agency was opened there by the Montreal Ocean Steamship Company, colloquially known as the Allan Line. By the 1880s the Allan Line had 400 local agents in Norway alone: merchants, inn keepers and schoolteachers, with railway or post office staff additionally circulating propaganda brochures. About 500 Icelanders registered to go by the first Allan boat to the USA (thirty-six others went to Brazil); and by the late 1880s, twenty-seven out of every thousand Icelanders had emigrated – the highest rate in any Nordic country. Throughout the main European ports, there were emigrant agents working for shipping companies, primarily on a commission basis, circulating brochures and advertising, offering differentiated prices for tickets (for the cheapness of tickets was crucial in people's life-changing decisions). They ran a network of local agents in the provinces as well as 'Yankees' – earlier migrants who had temporarily returned home, and were paid for shepherding new migrants on their outward journey to America.

Advertisements and propaganda issued by the steamship companies and their agents were enticing. There were poems like Andersen's expatiating on the productive wealth of America. In Greece, steamship companies canvassed rural districts, and posted advertisements in coffee houses and stores showing a liner steaming across the Atlantic. One agent circulated an extract supposedly from a Greek newspaper printed in New York describing how a poor boy from Thessaly had gone to Cincinnati, opened a small candy store and had in eight years amassed four factories and $200,000.

Croats who were bar owners in Chicago or Pittsburgh set up as steamship agents, and with the aid of confederates, organized transit routes from the villages of Croatia to their bar. Young Croatians on *Titanic* – Tomo and Mate Pokrnic from Bukovac, Ivan Strilic from Siroka Kula, three youngsters named Oreskovic from Konjsko Brdo, four agricultural workers from Kula named Cacic, all heading for south Chicago on tickets supplied by a Swiss agent, Johann Isidor Büchel – were doubtless on the bar-owner transit route. An estimated 600,000 Croatians went to the US between 1880 and 1914. Local agents exaggerated the abundance of work and levels of pay in America, induced peasants to sell their possessions or borrow money at up to 50 per cent interest in order to buy tickets, mustered a pack of new migrants, and launched them on a journey from the port of Fiume, via Genoa, to New York. In New York they were met by another agent in the chain, who shipped them on to their destination, where they were presented to a steel-plant foreman, civil works contractor or mine manager.[21]

There were about eighty Lebanese on board *Titanic* – part of an outflow that had begun over twenty years earlier. Because they migrated from the Ottoman province of Syria, which included Mount Lebanon until 1917, they were denoted as Syrians.[22] Mulberry trees were the chief plantation on Mount Lebanon's rocky soil, but silk prices fell and by 1896 emigration from 'Syria' – predominantly Maronite, Melkite and Eastern Orthodox Christians, with under 10 per cent Sunni or Shia Muslims – was estimated at 5,500 a year. By 1914 the figure was 15,000–20,000. Overall, between 1860 and 1914, some 350,000 went abroad: two-thirds to the USA, and most of the rest to South America. As elsewhere, the prosperity of men returning to their home villages sporting leather shoes and gold watch fobs – men who were fetching brides, revisiting families or retiring – provided an inducement to emigration. People were also encouraged to try their luck in America by letters home, often containing money remittances (worth an estimated £800,000 a year by 1910). Steamship company agencies opened in Beirut and Tripoli, and sent men into the villages to recruit cheap labour for America. A man who emigrated in 1895 with seventy-two others from his village recalled, 'It was like a gold rush.'[23] They all wanted to reach New York, although unscrupulous agents put them on ships destined for Canada, Mexico, even Australia. One of the dupes, Julián Slim Haddad, arrived in Mexico in 1902 aged fourteen speaking no Spanish: his son Carlos Slim, the telecommunications billionaire, was reckoned to be the richest man in the world in 2011.

At first only people engaged in commerce were given foreign travel permits, but these were issued to labourers after 1899 once Ottoman officials realized that stringency in issuing permits was a business incentive to middlemen to smuggle people abroad. By 1900 there were ten of these mercenary rascals, employing eighty people, bribing port officials and guards to let prohibited individuals (men without travel permits and Muslims of military age) out of the Ottoman Empire. Muslims of military age disguised themselves as Christian Lebanese to get abroad: other human contraband hid in the woods until the depths of night, and were taken in dinghies out to the ships. Soon the people smugglers diversified into tobacco, gunpowder, firearms, and made bigger money by fleecing Lebanese returning to the port at Beirut from abroad with their hard-earned savings. The stay-at-homes envied the initiative and success of the migrants, whom they liked to bully, rob, dispossess, and humiliate. Ottoman officials, military officers, local dignitaries, foreign consuls, shipping agents, porters and boatmen all battened on to the lucrative migrant business.[24]

Marseille, like Beirut, was a port burgeoning with travel agents living from the migration process. Travel agents ran coffee shops, grocery stores and boarding houses, and were used as intelligence brokers, steamship agents, bankers, letter writers, and interpreters. Their earnings depended on their renown for getting their paying clients through the formalities of Atlantic immigration. Some agents were honest. Some infiltrated their clients on board Atlantic steamers by bribing seamen or port officials. Still others swindled immigrants out of their savings, crowded them into insalubrious rooms, kept them in ignorance, and exploited their anxiety. For voyagers the port of Marseille was a place of overpowering sights and astonishing odours. 'Here,' wrote an excited traveller, 'are barrels, crates, beams, wheels, levers, tubs, ladders, tongs, hammers, sacks, cloths, tents, carts, horses, engines, cars, rubber tubing. Here is the intoxicating cosmopolitan smell you get when you store a thousand hectolitres of turpentine next to a couple of hundred tonnes of herring; when petroleum, pepper, tomatoes, vinegar, sardines, leather, gutta-percha, onions, saltpetre, methylated spirits, sacks, boot-soles, canvas, Bengal tigers, hyenas, goats, Angora cats, oxen and Turkish carpets exude their warm scents.'[25]

During the Italian mass migration of the 1890s, the shipping of migrants was piratical in its conduct. Emigration agents lured the rural peasantry onto small decrepit sailing ships or steamers – colliers, for example, built for hauling coal – operated (often only leased) by exploitative opportunists who were likened to slave traders. Agents lied to their clients, and sent them by the shipping line that paid the highest commission, but not by the safest or fastest ships, and sometimes not to the emigrant's chosen destination. Passengers were stowed in the hold alongside the cargo: competition was so keen that fares were as low as 60 lire. The slow passage of these steamers across the seas was marked by the jettisoning overboard of passengers' corpses. With 500 people packed into 500 cubic metres, sometimes thirty children might perish on a voyage. From 1903 US officials required a medical examination of migrants at ports of embarkation so that their Ellis Island immigration depot was not overwhelmed by emigrants held back as unfit. Rejected emigrants were sent home at the shipping companies' expense. To avoid this burden, employees of the Italian-operated but British-financed Prince Line were suborned into adding the names of passengers who had failed pre-embarkation health checks at Italian ports to the crew list. After paying further bribes on board, the sham crewmen were enabled to desert ship on arrival in New York. Ships thus crossed the Atlantic crewed by imposters who could not tell a rudder from a compass.

This compromised safety, although standards improved after the newly formed Lloyd Sabaudo line, with financial backing from the Italian royal family, began its Genoa-Naples-Palermo-New York service in 1907 using new ships distinguished by such patriotic names as *Principe di Piemonte* and *Regina d'Italia*.

What was the journey like for migrants?

Departing families caused a stir in their communities. The hamlet of Carclaze, above St Austell in Cornwall, had once been the site of the world's largest open tin mine. In the late nineteenth century it was a source of china clay; but after 1905, men left for American mining jobs, later summoning their wives and children. On a high point of the long, straggling village stood a Methodist chapel: there on the Sunday before a departure, the minister always recited the names of those leaving before the congregation sang, 'God be with you till we meet again'.[26] At Karlovac in Croatia, migrants attended church on the day before departure and, fighting their tears, received their priest's blessing. In the evening, they made a round of last visits to neighbours. After a sleepless night, they went through the village singing to express the sorrow in their hearts. When the train reached their station, as an observer wrote in 1910, 'how many tears and sobs, kisses and embraces! It was as heartbreaking a farewell as seeing off people condemned to die.'[27] All the villagers of Chanakhchi in Armenia turned out at the feast of Vartevar in 1910 to bid farewell to a party of migrants to Canada. 'The village priest said Holy Mass. The women were weeping so much you'd think they were offering their children as a sacrifice to the pagan gods.' They trooped together to a bridge, halted there and strained their eyes for a last glimpse of their village. Heavy mist obscured the view: then suddenly the mist dispersed to show the towering mountain of St Light. Blowing a kiss to the mountain, the migrants departed.[28]

On a Sunday morning in 1906 a Norwegian farm boy called Paul Knaplund stood on the deck of a runtish coastal steamer, waving goodbye to his parents and sisters, who were silhouetted against the eastern sky as they stood outside their house on the steep gaunt slope above the harbour. The Knaplunds lived on the island of

Saltstrung, across the fjord from Bodo, the provincial capital of Nordland, within the Arctic Circle. The propeller churned, the ship steamed down the fjord while Knaplund gazed at the dwindling family group. Slowly, each of his relations turned and trudged indoors with a heavy heart. Knaplund felt downcast and alone. Two steamer rides brought him to Trondheim, where a band of agents from rival Atlantic steamship companies waited on the quay to pounce on prospective emigrants. Both in Trondheim and during his journey to America, Knaplund 'felt that he was either just carrion for others to batten on or a sheep to be herded and pushed into the proper enclosure'.[29] In one respect Knaplund was exceptional. He was leaving Saltstrung not with the hope of making his fortune, but with the intention of improving his education. In this he succeeded, for decades later he became a doyen of American historians of British imperialism.

At Trondheim, the emigrants boarded *Tasso*, an old tub belonging to the Wilson Line, which ran cargo liner services between Hull and Scandinavia, and had made a fortune as a timber carrier. The Wilson Line constituted the biggest privately owned fleet of merchant ships in the world. It was owned by two brothers, who made Hull a port that vied with London and Liverpool, and amassed such a fortune that the elder brother received a peerage. The new Lord Nunburnholme bought the fine estate of Warter Priory from the last Lord Muncaster. He added a great baronial hall with marble staircase in an Italianate style, and a tall entrance clock tower: there were nearly a hundred rooms in the extended house. Warter was a millionaire's model village, in a green hollow of the Yorkshire Wolds, with bulging yew topiary interspersed among salubrious thatched cottages. The roads into Warter were bordered with clipped yew hedges, so that they resembled dark green tunnels. A pretty river ran down a chalk valley to fill the lake in Lord Nunburnholme's 300-acre park. It was a place of rare beauty and careful luxury 'which must have cost mints of money', noted a visitor whose bathroom was 'as big as an Eaton Square front drawing room'.[30] By contrast, *Tasso*'s third-class accommodation comprised two large rooms, one for men, the other for women, with thick sawdust on the floor to absorb vomit. The bunks were partitioned, each section accommodating four persons, with neither mattress nor sheets. They were supplied with blankets, which although recently laundered, still contained the carcasses of rats.[31]

On the evening of *Tasso*'s departure from Bergen for Stavanger, passengers were in festive mood; but Knaplund discovered that there is nothing like a crowd for intensifying a gloomy man's isolation. The decks and every nook below were crowded with leave-takers; innumerable toasts were drunk; the clinking of glasses, shouting of '*skaal*' and singing made an exciting din beyond anything he had experienced. 'Everyone seemed to have a host of friends, all were jolly and certain of finding at least one gold mine in America. As the ship glided from the quay, pledges of eternal friendship rang across the water. Only he seemed utterly alone.'[32]

Lord Nunburnholme's *Tasso* carried Knaplund across the North Sea to Hull. The emigrants were herded from the docks and piled into great horse-drawn vans which hauled them to the railroad station, Hull's townsfolk staring at them as if they were exotic beasts heading to a circus. Knaplund was excited, bewildered and overwhelmed by the sights, sounds and encompassing strangeness of the English port: 'the heavy horses with big fetlocks, the large wagons, the drivers' shouts in an unfamiliar tongue, the street signs, and the foreign-looking houses which made everything seem so alien.' For the first time in his life he travelled by train: everything the emigrants saw was new and absorbing. 'Coming from a country with few industries the passengers thought the pall of smoke over English cities dreadful; the countryside, on the other hand, was green and altogether charming. The patterns made by hedges attracted special attention, for Norway had nothing like it.'[33]

Knaplund relished his train journey, but the experiences of Mary Antin and her mother travelling from the Russian Pale of Settlement were frightening: 'we emigrants were herded at the stations, packed in the cars, and driven from place to place like cattle.'[34] Just as Hull confused Knaplund, so Mary Antin was disorientated by her first exposure to an urban maelstrom, Berlin. 'I grow dizzy even now when I think of our whirling through that city,' she recalled. 'The sights of crowds such as we had never seen before, hurrying to and fro, in and out of great depots that danced past us, helped to make it more so. Strange sights, splendid buildings, shops, people, and animals, all mingled in one great, confused mass . . . Round and round went my head. It was nothing but trains, depots, crowds – crowds, depots, trains – again and again, with no beginning, no end, only a mad dance! Faster and faster we go, and the noise increases with the speed. Bells, whistles, hammers, locomotives shrieking madly, men's voices, pedlar's cries, horses' hoofs, dogs barking.'[35]

Later the Antins underwent forcible decontamination. Mary's description of this dehumanizing experience seems to foreshadow the experiences of Jews on trains taking them to Nazi death camps almost half a century later. 'In a great lonely field opposite a solitary wooden house within a large yard, our train pulled up at last, and a conductor commanded the passengers to make haste and get out,' she recalled. 'He hurried us into the one large room which made up the house, and then into the yard. Here a great many men and women, dressed in white, received us, the women attending to the women and girls of the passengers, and the men to the others. This was another scene of bewildering confusion, parents losing their children, and little ones crying.' White-clad Germans shouted orders, accompanied by *Schnell! Schnell!* (Quick! Quick!), at travellers who were dazed, fearful and meek. 'A man came to inspect us, as if to ascertain our full value; strange-looking people driving us about like dumb animals, helpless and unresisting; children we could not see, crying in a way that suggested terrible things; ourselves driven into a little room where a great kettle was boiling on a little stove; our clothes taken off, our bodies rubbed with a slippery substance that might be any bad thing; a shower of warm water let down on us without warning.'[36] Finally the Antin party reached Hamburg, where they were 'once more lined up, cross-questioned, disinfected, labelled, and pigeonholed'. For a fortnight they were held in quarantine in crowded prison-like conditions, 'sleeping in rows, like sick people in a hospital; with roll-call morning and night, and short rations three times a day; with never a sign of the free world beyond our barred windows; with anxiety and longing and homesickness in our hearts, and in our ears the unfamiliar voice of the invisible ocean, which drew and repelled us at the same time'.[37]

Fiorello La Guardia was the US official overseeing the medical examination of prospective emigrants at Fiume after Cunard began its regular passenger service to New York in 1903. Emigrants carrying a bag crammed with all their worldly goods, with children tagging along behind their parents, became a popular spectacle in the small port, he recalled. 'Big shots would obtain permits from Hungarian officials to watch the scene, and there would often be as many as thirty or forty visitors. They would stand on the first-class deck where they could get a gallery view of the entire procedure.'[38] A visit by Archduchess Maria Josefa to watch the screening of migrants on *SS Pannonia* showed the social altitude of the spectators.

At Naples the tired, bewildered steerage passengers, who had been the prey of quayside cheats, thieves and extortionists, were herded onto little steam barges which took them to the fumigating station, half a mile across the harbour, by the breakwater. The emigrants were knocked about shamefully by seamen as they were herded aboard like cattle into a shambles, and packed so densely that it seemed the ship must capsize. There was similar havoc when steerage passengers struggled up the gangplank for embarkation. A man with the cosmopolitan name of Broughton Brandenburg, who travelled from Naples to New York in 1903 under the alias of Berto Brandi, recalled hundreds of men, women and children resembling beasts of burden as they mounted the gangway of *Prinzessin Irene*: 'some staggered under the weight of great cloth-wrapped bundles; others lugged huge valises by the grass ropes which kept them from bursting open because of their flimsy construction; and even the tots carried fibre baskets of fruit, straw-cased flasks of wine, cheese forms looped with string, and small rush-bottomed chairs for deck sitting'.[39] Every seventh or eighth person had been to America before, and had a group of from two to thirty friends, relations and neighbours travelling in his care.

There was terrific hubbub on *Prinzessin Irene*'s forward deck as over a thousand steerage passengers, with their baggage heaped about them, raised a tumult with their cries and created turmoil by dashing about. The stunted throng looked repugnant to watching Yankees. As she surveyed them, a first-class passenger (a Philadelphia clergyman's daughter) felt both guilt at being enviable to them and fear of the envious. She strove to demote them to the level of the emotionally insensible: 'These dirty, repulsive creatures really seem to show traces of the finer feelings; do you not think so, Agnes?' She pointed at a departing family bidding farewell to an old man with tears running down their faces, and conceded that they must be less brutish than they looked.[40] Others preyed on the eager suggestibility of the steerage rabble. Clustered alongside *Prinzessin Irene* lay an armada of 'bumboats selling melons, *fico-indias*, ship-slippers, caps, mirrors, razors, brushes, candy, wine, shawls, seasickness charms, toothache and stomach-ache medicine, knives, pipes, and numberless other things which the childish-minded emigrant imagines are necessary to life aboard ship'.[41]

The Barbarossa-class liner *Prinzessin Irene*, named after Kaiser Wilhelm's sister-in-law, was reckoned after its maiden voyage in 1900 to be the best emigrant-carrying ship in existence. Norddeutscher-Lloyd, its owner, was reputed to treat steerage better than most; but Brandenburg saw the crewmen treating the third-class people as 'inferior beings, to be knocked and pushed about'.[42] The purser was a heavy, strutting fellow, who charged into people like an angry bull, and cleared his way through them by hurling his bulk into the mass.[43]

Meal-times on *Prinzessin Irene* were unedifying: food was ladled out of 25-gallon tin tanks – one containing macaroni Neapolitan, the next large chunks of beef, the next red wine, the next boiled potatoes – to serve over a thousand steerage passengers. The food looked nauseating messed into heaps and was cold before everyone was served. The dough biscuits served for breakfast were 'as hard as a landlord's heart, and as tasteless as a bit of rag carpet'.[44] A former crewman with the Hamburg-Amerika line noted that the cooks and stewards made good money by the clandestine sale of food to third-class passengers.[45] On a Cunarder crossing from Liverpool to New York in 1913, the third-class food – roasted corn beef, sausage and mash, dubious eggs, tea tasting of soda, melting butter, ice-cream – was a poor preparation for Atlantic weather. The stewards sold seasick third-class passengers cups of Bovril, and hawked plates of ham and eggs saved from the second-class table.[46]

French and Italian ships had worse ventilation, food and over-crowding than English or German; and yet the German-American Edward Steiner denounced third-class conditions on Norddeutscher-Lloyd's new liner, *Kaiser Wilhelm II*, which had its maiden voyage in 1903 and won the Blue Riband across the Atlantic in 1904. 'The 900 steerage passengers crowded into the hold of so elegant and roomy a steamer as the *Kaiser Wilhelm II* . . . are packed like cattle, making a walk on deck when the weather is good, absolutely impossible, while to breathe clean air below in rough weather, when the hatches are down, is an equal impossibility. The stenches become unbearable, and many of the migrants have to be driven down; for they prefer the danger of the storm to the pestilential air below.'[47] Steiner objected that German steamship companies provided second-class passengers on *Kaiser Wilhelm II* with abundant outdoor deck space, and comfort-ably furnished cabins sleeping two to four passengers – while up to 400 passengers slept on tiered bunks in each sombre, frugal third-class compartment. Second-class passengers enjoyed a pleasant dining room, with nicely cooked and politely served food, 'while in the steerage the unsavoury rations are not served, but doled out, with less courtesy than one would find in a charity soup-kitchen'.[48] On some ships drinking water was grudgingly given. On the Dutch steamer *Staatendam*, steerage passengers were forced to steal water from second-class decks in night raids.

Stephen Graham travelled third-class on a Cunarder from Liverpool to New York in 1913. Each passenger was supplied with a spring bed, towel, bar of soap, and lifebelt. Berths were arranged two, four and six in a cabin. Married couples could have a room to themselves, but otherwise men and women were segregated, the different nationalities being put together. The small, box-like cabins were equipped with wash basins, but the water was not replenished after the first day of the voyage. There were lavatories where third-class travellers might wash in hot water, but the bathrooms were locked and never used. Cabins were steam-heated, so that if one's berth mates were dirty, the air was foul. Voyagers could refresh themselves in the clean air on the fore and after decks, except during storm weather, when they were battened down. During storms, the smell below was atrocious, for most people vomited profusely.[49] The walls bore notices warning that 'all couples making love too warmly would be married compulsorily at New York if the authorities deemed it fit, or should be fined or imprisoned'. Graham noted that 'the dirtiest cabins in the ship were allotted to the Russians and the Jews, and down there at nine at night the Slavs were saying their prayers while just above them we British were singing comic songs'.[50] Steerage passengers dreaded compulsory vaccination on deck for smallpox. Knaplund on *Caronia* watched young girls screaming and scampering away with sailors in pursuit. Their fear, he felt, was simulated: the sailors' chase of pretty Jewish girls delighted both hunted and their quarry.[51]

A vivid memory for Stephen Graham was the emigrants disgorging into his Cunarder's dining room to sit at twenty immense tables spread with toppling platters of bread. 'Nearly all the men came in their hats, in black glistening ringlet sheepskin hats, in fur caps, in bowlers, in sombreros, in felt hats with high crowns, in Austrian cloth caps, in caps so green that the wearer could only be Irish. Most of the young men were curious to see what girls there were on board, and looked eagerly to the daintily clad Swedish women, blonde and auburn-haired beauties in tight-fitting, speckled jerseys. The British girls came in their poor cotton dresses, or old silk ones, things that had once looked grand for Sunday wear but now bore miserable, crippled hooks and eyes, threadless seams, gaping fastenings.' The third-class dining room was like a fairground in the colour and variety of its costumes. Graham sat between a Russian peasant woman wrapped in sheepskin and a neat Danish engineer. Two American cowboys, a Spanish dandy and two Norwegians in voluminous knitted jackets shared their table. Nearby there were boisterous Flemings with huge caps and gaudy scarves, Italians who wore their black felt hats throughout meals, gentle Russian youths in shirts which womenfolk had embroidered, and gaunt, black-bearded Jewish patriarchs in long, loose gabardines.[52]

After these convivial meals, third-class passengers began to talk, dance, sing and play together, Graham said. 'The cabins were abuzz with chatter, and along the decks young couples began to find one another out and to walk arm-in-arm. Two dreamy Norwegians produced concertinas, and sat down in dark corners and played dance music for hours, for days. Rough men danced with one another, and the more fortunate danced with the girls, dance after dance, endlessly. The buffets were crowded with navvies clamouring for beer; the smoking rooms were full of excited gamblers thumbing filthy cards.' In the first deck mess room, the more respectable passengers sat and talked, or sang while someone played the piano. Above them, on the second deck, 'hooligans rushed about, and there also, in the many recesses and dark empty corners, young men and women were making love, looking moonily at one another, kissing furtively'. And out on the open deck were 'the sad people, and those who loved to pace to and fro to the march music of the racing steamer and the breaking waves'.[53]

EIGHT

Imported Americans

She and her man crossed the ocean and the years that marked their faces saw them haggling with landlords and grocers while six children played on the stones and prowled in the garbage cans.

One child coughed its lungs away, two more have adenoids and can neither talk nor run like their mother, one is in jail, two have jobs in a box factory.

Carl Sandburg, 'Population Drifts'

The peak of immigration into the US was 1907, when some 1,125,000 immigrants were admitted into the country. Henry Roth depicted a small steamer reaching New York in that year, delivering migrants from the stench and throb of steerage to the stench and throb of the city's tenements: its decks thronged by 'natives from almost every land in the world, the jowled close-cropped Teuton, the full-bearded Russian, the scraggly-whiskered Jew, and among them Slovak peasants with docile faces, smooth-cheeked and swarthy Armenians, pimply Greeks, Danes with wrinkled eyelids. All day her decks had been colourful, a matrix of the vivid costumes of other lands, the speckled green and yellow aprons, the flowered kerchief, embroidered homespun, the silver-braided sheepskin vest, the gaudy scarves, yellow boots, fur caps, caftans, dull gabardines. All day the guttural, the high-pitched voices, the astonished cries, the gasps of wonder, reiteration of gladness had risen from her decks in a motley billow of sound.'[1] Another first-time visitor to New York, in 1913, described his liner's progress past the tall, shabby warehouses, the greasy swirls of oil on the water and the hooting of the port. 'Round her snorted and scuttled and puffed the multitudinous strange denizens of the harbour. Tugs, steamers, queer-shaped ferry-boats, long rafts carrying great lines of trucks from railway to railway, dredgers, motor boats, even a sailing boat . . . All kinds of refuse went floating by: bits of wood, straw from barges, bottles, boxes, paper, occasionally a dead cat or dog, hideously bladder-like, its four paws stiff and indignant towards heaven.'[2]

Once steamers had docked, passengers had to endure customs inspections. Torrents of humanity poured along the companion-ways lugging their bundles when the steerage disembarked from *Prinzessin Irene* in 1903. A woman trying to mount a companionway with a child in one arm, a chair hooked over her other arm, which also supported a bundle, momentarily blocked the way. A livid German steward dragged her back, wrenched the chair off her arm, tearing her sleeve and grazing the skin off her wrist, and smashed the chair into splinters. The cowed woman went ashore sobbing. The dock employees were all German, some speaking only broken English, who shouted mongrel exhortations at the crowd to stand in line for baggage inspection. When the Italians did not understand, they prodded them with sticks. Brandenburg heard a German shouting in English at an Italian woman: 'I'll knock the brains out of a few of you dirty **** **** with this club! God damn your **** souls to Hell anyway! I'll break your neck, I'll fix you for buttin' in, you **** dago!'[3] After customs, third-class passengers who were not US citizens embarked on barges to the immigration station on Ellis Island. Dock employees were rough when transferring immigrants to the barges, shoving violently, jabbing them with sticks. A bargee herding his passengers swore as he explained his work. 'I'm driving these animals back . . . You've got to be rough with this bunch. I get so sick of handling these dirty bums coming over here to this country.'[4]

At Ellis Island, immigrants were received, medically examined, interrogated and winnowed: most were let pass, but some detained and ultimately returned to Europe. Ellis Island was an immigration depot built in New York harbour after a federal law of 1891 denied entry to the USA to paupers, polygamists and people with loathsome or contagious diseases. Anarchists, prostitutes, epileptics and beggars were added to the excluded categories by a law of 1903. In 1909, William Williams, the Commissioner of Immigration at Ellis Island, set a figure of $25, plus railway tickets, as the requisite minimum for prospective immigrants to possess (first- and second-class passengers underwent only perfunctory inspection). He wanted to restrict immigration from the Mediterranean and east Europe, especially aliens who might become a public charge: his rule hit Russian Jews particularly. A vituperative campaign against Williams by an American-German newspaper, perhaps instigated by a steamship company seeking relaxation of immigration rules, was amplified by the Hearst press during 1911, and he was driven to resign in 1912. He and other commissioners were honest men who fought shyster lawyers preying on immigrants, procurers who inveigled friendless women into prostitution, corrupt or brutal officials, and extortionists who used their food, currency exchange and luggage concessions at Ellis Island to abuse, cheat and rob confiding immigrants. A notable scoundrel, Barney Biglin, rose from being a luggage porter to a millionaire by obtaining, with backing from bent politicians, the Ellis Island luggage concession, which he abused. Biglin also secured a contract to transport hundreds of immigrants a day to Grand Central Station in covered wagons, at 50 cents a passenger, but had his men take them instead by subway, and pocketed 45 cents on each transaction. Williams was finally rid of him in 1912.[5]

Once landed from the barges at Ellis Island, passengers were herded to the examination hall, where they trailed down narrow aisles of iron railings suggestive of prison bars. 'Once more it was "Quick march!" and hurrying along with bags and baskets in our hands, we were put into lines,' Stephen Graham recorded of his processing through Ellis Island in 1913. One physician turned their eyelids inside out with a metal instrument, and another scanned faces and hands for skin diseases. 'We passed into the vast hall of judgment, and were classified and put into lines again, this time according to our nationality. It was interesting to observe at the very threshold of the United States the mechanical obsession of the American people. This ranging and guiding and hurrying and sifting was like nothing so much as the screening of coal in a great breaker tower. It is not good to be like a hurrying, bumping, wandering piece of coal being mechanically guided to the sacks of its type and size, but such is the lot of the immigrant at Ellis Island.'[6] Knaplund's memories of his arrival from Norway were similar. An apprehensive medley – the majority of them aged between 18 and 25 – filed like docile sheep to desks where inspectors studied their papers, inquired about their funds and destination. The immigrants were shoved a good deal, perhaps inevitably as few of them had a common language with the officials. Knaplund, like Graham, felt manhandled as a commodity rather than valued as a human. On the gallery running above the concourse he saw a scornful black charwoman gazing down on the milling mass of humanity beneath her: 'ever afterwards when he was treated condescendingly because of his foreign origin, he saw behind the face of the disdainful person the contemptuous expression on the countenance of the unknown Negress at Ellis Island'.[7]

Frank Martocci, an interpreter at Ellis Island before 1914, recalled that to speed the processing of bewildered immigrants, they were tagged with numbers. If a case aroused medical suspicion, or lacked $25 or convincing plans, Martocci continued, 'the alien was set aside in a cage apart from the rest, for all the world like a segregated animal, and his coat lapel or shirt marked with colored chalk, the color indicating why he had been isolated. These methods, crude as they seem, had to be used, because of the great numbers and the language difficulties.'[8] Another Ellis Island interpreter, during 1907–10, was Fiorello La Guardia, son of an Italian bandmaster and a Jewish mother from Trieste, who spoke English, Croatian, German, Hungarian, Italian and Yiddish and, as suited such a polyglot, was later elected Mayor of New York City. 'There were many heartbreaking scenes on Ellis Island. I never managed during the three years I worked there to become callous to the mental anguish, disappointment and despair I witnessed almost daily.' He regretted the enforcement of federal laws, introduced at the behest of labour unions in 1885 and 1903, excluding immigrants coming to the US for pre-arranged jobs, so-called contract labour. 'Common sense,' La Guardia said, 'suggested that any immigrant who came into the United States in those days to settle here permanently surely came here to work. However, under the law, he could not have more than a vague hope of a job.'[9] Amongst the Croatians on *Titanic*, for example, Bartol and Ivan Cor, labourers from Kricina, were both heading to Great Falls, Montana (a mushroom-growth new city, fuelled on hydro-electricity, where the Anaconda Copper smelter was the biggest employer and boasted the tallest smokestack in America). Matilda Petrinac, Ignjac Hendekovic, and Stefo Pavlovic, all from Vagovina, were destined for Harrisburg, Pennsylvania, with its steel-works and Hershey's chocolate factory. It beggars belief that they were voyaging thousands of miles on a vague hope of work in the smelter, or chocolate factory. Immigrants under interrogation had to reply carefully so that they were rejected neither for coming with the definite promise of work, in violation of the contract labour ban, nor for being clueless about jobs.

Archie Butt, a *Titanic* passenger, who accompanied President Taft on an inspection of Ellis Island in 1910, thought the questioning was unintelligent and unkind. The White House men were touched by the sight of a seventeen-year-old girl tending five smaller siblings while an immigrant officer interrogated their father with the object of proving that he was too ignorant to be admitted. Did the United States have a 'monarchical' government, he asked. His victim, not understanding, gave a muddled reply: Taft, feeling that a minority of Americans knew the word, asked the immigrant if he knew the name of the President, and was answered, 'Yes, sir; Mr Taft.'[10]

On average, around 1912, there were 2,000 detainees at any one time. They were kept in long halls lined by tiers of narrow iron bunks: those without beds had to sleep on benches, chairs or floors. A British physician, who was detained for four weeks on Ellis Island, penned an indignant account of his ordeal. 'A government by the people for the people has devised this means of humiliating and torturing its immigrants and visitors . . . Human beings from infancy to old age of all nations, creeds and classes are crowded together.' He was confined under guard with hundreds of others inside the same room with only six hours' exercise in the open air each week: less than criminals got in prison. Clothes had to be washed in hand basins, and plastered to the tiled walls of the living room for drying. The lavatories were filthy and flooded. Detainees were allowed a maximum of one visitor three times a week, though few received so many, and had no outside contact save by letter. 'The weekends are interminable – no movement, the offices closed, no post, no visitors,' the detainee continued. 'At the long tables during the day women weep for the discomfort of themselves and their children. Others lie with fever rather than report sick and be sent to Hospital which they dread, and because they will postpone their freedom of this awful place. Men are assaulted and threatened by the orderlies.'[11]

Detainees were fed from big pails filled with prunes and loaves of rye bread. 'A helper would take a dipper full of prunes and slop it down on a big slice of bread, saying "Here! Now go and eat!" The poor wretches had to obey,' Frank Martocci recalled. 'They moved along, their harassed faces full of fear . . . All they got to eat there was prunes or prune sandwiches: when you have it all the time, morning and evening, evening and morning, it becomes revolting.'[12]

The physician was detained at Ellis Island after being denounced by an American father whose daughter he wished to marry. In some cases, when young women arrived in America to marry their fiancés, Ellis Island interpreters would be told to take them to City Hall, where marriage ceremonies were performed by aldermen after payment of fees. On the occasions when Fiorello La Guardia undertook this task, the aldermen were drunk: they inserted nasty quips or lewd words into the marriage ceremony, 'to the amusement of the red-faced, "tin-horn" politicians who hung around to watch the so-called fun'.[13]

A ferry took Ellis Island workers to the depot each morning. Hundreds of others – relations or friends of immigrants expected that day, or already on Ellis Island – jostled and clamoured to get aboard too. As a native Italian, Martocci seemed a 'godsend to many of these people who, recognizing my nationality, would seize me by the coat, by the arm, and even by the neck, and insist on following me everywhere I went, babbling out their problems and pleading for aid. I did my best to keep clear of them in a kindly way, but sometimes I couldn't help but lose my patience.'[14] Some of the more discreetly behaved travellers in this boat were confidence-tricksters, perhaps with a braided cap secreted in their pocket or wearing a fake uniform jacket under their coat. Once inside the Ellis Island compound, they would masquerade as officials, demand to see an immigrant's money and then, exchanging a $50 US bill for an Argentine coin, vanish.

Henry Roth pictured the reunion of families on the New York quay. 'The most volatile races, such as the Italians, often danced for joy, whirled each other around, pirouetted in an ecstasy; Swedes sometimes just looked at each other, breathing through open mouths like a panting dog; Jews wept, jabbered, almost put each other's eyes out with the recklessness of their darting gestures; Poles roared and gripped each other at arm's length as though they meant to tear a handful of flesh; and after one pecking kiss, the English might be seen gravitating towards, but never achieving an embrace.'[15]

The reception in the Land of Liberty, even for those who were escorted by a guide, was often hostile. The courier of a group of Italian emigrant women recalled taking them on a streetcar from Battery Park to Broadway. 'Oh, what dirty, dirty wretches,' exclaimed a woman with a worn seal-plush bag, as she scrutinized the Italians. 'I don't see why they let these lousy dagoes ride on the same cars as other people have to use,' a stout man with gold-framed glasses objected.[16] The group was repulsed as 'dagos' when its guide tried to get rooms for his party in Bleecker Street hotels. They soon had the flayed looks of poor immigrants facing ill-disposed natives in an indifferent world.

Cheapskate boarding house runners duped immigrants with mean stratagems. Compatriots speaking the newcomer's language were the most dangerous because they could insinuate themselves into his confidence, cheat him in money-changing, lie about railway fares, send him to wrong destinations, betray him to a bad employer, or plunder his dollars.[17] This was why disinterested, protective couriers were desirable. At Grand Central Station in 1903 a bystander watched two dozen newly arrived Italians led by a stocky, prosperous-seeming man who gabbled Italian to the left and broken English to the right: 'they were tagged for Boston and other New England towns, and, bearing their heavy burdens of luggage and bundles, with faces drawn from weariness, eyes dull with too much gazing at the wonders of a new land, with scarce a smile among them except on the faces of the unreasoning children, they were herded together, counted off as they passed through the gate and taken aboard the train, much as if they had been some sort of animals'.[18]

In New York, an enterprising Cornish family ran the Star Hotel at 67 Clarkson Street, Brooklyn, as 'a sort of home away from home' and courier service for Cornish voyagers.[19] Its proprietor John Blake hailed from St Stephen-in-Brannel, a hamlet in the china clay country surrounding St Austell, where the countryside was dotted with white mounds resembling little snow-clad hills. He had married the daughter of a hotel keeper from whom he took over the Star. Their son Sid (born in New York in 1890) was its manager. 'When you land at New York stay at the Star Hotel,' advertisements in Cornish newspapers urged: 'the only Cornish house in New York, well-known and appreciated.'[20] Sid Blake also sent newsletters, naming recent guests at the Star, and retailing their stories, to English newspapers, including the *Cornishman* of Penzance, *Hayle Mail* and *Cornubian* covering the mining district of Redruth and Camborne. The Blakes were steamship and railroad agents who met Cornish migrants on arrival in New York, took them to their Star Hotel, and guided them on their way with their luggage to the station from where they caught their trains to westerly mining districts. They had local agents in Cornwall, such as the St Austell auctioneer called King Daniel and a Penzance shipping agent named Christopher Ludlow. It was doubt-less by the Blakes' advice that many Cornish emigrants, even from poor families, travelled second-class to America, and thus circum-vented strict inspection at Ellis Island. The Blakes also acted as travel agents for Cornishmen wishing to revisit home. In prompt answer to inquiries, they would provide sailing dates, ticket prices, and make bookings. Bridegrooms would travel back from their western mining district to the Star Hotel to meet their incoming brides: the couple would be married from the hotel with old man Blake acting as father-of-the-bride.

'If only we had some memoir of that hotel, some reminiscences of the life that passed through it, with its mingled gaiety and sadness, its chance encounters, its happy reunions and partings forever!' A. L. Rowse exclaimed in his study of Cornishmen in America. Rowse recalled that as an Edwardian boy in a village near St Austell, life in Butte, Montana was more familiar than London. Three cottages near his home were named Calumet, Butte and Montana by owners who had returned with their savings from the US. Miners returning from America were easily recognized at St Austell railway station: 'you could always tell them, they wore broad-rimmed hats, ill-fitting light grey suits, and tremendous watch-chains with gold nuggets hanging heavily from them'. A boy whose parents had returned to Cornwall after nine years at Butte recalled that their chief topic during meals was America. 'Mother and Father always talked about it, how different things were, how the houses were built and how people lived. Father talked for many an hour over the hedge with our next neighbour, Tom Nicholls, about America; he had also lived in Butte.'[21]

The intimacy between remote settlements in Cornwall and American mining districts was encouraged by local newspapers. The *Cornubian*, of Redruth, carried a regular column entitled 'Cornishmen Abroad', which gleaned news from foreign newspapers. In the week that it announced *Titanic*'s fate, it reported from Butte's *Tribune Review* that 'the little daughter of Mr & Mrs William Trenerry, of Dewey's Point, Walkerville, caught her index finger in a washing machine a few days ago, severely lacerating and breaking that member'; or from the *Keweenaw Miner* that 'Mr Richard H. Williams has suffered the loss of his horse. This is the second horse that has died on Mr Williams this winter . . . He has also lost a couple of cows. Considerable sympathy is expressed for him in his losses.'[22]

There was a similar 'Cornishmen Abroad' column in the *Hayle Mail*, which in the same week included such tit-bits as the business trip of Silas Chynoweth of Calumet to Ahmeek, Michigan, and from Butte that 'recently a jolly surprise party was given in honour of Mrs William Johns, by Mr & Mrs Edward Champion Hall, 613 West Granite Street . . . an event long to be remembered. The beautiful home was decorated with choice cut flowers. Vocal and instrumental music added to the evening's enjoyment.'[23]

A lacerated finger, a dead horse, cut flowers made news because life was so tedious. 'The men did nothing between sleep and work, except when emergency arose,' Newton Thomas wrote of emigrant copper miners in Michigan, 'and the one emergency in winter-time was more wood' – for they lived in a stove-centred world. 'They sat about, paperless, bookless, smoked and talked, or – smoked and dreamed. They discussed the superiority of the English lever to Swiss watches; how best and quickest to color a meerschaum or common clay pipe, and the brand of tobacco to do with it; Cornish wrasslin,' the Cornish pasty, and Cornish cream.'[24]

On ship, the migrants had been dazed by the throb of the screw and the rush of the parting waters. On land, they were shaken by every jolt and rattle of the trains carrying them to their new lives. Knaplund recalled long days gazing at the countryside as he travelled by train from New York via Buffalo, Chicago and McIntire, Iowa, to Ostrander, Minnesota. 'Railroad stations and the houses nearby seemed surprisingly dingy for this wealthy land. Perhaps America, too, had her poor. This was a disquieting thought for immigrants who all expected to make a fortune.'[25] Newton Thomas depicted the arrival in Michigan's copper belt of a group of Cornish miners. They had journeyed from Chicago on a slow train through a Hiawatha landscape of misty lakes and forests of aspen, laurel and pine. 'The boys were tired. They were dishevelled; they felt disrespectable without shame. For four days they had ridden the cane-seated coaches from New York; and they had not washed since the train left Chicago the preceding morning. The washrooms of the day coaches had discouraged them. They had slept each night, bent and knotted, in the discomfort of the car seats, without undressing. They were hungry.'[26] Sinclair Lewis described a similar journey: a long, low line of carriages trundling through Minnesota, under the rolling clouds of the prairie, on a hot, dusty September day.

> No pillows, no provision for beds, but all today and all tonight they will ride in this long steel box . . . They are parched and cramped, the lines of their hands filled with grime; they go to sleep in distorted attitudes . . . They do not read; apparently they do not think. They wait. An early-wrinkled, young-old mother, moving as though her joints were dry, opens a suitcase in which are seen creased blouses, a pair of slippers worn through at the toes, a bottle of patent medicine, a tin cup, a paper-covered book about dreams which the news-butcher has coaxed her into buying . . . A large brick-colored Norwegian takes off his shoes, grunts in relief . . . An old woman whose toothless mouth shuts like a mud-turtle's, and whose hair is not so much white as yellow like mouldy linen, with bands of pink skull apparent beneath the tresses, anxiously lifts her bag, opens it, peers in, closes it, puts it under the seat, and hastily picks it up, and opens it, and hides it all over again . . . Two facing seats, overflowing with a Slovene iron-miner's family, are littered with shoes, dolls, whisky bottles, bundles wrapped in newspapers, a sewing bag. The oldest boy takes a mouth-organ out of his coat-pocket, wipes the tobacco crumbs off, and plays 'Marching through Georgia' until every head in the car begins to ache.[27]

When Knaplund reached his destination in Minnesota, he first noticed the trees: blue spruces lined one side of the drive from the road to the farmhouse, with maples on the other, while before the house stood tall, erect Norway pines so different from the stunted aspens and birches of his home fjord. He had imagined that an American farmstead would resemble a Norwegian merchant's country estate; but instead of a commodious, airy dwelling and large, proud barns, he was startled to find a small white wooden house abutting dilapidated sheds thatched with rotting straw and so flimsy that it looked as if they might be blown down by the grunts of the sow rootling in the mud. The one big downstairs chamber of the farmhouse served as living room, dining room, kitchen and bedroom for a venerable widow. It all seemed shockingly meagre.[28]

There were a dozen young Armenian men on *Titanic* with a tradition of sojourning – quitting their villages for years at a time and remitting funds home. Often, before a youth's departure, he was married off by his parents to a local girl as a way of ensuring his return to his birthplace. As Armenians learned the routes and mastered survival skills after 1895, they discounted distances, costs, dangers and hardships as time and again they traversed the Atlantic. One man from Keghi sojourned on his first trip at Pontiac, Michigan, at Erie, Pennsylvania on his second crossing, and Brantford, Ontario on his third. By relentless effort, migrants restored some prosperity to Keghi and remitted funds which spurred migration, especially after 1909, when the Turks relaxed travel restrictions. With remitted money, families could discharge debts, buy land, improve farms and houses (by adding a second storey or installing glass windows), erect another house to ease overcrowding, open shops, provide dowries, pay the military-exemption tax, build village schools and churches. This inflow of money enabled Armenians to import food in times of famine, and hire mercenaries to pursue thieves who rustled their sheep or stole their crops. In these poor, backward districts, Armenian Christians were already resented by their Kurd and Turk neighbours for their religious dissent, success as traders, aspiration for political freedom, and enthusiasm for modernizing, secular influences. Keghi village economies were vulnerable to business fluctuations half a world away: a lay-off of workers at the Pratt & Letchworth Malleable Factory in Brantford could undermine the village prosperity of Astghaberd. Just as Butte was a talking point in St Austell, so Brantford, Hamilton, Detroit, Troy, St Louis, Granite City, and Corey, Alabama were part of the daily chaff and long-term hopes of Keghi villages. Money and newspapers remitted to the villages served to Americanize Keghetsi. So, too, did American consumerism and artefacts: Singer sewing machines, Yankee dolls, posters of Roosevelt and Taft.[29]

If some immigrants became Atlantic commuters, others vanished forever into the scramble of American life, where everyone grabbed and took their chance. After a goodbye service in a Methodist chapel in Cornwall, for a family departing after the closure of a mine, a woman came forward sadly: 'My boay Jan be awver there, somew'ere. If you see un, tell un Mother would like to 'ear from un.'[30] Before the Antins left Russia, the village wig-maker beseeched their mother to trace a missing son: 'Emigrated to America eighteen months ago, fresh and well and strong, with 25 rouble in his pocket, besides his steamer ticket, with new phylacteries, and a silk skull-cap . . . sent one letter, how he arrived in Castle Garden, how well he was received by my uncle's son-in-law, how he was conducted to the baths, how they bought him an American suit, everything good . . . and since then not a postal card, not a word, just as if he had vanished, as if the earth had swallowed him. *Oi, weh!*'[31] They disappeared in the anguish of defeat, as an unknown Armenian diarist, from East Providence, Rhode Island, writing in 1915, showed in his craving for oblivion. 'What to do? Live or die? Today again I feel abandoned . . . I hate everything . . . I hate my life, my love, my heart, my life and soul, my body and whole being . . . Ah, cursed is the foreigner when you don't have even a cent. You're thrown out of your room and your acquaintances forsake you . . . Your appearance gives the impression of a thief and the passer-by looks at you with hatred and fear. What to do? There is no job. Absolutely no work. To live or to die?'[32]

In Chicago, Germans settled north of the Loop, Poles in the north-west of the city, Italians and Jews west, Bohemians south-west, and Irish south. Somerset Maugham's description of Chicago's Wabash Avenue catches the harsh speed of the polyglot city with its tall, dingy buildings scarred by ramified fire escapes like parasitic growths. 'Long lines of motors along the kerbs. The dull roar of trains on the elevated, the hurried, agitated string of streetcars as they thunder along crowded with people, the sharp screech of motor horns and the shrill, peremptory whistle of the cop directing the traffic. No one loiters. Everyone hurries . . . The mixture of races,

Slavs, Teutons, Irish with their broad smiles and red faces, Middle-Westerner, dour, long-faced, strangely ill at ease, as though they were intruders.'[33] The city of migrant workers is vividly evoked in Carl Sandburg's sequence of 'Chicago Poems'. In 'Child of Romans' he depicts an Italian working a ten-hour day levelling the clinkers on a railway-line:

> The dago shovelman sits by the railroad track
> Eating a noon meal of bread and bologna.
> A train whirls by, and men and women at tables
> Alive with red roses and yellow jonquils,
> Eat steaks running with brown gravy,
> Strawberries and cream, éclairs and coffee.

There were no strawberries or éclairs for a young Serb called Nikola B who settled in Pennsylvania in 1905. Born in 1889, the sixth child in his family, his father owned five hectares of land, two cows, three pigs, and two horses, which he took with him each year when he left with his sons to work on farms in Hungary. In 1902, Nikola's uncle and his cousin left for America with other men from Cvijanović. They settled in Johnstown, from where they sent letters and photographs: 'They looked well and I decided to go.' In 1905, Nikola reached Johnstown, where he joined his relations in a boarding house. 'I was frightened of everything, different country and different people, and I never saw such big factories. My uncle told me every-thing, what to do, how to behave, what to say.' His uncle took him to the coal mine supplying Cambria Company mills. 'Soon this hard work began to weigh very heavy on my shoulders. I regretted my coming to America and more and more missed home. All day I sweated in exhausting labor, seeing no sun, only darkness, water up to my ankles, from morning till night.' In 1908, Nikola returned to his village, 'but there was nothing there for me, same poverty, same hardship as when I left'. Two years later he was back in Johnstown with his younger brother. They worked as 'buddies' in the mine making $11 a week if they toiled eleven to twelve hours a day. 'It was terribly hard work, coal-mine, back-breaking, dirty, awful. But I still preferred it here, thought it was better. I saw here some future, and at home there was none.' Workers were laid off in Johnstown in 1913, and Nikola journeyed to Steubenville, Ohio, where there was a colony of Serbs from Kordun, but failed to find work there. After various reverses, Nikola got a job in a gang of Serbs working in a blast furnace back at Johnstown. In the 1920s he opened a grocery store, which failed through bad credit, and returned to Cambria to work in the mechanical department. 'It was not bad then, we had electricity and water in the house, and plenty of food on the table, and we dressed nice, American.'[34]

To dress nice is a good ambition; but it was hard to satisfy in the environment of Johnstown coal mines and blast furnaces. After Clay Frick masterminded the defeat of the strikers at the Homestead steelworks in 1892, steel masters downgraded skilled men. In the twenty years between Homestead and *Titanic*, the pay of unskilled steel-mill labourers rose as that of skilled steel workers plunged, sometimes by up to 70 per cent. Men could keep their losses in earnings under 30 per cent only by working longer hours at a more intense pace. Steel-mill organization before the Homestead strike had resembled that of workshops in which authority was dispersed among semi-autonomous craftsmen; but increasingly, after Homestead, there were hierarchical lines of command which sharply differentiated labourers from supervisory managers. Craftsmen ceased to lead the work team or train newcomers: instead, clerks and engineers issued orders to machine tenders. The skilled, for whom machine-tending seemed brutalizing, became vastly outnumbered by semi-skilled labourers to whom mechanization and regimentation were less objectionable.

'Hunkies' took over semi-skilled steel-mill work: Bosnians, Croats, Serbs, Slovenes, Slovaks, Lithuanians, Hungarians, Ruthenians, Bohemians, Romanians, Poles, Ukrainians and Russians were recruited to work in steel mills alongside Italians and Southern Blacks, replacing Irish, German, Welsh and English. *Titanic*, for example, transported four labourers from Batic in Bosnia who were expecting jobs in Harrisburg, Pennsylvania, where Bethlehem Steel had a great works: employers, according to a turn-of-the century report of Pittsburgh, preferred Slav and Italian workers to English-speaking applicants because of 'their habit of silent submission, their amenability to discipline, and their willingness to work long hours and overtime without a murmur'.[35] Disempowered emigrants did not share the craftsmen's resentment of lost status, and had less reason to feel injured by the swarm of clerks and supervisors, monitoring and tabulating productive efficiency.[36] Edward Steiner visited Hunkies in a steel mill. 'Half-naked, savage-looking creatures darted about in the glare of molten metal, which now was white, "like bitten lip of hate", then grew red and dark as it flowed into the waiting moulds . . . I watched them day after day coming from their work, wet, dirty and blistered by the heat; dropping into their bunks at night, breathing in the pestilential air of a room crowded by fifteen sleepers, and in the morning crawling listlessly back to their slavish task.'[37]

In this hard world the 'padrone' system had a part. A padrone was an ethnic boss who spoke English, recruited workmen from his native land, advanced their passage money to America, charged commissions for finding them jobs, and received further payment from employers. Most often they were Greek, Italian, Austrian, Bulgarian or Mexican. Sometimes a padrone provided men with bed, food and minimum wages, and, treating them as indentured servants, kept anything else they earned. The better class of padrone were community leaders who helped with language problems or mediated disputes, while others were brigands who bilked their compatriots when the latter remitted their savings to their villages. A helpless, ignorant immigrant, without resort to reliable, wised-up relations or friends, might have to rely on a money-grubbing compatriot for help in seeking a pedlar's licence or completing his naturalization papers, and in arranging to bring relations to the States. These shysters charged high fees for easy services.

Theodore Saloutus, in his magisterial work *The Greeks in the United States*, has chronicled the world of padrones. An enterprising

Greek-American would write to family or neighbours in Greece, vaunting his prosperity, and offering to arrange transport and accommodation for ambitious youths. He might revisit his home province regularly to stand as godfather at baptisms or best man at weddings, or instruct his male kin in Greece to represent him in this way, with the aim of raising momentum for recruitment drives. Greek parents, often concerned more with the earning power of their sons than with their education, were keen to place youths in work, and instructed them to be obedient and dutiful. The boy was given a steamship ticket to America, with $25 in cash needed for his interrogation at Ellis Island. A mortgage was put on the father's property, representing whatever his boy had received in cash plus an amount equivalent to one year's wages. Passage money was advanced on the understanding that the boy was to remain under the padrone's control for a year.

Boys were sent by padrones to destinations far from Ellis Island, for those with destinations near the port of entry were more likely to be detained for close interrogation. In such cases, the youth's American family or sponsors were compelled to come to justify his case before officials. Youths with destinations far from New York had more lenient investigation, as there was little prospect of summoning sponsors from thousands of miles away. Chicago was therefore a common destination for Greek boys, even if their padrones operated in eastern states. In Chicago, youths were told to report to a Greek barkeeper who issued directions to their final destinations. In the bars and eating-places on South Halstead Street, a youth was bound to meet a relation or neighbour of his father's.

Padrones typically controlled flower, fruit and vegetable pedlars and shoeshine boys, and supplied labour for railway-building and mining. In Chicago, boys went to houses and apartment blocks with fruit and vegetables while the padrone guarded his stock on the street. Boys learnt the English names and prices of their wares, and were more welcome by women in their homes than coarse, slouching adults. They lived in crowded basements or unventilated rooms – sometimes above stables. The Greek boys, generally prettier, who were used as flower pedlars in parks and shopping streets, especially in New York City, were better paid and treated.

Greeks took up shoe-shining (previously the preserve of Italians and Blacks) in the 1890s. They had booths and chairs in the street, and stands near hotels, restaurants, saloons, amusements and stations. Greeks who had amassed a little money in America began to import youths to work for them as shoe-shiners. Greek shoeshine boys worked seven days a week, getting up early in order to reach the parlours which opened after six in the morning, working till nine or ten at night, and for longer hours at weekends. After closing, youths still had to mop the floor, clean the marble stand, take the shoe-shining rags home, where they washed and dried them for the following day. Padrones discouraged them from talking openly to inquisitive compatriots having their shoes shined, or from learning competent English: the more ruthless of them monitored the youth's incoming and outward mail so as to stop tales of maltreatment from circulating in Greek villages. The average wage paid by a padrone was $110 to $180 a year: it was estimated that padrones made $100 to $200 a year for each boy, or $300 to $500 in some locations in big cities.

Sometimes Greeks were hired as strike-breakers without realizing the implications, for they barely understood English and lacked community nous. One flagitious case involved Bingham Canyon, the Guggenheims' copper mine south-west of Salt Lake City. Dan Jackling, the Guggenheims' manager, ran Bingham as 'a virtual slave-camp, backed up by the Utah state militia', as the family historian concedes.[38] Greeks, mainly Cretans, were the largest nationality working in the mine – supplemented by Italians, Austrians, Finns, Bulgarians, Swedes, Irish, German, Japanese and English. They were controlled by a padrone, Leonidas Skliris from Sparta, who had settled in Salt Lake City in 1897. Skliris had recruiting agents in Greece, and advertised in Greek newspapers in America. He was remunerated with an initial fee by labourers for whom he found work, and sometimes by further monthly exactions. He was said to charge an initial fee of about $20 for a job for a man, and a monthly fee of $1 or $2 to buy clothes or gifts for the foreman. In spring or fall Skliris might solicit a $10 fee ostensibly to prevent a man's discharge.

In 1912 a strike at a smelter in Murray, Utah was broken by strike-breakers procured by Skliris. This infuriated the Bingham miners, especially the Cretans, who joined the mining union with the hope that they would thereby be released from Skliris' yoke. A strike erupted, strikers armed with guns occupied high ground on the canyon side from which they could repel strike-breakers, and Governor William Spry came from Salt Lake City with seventy-five armed deputies to oust the strikers from their stronghold. Skliris meanwhile collected a gang of mainland Greek strike-breakers to defeat the Cretan-led strike until forced to flee to Mexico when miners brought charges of extortion against him. Strikers armed with rifles and nitro-glycerine seized control of the mine and fought militiamen and Guggenheim security guards. Two miners were killed before the strike fizzled out in bitter despair, and the mine was reopened with Mexicans.

Many migrants flailed and wilted in this harsh world, and returned to Europe. Many, indeed, had always intended to do so. Croatians toiling in America's mills, factories, mines and construction sites longed for the Adriatic shore, islands, mountains, hills, fields and woods of their native land: 'almost every Croatian immigrant, except those who married American-born women and some who became rich, wanted to die at home'.[39] The elders of communities on the Hungarian plains were appalled if a youngster proposed to become a factory worker in Budapest. America, they said, was less foreign and remote than Újpest: though men often returned from America, they seldom did from the capital.[40]

About 20 per cent of Nordic people who had migrated to the US returned to their homelands. Re-migration rose during American economic crises, so that Sweden's peak year of returnees (1894) followed the US financial crisis of 1893, and Norway's peak year (1908) ensued from the Wall Street panic of 1907. Many emigrants had always planned to return from the States after accumulating some savings. Often returnees had success stories to tell; but others had disliked American work conditions, or spoke of homesickness. Returnees from America, accustomed to rapid movement and enthused by change, found themselves in communities with antique, immobile customs, often consecrated by sclerotic churchmen. Ineluctably, there was a clash of values. Karl Staaf, a Minnesota farmer, told Knaplund: 'It took three trips to Norway to make me satisfied with America.'[41] Ignazio Silone records that Italians who returned to his district from America did not fare well. 'Those who managed to accumulate some bank-notes between their vest and their shirt (on the side of the heart) and returned to Fontamara in a few years lost their small savings on the parched and barren soil of their native place and relapsed into the old lethargy, preserving like a vision of paradise lost the memory of a life glimpsed beyond the sea.'[42]

At least one-third of Croatians returned from the US to their homeland with their 'krvavo zaradjeni dollar' (bloody-earned dollar). Some – crippled or debilitated miners and steel workers – had no choice but to return. Others crossed the Atlantic ten times or more, bearing tales of American riches. Thousands of Croatian villages became divided into two groups: those who stayed at home and those who had been to America. Returnees were show-offs, conspicuous in different clothes and attitudes, carrying themselves independently (some said strutted). Their work was better organized, they introduced agricultural innovations or started businesses, and respected education. They spiced their Croatian speech with English words or phrases, and in some Dalmatian villages, American-English became the second language. Life in a republic had made them impatient with traditional deference: Austro-Hungarian and Croatian officials were scandalized by their insolence in refusing to remove their hats in government offices. Many chafed at the rustic living standards and slow tempo of village life, and returned to America. The return of Amerikantsi to Croatia meant that overdue taxes and debts were paid, extra fields, better tools and more cattle were bought, phylloxera-smitten vineyards were grubbed up, immune vines planted, churches were repaired, schools and hospitals were built, cripples and political prisoners aided. Money was given to political exiles and anti-Hapsburg political groups. In the villages, new houses were erected, streets were paved, bridges improved. Sewing machines became common in homes. There was civic pride: sometimes a library was opened, volunteer fire brigades started, church bells bought, even though many who returned from America defied the village priest, and outraged their God-fearing neighbours, by declaring themselves free-thinkers.[43]

A German-American travelling on an eastward-bound steamer returning Greeks, Spaniards, Swiss, Germans, Macedonians, Montenegrins, Hungarians, and Lebanese to their homelands noted their command of English varied from complete fluency down to the ability to swear: 'American "cuss words" are among the first things picked up and the last forgot.'[44] Another German-American, Edward Steiner, described his journey to Europe with bitter, broken men and quashed, slatternly women – the failed sojourners. 'It is an awful country!' a Hunkie exclaimed to him. 'They do not stop to eat nor sleep, and they drive one as the water drives the village mill. They build a house one minute and tear it down the next; the cities grow like mushrooms and disappear like grass before a swarm of locusts. The air is black in the city where I lived; black as the inside of the chimney in my cabin, and the water they drink looks like cabbage soup. The cars go like a whirlwind over the *puszta* and I should rather stand among a thousand stampeding horses, than on one of those dreadful street corners. How terribly those whistles blow in the morning and how dark and dismal are those [work]shops, where they eat up iron and men . . . The heat outside burns and the heat inside blisters, and when it is cold, it freezes the blood. No, no,' and he groaned in terror at his memories, 'no more America for me.'[45]

PART TWO

On Board

He explored the steamer. It was to him, the mechanic, the most sure and impressive mechanism he had ever seen; more satisfying than a Rolls, a Delaunay-Belleville, which to him had been the equivalents of a Velásquez. He marvelled at the authoritative steadiness with which the bow mastered the waves; at the powerful sweep of the lines of the deck and the trim stowing of cordage. He admired the first officer, casually pacing the bridge. He wondered that in this craft which was, after all, but a floating iron egg-shell, there should be the roseate music-room, the smoking room with its Tudor fireplace – solid and terrestrial as a castle – and the swimming pool, green-lighted water washing beneath Roman pillars. He climbed to the boat deck, and some never-realized desire for seafaring was satisfied as he looked along the sweep of gangways, past the huge lifeboats, the ventilators like giant saxophones, past the lofty funnels serenely dribbling black woolly smoke, to the forward mast. The snow-gusts along the deck, the mysteriousness of this new world but half-seen in the frosty lights, only stimulated him. He shivered and turned up his collar, but he was pricked to imaginativeness, standing outside the wireless room, by the crackle of messages springing across bleak air-roads ocean-bounded to bright snug cities on distant plains.

Sinclair Lewis, *Dodsworth*

NINE

First-Class

Complete freedom consists of being able to do what you like, provided you also do something you like less.

Italo Svevo, *Zeno's Conscience*

Monarchs and princes travelled in state, but when journeying abroad for pleasure, staying at the local Ritz, disguised themselves under incognitos in order to limit ceremonial duties.[1] Kings of finance also travelled in state, but never cared who knew their names. Washington Irving's account of early-nineteenth-century Montreal money men attending the Northwest Company's annual meeting at Lake Superior shows the imposing train and ostentatious comforts that they required. 'They ascended the rivers in great state, like sovereigns making a progress: or rather like Highland chieftains navigating their subject lakes. They were wrapped in rich furs, their huge canoes freighted with every convenience and luxury, and manned by Canadian voyageurs, as obedient as Highland clansmen. They carried up with them cooks and bakers, together with delicacies of every kind, and abundance of choice wines for the banquets which attended this great convocation.' They were happiest of all if they could persuade 'some titled member of the British nobility to accompany them on this stately occasion, and grace their high solemnities'.[2]

The stately progress of crowned heads and business chieftains demanded all that was costly and conspicuous. But whereas monarchs expected panoply which enthroned precedent, reverence and continuity, the rulers of twentieth-century business spurned tradition: their voices were raised for speed, movement, novelty, instability. Their money went on sudden disjunctive choices that unsettled everyone else. Impulsive, peremptory decisions were expensive, and thus a proof of power. They made a bonfire of other people's arrangements so that the blazing resplendence of their own reputations would be seen for miles. To show the tempo of her protagonists, Edith Wharton included a last-minute dash from Paris on a White Star liner at the close of her novel, *The Custom of the Country* (1913). Elmer Moffatt, the 'billionaire Railroad King', tells his ex-wife Undine Spragg, whom he intends to remarry, that he is expected at a board meeting in Apex City, and will have to cable for a special train to get him there from New York, 'but I'll have a deck suite for you on the *Semantic* if you'll sail with me the day after tomorrow'.[3] Sailing the day after tomorrow, or cancelling a voyage leaving the day after tomorrow, was part of life's satisfaction.

Clay Frick, who visited Europe most years, travelling on Atlantic liners with his wife, children and entourage, cancelled his reservation of *Titanic* suite B-52 because his wife had sprained her ankle. Pierpont Morgan took over Frick's booking, but then cancelled because he preferred to oversee the shipment of his Paris art collection to America. George Vanderbilt cancelled his booking for himself and his wife on the day before departure, although his servant Frederick Wheeler travelled second-class with their luggage, and perished with it. Milton Hershey, the Pennsylvania chocolate millionaire, cancelled his reservation. Robert Bacon, the outgoing US Ambassador to France, had booked to embark at Cherbourg with his wife; but they were forced to defer their return as his successor had delayed his arrival. Frick and Morgan were two of the most hard-headed men in America, and Vanderbilt one of the most gracefully romping: they were united in their abrupt jettisoning of well-laid plans. There were others, such as John Weir, retired president of the Nevada-Utah Miners & Smelters Corporation, wishing to travel from his native Scotland to inspect mining properties in California, who were forced to transfer to *Titanic* because of the coal strike.

Many first-class *Titanic* voyagers met the beau ideal of upper-class manliness, which was to be frank, fresh and sporty, and to live with a *modest* swagger. These included William Carter, of Bryn Mawr, Pennsylvania, the thirty-six-year-old polo-playing scion of a Philadelphia family, who had taken Rotherby House in Leicestershire for the hunting season. Carter divided his time between Philadelphia, his estate at Newport and the English hunting shires. His wife – formerly Lucile Polk of Virginia – turned heads in Philadelphia and Newport society by her daring costumes and four-in-hand driving. Husband and wife, who were prominent followers of the Quorn hunt, travelled with their two children, plus a valet, lady's maid and chauffeur. On board, Carter hailed another broad-shouldered sportsman, Clarence Moore, master of the Chevy Chase hunt, who had been in England buying foxhounds. Moore was a Washington stockbroker who farmed in Maryland and owned land in Virginia. For sporting gentlemen like Carter and Moore, it was deadly to keep still. They always had to be on the move: riding, jumping hedges, tramping fields with a gun, clambering aboard yachts, strolling on bosky paths with a lady, circling the pockets of a billiard table with the men. The card table provided a permissible sedentary diversion. So, too, did the deep chairs of the smoking room with its array of bottles that brought a thumping resonant end to the men's evenings.

A member of Caroline Astor's Four Hundred described her set in the period before 1914. 'Breathless rushes across continents – One country blending into another – journeys by car, by boat, by train – Paris – Newport – New York. Paris again – London – Vienna – Berlin – the Riviera – Italy. Champagne years, colourful, sparkling, ephemeral . . . Always entertaining, being entertained, the same scene in a new setting.'[4] There was speeding bustle as they chased Italian masters, English butlers, Austrian musicians, French chauffeurs, Spanish dancers and Paris dressmakers; but their vagrancy, like that of the Jet Set half a century later, was as aimless as that of tramps. They chattered about new motors, new fashions, new restaurants, new health fads and new marriages in a stifling airtight atmosphere. They scattered all the little words by which the rich recognized, comforted and affirmed one another: Ballets Russes, Consuelo, Grand Duke, Grand Slam, Hollandaise, Poiret, Rumpelmayer, Sobranie, Standard Oil, the Uffizi, the Racquet, the Nile, Marconigram, Rolls, *Olympic*, Ritz.

'Ritzonia' was the epithet coined by Bernard Berenson, who sold Italian pictures to American millionaires, to describe the unreal, mortifying sameness of their luxury. 'Ritzonia,' he wrote in 1909, 'carries its inmates like a wishing carpet from place to place, the same people, the same meals, the same music. Within its walls you might be at Peking or Prague or Paris or London and you would never know where.'[5] Feverish movement provided the tempo of Ritzonia, as Edith Wharton told Berenson. 'Yes, it's very nice to be petted & feasted – but I don't see how you can stand more than two or three weeks of that queer rootless life. I felt my individuality shrivelling a little every day, till I had somehow the feeling of being a mere "jeton" [counter] in a game, that hurried & purposeless hands were feverishly moving from one little square to another – a kind of nightmare chess without rules.'[6] Henry James in 1904 described life in the hotels, liners and marble pleasure palaces of Ritzonia. 'Every voice in the great bright house was a call to the ingenuities and impunities of pleasure; every echo was a defiance of difficulty, doubt or danger; every aspect of the picture, a glowing plea for the immediate, and as with plenty more to come, was another phase of the spell. For a world so constituted was governed by a spell, that of the smile of the gods and the favour of the powers.'[7] It was with this impregnable spellbound assurance that first-class passengers boarded *Titanic*.

Over-dressing, said Ben Hecht, was the only art that Americans ever perfected. Each spring American plutocrats wrested the latest dresses and hats from their Paris makers. Only spring fashions mattered to the women of Ritzonia: within months the latest trends had been so meticulously detailed in American women's magazines such as *Butterick's* and the suggestively titled *Elite Styles*, that every Main Street dressmaker and amateur seamstress was purveying a version of Rue des Pyramides *modes*. The Paris spring fashion of

1912 was a voluminous looped silk overskirt called a pannier, which if carefully cut and drawn in tightly about the feet could make a woman look more slender than the reality. 'It is a clever deceit,' wrote the *Philadelphia Inquirer*'s Paris correspondent on 13 April. 'Never has the fashionable woman worn less. She wears her chemise, a dainty silk affair, so thin that it takes scarcely any room beneath her corsets. The corsets are long enough to insure protection against the cold, and so she wears with them only a bust supporter of English eyelet embroidery, which ends above the waistline, and then a tiny pair of knickerbockers generally in white or pale pink China silk, which are fitted closely at the waist-line.'[8]

The couturier and *Titanic* passenger Lady Duff Gordon, with shops in Paris, London and New York, was a pioneer in using panniers as concealing draperies. She recalled Paris in 1912 as a city where the 'luxury trades were kept alive by the princely expenditure of American millionaires and Russian grand dukes'.[9] Charlotte Cardeza, who occupied a suite with its own promenade deck, was one such Croesus. She travelled with fourteen steamer trunks, four suitcases, three crates and a medicine chest. These contained, with other items, seventy dresses, ten fur coats, ninety-one pairs of gloves and twenty-two hatpins, with a total value of £36,567. Mrs Cardeza was the daughter of the industrialist Thomas Drake, who in 1866 founded the Fidelity Trust Company. Having divorced her rich husband, she lived in a stylish house, Montebello, at Germantown. She was returning from Hungary, via Paris, with her bachelor son, Thomas Drake Cardeza, an unobtrusive director of his grandfather's Fidelity-Philadelphia Trust, who had trained himself to mimic other men's airs of distinction, but had neither contours nor colours of his own. For Charlotte Cardeza, there was no thrill in buying life's mundane necessities, but it was voluptuous joy to buy Paris luxuries which she did not need.

There were Canadian counterparts to the Cardezas called the Baxters. Hélène Baxter was the widow of 'Diamond Jim' Baxter, a Quebec financier who had built the first shopping mall in Canada before his imprisonment in 1900 for embezzling large sums from his bank. She had protected most of her husband's fortune and, after staying with her son and daughter at the Elysée Palace Hotel in Paris, was returning with them to North America. Their tickets were amongst the most expensive. Her twenty-four-year-old son Quigg Baxter had been a star hockey player, was full of animal spirits and, travelling in B-60, quietly installed his girlfriend in C-90. She was a Belgian cabaret singer called Berthe Mayné, but was travelling under the name of Madame de Villiers – a name taken from that of a previous lover who had enlisted in the Foreign Legion.

George and Eleanor Widener had gone to Paris with their daughter to buy her trousseau for her forthcoming wedding: although she remained in France, they carried her purchases with them. Eleanor Widener was an inveterate Paris shopper, and twenty-five years later died during an expedition to a Paris boutique. Men, too, travelled with great trains of luggage. The American presidential aide Archie Butt, who visited Europe for six weeks, took seven trunks. As well as his Renault car, Billy Carter lost sixty shirts and twenty-four polo sticks when *Titanic* sank.

The White Star stewardess Violet Jessop recalled embarkation day of an Olympic-class liner. 'Everywhere there was tension,' she wrote. 'As the passengers began to arrive, the volume of noise increased to a crescendo that seemed as if it could only end in madness . . . That babble even blotted out thought, as perspiring masses of smartly dressed, over-scented humanity surged together; yet here and there, a silent pathetic farewell was taking place. Everybody was totally oblivious of the distracted stewards vainly attempting to move enormous pieces of baggage through the crush. Those in charge shouted orders, and room bells rang impatiently for drinks, while stewardesses' additional bugbear – flowers to arrange – arrived with the regularity of snowflakes. Boxes of every size were piled mountain-high.'[10] Ida Straus, whose husband owned Macy's department store in New York, found a basket of roses and carnations waiting in her cabin, a parting gift from Catherine Burbidge, whose husband's family owned Harrods in London – 'all so beautiful in color and as fresh as though they had just been cut'.[11] Women passengers would receive over a dozen boxes of flowers on sailing day, and expect their exasperated stewardess to conjure eight or ten tall vases.

Many women in first-class had abrasive grandeur: they spoke as if they always required special arrangements. Once on board, their faces set in an expression of unchallenged superiority, for they had only themselves to put first. In their cabins, they conned the Passenger List, which was printed as a booklet, to see which of their friends and rivals were travelling on the same ship. Later, when two acquaintances met in the lounges or on deck, they could pretend to be amazed by the discovery that they were both on board, and entranced by the sound of one another's voices.

First-class was crammed with nouveaux riches. Edward Steiner, who on different Atlantic crossings sampled both steerage and first-class, described first-class as encumbered by shop-worn men with unknown names. 'The passengers were walking on tiptoe; many of them trying to adjust themselves to these labyrinthine luxuries,' Steiner noted. 'Critically, almost with hostility, each passenger measured the other; the tables were buried beneath loads of flowers which were in the first melancholy stages of decay; so that all of it reminded me of a palatial home, to which the mourners have returned from a rich uncle's funeral.' No-one spoke to him. There was an atmosphere of aggressive insecurity. A man recoiled as if he had been hit with a sledgehammer when Steiner uttered a commonplace about the weather. 'I learned later that he occupied a thousand-dollar suite of rooms and that his name was Kalbfoos or something like it. In choosing his seat at the table, I heard him remark to the head steward that he did not want to sit "near Jews", nor any "second-class looking crowd".' Mr Kalbfoos's wish was impossible to accomplish. 'More than a third of the passengers were Jews, and more than two-thirds were people whose names and bearing betrayed the fact that they were either the children of immigrants, or immigrants themselves.' Under V, in the passenger list, Vanderbilt stood at the head, but with Vogelstein immediately under him. 'Between such American or English names as Wallace or Wallingford, were a dozen Woolfs and Wumelbachers, Weises and Weisels,' Steiner recorded. 'I need not tell you of the multitude of the Rosenbergs and Rosenthals there were in our cabin. Mr Funkelstein and Mr Jaborsky were my room-mates. First cabin after all is only steerage twice removed, and beneath its tinsel and varnish, it is the same piece of world as that below.'

On *Titanic*, German-Americans and Jewish Americans were abundant in first-class accommodation, although not beloved by their fellow passengers. Henry Stengel, principal of the firm of Stengel & Rothschild, leather merchants, from Newark, New Jersey; John Baumann, a New York importer of South American rubber; the young diamond dealer Jakob Birnbaum, originally from Cracow but based in San Francisco and a regular visitor to Antwerp; William Greenfield the New York furrier; Samuel Goldenberg the Broadway lace importer; Henry Harris the theatrical producer; Herman Kleber the hop merchant from Portland, Oregon; Adolphe Saalfeld a perfumer based in Manchester; Abram Lincoln Salomon the Manhattan stationer; Martin Rothschild the garments merchant; and George Rosenshine, New York importer of ostrich feathers, were among the passengers who reminded the class-conscious that first-class was only steerage twice removed. Some of these were showy spenders having their top moment: men who needed to put up a front to prove that they were never going to be kicked around again.

Playing poker with a high spirit was a masculine rite of passage in first-class Atlantic crossings. The staking of large sums was a display of status: wherever rich men gathered, there were poorer men, too, adepts at sleight-of-hand, subterfuge and connivance. Notices on *Titanic* warned that the first-class saloons of liners were infested by card sharks, and unavailingly sought to discouraging gambling. Harry ('Kid') Homer, a professional gambler, originally from Indianapolis, was a first-class passenger on *Titanic*, and a gaunt, hard-faced rogue he looks in his photograph, with all the facial charm of a prison guard. A former Los Angeles car salesman turned professional gambler named George Brereton was also known as 'Boy' Bradley and travelled under the alias of George Brayton. Charles Romaine, originally from Georgetown, Kentucky but now of Anderson, Indiana, was another gambler travelling under a disguised surname.

The first-class lounges were action zones, too, for confidence tricksters, with their squalid dedication and vindictive traps. Alfred Nourney, calling himself Baron von Drachstedt, ostensibly a salesman of fast cars, upgraded from second-class to first-class, where he moved with the care of a spy who had infiltrated a hostile camp. He was a slippery youth who took his cues quickly, and was ready for any chances offered. It is suggestive of Nourney's targets that he insinuated his way into a card game with Greenfield the furrier and Henry Blank, of Glenridge, New Jersey, who had been visiting Swiss watchmakers and dealers in precious stones in Amsterdam.

'It is a stratified society,' Steiner continued, 'and the lines are dollar-marked.' Stewards assessed the size of men's bank accounts by the contents of their wardrobes, and placed passengers accordingly. 'Around the captain's table are gathered the stars in the financial firmament; those whom nobody knows, who travel without retinue, are at the remote edges of the dining room, far away from the limelight.' This was different from the equality of steerage, where 'everybody "gets his grub" in the same way, in the same tin cans, "first come, first served"; and all of us are kicked in the same unceremonious way by the crew'.[12] It was not as if the table manners were reliably superior in first-class. Steiner saw plutocrats eating blueberry pie off their knives and frowning in confusion at the little bowls of rose water set before them. Some American success stories not only lacked table manners, but did not know how to dress. 'The new rich used to come secretly to me to be coached, not only in the art of dressing, but in the art of wearing beautiful clothes,' Lady Duff Gordon confided. Englishwomen paid as much as 20 guineas for a consultation, and in New York she received five times that sum from wives of 'self-made men' who felt incapable of appearing in society until they had been drilled.[13]

In the childish belief, held by many rich people, that they could dupe their staff, newly embarked first-class passengers used to tell their stewards, 'I am a friend of the President of this line.' Violet Jessop, who was seldom outsmarted by those she served, used to reflect what a lucky man Bruce Ismay was to have so many thousands of friends.[14] On *Titanic*, first-class accommodation was filled to 46 per cent of capacity: a sure indication that there was over-capacity in the Atlantic steamship business. The liner's 337 first-class passengers were estimated to be worth $500 million.

Richest of all was John Jacob Astor. A photograph survives of him entraining at Waterloo station for Southampton: a man of forty-seven, looking straight at the camera, his bearing stiffened by high confidence in himself and his purposes, Astor resembles a conventional ruling-class Englishman, with his trim moustache, erect bearing, bowler hat, rolled umbrella and overcoat with velvet collar. He had the consistency that comes from never being flurried, and that makes for calm, commanding dignity. His ends were reached with a distinctive mixture of reserve and subdued determination. 'He knew what he wanted and how to get it,' according to the family lawyer, who extolled Astor's 'inexhaustible energy all through his life, which he lived in his own way, not in your way or mine, but his.'[15]

Jack Astor was the unchallenged owner of much of New York, and did not need to shout for attention. In 1891 he had married Ava Willing, 'quite the most beautiful woman in the world',[16] but frigid and insolent. It was for her a worldly, showy marriage; but she had neither grace nor gratitude for her situation. Her guests at Ferncliff, the Astors' country estate at Rhinebeck, were, like her, fanatical bridge-players, who spent their waking hours with eyes fixed on cards. 'Their host, who detested bridge and was far more at home going at top-speed in his new racing-car . . . shambled from room to room, tall, loosely built and ungraceful, rather like a great overgrown colt, in a vain search for someone to talk to.' In the evenings he would dress immaculately for dinner, and go downstairs to entertain his guests, only to find everyone scurrying upstairs for a hasty, last-minute change of clothes. 'They would all be late, which annoyed him intensely, for he made a god of punctuality, and the probability of a spoilt dinner did not improve his temper, for he was a notable epicure. The house would come down to find him, watch in hand, constrained and irritable.' Dinner with his wife was uncomfortable. 'Never a brilliant conversationalist, he would be wanting to discuss what Willie Vanderbilt's new car was capable of doing, or whether the chef Oliver Belmont had brought back from France was really better than his own. Instead, he had to listen to interminable *post mortems* – "You should have returned my lead . . ." "You should have played your queen . . .".'[17]

At the height of the Progressive Era this great slum landlord refused to ameliorate the conditions which his tenants were forced to endure. He opposed the development of north Manhattan to alleviate the density of the slums, for his rental income would fall if the tenements were less congested. Working at a roll-top desk behind the barred windows of the Astor Estate Office – the window of his plain room looked across a small court to a blank brick wall – Astor was nevertheless at the forefront of developing New York City into a forest of skyscrapers. He was a builder of *Titanic*'s on terra firma. The liner as floating luxury hotel owed much to his decision to build the Astoria half of the Waldorf-Astoria Hotel. This delivered a new concept in hotels: instead of corridors lined by bedrooms, to which weary travellers went to sleep, he devised something akin to a club-house, with an elegant bar, tea room and lounges where businessmen met and made deals, and sportsmen slapped one another's backs and bought rounds. For some of *Titanic*'s first-class passengers, the Astor hotels were home – and the ship rather like home with four funnels added. Ella White, when she was not in Europe or at her summer apartment at Briarcliffe Lodge, a sumptuous sham-medieval hotel in Westchester County, lived in the Waldorf-Astoria.

For years Astor shuffled dejectedly in his wife's chill shadow. He waited until the death of his mother before trying to settle terms for a divorce – finally achieved in 1909. Two years later he married Madeleine Force, the eighteen-year-old daughter of a Brooklyn businessman. Life for the young bride promised to be like a never-empty box of chocolates, but was quickly knocked awry. Astor failed to realize that his riches, capacities, handsome gloss, hale physique, added to the unspoilt beauty of his ductile child bride, would make the pus ooze from every envious sore. There was a boycott of the reception he gave at his house in Fifth Avenue to introduce his bride to his friends, who ignored the Astors in their box on the opening night of the new season at the Metropolitan Opera House. Faced with ostracism, they abandoned their planned charm offensive of dinners, dances and balls, and wintered in France and Egypt. By April 1912 she was four months pregnant, and the Astors were returning to America for the confinement. They were elated at the pregnancy yet soberly set on their social rehabilitation. His retinue on *Titanic* comprised his valet Victor Robbins (altogether there were thirty-one personal maids or valets on board), his wife's maid Rosalie Bidois (from the Channel Islands), an American nurse, Caroline Endres, hired to care for her during the pregnancy and his Airedale dog, Kitty.

Apart from the Astors, there were at least six sets of honeymooners in first-class. Daniel Warner Marvin, aged nineteen, son of the owner of the Biograph Cinema Company, was returning to America with his bride Mary Farquarson, aged eighteen. Lucien P. Smith, aged twenty-four, of Huntington, West Virginia, had recently married eighteen-year-old Mary Eloise Hughes: she bore his posthumous son in December 1912. Victor de Satode Peñasco y Castellana, aged eighteen, from Madrid, was going to America with his new wife Maria Josefa Perez de Soto y Valleja, aged seventeen. John P. Snyder, aged twenty-three from Minneapolis, was returning from his European honeymoon with Nelle Stevenson, aged twenty-two. Dickinson Bishop, heir to the Round Oak Stove Company, had married in November 1911, and embarked at Cherbourg with his wife Helen after a tour of Mediterranean Europe and Egypt. One newly married couple were both verging on the age of fifty: Dr Henry (or Hyman) Frauenthal, with a high-domed baldness and fulsome black beard, had married in France, as recently as 26 March, Clara Heinsheimer from Cincinnati. They were travelling with his brother Gerry (or Isaac) Frauenthal, a New York lawyer.

'The faster and bigger the ship, the less likely one is to speak to strangers,' Emily Post adumbrated in her *Etiquette* manual. 'Because the Worldlys, the Oldnames, the Eminents – all those who are innately exclusive – never "pick up" acquaintances on shipboard, it does not follow that no fashionable and well-born people ever drift into acquaintanceship on European-American steamers of to-day, but they are not apt to do so. Many in fact take the ocean-crossing as a rest-cure and stay in their cabins the whole voyage. The Worldlys always have their meals served in their own "drawing-room", and have their deck-chairs placed so that no-one is very near them, and keep to themselves except when they invite friends to play bridge or take dinner or lunch with them.'[18] This gives an accurate picture of the Astors on *Titanic*. One acquaintance to whom they were cordial was Margaret Brown. Colonel Astor had met her five years earlier in Lucerne, and they converged again in Cairo. From Egypt she travelled with them to Paris, and then hearing that her infant grandson was lying sick in Kansas City, determined to take an early boat home.

Margaret Brown had been born in 1867 to Irish immigrants in a hovel in Denkler Alley, Hannibal, Missouri – a halt on the railroad to the California goldfields. Her father fired the coke furnaces in Hannibal's gas works. At the age of thirteen she began working with other Irishwomen in a tobacco factory – probably stripping tobacco leaves. Her brother Daniel had settled in the mining boom-town of Leadville, Colorado, where the Guggenheims had laid the basis of their fortune. At the age of eighteen she went west to Leadville, where she lived as Daniel's cook-housekeeper. Next she worked in the carpet and drapery department of a Leadville store sewing carpets and draperies. In 1886 she married J. J. Brown, an Irishman from Pennsylvania, who had worked as a miner in the Black Hills of South Dakota before trying his luck at Leadville. His best man was his barber; her bridesmaid was a maid-of-all-work in a miners' boarding house. They went to live in a two-room cabin on Iron Hill, also known as Stumpftown, hard by the mines: other nearby settlements were called Finntown, Ibex City, Chicken Hill and Strayhorse Gulch, and served, it seems, by one water pump each. In 1893, J.J. struck gold in Little Jonny Mine, which soon produced 135 tons of gold ore daily. The millionaire J.J. bought more mining properties in Colorado, Utah and Arizona, and an imposing house in Denver.

As Irish working-class Catholic millionaires, the Browns did not become overnight darlings of Denver society, but the extent to which they were shunned has been exaggerated. It is true that a Denver socialite had recently declared: 'The world is full of dowdy, ill-bred women who fancy that if only they had money enough they could take society by storm.'[19] Margaret Brown, however, was not dowdy: inclined to chubby cheeks, perhaps, but with a strong, smiling and confident face, her laughing blue eyes set under luxuriant dark hair; not finished like a debutante, certainly, but shrewd, clear-headed, inquisitive and amusing. She made the most of her chances. The Browns first visited Europe in 1895: sailed to Naples, toured Italy for several months, dallied in Paris, tried the British Isles. She discovered an aptitude for foreign languages (acquiring fluent French) and a love of Paris. Margaret Brown was twenty-six when her husband started to make millions: too late for her to resemble Astor or Vanderbilt heiresses, who were both bullied and pampered by men, held too tight by silken lassos to wrench life into their own free pattern. Other women with self-made husbands often became snobs on the edge of good society, or scared cats, but she was neither heartless nor shallow. She proved a benefactor to all America when, after 1903, she helped a reforming judge to establish the US's first court for juveniles. She was a founder of the Denver Women's Club, which promoted education and advocated suffrage for women, and after 1912, when her name had national recognition as a *Titanic* survivor, she drew a large audience when she spoke at Women's Suffrage headquarters. Her hard-drinking husband suffered a bad stroke, as a result of which his temper deteriorated, and they signed a separation agreement in 1909. She forsook Denver for New York and Newport; but spent much time travelling in Europe.

Leadville, Colorado was Margaret Brown's common denominator with her fellow passenger Benjamin Guggenheim, the most personable of the seven brothers. He was the first of them to attend college, the first to work in mining, the first to leave the family business, the first to collect good paintings and the first to gallivant. He renounced capital of $8 million when he left the family business in 1901, but took a share of the profits with him, and four years later inherited his cut of his father's fortune. At first, Ben Guggenheim lived with his wife Florette and three daughters in a pretentious, tomb-like house on a corner of Fifth Avenue. His wife busied herself by holding muffled, listless tea parties and stilted bridge drives. Guggenheim had never felt marriage would provide full satisfaction for his claims on life. He was the rare sort of philanderer who liked women and understood them. He kept a slim brunette nurse in the Stygian house, ostensibly because her massage warded off his neuralgia, but eventually decided that marvellous regions lay waiting to be explored in Paris, where he took an apartment. The Fifth Avenue household was designed to look immutable, but the Guggenheims cared no more for permanency than the J. J. Browns at Bear Creek, and in less than ten years it had been dismantled, and its occupants dispersed.

In Paris, Ben Guggenheim tripled his emotional capital even as he lost millions by rash investments. Unlike his brothers, Ben had pale skin, delicate rather than big bones, light eyes, with the dandyish elegance of a cosmopolitan European rather than the chunky gravity of a Jewish, German-American millionaire. He was too proud and cheerful a man to play the sneak. In Paris, he had open love affairs with a marquise before finding a singer, Léontine Aubart. His wife in New York thought of divorcing him, but she was a money-loving woman who was persuaded by the other Guggenheim brothers that divorce would hurt the family name, thereby harming the business, and therefore reducing her income. By 1912 she lived with her daughters in a spacious suite at Jack Astor's St Regis hotel, screened, as they thought, from all unforeseen contingencies until that dark day when Solomon Guggenheim, outside a theatre on Broadway, was halted in his steps by a news-vendor's cry, '*Extra! Extra! The Titanic sinks!*'

Guggenheim travelled with an entourage of Léontine Aubart, her maid Emma Sägesser, his valet Victor Giglio – all aged twenty-four – together with his thirty-nine-year-old chauffeur René Pernot. Guggenheim, returning with his mistress, was bathed in the lurid greenish light of a dubious reputation: it is doubtful whether he and

Léontine Aubart had more than negligible contact with the respectably married American couples thronging the lounges and decks who recognized them. Probably he and his mistress kept apart with proud discretion. George Rosenshine, the ostrich feather dealer, was also travelling with his mistress, Maybelle Thorne; he cloaked himself under the alias of George Thorne, but was known to passengers such as Irene (Renée) Harris, wife of the theatrical producer.

Guggenheim had little contact on board with Isidor Straus, to whom he was related by marriage. Straus had been born in Bavaria in 1845: his family emigrated in 1854 to Talbotton, Georgia, where he started his working life as a clerk in his father's dry goods business. As an agent commissioned to obtain supplies for the Confederate government, he ran the blockade of Europe. After the civil war, he worked in a Liverpool shipping office, moved to New York City, and in 1896 became co-proprietor with his brother of Macy's. Straus was careful, systematic, equable, dignified and industrious: he had intuitions which enabled him, without any forceful assertion of will, to sense where profits lay. Straus was travelling with his wife, Ida. 'These two so openly adored one another that we used to call them "Darby and Joan" on the ship,' recalled Lady Duff Gordon. 'They told us laughingly that in their long years of married life they had never been separated for one day or night.'[20] Also in Straus's party was his valet, John Farthing, and Ida's maid, Ellen Bird, a shepherd's daughter from Norfolk, who had been hired a few days before embarkation. They were delighted with their accommodation. 'What a ship!' Ida Straus exclaimed as they steamed for Cherbourg. 'So huge and so magnificently appointed. Our rooms are furnished in the best of taste, and most luxuriously, and they are really rooms not cabins.'[21]

There was no counterpart of Europe's *haute juiverie* in America. Neither Guggenheims nor Strauses had any hope of the acceptance in society enjoyed by the Sassoons and Rothschilds, or King Edward VII's trusty Sir Ernest Cassel (who tried to stop the sale of White Star to Pierpont Morgan to please the monarch). However intelligent, inventive, generous and charming, Jewish Americans had no chance of assimilation except – like Henry Harris – in showbiz. A respected

American sociologist had written in 1906 of Jewish districts: 'It is a haggling, bargaining, pushing, crowding, seething mass . . . cowed by fear, unmanned by persecution; a thing to jeer at, to ridicule, to plunder and to kill.' Many Jews, he charmingly explained, conceded their 'racial faults', and accepted that their 'people are greedy, greasy and pushing, or doggedly humble; as might be expected of hunted human beings, who for 2,000 years have known no peace, wherever the cross overshadowed them'.[22] This was the bigotry with which Guggenheim and Straus (to say nothing of Jakob Birnbaum, George Rosenshine and Abram Lincoln Salomon) had to contend.

There were two family parties led by North American railway colossi on board *Titanic*. John Borland Thayer, vice-president of the Pennsylvania railroad, the largest American railroad measured by traffic and revenue, was returning from a visit to a diplomatist friend posted in Berlin, accompanied by his wife Marion, 'one of the handsomest women in Philadelphia',[23] their teenage son John B. Thayer junior, known as 'Jack', and his wife's maid Margaret Fleming. Thayer was also a director of the Long Island railroad and other concerns, and an expert in managing freight traffic. The other railway titan was Charles M. Hays, president of Canada's Grand Trunk Railway, a stocky, heavily bearded, pomaded man whose expansive ambitions and wish to make his will inexorable had left him looking careworn.

Born at Rock Island, Illinois in 1856, Hays began as a railway clerk with the Atlantic & Pacific railroad in St Louis, Missouri. He moved to Montreal in 1896 as general manager of Canada's heavily indebted Grand Trunk Railway, and gained a reputation for invincibility after imposing reforms which coincided with the boom years of 1896–1913. As general manager (and president from 1909), he impressed, at times captivated, the Canadian Prime Minister, Sir Wilfrid Laurier. Hays's working week was filled with swift, obligatory action: he believed in big decisions and unfaltering purposes. In every predicament he chose the course that demanded the greatest energy. Risk was his stimulant. He convinced Laurier that Canada needed a second trans-continental railway route, running along a less populous northern route to the existing Canadian Pacific Railway, and extracted a large government subsidy towards the cost of building one.

Building of the Grand Trunk Pacific Railway began in 1903. Hays determined that Grand Trunk Pacific would be a *Titanic* of railways, built to the highest standards. However, his perfectionism slowed completion of the project, and by 1912 the company's debts were immense. Hays's solution – which smacks of blind obstinacy or unreasonable pride – was to spend more money by upgrading rolling-stock, laying double tracks and building luxurious hotels in the great cities. The first of these hotels, Château Laurier in Ottawa, had recently been completed, and Hays needed to attend its ceremonial opening later in the month. Ostensibly, he had visited Europe to study Ritzonian hotels, with a view to improving the projected Grand Trunk hotels, but his most pressing task was to reassure his London board and British investors. Some considered that Hays had deceived his London directors about the Grand Trunk Pacific project: his policies certainly lured the railway headlong towards insolvency. In 1919, GTP defaulted on its borrowing and went into receivership, which soon necessitated the nationalization of the whole network. Hays's tactics and targets closed in ignominious failure.

Hays was travelling with his wife Clara, her maid, Mary Anne 'Annie' Perrault, his daughter Orian (aged twenty-seven), her stockbroker husband Thornton Davidson, and Vivian Payne, a fatherless boy of twenty-two, who after a shining career at Montreal High School had become Hays's protégé and personal secretary. Thornton Davidson was the son of Sir Charles Davidson, Chief Justice of Quebec: the family were staunch Protestants, and the elder son Shirley Davidson, one of Canada's best racing yachtsmen, drowned himself in a suicide pact on the St Lawrence River in 1907 with his Catholic fiancée, whom the judge forbad the boy to marry. Thornton Davidson had a square face with a tenacious, emphatic and uncompromising look. He ran his own brokerage firm in Montreal, and was one of those stockbrokers whose success was compounded of force and ease: he was a sporty clubman who pressed palms, exchanged confidences and made deals as a member of the Racquet Club, the Montreal

Hunt Club, Montreal Jockey Club, Montreal Polo Club, Montreal Amateur Athletics Association and the Royal St Lawrence Yacht Club.

This was an exciting era to be a Canadian stockbroker, especially if one was not restrained by obtrusive scruples. Canada's first burst of industrialization occurred in textiles, brewing, flour-milling, iron, rolling-stock and farm implements. Its second-wave of industrialization, during the Laurier boom era of 1896–1913, derived from steel, precision machinery, cement, chemicals and electric power generation. It was during this boom that the embezzling banker 'Diamond Jim' Baxter amassed the fortune that allowed his widow Hélène to travel so royally with her children on *Titanic*. After 1909, Canada was in the throes of a merger boom, with promoters floating new businesses and creating paper millionaires. There was a lot of sudden, showy, precarious opulence in the sphere of Hays and Davidson. Bernard Berenson visited Montreal in 1914: 'the one thing these provincial millionaires think of,' reported his wife, 'is to build ultra hideous brown-stone houses (here the stone is a gloomy slate-colour) and hang in their multifarious and over-heated rooms a vast collection of gilt-framed mediocre pictures, often spurious and almost always, even if authentic, poor. The usual acres of Barbizon output greet us here, some of your beloved Rembrandts, a few real Goyas and fake Velásquezes, endless "English School" and "French XVIII Century" pictures, Japanese knickknacks enough to bury you – and all dreary and horrible, and affording endless satisfaction to their owners.'[24]

The collecting bug was well represented on *Titanic* by the Wideners. Old Peter Widener, the Philadelphia tramway millionaire and associate of Pierpont Morgan in IMM's takeover of White Star, amassed a collection of paintings at Lynnewood. His son Joseph collected promiscuously, too, while his other son George cheerfully paid for his wife's collection of silver and porcelain, and his young grandson Harry was in 1912 shaping up to become America's finest bibliophile.

Young Americans reared at empyrean social heights, like Harry Widener, began crossing the Atlantic on the fastest steamers of the most expensive lines when they were small children. Edith Wharton described a youth called Troy Belknap who from the age of six had embarked in New York for Europe every June. His family would alight at New York docks from a large silent car, he would kiss his father goodbye and shake hands with the chauffeur who was his special friend, and mount the gang-plank in file behind his mother's maid. On board one steward would carry off his mother's bag while another led away her French bulldog. Then for 'six golden days Troy . . . ranged the decks, splashed in the blue salt water brimming his huge porcelain tub, lunched and dined with the grown-ups in the Ritz restaurant, and swaggered about in front of the children who had never crossed before and didn't know the stewards, or the purser, or the captain's cat, or on which deck you might exercise your dog, or how to induce the officer on the watch to let you scramble up a minute to the bridge.' On the seventh morning they would reach Cherbourg, and Troy Belknap would traipse down the gang-plank with his mother, and her maid, and the French bulldog, towards a smiling, saluting French chauffeur (to whom he was as devoted as to the New York driver). 'Then – in a few minutes, so swiftly and smilingly was the way of Mrs Belknap smoothed – the noiseless motor was off, and they were rushing eastwards through the orchards of Normandy . . . beautiful things flew past them; thatched villages with square-towered churches in hollows of the deep green country, or grey shining towns above rivers on which cathedrals seemed to be moored like ships.'[25] Troy Belknap almost seems modelled on Harry Widener, who embarked at Cherbourg on *Titanic* with his parents: they had been staying at the Ritz in Paris, and were travelling with their servants Edwin Keeping and Emily Geiger.

Harry Widener had been born in Philadelphia in 1885. He had a rational, ordered childhood which left him confident and untroubled. 'The marvel is that Harry is so entirely unspoiled by his fortune,' a visitor to Lynnewood said. It was at Harvard in 1906 that he began buying Charles Dickens first editions, as well as folio works by Jonson, Beaumont and Fletcher. With the help of his mother, in 1907, he bought a first folio Shakespeare for the highest price then known for a folio of its kind. He may have relished the eager exchange of heretical ideas when he was a Harvard boy, but after college his course was conventionally disciplined. An investment manager in his grandfather's business, he crossed to Europe several times each year, and when in London, scouted the rare book dealer Bernard Quaritch's shop or lunched him at the Ritz. 'So many of your American collectors refer to books in terms of steel rails; with Harry it is a genuine and all-absorbing passion, and he is so entirely devoid of side,' Quaritch said. 'Had he lived, he would no doubt have gathered one of the most remarkable libraries in America. He was a most amiable young man & greatly liked by everyone who came into contact with him.'[26] Several rare books lately bought by him had already been remitted to America on *Carpathia*; but he was carrying with him a copy of the rare 1598 edition of Francis Bacon's essays, which he had bought from Quaritch a fortnight earlier for £260. Its money value was infinitesimal compared with the pearls with which his mother was travelling, which were insured for £150,000.[27]

French bulldogs, it will be noted, played a part in Troy Belknap's Atlantic crossings – appropriately, for this muscular, compact, frisky and bat-eared breed provided fashionable trophies for Americans returning from Paris. French bulldogs were the *Titanic* dogs. A French bulldog, Gamin de Pycombe, belonging to Robert Daniel of Philadelphia, was last seen swimming for its life in the ocean. Moreover, the greatest American force in the world of French bulldogs, Samuel Goldenberg, boarded at Cherbourg with his wife Nella. In 1902 he had bought in France a dog, Nellcote Gamin, which he imported to his kennels at Riverdale-on-Hudson, where it became the progenitor of most French bulldogs in America. In 1905, having just turned forty, Goldenberg retired from his business as a New York lace importer to live in Paris, where he founded the French Bulldog Club of Paris. He was travelling to New York so that he could judge the French Bulldog Club of America's show at the Waldorf-Astoria on 20 April.

At Cherbourg, Henry Harper, scion of the American publishing family, boarded with his Pekingese, Sun Yat-sen, and handsome Egyptian dragoman, Hammad Hassab; Margaret Hays, Elizabeth Rothschild and Philadelphia attorney William Dulles each boarded with a Pomeranian; and Helen Bishop had a lapdog, Frou-frou, which she had bought in Florence on honeymoon. The Astors had their Airedale, and a spinster called Ann Isham, a Chicago lawyer's daughter who lived in Paris, may have been accompanied by a Newfoundland or Great Dane; William Carter by a King Charles spaniel, and Harry Anderson by a chow.*

Lapdogs were objectionable to Francis Millet, a sixty-five-year-old American painter, the head of the American Academy in Rome, who was returning from attending a ceremony there honouring a benefaction to the Academy by Pierpont Morgan. 'Queer lot of people on the ship,' Millet wrote in a letter posted at Queenstown. 'Looking over the list I only find three or four people I know but there are . . . a number of obnoxious, ostentatious American women, the scourge of any place they infest, and worse on shipboard than anywhere. Many of them carry tiny dogs, and lead husbands around like pet lambs. I tell you the American woman is a buster. She should be put in a harem and kept there.'[28]

Millet was an interesting man. Born in Mattapoisett, Massachusetts in 1846, he served as a drummer boy and surgical assistant with Union troops in the Civil War. After a shining career at Harvard, he worked on the *Boston Courier*, but lithography and sketching were his avocations, and he forsook journalism to attend the Royal Academy of Fine Arts at Antwerp, where he was awarded a gold medal. He was a hardy traveller who acted as a war correspondent during the Russo-Turkish conflict of 1877–78. Millet's friend Henry James spoke of 'his magnificent manly self . . . irradiating *that* beautiful genius and gallantry'.[29] He published travel reportage, essays, short stories and a translation of *Sebastopol Sketches*, Tolstoy's fictionalized account of his Crimean war experiences. Murals at Baltimore

---

*Harper's Pekingese, the Rothschilds' Pomeranian and the Hays' Pomeranian all escaped in lifeboats.

Customs House, Trinity Church, Boston and other public buildings were painted by him. Photographs of Millet show a quietly handsome, distinguished man with an unwavering look and a calm, determined manner with no fierceness or bravado.

Millet owned a property at East Bridgewater, Massachusetts, but also shared a house in an old-fashioned district of Washington DC with President Taft's military adviser, Archie Butt, who was nineteen years his junior. They had left America together for Italy on 2 March on the Norddeutscher-Lloyd steamship *Berlin*. 'If the old ship goes down, you will find my affairs in shipshape condition,' Butt told his sister-in-law on the eve of departure.[30] He was the cynosure of every eye on the deck of the *Berlin* – fascinating a deaf-mute sponge merchant from Patras – because of his glorious apparel: bright copper-coloured trousers with matching Norfolk jacket, fastened by big ball-shaped buttons of red porcelain, a lavender tie, tall bay-wing collar, derby hat with broad brim, patent leather shoes with white tops, a bunch of lilies in his buttonhole and a cambric handkerchief tucked in his left sleeve.[31] The two men returned to America together (Butt in cabin B-38, Millet in cabin E-38), although Butt boarded at Southampton and Millet some hours later at Cherbourg.

Their affection for one another was undying, as was recognized when the memorial fountain erected, by Joint Resolution of Congress, on Executive Avenue in Washington DC was named the Butt-Millet fountain. 'Millet, my artist friend who lives with me' was Butt's designation of his companion: their only recorded discord was over Millet's choice of wallpaper for their shared home. 'Both my bedroom and dressing-room are walled with red and pink roses, from buds to full-blown flowers, and even when I shut my eyes I seem to see them tumbling over each other,' Butt had lately complained. It put him in mind of Elagabulus, the Roman Emperor who outraged the Praetorian Guard by treating a blond slave charioteer, Hierocles, as his husband. 'That artistic if somewhat decadent gentleman,' Butt recalled, 'when he wanted to rid himself of certain enemies both male and female, invited them to a feast and, after he had withdrawn, let down a shower of roses from the ceiling. They played with them at first and pelted each other with them, but they continued to fall until they were smothered to death by them.'[32]

The Butt-Millet household was staffed by Filipino boys. In 1911 'a very delightful person' named Archie Clark-Kerr came to live there, 'a sensible youth [who] only wanted to be let alone, not to be discussed every time he batted an eye'.[33] Kerr (born in Australia, where his father owned a sheep station, but histrionic about his Scottish ancestry) was a high-spirited, playful attaché at the British Embassy who opened Butt's eyes: 'did you know that the kilt is worn without any drawers? I never knew it before Archie Kerr came to live with me.'[34] (Thirty-five years later Kerr returned to Washington as British Ambassador: he had been created Lord Inverchapel, taking as his heraldic supporters two full-frontally naked Greek athletes, suggestively juxtaposed with a Latin motto which could be rendered 'Though shaken, I rise.' As ambassador, Inverchapel alarmed the prudes of the American security services by going to stay in Eagle Grove, Iowa with a strapping farm boy whom he had met in Washington.) Butt, too, enjoyed masculine vigour: John Tener, the Major League baseball player who became Governor of Pennsylvania in 1911, he described appreciatively as 'a big, stalwart man, handsome as a Greek athlete'.[35]

Butt had been born in Augusta, Georgia in 1865 a few months after the surrender of the Confederates in the Civil War, and remained an unrepentant Southerner. He graduated from university in Tennessee, and like Millet, started as a journalist – acting as Washington correspondent for Southern newspapers. On the outbreak of the Spanish-American war he joined the army, and later served in the Philippines, where he impressed President Theodore Roosevelt and the Secretary of War, William Taft. Butt was recruited to the White House as presidential aide-de-camp, and remained as military aide when Taft succeeded Roosevelt as President in 1909. A strongly built man who looked impressive in his spurs, plumed hat and elaborate uniform ('dressed in raiment which puts out the eye of Rembrandt', as Taft said),[36] Butt acted as the President's chief of protocol, secret-keeper and buffer.

Butt was loyal, disinterested, affectionate and sympathetic. He liked to be useful, popular and amusing: though a modest man, he had a swelling sense of accomplishment when his arrangements, introductions and discreet advice went off perfectly, as they usually did. Butt misplayed shots in order to revive the golf-mad President when he was disheartened, sat up late playing bridge with him, laughed at his dull legal jokes, mitigated his boredom during official lunches for Sunday School teachers, ate the horrible meals which the obese President liked (broiled chicken, hominy and melon for breakfast; fish chowder, mustard pickles, baked beans and brown bread for lunch), salved the dignity of visiting politicos who did not know how to eat artichokes or cucumbers, mollified the President when saucy brats yelled 'Hello, Fatty' at him. Butt's hospitality was delightful. 'People come early to my house and always stay late and seem merry while they are here,' he wrote. At his New Year's Eve party – attended by Taft, Cabinet members, ambassadors, generals, Supreme Court judges and 'the young fashionable crowd' – he served nothing more elaborate than eleven gallons of eggnog, whipped by his Filipino boys, with hot buttered biscuits and ham served by his black washerwoman.[37]

Butt and Millet, both ex-journalists, would have noticed that W. T. Stead, England's most notorious newsman, was on board with them. Working alone in his cabin during the day, but dominating his table at meal times, Stead was indefatigable, unstoppable and impossible to ignore. For thirty years he had been a public performer – all sonority, phrase-making and frontage. Appointed in 1883 as editor of a London evening newspaper, where he promoted a raucous, jarring tone, he had the journalist's knack of transmuting shoddy second-hand ideas into high-coloured first-class emotions. A press stunt by him in 1883–84 resulted in the calamitous decision to send General Gordon, with his messianic death wish, to Khartoum. Next he started a press agitation about naval supremacy which resulted in the British government resolving in 1889 to maintain enough battleships to equal the combined strength of the two next largest navies in the world – then French and Russian – at the cost of tens of millions. Germany retaliated with a vast naval building programme, the European arms race began, and by 1921 debt-ridden Britain was conceding naval supremacy to the United States. Another of Stead's stunts, entitled 'The Maiden Tribute of Modern Babylon', exposing the prostitution of young girls, provoked the passing of the Criminal Law Amendment Act of 1885. This raised the age of consent for girls from thirteen to sixteen years, while another provision tightened the criminal laws against homosexuality, enabled the prosecution of Oscar Wilde, and exercised a baneful influence until long after its repeal in 1967.

There was no restraining Stead's inquisitive energy, his prurience and his rush to judgement. He lived in a flurry of telegrams. Everything and everyone was his business and, once he had reported it, everyone else's business too. He had high enthusiasms, intense sympathies, found so many activities to denounce and so many people to decry. Like most columnists, he was never happier, because it was never easier work, pouring contumely on his fellow citizens, especially if he could claim a finer conscience than them, or use their sexual impulses to have them degraded or outlawed. He claimed to be maintaining a vigilant public opinion by his press stunts, but he was too excitable to have a sense of proportion, and indeed he would have been a less successful editor if he had been calm or proportionate. Stead testified to the Royal Commission on Divorce in 1910 that he was 'a puritan, and proud to bear the name'. This impelled him to humiliate people whom he thought immoral: personal privacy, indeed, tended to immorality. 'The simple faith of our forefathers in the All-Seeing Eye of God has departed from the man-in-the-street. Our only modern substitute for him is the press. Gag the press under whatever pretexts of prudish propriety you please, and you destroy the last remaining pillory by which it is possible to impose some restraint upon the lawless lust of man.'[38]

Stead's blaring publicity made him the darling of journalists in the newspaper offices, compositors in the print rooms, messenger boys in the corridors, newsboys on the streets. 'His strength was in a flaming certainty, which one only weakens by calling sincerity,'

G. K. Chesterton wrote of Stead. 'His excess, we may say with real respect, was in the direction of megalomania; a childlike belief in big empires, big newspapers, big alliances – big ships.'[39]

President Taft had invited Stead to address a pompous conference on peace to be held in Carnegie Hall on 21 April 1912; and it was for this reason that the old mountebank booked passage on *Titanic* – doubtless also to write a sensational account of its maiden voyage. The liner seemed as firm as a rock, and the sea was as flat as a millpond, he reported in a letter sent from Queenstown. He spent productive hours working in his cabin beyond reach of time-wasters with their pesky telephone calls and disruptive visits. At meal times, though, while businessmen at adjacent tables shoved along the talk as if they were straining to shift heavy boulders, he held his table spellbound with anecdotes of great men and views of great events told in his loud, cheery voice. Stead's Puritanism, as well as his radicalism, would have made him anathema to some English passengers, who 'cut' him. Certainly, his views were at odds with the Duff Gordons: the incarnation of worldly duplicity, he would have thought them; and a self-centred, verbose old bore they would have found him.

Sir Cosmo Duff Gordon was a baronet who fenced for England in Lord Desborough's Olympics of 1908, played excellent bridge, had a fine singing voice, and seemed valiant for having lost an eye in a shooting accident. He was a tall, clean, well-groomed Englishman, but so drilled in the stiff conventions of his set as to have shed any originality. Oscar Wilde quipped that originality means concealing your origins, but those of Sir Cosmo – schooling at Eton, inheriting estates in Scotland and Wales when he was barely thirty – were indelible.

During the 1890s Sir Cosmo had wished to marry, but his mother opposed the match because his prospective bride, Lucy Wallace, ran a Mayfair shop which sold sexy lingerie and, worse still, was a divorcée. He contented himself with investing in her shop, and married her in 1900 after the old lady's death. Lucy Duff Gordon boasted of her conception early in her parents' marriage while her father was working as a bridge builder in Rio de Janeiro. 'In the glamour and wonder of the first love of these young, vital beings, I was conceived. The torch they handed to me was lighted at the flame of passion, and the rapture and the joy of their romance was rekindled in my own eagerness for emotional experience. This, I think, is the only way in which children should be brought into life; there are too many mediocre, colourless men and women about the world to-day, born of a union which was neither that of passion nor of great love.'[40] Few first-class White Star passengers would have admitted such incendiary sentiments. After her father's early death, she was sent to live with her maternal grandparents on a ranch near Guelph, Ontario. Grandmother Saunders, in her stiff, black silk dresses and snowy, lace caps, was a terrifying antiquity who instilled severe rules of etiquette. 'Ladies,' she would say, 'do not show emotion or cry. The common people can find that a relaxation.'[41]

At the age of eighteen, in Europe, Lucy married James Wallace, but after six years of marriage he absconded with a girl who danced in pantomime. Family friends tut-tutted when she insisted on a divorce after which, penniless, she became a dressmaker in Mayfair. 'I was one of the first women . . . of my class to go into the business world, and I lost caste terribly in doing so.'[42] Her standing only rose when it became known that an ultra-respectable dowager, Adeline, Duchess of Bedford, had bought her satin corsets and introduced clients with resonant names, the Countess of Dudley, the Countess of Clarendon.

Until the advent of Maison Lucile, a Mayfair dressmaker provided a few hard chairs, some unflattering mirrors and a tight little fitting-room hidden away. The dresses were displayed on models stuffed with sawdust and sporting gruesome wax faces. When live models were introduced from Paris, the models stood still in fixed poses, because it was thought indecent for them to parade about. As a guarantee of respectability, ambulant models were chosen for their plain looks. To prevent them showing their inflammatory ankles, necks or forearms, they were encased in dingy black satin smocks, stretching from chin to feet, and then displayed delicate evening dresses over the puritanical black. On their feet were black-laced boots. Lady Duff Gordon was the insurrectionist who determined to have 'glorious, goddess-like girls' parading in her designs on a stage hung with olive chiffon curtains as background, showing off the dresses to an admiring audience of women. She taught good posture to her models by making them walk with books balanced on their heads. 'I watched them develop a hundred little airs and graces, watched them copy the peeresses and actresses who came into my saloons.'[43] She gave each of her dress creations an individual name: '"When Passion's Thrall is O'er", "Give Me Your Heart", "Do You Love Me?", "Gowns of Emotion", "The Sighing Sound of Lips Unsatisfied", I called them, and they caught the fancy of all those women who sat and watched the girls from Balham and Bermondsey showing them how they ought to walk.'[44]

Lady Duff Gordon was the pioneer of sexy underwear. She hated the thought of her creations being worn over 'the ugly nun's veiling or linen-cum-Swiss embroidery which was all that the really virtuous woman of those days permitted herself'. Instead she made under-clothes 'as delicate as cobwebs and as beautifully tinted as flowers, and half the women in London flocked to see them, though they had not the courage to buy them at first . . . Slowly one by one they slunk into the shop in a rather shamefaced way and departed carrying an inconspicuous parcel, which contained a crêpe-de-Chine or a chiffon petticoat, although one or two returned to bring the new purchases sorrowfully back because a Victorian husband had "put his foot down".'[45]

At Christmas 1909, Lady Duff Gordon went to New York, staying at the Waldorf-Astoria, and arranged to open a shop there. Her title ensured its immediate success. 'The one thing that counts in America is self-advertisement of the most blatant sort . . . Impress them with your ancestry, impress them with your possessions, with your bank-book, with the price you paid for your car, or your dog.'[46] She booked orders for a thousand gowns, and was stunned by the amounts that Americans would pay. 'I was invited to every ball and party given by members of "The Four Hundred" . . . I could hardly put my nose outside my hotel without encountering pressmen and photographers; my telephone kept ringing all day.'[47]

In 1911, Lady Duff Gordon opened her Paris shop, and launched a fashion for wearing coloured wigs, *têtes de couleurs*, as they were called, to match evening dresses: a rose pink wig for a dress of deeper pink, a jade green wig with a dress of emerald. This innovation she recalled as 'a folly . . . in keeping with all the extravagances and exaggerations of a pre-War Paris basking in the sunshine of its last seasons of brilliance.'[48] She bestowed professional names on her models: Gamela, Corisande, Phyllis. When they strolled in the Avenue des Champs-Elysées or lunched at Voison's, a crowd of rich men admired and petted them. They could ask for anything. 'Be sure of what you want,' she advised them. 'If you want to marry, be as good as gold. If you don't, be expensive.'[49]

A different type of modern young woman from Gamela or Corisande was sharing cabin E33, at a cost of £55, with her mother. Elsie Bowerman, who was twenty-two, had recently graduated in medieval and modern languages from Girton College, Cambridge, and had previously been a pupil in the early years of a great pioneering girls' boarding-school, Wycombe Abbey. The school was renowned for producing cheerful, dauntless, productive and fulfilled young women: Elsie Bowerman conformed to type. She had joined the suffragettist Women's Social and Political Union while at Girton, and carried a Pankhurst banner in the great Hyde Park demonstration for women's votes. Her mother (the widow of a Hastings property landlord) was also a campaigner for women's political emancipation, and ran her local branch of the Women's Tax Resistance League. Elsie Bowerman was to be the first woman election agent at the earliest general election at which women were permitted to be parliamentary candidates – for Christabel Pankhurst, at Smethwick, in 1918. After the enactment of laws suppressing sexual bars in the professions, Bowerman became one of the first Englishwomen to qualify as a barrister in 1924. She was, among other distinctions, the inaugural woman barrister to plead at that historic London court, the Old Bailey.

*   *   *

How did first-class passengers fill their time at sea? On the first day they made exploratory forays about the first-class decks to orientate themselves. They called at the post room to inquire of the postmaster about postal arrangements. They established how to send Marconigrams, scanned the shelves of books in the library, and enjoyed the comforts of their cabins. After the first hours' novelty, they ambled about, lounged in chairs, listened to the bandsmen, chatted and gossiped with old friends and shipboard acquaintances, eyed potential business contacts, wrote letters, ate gargantuan meals, looked at the sea and the weather, and took bets on the exact time of arrival. Fitness fiends used the gymnasium, steam baths, racquets court and swimming pool. In the evening there were concerts in the lounge on D Deck. There was heavy use of the Marconi telegraph facilities: messages were sent predicting arrival times, salutations from passengers proud to show their friends that they were on *Titanic*, and business instructions. On Sunday afternoon, Isidor and Ida Straus exchanged Marconigrams with their son and his wife, who were passengers on *Amerika*, as it passed near *Titanic* on its way to Europe.

'Life on the *Titanic*,' Renée Harris recalled, 'was expensive and gay.'[50] She and her impresario husband belonged to a set that played cards, so she did not see any dancing. Unless onboard dancing was sedate, it attracted scowls. On the *Olympic* in 1912 the Duchess of Sutherland, Lord Winterton, several young blades and some pretty Americans improvised a party displaying a new dance, the Turkey Trot. Their tough smart exclusiveness excited the envy of other travellers who were made to feel their inferiority: as Winterton noted next day, 'the "Turkey Trot" party has rather offended the rest of the first-class passengers, which is regrettable!! Nevertheless, we had another one after dinner, and followed it up with a supper in the restaurant.'[51]

There is unanimity about *Titanic*'s calm seas and deceptive lulling comforts. 'At all times,' recorded Dr Washington Dodge of San Francisco, 'one might walk the decks, with the same security as if walking down Market Street, so little motion was there to the vessel.

It was hard to realize, when dining in the large spacious dining saloon, that one was not in some large, sumptuous hotel.'[52] Colonel Archibald Gracie IV, after whose family Gracie Mansion in New York is named, enjoyed himself as if he was in 'a summer palace on the sea-shore, surrounded with every comfort – there was nothing to indicate that we were on the stormy Atlantic Ocean'.[53] Frank Millet was delighted by his first-class cabin: with its walk-in cupboard in which to hang his suits it was 'the best room I have ever had in a ship'. Luxury liner travel, he added, was 'not like going to sea'.[54]

'Like everyone else I was entranced with the beauty of the liner,' recalled Lady Duff Gordon, who felt gleeful when strawberries were served for breakfast. 'Fancy strawberries in April, and in mid-ocean,' she told her husband. 'Why, you would think you were at the Ritz.'[55] Other women had similar reactions. 'Once off, everything seemed to go perfectly,' Mahala Douglas described afterwards. She was travelling with her husband Walter Douglas, owner of a starch works at Cedar Rapids, Iowa: he had retired on 1 January 1912, having reached the age of sixty, and they marked this event with a three month, once-in-a-lifetime European tour. 'The boat was so luxurious, so steady, so immense, and such a marvel of mechanism that one could not believe one was on a boat – and there the danger lay. We had smooth seas, clear, starlit nights, fresh favouring winds; nothing to mar our pleasure.' The Douglases had recently built a Frenchified mansion at Lake Minnetonka, for which they had bought objects during their European tour, and were looking forward to retirement there. Sunday was 'a delightful day; everyone was in the best of spirits; the time the boat was making was considered very good, and all were interested in getting into New York early.'[56]

It was the practice for first-class men to attach themselves as shipboard protectors to women who were travelling without husbands, fathers, brothers or sons. They ate with them, strolled on deck together, attended concerts and made amiable talk. On *Titanic*, where her friends the Astors were aloof and preoccupied with one another, Margaret Brown spent hours with Emma Bucknell, the widow of a Pennsylvania land speculator, and projector of gas works and water works, whose benefaction saved the university outside Lewisburg, which was renamed Bucknell in his honour. Emma Bucknell built a Greek revival house at Clearwater, Florida, where she wintered, and spent her summers at her private camp at Upper Saranac Lake, a village in the Adirondacks. She boarded *Titanic* at Cherbourg after visiting her daughter Margaret, who had married Daniel, Count Pecorini, an intrepid Oriental traveller who collected jade and wrote a monograph on Japanese maple. Her maid Albina Bazzani was a servant supplied by the Pecorinis in Italy. Mrs Brown and Mrs Bucknell were often squired by Arthur Jackson Brewe, a Dublin-trained physician specializing in nervous diseases with a practice in Philadelphia.

Then there was 'Mrs Candee's Coterie', as it described itself. Helen Churchill Candee was an American writer and decorator who boarded at Cherbourg. Friends in England had recommended her to the care of Colonel Gracie, who sought her out and paid her the compliment of attention. She gathered a group of male adherents: Gracie, his friend James Clinch Smith, together with a Buffalo architect named Edward Kent, a roly-poly Irish-Canadian engineer, Edward Colley, a young Swede named Mauritz Håkan Björnström-Steffansson, and Hugh Woolner. The last two men were alert, inscrutable, predatory – quick to scent a game, and always ready to play.

James Clinch Smith had celebrated his fifty-sixth birthday a few days before embarkation. His family had been the chief proprietors of Smithtown, on the north shore of Long Island, since the seventeenth century. He was thus born into the fast-vanishing American ruling class: 'A gentleman with his mansion, coach-houses, stables, hunters even and plantations on Long Island,' as Ford Madox Ford recalled, 'presented to the rest of his nation an image for emulation such as no class of person could lately, in spite of Standardisation, aspire to being.'[57] Smith's parentage showed the social flux of nineteenth-century America, for his mother's uncle was Alexander Stewart, owner of New York's first department store and builder of a stupendous marble house on Fifth Avenue that had exemplified *nouveau riche* euphoria. Smith graduated from Columbia University Law

School in 1878, and practised law on Wall Street and in the Stewart Building at Broadway. He was elected to smart clubs, was an expert yachtsman, won prizes at the New York horse show, and built his own racetrack at Smithtown. In 1895 he married Bertha Barnes of Chicago: in addition to New York and Long Island, the couple had a Newport home, The Moorings, overlooking the harbour. His wife was musical, and in 1904 they moved to Paris, where she organized an all-women orchestra and he was popular with compatriots who savoured his dry humour. Smith returned to America at least once a year, and in 1906, while attending a musical comedy at Madison Square Garden, witnessed the murder of his brother-in-law, the architect Stanford White, by Harry Thaw. Strains developed in the Smith marriage, and he returned to Smithtown; but in January 1912 he backtracked to Paris, where the couple were reconciled. They agreed to return to live together at Smithtown: he was returning to make improvements in the amenities there before her arrival.

Mauritz Björnström-Steffansson was a twenty-eight-year-old chemical engineering graduate of Stockholm Institute of Technology, and son of a leader of the Swedish wood pulp industry. He was a sharp, determined young man who knew how to advance his interests in a balanced manner, and had first crossed the Atlantic in 1909 intent on becoming a rich, well-placed New Yorker. In this he succeeded, for in 1917 he was to marry Mary Eno Pinchot, heiress to a New York wallpaper and timber fortune, to whom he had reportedly been introduced by Helen Candee. The marriage fixed him in a political and business nexus including Gifford Pinchot, the conservationist Governor of Pennsylvania, and the English diplomat Lord Colyton. Steffansson's cold pursuit of money elbowed aside mellower traits or more sensual appetites. During the 1920s he amassed holdings in the Canadian paper and pulp sectors, and bought real estate around Park Avenue in New York before its remunerative redevelopment with apartment buildings and hotels.

If Björnström-Steffansson was hawk-like, Hugh Woolner was vulpine. Aged forty-five, he was the son of an eminent sculptor, and a cousin of Evelyn Waugh. He graduated from Trinity College,

Cambridge in 1888, and was elected a member of the London Stock Exchange in 1892 at the age of twenty-six. In 1893, using £7,000 inherited from his father, he founded the firm of Woolner & Co. in the City, and dealt chiefly in mining shares. His interests included Kalgoorlie Electric Power & Lighting Corporation, which was promoted to supply electricity to gold mines in Western Australia, and Sterkfontein Gold Estates, which found lime rather than gold in its Transvaal properties. In 1905, together with George Baker, Woolner formed Great Cobar, a mining company with copper and coal properties in New South Wales and nominal capital of £1,500,000. By way of promotion profit, Woolner's firm received shares and debentures worth £34,110, and was lifted from insolvency to affluence.[58]

In March 1907, in Woolner's words, 'one Montmorency, notorious in the City but unknown to me, known also as Nassif, placed orders with us for purchase of Great Cobar shares to the extent of over £70,000 for which he paid & gained my confidence'. A month later Montmorency telephoned from Paris with further orders: as a result Woolner bought Great Cobar shares worth £122,473 (the equivalent a hundred years later of nearly £10 million computed from the retail price index). These lavish purchases may have been a 'ramp' intended to boost the value of the shares before dumping them. Woolner paid about £11 per share, but when Montmorency defaulted and never paid a sixpence, he could not settle the debts. Although Baker of Great Cobar promised to aid Woolner as the stockbroker unloaded shares in small parcels, he joined a bear market against Great Cobar shares, the price of which fell. Woolner sold at an average price of about £4½ per share, sustaining a loss exceeding £70,000. In November 1907 he and his partner were hammered on the Stock Exchange, where their debts were about £5,600, with assets around £2,000.[59]

Now, whichever way he turned, Woolner saw the smirking face of trouble. Baker sued his firm and obtained judgement for £11,702 (the equivalent of nearly £1 million in today's values). In 1908 he became chairman of the New Gutta Percha rubber company, but had to borrow money from his mother and spinster sisters secured on shares in Gutta Percha and the Bohemia Mining Corporation

– another of Baker's companies, promoted to mine tin and wolfram, but where the mineshafts were flooded after the pumps failed. In 1908–09 Woolner borrowed £9,600 from Elizabeth Forster, a rich old spinster living in Palace Green, Kensington. He visited Cheyenne, Wyoming, and became chairman of Casper & Powder River Oilfields, which held oil rights in the state; but he was stuck in a glutinous mass of debt. In July 1909, at the instigation of his enemy Baker, he was adjudged bankrupt with assets of £21 and liabilities of £65,417 (the equivalent of £5 million a century later), and forced to resign from Gutta Percha and Casper & Powder. He was discharged from bankruptcy on payment of just £1,000 in 1910, and thus freed to become a company director again.

Woolner was a towering, suave man who evidently coaxed old Miss Forster into signing a new will in January 1912. Under its provisions, she bequeathed a quarter of her estate to him, £400 to his soldierly son Christopher and £200 each to his daughters. After her death in 1915, her estate was proved at £369,566 net. Her nieces, legatees of an earlier will, contended that because of senile decay, she was incapable of comprehending the contents of her will, and had been influenced by Woolner. The case was settled in 1917 with the 1912 will upheld.[60]

After inveigling Elizabeth Forster into signing her will, Woolner in February 1912 went to New York on *Baltic*. The attraction in New York may have been Mary 'Maisie' Dowson, widow of an American, whom he was courting and was to marry in August. She was eldest daughter of Lucas Ionides, a London stockbroker and art connoisseur: the marriage may have improved his credit if not his reputation. His mother died on 9 March, and he hurried back from New York to attend her funeral. His return to the United States was on a first-class ticket costing £35 10s. Woolner, then, when he boarded *Titanic*, was the victim of his own temerity, an ex-bankrupt who had learnt in hard times to dive beneath insults.

For every Widener or Hays on *Titanic*, there were half a dozen pretenders whose silky assurance was a precarious facade. Woolner had a Californian counterpart in Washington Dodge, a physician who had entered San Francisco politics in the 1890s, and served four terms as Assessor of the city. Dodge had been president of the Continental & Building Loan Association 'when that concern stirred up Californian politics in 1905 by setting a trap which involved many members of the legislature in bribery charges'.[61] When he boarded *Titanic* he was on the brink of leaving politics, at the age of fifty-two, to become president of the Federal Telegraph Company, and vice-president of the Anglo-London & National Bank. There was as much devious business in telegraphs as in city politics. Dodge was forced to resign from his Federal Telegraph presidency in 1919, and was being sued for Stock Exchange manipulations when some months later he shot himself. In 1912 he was travelling with his young wife Ruth, and their four-year-old son 'Bobo', Washington Dodge junior.

Emily Post described a familiar type of Atlantic voyager who conned the passenger list with the avidity of a bird pecking at worms. 'You have scarcely found your own state room and had your deck-chair placed, when one of them swoops upon you: "I don't know whether you remember me? I met you in 1902, at Contessa della Robbia's in Florence." Your memory being woefully incomplete, there is nothing for you to say except, "How do you do!" If a few minutes of conversation, which should be sufficient, prove her to be a lady, you talk to her now and again throughout the voyage, and may end by liking her.' If these over-friendly pests proved objectionable, well-bred Americans should engross themselves in a book, or confine their replies to monosyllables.[62] Dawn Powell also described a mid-west American determined on scraping shipboard acquaintance with 'the best names in the travelling universe'. In *A Time to be Born* she depicted a mother and daughter who were social masochists: 'it gave them a feeling of accomplishment and progress to wear down snubbing, and they felt there was something secretly the matter with someone who did not make use of his or her position to be arrogant. The merest Astor had only to step on them firmly to utterly enslave them.'[63]

Some passengers did not want to pick up new acquaintances,

or pay attention to others: the honeymooners and mourners, especially. Perhaps the saddest *Titanic* party were the Ryersons. Arthur Ryerson, of Haverford, Pennsylvania, an attorney and steel maker aged sixty, who boarded at Cherbourg with his wife Emily, was hurrying to Cooperstown, New York, after their eldest son Arthur Learned Ryerson had been killed in a motoring accident at Bryn Mawr. (He was being driven by a college chum on the Chester road when a front wheel hit a stone, so that the car swerved suddenly: both youths were thrown out and fatally injured.[64]) The Ryersons were accompanied by their surviving children, aged between twenty and thirteen, Suzette, Emily, and John, and by Mrs Ryerson's maid, Victorine Chaudanson, from Le Teil, a little port on the river Rhône specializing in the transit of chestnuts out of Ardèche. A railway station had opened there in 1876, a year after Chaudanson's birth, and the de luxe carriages of the Compagnie des Wagons-Lits flashed through Le Teil on their journeys between Paris and the Riviera. Now the maid was experiencing first-class luxuries herself.

Three American sisters, originally named Lamson, boarded at Southampton, having attended the funeral on 9 April, at nearby Fawley, of their eldest sister Elizabeth: she had died a fortnight earlier at her home, 60 Avenue Victor Hugo, in Paris, and was widow of Sir Victor Drummond, a diplomatist attached to the Courts of the Kings of Bavaria and Wurttemberg at Munich and Stuttgart. The sisters – Caroline Brown, Malvina Cornell, and Charlotte Appleton – were in their fifties, and accompanied by a considerate spinster in her thirties, Edith Evans. Colonel Gracie put all four women under his ocean-bound protection.

Lady Duff Gordon took her evening meal in the first-class dining saloon on Sunday night. 'We had a big vase of beautiful daffodils on the table which were as fresh as if they had just been picked. Everyone was very gay, and at the neighbouring tables people were making bets on the probable time of this record-breaking run.'[65] The repast, indeed, was enough to make any diner sanguine:

Hors d'Oeuvres Variés

Oysters

Consommé Olga

Cream of Barley

Salmon, Mousseline Sauce, Cucumber

Filets Mignon

Sauté of Chicken Lyonnaise

Vegetable Marrow Farcie

Lamb with mint sauce

Roast duckling with apple sauce

Sirloin of Beef with Chateau potatoes

Green peas

Creamed Carrots

Boiled Rice

Parmentier & New Potatoes

Punch Romaine

Roast Squab & Cress

Cold Asparagus Vinaigrette

Paté de Foie Gras

Celery

Waldorf Pudding

Peaches in Chartreuse Jelly

Chocolate & Vanilla Éclairs

French Ice Cream

The à la carte restaurant was favoured by those old-money Americans who viewed with barely dissimulated repugnance the upstart Americans who populated the dining saloon. George and Eleanor Widener's last dinner party was served there by discreetly flitting waiters; Captain Edward Smith, Harry Widener, Archie Butt, William and Lucile Carter, and John and Marion Thayer were their guests. People like the Wideners and Thayers recognized each others' passwords: the men spoke the same language, drew on the same stock of ideas about business, politics and recreations, used the same weights and measures to value men and events. They were America's self-renewing ruling class.

In dress, too, Wideners and Thayers respected strict conventions. They thought of how they would look to other people rather than of their own selfish comfort. 'On the de luxe steamers,' Emily Post wrote, 'nearly every one dresses for dinner; some actually in ball dresses, which is in worst possible taste, and, like all overdressing in public places, indicates that they have no other place to show their finery. People of position never put on formal evening-dress on a steamer, not even in the *à la carte* restaurant, which is a feature of the *de luxe* steamer of size. In the dining saloon they wear afternoon house dresses – without hats – for dinner. In the restaurant they wear semi-dinner dresses. Some smart men on the ordinary steamers put on a dark suit for dinner after wearing country clothes all day, but in the *de luxe* restaurant they wear Tuxedo coats.'[66] It is easy to bridle or scoff at these dress codes, but they were part of the curbs and conventions which America's East Coast social leaders upheld as part of their discipline, cohesive identity and self-respect.

Thayer junior was seventeen years old, a slim boy with good skin, who expected to have a smooth, seamless life. He spent part of Sunday on deck with his parents enjoying the Atlantic billows. They stopped to talk to Bruce Ismay, and Charles Hays. In the evening, too, while his parents dined with the Wideners, he took a few turns on deck. 'I have never seen the stars shine brighter; they appeared to stand right out of the sky, sparkling like cut diamonds. A very light haze, hardly noticeable, hung low over the water. I have spent much time on the ocean, yet I have never seen the sea smoother than it was that night; it was like a mill-pond, and just as innocent-looking, as the ship rippled through it. I went onto the boat deck – it was deserted and lonely. The wind whistled through the stays, and blackish smoke poured out of the three forward funnels . . . It was the kind of a night that made one feel glad to be alive.'[67]

TEN

Second-Class

In the course of history those who have not had their heads cut off and those who have not caused others' heads to fall leave no trace behind. You have a choice of being a victim, a tyrant or a nobody.

                              Paul Valéry, *Analects*

If first-class on *Titanic* resembled a floating Ritz designed to gratify American millionaires, second-class was a floating Lyons Corner House to soothe the English genteel. The first Lyons Corner House – the brainchild of Montague Gluckstein – had opened in 1909 just east of Piccadilly Circus, near his famed Trocadero restaurant. Gluckstein aimed to provide restaurants offering a wide range of comforting food at low prices in agreeable surroundings. Theodore Dreiser, venturing into the first Lyons Corner House in 1912, was 'struck with the size and importance of it even though it was intensely middle class. It was a great chamber, decorated after the fashion of a palace ballroom, with immense chandeliers of prismed glass hanging from the ceiling, and a balcony furnished in cream and gold where other tables were set, and where a large stringed orchestra played continuously during lunch and dinner. An enormous crowd of very commonplace people were there – clerks, minor officials, clergymen, small shop-keepers – and the bill of fare was composed of many homely dishes such as beef-and-kidney pie, suet pudding, and the like – combined with others bearing high-sounding French names.' In the early years the waitresses in starched uniforms were all called Gladys and moved with stately dignity so that Dreiser found

193

the service slow by American standards: it was only in the 1920s that a friskier generation of Corner House waitresses became known as 'nippies' because they darted about so sharply. He enjoyed listening to the music, watching the customers – the English curate under his shovel hat and the tightly buttoned clerk – being led to their tables, and analysing the social spheres that Lyons Corner Houses represented.[1]

Second-class passengers on *Titanic* were like a sample of Dreiser's fellow diners: clergymen, teachers, hoteliers, engineers, shopkeepers, counter-jumpers, clerks. In second-class there were chauffeurs whose employers were travelling first-class – one of them was an instigator of pillow fights on F Deck. There were workmen, such as a glass-blower from the lower-middle-class London suburb of Forest Gate, heading for New York, and a young bricklayer from Catford heading for Detroit. Harry Rogers, aged nineteen, formerly a waiter at the Bedford Hotel, Tavistock and the Angel Hotel, Helston, 'was sailing for Wilkes-Barre, Pennsylvania, where he has several uncles and aunts, and intended to turn his hand to anything that came along. He was a smart and steady young fellow. He had intended to travel by another liner, but the sailing was cancelled on account of the coal strike.'[2] Second-class passengers, in White Star's oceanic Lyons Corner House, were seldom hectoring or braggart people. Some of them stood at the furthermost brink of gentility: the parties of Cornish migrants, for example, could easily topple into the abyss of poverty.

'The second cabin,' Robert Louis Stevenson had reported after his Atlantic crossing in 1879, 'is a modified oasis in the very heart of the steerages. Through the thin partition you can hear the steerage passengers being sick, the rattle of tin dishes as they sit at meals, the varied accents in which they converse, the crying of their children terrified by this new experience, or the clean flat smack of the parental hand in chastisement.'[3] The improvements in transatlantic conditions that were achieved in the next quarter century owed much to White Star, which unlike Cunard and the Germans gave priority to ship-board amenities rather than speed. Their second-class accommodation was situated atop rather than amidst steerage, and was gentrified to the Lyons Corner House standard. Arnold Bennett, who crossed the Atlantic as a first-class passenger in 1911, found the second-class accommodation impressively spacious. Propellers and engines were audible, but otherwise second-class resembled a reduced first-class, with 'many obviously well-to-do men' in the smoking room.[4] A guide to Atlantic liners published in 1913 noted that the demarcation between first-class and second-class passengers was less sharp than between second-class and third-class. Second saloon comforts tempted travellers who might have travelled first to economize on their fares: moreover, in second, 'certain established conventions, such as dressing for dinner, are not observed'.[5]

Bennett's descent into second-class was exceptional. 'It is a gross breach of the etiquette of the sea life, and a shocking exhibition of bad manners and low inquisitiveness, for passengers to visit unasked the quarters of an inferior class,' the 1913 guide insisted.[6] There were indeed signs on *Titanic*, at the doors connecting the second- and third-class decks, prohibiting people from moving between their classes.[7] The condescension of passengers on slumming expeditions had been resented by Stevenson when he travelled steerage. 'There came three cabin passengers, a gentleman and two young ladies, picking their way with little gracious titters of indulgence, and a Lady-Bountiful air,' he described. 'We were in truth very innocently, cheerfully, and sensibly engaged, and there was no shadow of excuse for the swaying elegant superiority with which these damsels passed among us, or for the stiff and waggish glances of their squire. Not a word was said; only when they had gone . . . we had been made to feel ourselves a sort of comical lower animal.'[8]

In second-class on *Titanic* there were a good number of 'well-to-do men', to use Bennett's phrase, who had not needed to shove and squirm their way forward in life. These included Erik Collander, the young technical director of a Helsinki paper mill, and Hull Botsford, of Orange, New Jersey, a graduate of Cornell School of Architecture, designer of railway stations and railway bridges, who had been studying European styles and construction techniques. Denzil Jarvis, originally from Breconshire in Wales, managing partner of an engineering firm, Wadkin of North Evington, employing about a hundred people, was embarking on a six weeks' business trip to America: he lived with his wife and two adolescent sons in Stoneygate, the most expensive suburb of Leicester, in an imposing modern villa, The Crest, an airy three-storey red-bricked building with big bay windows, turreted balconies and high chimneys. He was an ambitious, striving man, who had given his younger son the forename of Wellesley in honour of his great military hero, Arthur Wellesley, Duke of Wellington.[9] Ernst Sjöstedt, a Swede who had worked for the great steelworks of Schneider-Creusot in France and Bethlehem Steel in Pennsylvania, had been a senior manager at the Lake Superior Steel Company at Sault Ste Marie in Ontario since 1904. The inventor of the Sjöstedt sulphur roaster and the Sjöstedt electric smelting furnace, he was returning from Gothenberg which he had visited at the request of the Canadian government's Mining Department to report on methods of extracting copper sulphite ore. Denzil Jarvis and Ernst Sjöstedt were just the type to feel uncomfortable dressing for dinner, impatient of gushing, over-emphatic millionaire's wives, and disgusted by their painted faces.

Lower in the social scale were the sort of men whom Somerset Maugham had encountered after he crossed the Atlantic, on the Cunarder *Caronia*, in 1910. Maugham stayed initially in the exclusive purlieus of the St Regis hotel before visiting other cities and backwaters. 'I often asked myself what sort of men those were whom I saw in the parlour-cars of trains or in the lounge of a hotel, in rocking-chairs, a spittoon by their side, looking out of a large plate-glass window at the street . . . In their ill-fitting, ready-made clothes, gaudy shirts and showy ties, rather too stout, clean-shaven, but wanting a shave, with a soft hat on the back of their heads, chewing a cigar, they were as strange to me as the Chinese.' This category of *Titanic* second-class traveller – men determined not to stay where they started economically – included Frank Maybery, a realtor at Moose Jaw, Saskatchewan, and Thomas Myles, in a similar business at Cambridge, Massachusetts. Maugham decided, after several visits to the United States, that the common notion that the great republic was free of class distinctions was 'hokum'. One day, out West, he was asked to lunch with a woman worth $20 million. 'I have never seen a duke in Europe treated with such deference as she was. You might have thought that every word that issued from her opulent lips was a hundred-dollar bill that the guests would be allowed to take away with them.' The American notion that one man is as good as another was 'only a pretence', he felt. 'A banker will talk in the club car of a train to a travelling salesman as though they were equal, but I am not aware that he will dream of asking him to his house. In such communities as Charleston or Santa Barbara the travelling salesman's wife, however charming and cultivated, will never succeed in making her way into society. Social distinctions in the final analysis depend upon money.'[10]

The pretence that one man is as good as another led Americans to treat liner crew with a politeness that was applauded by Violet Jessop, stewardess to second-class passengers on the New York run of White Star's *Majestic*. American passengers, although demanding, were appreciative. 'Even those I learnt on better acquaintance to dub "holy terrors" were somehow approachable and human. They acknowledged you as an individual, invariably gave you your name, even went to the trouble of demanding to know it at the first moment of meeting.' Americans expected her to make their trip comfortable, but recognized that her work was arduous. 'Most Americans want to absorb every new fad as soon as it appears,' Jessop recalled. 'As a result, they are often left in a state of hectic unrest which naturally transfers itself to those around them.' When liners reached their destination, Americans rang to bid goodbye to the steward or stewardess, tip them well, and shake hands heartily. Passengers of other nationalities, by contrast, expected stewards 'to hang about like beggars outside a church, waiting for alms', and usually proffered a niggardly tip.[11]

On *Titanic*'s maiden voyage, two cranky American women, claiming to be mother and daughter, chided and vexed the stewards. Perhaps they were plaintive eccentrics, rather than trouble-makers trying to extort compensation, but their protests on the first day of their voyage were discordant and relentless. The elder woman had been born Lucinda ('Lutie') Temple in 1852 in Lexington, the 'Horse Capital of the World', in Kentucky's Bluegrass Country. In 1870 she had married Samuel Parrish of Lexington. They lived there and in the nearby horse-breeding centre of Versailles for many years. In her fifties, she became an inveterate globe-trotter, often accompanied by Imanita Shelley, aged twenty-five in 1912, who was described as her daughter, although her maiden name was Hall. Mrs Shelley hailed from Deer Lodge, a junction of the Chicago, Milwaukee, St Paul and Pacific railroad system, where life was dominated by long trains lumbering through and by the over-crowded, squalid Montana state prison. An older woman from a milieu of stables and race tracks travelling with a younger woman from the drabbest of convict settlements should arouse mistrust. One imagines Lutie Parrish with a rasping voice and skin like dirty leather, and Imanita Shelley with a sharp pixie face and lashing tongue. There were surely paltry scams lurking in their history. Lutie Parrish, the older woman, died in Hawaii in 1930, but Imanita Shelley continued to shift around the country, living successively in Montana, Kentucky, Missouri, Oregon, California, Washington, and Hawaii.

The two women boarded together at Southampton on a ticket costing £26. Unlike other passengers, they did not find *Titanic* all ship-shape. Instead, they were contentious and disobliging. This is clear from an affidavit that Imanita Shelley later tendered to the Senate investigation of the sinking, in which she recounted her grievances against White Star. She and Lutie Parrish had embarked on 10 April, 'having purchased the best second-class accommodation'; but instead of being assigned commodious berths, 'were taken to a small cabin many decks down in the ship, which was so small that it could only be called a cell. It was impossible to open a regulation steamer trunk in said cabin. It was impossible for a third person to enter said cabin unless both occupants first of all crawled into their bunks.' The two women sent their stewardess to the purser entreating transfer to the accommodation for which they had paid. He responded that nothing could be done until the ship had left Queenstown with its full load of passengers. After Queenstown, Lutie Parrish made eleven trips to the purser demanding transfer: he must have been in turn solicitous, numbed and exasperated by her importunities. At nine that evening, no-one having taken them to better quarters, Imanita Shelley sent a note to the purser declaring that 'she was very ill and, owing to that freezing cold of the cabin, was in great danger', and if neither the purser nor Captain Smith would help, 'she would have to wait until reaching America for redress, but most assuredly would claim damages if she lived to reach her native land'. Four stewards, fervent with apologies, then appeared to carry her to a better cabin.

John Simpson, the physician responsible for second- and third-class passengers, who had become a ship's doctor because the strain of his Belfast practice had injured his health, was supposedly fearful that Imanita Shelley's tonsillitis would turn to diphtheria, and confined her to her cabin. This cabin, though roomy, was, she claimed, inferior to Cunard cabins, seemed half-finished, and intolerably cold. When she and Lutie Parrish complained about the chill, the steward replied that the second-class heating system was broken, except in three cabins where the heat was so intense that the purser had ordered the heat to be shut off: 'consequently the rooms were like ice-houses all of the voyage, and Mrs L. D. Parrish, when not waiting on her sick daughter, was obliged to go to bed to keep warm'. This was not the end of the women's voluble remonstrance. They claimed that fixtures in the women's lavatories were still in crates, that their stewardess could not get a tray to serve Mrs Shelley's meals in her cabin, and brought the plates and dishes by hand one at a time, 'making the service very slow and annoying. The food, though good and plentiful, was ruined by this trouble in serving.' Although both steward and stewardess repeatedly appealed for a tray, none was obtained: 'there seemed,' said Imanita Shelley, 'to be no organization at all'.[12]

These complaints are not typical. 'It is lovely on the water, & except for the smell of new paint, everything is very comfortable,' wrote Marion Wright (a farmer's daughter from Yeovil going to marry a fruit farmer in Willamette Valley, Cottage Grove, Oregon), during the journey from Cherbourg to Queenstown. 'The food is splendid . . . the vessel doesn't seem a bit crowded, and there are dozens of tables empty in the dining saloon.'[13] Most voyagers appreciated that the second-class cabins had been designed to have as much natural light as possible. Their brightness was enhanced by the white enamel walls. Mahogany furniture was covered with hard-wearing, fire-resistant woollen upholstery, and linoleum covered the floor.

Marion Wright saw so many empty tables because *Titanic* carried only 271 second-class passengers, representing 40 per cent of capacity: another sign that the competition between Cunard, German shipping lines and Pierpont Morgan's trust was creating unprofitable duplication. These 271 included hardened travellers who were accustomed to heavy traffic about the world. Hans Givard, aged thirty, son of a Danish crofter, worked in both the US and Argentina, but returned annually to his native Kølsen. Ralph Giles, aged twenty-five, had been a wholesale draper in Exeter, where his father was a bookseller and his mother kept a lodging house, before becoming junior partner in a company importing French millinery to New York: he regularly travelled to and from Paris. A Jewish Russian in his fifties, Samuel Greenberg, who had lived in the Bronx for three years, travelled regularly from New York to South Africa on behalf of his employers. Second-class passengers came from all corners of the globe. A middle-aged civil servant, Masabumi Hosono, was the solitary Japanese. Arthur McCrae, the illegitimate descendant of Scottish dukes, was an Australian mining engineer whose recent postings had been to equatorial Africa and a freezing district of Siberia. James McCrie was a petroleum engineer hastening from Persia (where the first Middle Eastern oil wells had begun pumping crude oil in 1908) to Sarnia, the Canadian port on Lake Huron, where one of his children had galloping tuberculosis.

Joseph Laroche was the only black man on *Titanic*. He had been born in Haiti in 1886, had left in his youth for France, hoping to qualify as an engineer, but had been prevented by racial prejudice from obtaining decent work. In 1908 he had married a Frenchwoman, Juliette Lafargue: they had two daughters, and she had just begun a third pregnancy. The distinct appearance of the children was already attracting objectionable comments and gestures in France. Laroche could no longer face the struggling, screwing, stinting of life, so was retreating with his family to Haiti, where he hoped to forget the bigotry and secure remunerative work. The Laroches would not have received exemplary treatment on *Titanic*. Bertram Hayes recalled an Atlantic voyage on *Britannic* when the passengers included a black man who was a prize-fighter: 'he was a decent, self-respecting man . . . and if it had not been for his colour would have been even more popular on board than he was'.[14]

Among many married women, there was little racking of the brains for something to say at table or in the saloons: their talk was not confined to the exchange of recipes and sewing patterns, or anecdotes of children's illnesses and church outings; they could share their delight in being at sea on an Olympic-class liner, and their plans and apprehensions about their new life in the New World. Aloofness or mistrust seems to have been rare among young women at sea. Alice Phillips, for example, was a girl of twenty travelling with her father. They came from the Devon coastal resort of Ilfracombe: Robert Phillips had been a barman in the Royal Clarence Tap and then a fishmonger there. After his wife's recent death, he had resolved on a fresh start with a brother in New York. On the first day of the voyage, the Phillipses shared a table in the dining saloon with a family called Herman from Castle Cary in Somerset. Sam Herman had been a butcher, and proprietor of the Britannia hotel, and was emigrating to Bernardsville, New Jersey with his wife, twin daughters of twenty-four, and a fourteen-year-old boy who lived with them. The three young women struck up an immediate shipboard friendship full of prattle and laughter.

One can imagine the docile inquisitive sympathy between young women sharing a cabin. Nora Keane, Susan Webber and Edwina

Troutt shared a cabin on E Deck. Nora Keane ran a shop in Harrisburg, Pennsylvania with her brother, but had spent four months visiting her mother in County Limerick. Susie Webber, a Cornish farmer's daughter, was emigrating to join her nephew in Hartford, Connecticut as his housekeeper. Edwina 'Winnie' Troutt, aged twenty-seven, came from Bath. After working in her brother-in-law's tobacconist shop, she had gone to America in 1907, working as a waitress and servant, and was returning to Auburndale, Massachusetts from a holiday in Bath to help her sister who was heavily pregnant. She had been transferred from *Oceanic* as a result of the coal strike, and boarded with a ticket costing 10 guineas.

Wage-earning husbands were the unassailable leaders of the family groups on *Titanic*. Their wives were treated more as their human appendages than as autonomous voyagers. At sea, as on land, patriarchy was the model for families like the Collyers. Harvey Collyer, a grocer at Bishopstoke in Hampshire, was emigrating with his wife and daughter. Several years earlier some friends had gone to Payette, Idaho where they prospered on the orchards they bought there. In enthusiastic letters to the old country, they urged the Collyers to join them. When Charlotte Collyer evinced symptoms of tuberculosis, she and her husband decided to buy a farm in the same gentle valley as their friends. Payette, with a population of about 2,000, was also known as Boomerang, because it was the location of the turntables of the Oregon shortline railroad: it was salubrious because it was the end of the line. The leave-takings from Bishopstoke were gratifying for Harvey Collyer, but distressing for Charlotte. He had been verger, bell-ringer and sometime parish clerk of the local church: she had been in service in the vicar's household. On the afternoon before departing for Southampton, their Bishopstoke neighbours turned out to bid them godspeed. Some of the congregation sat Collyer under an old tree in the churchyard, climbed into the belfry and rang St Mary's church bells with gusto for an hour. He was delighted by the tribute, though his wife felt the poignancy keenly.

Collyer carried all their savings, including the proceeds of his shop, in bank notes secreted in the inside pocket of his jacket. From Queenstown he sent a letter, dated 11 April, to his parents, which shows his proud excitement at their coming adventure. If his wife still wore a closed, stricken face, he said nothing of it:

My dear Mum and Dad,

It don't seem possible we are out on the briny writing to you. Well dears so far we are having a delightful trip the weather is beautiful and the ship magnificent. We can't describe the tables it's like a floating town. I can tell you we do swank we shall miss it on the trains as we go third on them. You would not imagine you were on a ship. There is hardly any motion she is so large we have not felt sick yet we expect to get to Queenstown today so thought I would drop this with the mails. We had a fine send-off from Southampton . . .

Lots of love, don't worry about us. Ever your loving children Harvey, Lot & Madge.[15]

By the time that he wrote this letter, Collyer had savoured the second-class breakfast served on 11 April. It had the range of a Lyons Corner House slap-up.

Fruit	Grilled Sausage,	Conserve
Rolled Oats	Mashed	Marmalade
Boiled Hominy	Potatoes	Tea
Fresh Fish	Grilled Ham,	Coffee
Yarmouth Bloaters	Fried Eggs	Watercress
Grilled Ox	Fried Potatoes	
Kidneys and	Vienna & Graham	
Bacon	Rolls	
American Dry	Soda Scones	
Hash Au	Buckwheat Cakes,	
Gratin	Maple Syrup	

There was no-one on the second-class decks sulking and railing at life's hardships, especially after such a breakfast. The lower echelons of second-class passengers, when they were working in their home towns, often endured aching, jostled journeys on public transport; but here on *Titanic* there was none of the buffeted, shabby side of life. These were people with clothes that were neatly mended and brushed. Commuters faced every day, in cramped proximity, insulting evidence of their limitations, but *Titanic* opened to them a world of expansive possibilities. There were people in second-class, beneath the status of Hull Botsford or Denzil Jarvis, for whom life had brought disappointments, and those quiet little successes that no-one else noticed. They were covered with an enamel of good humour, and equipped with different appearances for different times. Second-class saloons on Atlantic liners had a magnanimous temper. They were not places for mean-minded types who stayed in their old districts, peering over fences with envious eyes, relishing their neighbours' misfortunes as visitations intended to keep uppity people in their place, and resolved to show their superiority in the pettiest ways.

After the first breakfast, Samuel 'Jim' Hocking, a confectioner from Devonport who at the age of thirty-six had determined to join his brother in Middletown, Connecticut, sat down to write a letter to his wife Ada, who intended to follow him with their children when he was settled. 'It is a lovely morning with a high wind but no heavy seas, in fact it has been like a millpond so far but I expect we shall get it a bit stiffer in the Bay of Biscay if this wind continues. This will be the ship for you, you can hardly realize you are on board except for the jolting of the engines that is why it is such bad writing. I am longing already for you to have a trip. I wish it had been possible for us all to come together, it would have been a treat.' But he was sure that 'when you come out, and I hope it will not be long, you will be able to manage with the two children splendid' if they travelled on *Titanic*. A married couple from Cornwall had struck up a shipboard friendship with him. 'I am pleased I have met someone nice, in fact you don't meet anyone rough second-class. I have a bunk to myself which is pretty lonely but still I would rather be alone than have a foreigner who I could not talk to.' He missed his Ada and 'the kiddies. I suppose they ask for me? You must get out a good bit and the time will pass quicker. Tell Penn his fags are my only comfort and I am smoking a few!' The close of his letter is particularly touching:

> We are getting pretty close to Queenstown and I am afraid of missing the post, so with heaps of kisses to you and the children, and best respects to Mabel and all at home.
> I am your ever loving husband
> Jim
> xxxxxxxxxxxxx divide these between the three
> Everybody tells me I shall not regret the step I have taken so buck up and we shan't be long.[16]

Henry Hodges, aged fifty, a Southampton dealer in musical instruments travelling on a £13 ticket, sent a postcard from Queenstown to a friend in the local Conservative Association: 'You don't notice anything of the movement of the ship. Up on top deck there are twenty boys marching round and singing. Others are playing cards and dominoes; some reading and some writing. Everything is quite different from what we thought to see at sea.'[17] Hodges was the type of passenger – an ample, cigar-smelling man travelling alone – who spent a lot of his evenings in the fusty smoking room playing cards. The second-class smoking room on *Titanic*'s B Deck, with its oak furniture and panelling, and dark green morocco upholstery, met the standards of first-class accommodation on the previous generation of Atlantic liners. 'The card room is sought because it suggests the sea less than any place else on the ship,' Theodore Dreiser wrote after his Atlantic crossing in April 1912. Its air was stale and smoky, the bids, wins and throw-ins of the gamblers all made in subdued voices, while outside the fog horn mooed like 'some vast Brobdingnagian sea-cow wandering on endless watery pastures'. Even under electric lamps, with attentive stewards serving relays of drinks, it was hard for passengers to forget 'the sound of the long, swishing breakers outside speaking of the immensity of the sea, its darkness, depths and terrors'.[18]

Few passengers were too queasy to eat their heavy meals. At first, people sat outside, in steamer chairs, wrapped in rugs, the pages of their books and magazines ruffled by the fresh westerly and south-westerly wind. Children like the Navrátil brothers scampered on deck. But going outside after Sunday lunch, as they steamed towards Newfoundland, passengers felt cut by the biting wind. Many retreated to the second-class library on C Deck to read or write. Women sat there opening their hearts to novels with salutary moral purposes: men reached to the shelves for formulaic detective stories or books that were heavy with solid, reliable facts.

One of the library occupants was Lawrence Beesley, the Dulwich College science master seeking new chances in America (his small son grew up to marry Dodie Smith, the author of *A Hundred and One Dalmatians*). 'The Library was crowded that afternoon, owing to the cold on deck,' Beesley recounted, 'but through the windows we could see the clear sky with brilliant sunlight that seemed to augur a fine night, and the prospect of landing in two days, with calm weather all the way to New York, was a matter of general satis-faction amongst us all. I can look back and see every detail of the library that afternoon – the beautifully furnished room, with lounges, armchairs, and small writing or card tables scattered about, writing bureaus round the walls of the room, and the library in glass-faced shelves flanking one side – the whole finished in mahogany relieved with white fluted wooden columns that supported the deck above.' Sitting near him were two young American women dressed in white: one returning from India, the other a school teacher 'with a distin-guished air heightened by a pince-nez'. They chatted with a shipboard acquaintance from Cambridge, Massachusetts, 'genial, polished, and with a courtly air towards the two ladies'. As they talked, a child clasping a large doll interrupted their conversation.[19]

Elsewhere in the library, a pert young Frenchwoman, Henriette Yrois, sat playing patience under the admiring scrutiny of her middle-aged companion. This was William Harbeck, aged forty-eight, from Toledo, Ohio, who had made his mark filming the aftermath of the San Francisco earthquake of 1906. More recently, he had been hired by the Canadian Pacific Railway to make documentary films about the stretch of western Canada that was to be served by Charles Hays' ill-starred railroad-building project. This had taken him to Paris to consult Léon Gaumont, the famous cineaste, about film-shooting on location. Harbeck was probably filming a documentary about the maiden voyage, for he recorded the liner's departure from Southampton, and his luggage included cine cameras with 110,000 feet of film. Henriette Yrois, boarding at Southampton with him, gave her address as 5 Rue des Pyramides, one of the smartest shopping streets in Paris, with arcaded pavements and shining shop fronts that were a famous enticement to rich Americans. As a cynic would have realized, the pair were too acutely aware of one another to be a married couple. Neither survived the calamity, although his body was recovered clutching her purse, which contained his wedding ring. His real wife did not pay for a headstone for his grave.

Charlotte Collyer, the grocer's wife heading for Idaho, recounted her memories of her Atlantic crossing when they were fresh. '*Titanic* was wonderful, far more splendid and huge than I had dreamed of. The other crafts in the harbour were like cockle-shells beside her, and they, mind you, were the boats of the American and other lines that a few years ago were thought enormous. I remember a friend said to me, "Aren't you afraid to venture on the sea?", but it was I who was confident. "What, on this boat!" I answered. "Even the worst storm could not harm her." Before we left the harbour, I saw the accident to the *New York*, the liner that was dragged from her moorings and swept against us in the Channel. It did not frighten anyone, as it only seemed to prove how powerful the *Titanic* was. I don't remember very much about the first few days of the voyage. I was a bit seasick, and kept to my cabin most of the time. But on Sunday April 14th I was up and about. At dinner time I was in my place in the saloon, and enjoyed the meal, though I thought it too heavy and rich. No effort had been spared to give even the second cabin passengers on that Sunday the best dinner that money could buy. After I had eaten, I listened to the orchestra a little while, then at nine o'clock or half past nine I went to my cabin.'[20]

Second-class on *Titanic* was replete with neat, sprightly, sententious vicars, priests, ministers and missionaries. In the library on that Sunday afternoon Beesley, who was a disciple of Mary Baker Eddy's *Science and Health* and became a Christian Science practitioner, watched two Catholic priests. One was reading quietly. He was Father Thomas Byles, who was travelling to New York to officiate at his brother's wedding, and had transferred to *Titanic* because of the coal strike. Byles came from a family of Bradford radicals and reformers. A gifted mathematician, he went to Balliol, Oxford to prepare for the Anglican ministry, but converted to Catholicism. He studied at Rome, took charge of the Catholic mission at Kelvedon, Essex, in 1903, proved a pious, upright man, and was made incumbent of St Helen's, Ongar in 1905. 'The Rev Father was very popular and highly esteemed by the members of the community in his district,' the *Epping Gazette* stated during the murky week when Byles had been reported missing but was not yet confirmed as dead. 'He is devoted to his flock, and there has been a largely increased attendance at the services since he came to Ongar.'[21] The other Catholic priest espied by Beesley was Joseph Peruschitz, aged forty, dark and bearded under a broad-brimmed hat. He had been ordained at Munich and, having spent Holy Week at the Benedictine cloister near Ramsgate, was travelling to Minnesota where he was to be principal of a Benedictine school.

The busiest clergyman was the Reverend Ernest Carter. Born in 1858, Carter was a graduate of St John's College, Oxford who had taught at Godolphin School, Hammersmith before taking holy orders. In 1890 he married Lillian Hughes, daughter of Thomas Hughes, author of *Tom Brown's Schooldays*, and a woman who perpetuated her father's zeal for social reform. Carter was vicar of St Jude's church, Commercial Street, the teeming crime-ridden thoroughfare linking Spitalfields to Whitechapel High Street. 'In this Whitechapel Ghetto the English visitor almost feels himself one of a subject race in the presence of dominant and overwhelming invaders,' a commentator noted shortly before Carter took over the parish in 1898. Whitechapel's sidestreets were as wretched as those of a *shtetl*, 'the poorest and densest population of the British Isles, packed together in a state of inhuman, solid and sodden poverty'.[22]

Carter was undaunted by the fact that his choir sometimes outnumbered his congregation. 'Not specially gifted intellectually, he took a Pass degree here,' an Oxford man recalled of Carter, 'and could not be called an exceptional preacher. None the less, he had made his mark in the East End of London; as vicar of St Jude's, Whitechapel, he had a most difficult and disheartening task to face, for his parishioners belonged mainly to the Jewish colony which crowds that quarter of London.'[23] A member of the diocese described Carter as 'a man of moderate attainments, of which the most striking was his sincere modesty about the rest', but admired the variety of his good works. 'To all these he brought a merry enthusiasm which made it impossible for any gloom to settle down on any cause, however desperate, with which he was associated.' He and his wife regarded Christianity as an instrument of social progress, and every week at their vicarage, they gathered an earnest little discussion-group of reformers. After someone had read a discussion paper, the questions for consideration were formulated by Lillian Carter, 'the keen-eyed, beaming lady, who was the very soul of the class and the light of their being'.[24]

The Carters boarded *Titanic* together with tickets costing £26. After supper on the Sunday evening of 14 April, Carter held a hymn service for some hundred passengers in the second-class dining saloon – an oak-panelled room, with mahogany furniture, crimson leather upholstery, linoleum flooring and a handy piano near the sideboard. Carter asked the assembled company which hymns they wished to hear, and preceded each hymn with a history of its author and composition. Douglas Norman, a twenty-eight-year-old electrical engineer from Glasgow who was joining his brother on a fruit farm in the foothills of the Rockies, played the piano. Marion Wright, en route to her farmer fiancé in Oregon, sang solo 'Lead Kindly

Light' and 'There is a Green Hill Far Away'. There were renditions of 'Eternal Father, Strong to Save' (also known as 'For Those in Peril on the Sea') amongst others: the final hymn was 'Now the Day is Over'. At about ten, as stewards laid out coffee and biscuits, Carter drew the proceedings to a close by thanking the purser for the use of the saloon and added that the ship was unusually steady and how everyone was looking forward to their arrival in New York.

Another clergyman of interest was Charles Kirkland. He had been born in 1841 in the Miramichi lumber district of New Brunswick abutting the icy Gulf of St Lawrence. As a young man he was a master carpenter and cabinet-maker in the little fishing seaport of Richibucto. About 1870 he crossed the Canadian-US border to live in the settlement at Baring, Maine. Maine was no gentler than New Brunswick: a damp state where the short summers were followed by cold north-easterly storms. The soil was meagre, as the result of glaciations, and though there was some good potato-growing, with fat barns and comfortable farmhouses, Kirkland's segment of the state was covered by poor bushy fields and straggling woods of white pines, black spruce, pointed firs, swamp maples and alders. The stony uplands grazed by sheep were described by Sarah Orne Jewett, a Maine contemporary of Kirkland's, as 'the wildest, most Titanic sort of pasture country'.[25]

Kirkland converted to the Free Will Baptist faith, and needed no training in a theological college before setting up as a pastor in this sect. He held revivalist meetings in Maine communities, and served as a Baptist pastor for Penobscot and Hancock counties. Penobscot, on the zigzagging Maine coastline, had a protected natural harbour: Maine people were the great navigators of the nineteenth-century United States, crossing the globe in fragile craft. 'They shame the easy voyager of the North Atlantic and the Mediterranean; they have rounded the Cape of Good Hope and braved the angry seas of Cape Horn in small wooden ships,' wrote Jewett. 'The sea captains and the captains' wives of Maine knew something of the wide world, and never mistook their native parishes for the whole instead of a part thereof; they knew not only Thomaston and Castine and Portland, but London and Bristol and Bordeaux, and the strange-mannered harbours of the China Sea.'[26]

Mortality dogged Kirkland: while pastor of Mattawamkeag in Maine, he lost three children in an influenza epidemic; while pastor at Danforth, on the Maine-New Brunswick border, his wife died; and he outlived other children. Lonely and disheartened, he married a Danforth divorcée over twenty-five years his junior in 1898. The marriage soon failed, and he became an itinerant preacher, living partly with a married daughter in the township of Bradford, Maine, but travelling about proclaiming his Christian message. During 1911 he preached at Moose Jaw, Saskatchewan before proceeding to Glasgow at the end of the year. This seems to have been his first crossing of the Atlantic, at the age of seventy – prompted by a belief that he was entitled to money from an uncle's estate. Even for a man acclimatized to Maine, Scotland seemed dismal. He wrote a sprawling, ill-punctuated letter from Scotland to his daughter early in 1912: 'I could not live here. This is the worst country I ever struck. Everything is tied up on account of the coal strike.' But he left Glasgow, crossed Ireland, and embarked on *Titanic* at Queenstown – wearing an obvious toupee.[27]

Aside from Kirkland, two Englishmen in second-class were Baptist ministers: the Reverend Robert Bateman was engaged in missionary work at Jacksonville, Florida and was accompanying his widowed sister-in-law Ada Ball who was to help him there; and the Reverend John Harper, travelling with his small daughter, on his way to address revival meetings at the Moody Church in West Chicago. Charles Louch, a fifty-year-old saddler from Weston-super-Mare, and prominent Wesleyan preacher in his district, was going out with his wife to visit his brother in California.

The non-English clergy included William Lahtinen, from Viitasaari, Finland, aged about thirty. He and his wife Anna, who had been brought up in the US by Finnish parents, were heading for Minneapolis. There was, too, a priest entering enforced exile. Juozas Montvila, aged twenty-seven, originally from Marijampolė in Lithuania, had attended the seminary in a great white-stoned turreted monastery at Sejny (Seinai), a town which had been stripped of its ancient privileges because of its complicity with opponents of the imperial Russian government. Montvila was ordained in 1908, but subsequently forbidden to undertake pastoral work by the Russian authorities because of his objectionable political sympathies. He was therefore emigrating to lead a Lithuanian parish in America. Reports that he was an eloquent writer and sensitive artist seem convincing: a surviving photograph shows a keen-faced, dedicated-looking ascetic. Byles, Peruschitz and Montvila celebrated Mass every morning on board.

There were three American missionary parties, too. The largest, and most stressed, was led by Nellie Becker, wife of an American missionary, who was working with orphans in the Guntur district of Andhra Pradesh on the coast of the Bay of Bengal. The wives of American missionaries led abject, desperate, lonely lives. They were exiled in hostile climates, terrains and populaces, enduring the stink of sewage, bad food and filthy labourers, with the constant fear of losing their children in epidemics. 'I have no more children to give away to God now,' cried the wife of an American missionary in China after losing four children to diphtheria or cholera.[28] Nellie Becker was gripped by well-grounded fears for her children. Her little son Luther had died at Guntur a few years earlier, and with her surviving one-year-old son Richard, whose deteriorating health had alarmed her, and daughters aged four and twelve, she was scuttling back to her hometown, Benton Harbor, built on swampland reclaimed from the Paw-Paw River, outside Kalamazoo in Michigan.

The missionary Albert Caldwell was strikingly handsome. He had been born in an Iowa settlement, Sanborn, in 1885, and attended a college in Kansas City where students received free tuition and board in return for working half-days on its farm, electrical workshop or printing press. There he met Sylvia Mae Harbaugh. After graduation, they married in 1909 in a teetotal resort town, Colorado Springs, and went to Siam under the auspices of the Presbyterian Board of Foreign Missions to teach in the Bangkok Christian College for Boys. Their son, Alden Gates Caldwell, was born in Bangkok in 1911. Early

ABOVE The spick-and-span drawing hall at Harland & Wolff's Belfast shipyard. It was here that the plans for the *Titanic* were drawn with immaculate precision.

BELOW A steel gantry, which resembled a vast, weird guillotine, being erected over the shipyard berth where the *Titanic* was to be built.

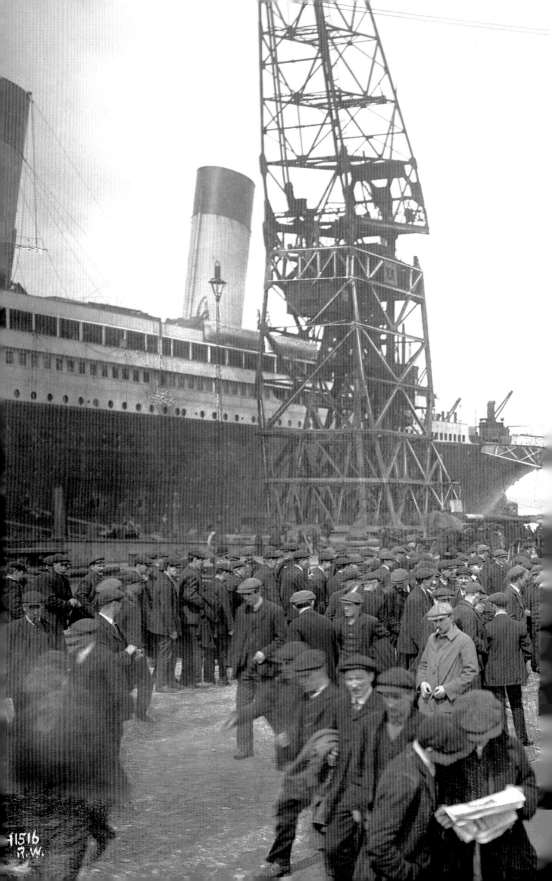

RIGHT Lord Pirrie, Harland & Wolff's autocrat (*left*), and Edward Smith, White Star's most trusted captain, on board the *Olympic* in 1911.

MAIN IMAGE Harland & Wolff workers on the *Titanic*'s sister-ship, the *Olympic*. The shipyard was so rough that the Belfast police did not dare to set foot in it.

ABOVE Lord Pirrie (*left*) and White Star's chairman Bruce Ismay on the *Titanic* before its launch. Both men were answerable to Pierpont Morgan in New York.

MAIN IMAGE Three tugs escort the *Titanic* through Belfast Lough. Once in the Irish Sea the liner made steam for Southampton.

The first minute of the world's most notorious maiden voyage: the *Titanic* leaving White Star's dock at Southampton.

ABOVE The *Titanic*'s Café Parisienne, where first-class passengers were 'sprinkled with liqueurs and ices', according to G.K. Chesterton. He thought it a refinement too far.

BELOW First-class accommodation on the *Titanic* was a hodge-podge of styles. This parlour suite on B Deck was said to be in the 'Old Dutch' manner.

ABOVE Crowds of Irish migrants waiting on White Star's quay at Queenstown, Co. Cork for a tender to take them to the liner that would carry them to America.

RIGHT William Murdoch (*right*) and Charles Lightoller (*centre*), First and Second Officers, looking down at a tender alongside the *Titanic* at Queenstown. When the crisis came, these two men superintended the loading of the lifeboats.

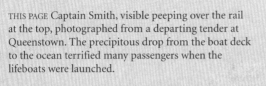

THIS PAGE Captain Smith, visible peeping over the rail at the top, photographed from a departing tender at Queenstown. The precipitous drop from the boat deck to the ocean terrified many passengers when the lifeboats were launched.

OPPOSITE TOP 'A half-hour in the gymnasium helped to set one's blood coursing freely,' said one fitness fiend.

OPPOSITE BOTTOM The Promenade (or 'A') Deck, from which Lifeboat 4 left with its cargo of American millionairesses and Cornish housewives, and from which Hugh Woolner jumped for his life.

ABOVE Second-class passengers sauntering on the boat deck – 550 feet long. The lifeboats are clearly visible on the left of the picture.

LEFT Lifeboat 14 towing Collapsible Lifeboat D (the last lifeboat to be lowered) towards their rescuers on the *Carpathia*. 'The rescued came solemnly, dumbly, out of a shivering shadow,' said *Carpathia*'s captain.

ABOVE Crowds outside White Star's Southampton office, checking lists of survivors and awaiting fresh bulletins. 'Women sobbed aloud, while tears glistened in the eyes of rough and hardy sea-faring men.'

BELOW Bathroom steward Sam Rule (*left*), safe back in Plymouth, but mourning the 'little lads' who were lift-boys and bell-boys. He would have bundled them in with the women if he could have.

ABOVE Able Seaman Horswill escaped in
Lifeboat 1. It has been suggested that he
and his wife are examining his cheque from
Sir Cosmo Duff Gordon.

OPPOSITE TOP Surviving crew members reach
Southampton Docks.

OPPOSITE BOTTOM White Star men attend a
memorial service in Southampton.

A corpse retrieved from the Atlantic by the cable-ship *Minia* is prepared for its coffin.

in 1912 the Caldwells left Siam with their baby, heading for a tiny place called Roseville, Illinois. In Naples, on their journey through Europe, they saw an advertisement for *Titanic*, and determined to buy tickets on it – costing £29. Caldwell in old age recalled the second-class saloons as thronged with carefree passengers. He recalled no apprehensions or anxiety: the calm sea helped everyone to enjoy their Atlantic crossing; and after years in Siam, he appreciated the abundance and quality of the meals.

Finally there was Annie Clemmer Funk, a Mennonite missionary returning on her first furlough after five years in the Jangjir-Champa district of the central Indian state of Madhya Pradesh (often called the Heart of India). Miss Funk had been born in Pennsylvania in 1874. Her father was deacon at his local Mennonite church. She attended the Mennonite Training School in Northfield, Massachusetts before toiling in the immigrant slums of Chattanooga, Tennessee and Paterson, New Jersey. In 1906 she was sent to India as the first female Mennonite missionary, serving in Janjgir-Champa, where she learnt to speak Hindi and taught girls in a one-room school. Mennonite tenets required literal obedience to New Testament commandments, and strict adherence to the ethics of Christ, especially self-denial, self-renunciation and sacrificial martyrdom. They renounced aggression and violence; were active in humanitarian works; and shunned Catholicism, worldliness and luxury. Mennonite women wore austere dresses with modest bonnets, shawls and veils.

In 1912 Miss Funk was summoned home by a telegram announcing her mother's illness. She entrained for Bombay, where she embarked on *Persia*, a P&O steamship plying between England and Australia, which was torpedoed by a German submarine off Crete three years later. *Persia* carried her to Marseille, from where she hastened by trains to Liverpool, where she was booked on the American Line's *Haverford*, which ran the Liverpool-Philadelphia route. As its crossing was delayed by the coal strike, she transferred to *Titanic* on a second-class ticket costing £13. The Friday of her voyage marked Miss Funk's thirty-eighth birthday.[29]

Annie Funk was an inspiring woman with a creed of personal

service and sacrifice. She was surely unaware that in second-class there were several adulterers, a child kidnapper, and a handsome bachelor with his Ganymede. There were doubtless tricksters, too, seeking targets. They seem to have missed Leopold Weisz, aged thirty-three, who had left the Jewish quarter of Budapest to study ornamental stone-carving in England, before moving in 1911 to Montreal where he was employed to carve friezes on newly built bank and museum buildings. He had returned to Europe to collect his Belgian wife to begin a new chapter in Montreal, and was carrying a fortune in life-savings. Tens of thousands of dollars were sewn inside the lining of his suit, and gold bullion secreted in his black Astrakhan coat with its fur collar.

Michel Navrátil, the kidnapper, had been born in Sered, a market town in southern Slovakia. From Sered there was a railway running to Bratislava, Slovakia's major city, with its multifarious population of Austrians, Czechs, Germans, Jews and Slovaks. Sered, too, had a busy traffic of barges and rafts carrying timber and salt along the river Váh, a tributary of the Danube. These easy transport links perhaps induced Navrátil to travel, first into Hungary and then to the French Riviera, where at Nice he became a women's tailor with an elegant clientele. This was not an end to his journeying, for in Westminster, on 26 May 1907, he married an Italian, Marcelle Caretto. They had two sons, Michel and Edmond, known as Lolo and Momon, born at Nice in 1908 and 1910. His wife found that he had an odd temper, and he accused her of having a lover. The couple separated, and while they were in the process of divorcing, the boys lived with a cousin of their mother's. At the start of April 1912, Navrátil collected the boys from this cousin, and absconded with them. He left his wife a cruel note – 'You will never see the children again: but never fear about them, for they will be in good hands' – and sent a further letter posted in Austria to mislead her, but she knew that he had fled to London. He had often spoken of going to America, and bought second-class *Titanic* tickets costing £26 under his assumed name of Louis Hoffman, taken from the *copain* who had helped him to vanish.[30]

This tailor accustomed in boyhood to Danube barges boarded the great liner at Southampton with his two stolen boys. The elder child always remembered his thrill at playing on deck and looking down the awesome length of the ship – and eating eggs with his father for breakfast. Navrátil implied to fellow passengers that he was a widower, and seldom relaxed his control of his sons. He was armed with a revolver. On one occasion, he diverted himself by playing cards, and left the boys in the charge of Bertha Lehmann, a Swiss waitress who ate meals at the same saloon table. She was on her way to join her brother in grandiloquently misnamed Central City, a hick settlement on the outskirts of Cedar Rapids, Iowa.

As to the adulterers, Henry Morley, aged thirty-nine, was a citizen of Worcester, a confectioner with branches in Worcester, Birmingham and Bristol – as well as a wife and child in Worcester. He eloped on *Titanic* with a nineteen-year-old Worcester girl, Kate Phillips: they travelled under the name of Mr & Mrs Marshall. Similarly, Harry Faunthorpe, also aged about forty, a Lancashire carrot and potato salesman, was heading for Philadelphia with 'Lizzie' Wilkinson, aged twenty-nine, his mistress rather than wife. They seem to have told fellow passengers that they were recently married, and honeymooning or starting a new life in California.

Joseph Fynney, principal of the firm Joseph Fynney & Co., rubber merchants, of Brown's Buildings in Liverpool, was on one of his recurrent visits to his widowed mother in Montreal. He was a hand-some, dark-haired bachelor in his mid-thirties with a keen, alert expression and shrewd eyes who enjoyed the company of youths and worked with delinquent youngsters. 'Well-known and highly respected in Liverpool,' reported an obituarist, 'his cheery and bright disposition endearing him to all who knew him. Mr Fynney took an interest in the work of St James's Church, Toxteth, particularly in connection with the Young Men's Club, and matters appertaining to the welfare of boys and young men.'[31] On each visit to his mother in Canada, he took a teenage companion: in 1912 it was a sixteen-year-old apprentice cooper, Alfred Gaskell, of 20 Dexter Street. In other circumstances, Fynney might have been a first-class voyager, but it was impossible for him to bring a working-class lad onto the same decks as Astors or Cardezas. The incongruity between the past experiences, future prospects, physical grace and easy manners of young Jack Thayer and Alfred Gaskell would have been too pointed. Each second-class ticket bought by Fynney cost £26.

There were several travelling parties on the second-class decks, notably groups from Hampshire, Guernsey and several from Cornwall.

From the hamlet of Fritham in Hampshire came three Hickman brothers and four of their friends. There was little at Fritham except ancient woodlands and the Schultze gunpowder factor, which had been located deep in the New Forest so as to limit loss of life in any accidental explosions. At the age of twenty Leonard Hickman had emigrated in 1908 to Neepawa, Manitoba, where he prospered working as a farmhand on a mixed-grain farmstead called Eden. He returned to Fritham for Christmas of 1911 intent on persuading the entire Hickman family of eleven to move to Eden. Because of the coal strike, only three brothers could get an immediate passage: Leonard, his elder brother Lewis (who worked in the gunpowder factory) and twenty-year-old Stanley. They travelled with four young companions from Fritham on a single ticket costing £73 10s – all of them upgraded from third-class on another ship to second-class on *Titanic*. All seven Fritham men perished.

Over a dozen passengers from Guernsey travelled second-class on *Titanic*. There was a party led by William Downton, a well-established quarryman of Rochester in upstate New York. Downton was chaperoning his young ward Lillian Bentham, who was heading for Holley, a village on the Erie Canal in the north-west of the state. The other Guernsey party members were another quarryman; a carpenter-joiner, who had made an earlier trip to the US in 1907, with his wife and her two younger brothers, who were both carters; a young man who worked on his father's smallholding; and the young daughter of a railwayman, heading for Wilmington, Delaware, where her uncle was a grocer. Three men in their early or mid-twenties were leaving Guernsey for a new life in America: a quarryman's driver, a young ledger clerk at a general store, and a horse trainer who had transferred from *Olympic*, and was heading for a horse breeders' in Minnesota (there was a demand for English grooms as horse trainers and riding instructors on American stud farms). Lawrence Gavey, aged twenty-six, was returning to Elizabeth, New Jersey, where he had settled five years earlier: he was a travelling fitter employed by a Rockefeller company, known for 'his unfailing bonhomie and cheerful spirit'.[32] An older second-class Guernsey man was a sixty-eight-year-old farmer, trustee of the Ebenezer Wesleyan chapel, member of the *Central Douzaine* of St Peter Port, and visiting his daughter in Rhode Island. He was travelling with a widower aged seventy-three, retired as both coach painter and boots shop proprietor, who was going to visit his sister in Toledo, Ohio. They were both Lyons Corner House sorts. None of the second-class Guernsey men survived.

The largest grouping of all in *Titanic*'s second-class decks was Cornish. They banded together, looked askance at the English and, with impassive faces, subjected them to banter. The route from Cornwall was well trekked with recognized staging posts on the way. At Southampton there was Berriman's hotel, run by a friendly Cornishwoman, and catering to Cornish voyagers, while in Brooklyn, John and Sid Blake ran the Star Hotel as a hospitable halt for Cornish coming in and out of America. 'We were expecting to be very busy when the *Titanic* docked as there would be quite a number of Cornish people who would wait for the honour of travelling on her for her maiden trip,' Sid Blake recorded. 'We had received personal letters from several people requesting us to meet them on their arrival, and assist them through the Customs. I meet all steamers sailing from Southampton, and whenever possible I see that Cornish passengers are looked after properly, baggage labelled right, etc., and that they are placed on their proper train for the West in good time. Besides, I always meet old friends who have gone home a few months before on a visit. It feels good to shake hands with them again, and hear them say, "There is no place like Cornwall".'[33]

Two separate parties were travelling from Penzance to Akron – a boom-town of the epoch, prospering since the Goodyear Tire &

Rubber Company had been founded there in 1898, and thriving after Firestone Tire & Rubber had opened its plant two years later. The pervasive smell of rubber was unpleasant after the sea breezes of Penzance, but rubber connoted modernity and good money. Often Cornishmen went out to the US alone, sending for their wives and children when they had saved enough money for tickets. Arthur Wells and his brother-in-law Abednego Trevaskis had migrated to Akron two years earlier. Now Addie Wells, daughter of a blacksmith and fish-packer, wife of Arthur Wells and sister of Trevaskis, was joining them with her two toddlers and household linen. A larger party was led by George Hocking, originally a Penzance baker, latterly a watchman in a rubber factory at Akron, who had returned home to collect his mother Eliza Hocking, his sisters Nellie Hocking and Emily Richards, together with his small nephews William and George Richards. Nellie Hocking was on her way to marry a man in Schenectady. Emily Richards was joining her husband in Akron. George Hocking had sung in the YMCA choir at Penzance, which turned out to sing the party joyously on their journey. No doubt the provident Cornishwomen had packed the ingredients for a picnic fit for Cornish travellers, with pasties and the brightly coloured, aromatic saffron buns relished by the Cornish.

George Hocking shared his cabin with an old Penzance school fellow, Harry Cotterill, who lived with his widowed mother, had just completed his apprenticeship with a Penzance builder, and had decided to go to Akron for work. The third boy berthing with them was Percy Bailey. Born in 1893, reared in Penzance, a butcher's boy in the town, Bailey was proceeding to Akron where he was to stay with a friend of his father and begin work as an apprentice butcher. Bailey initially booked on White Star's *Oceanic*, but transferred when he heard that his friends Cotterill and Hocking had tickets on *Titanic*. He arrived in Southampton on 9 April, and boarded next morning. He started on his voyage full of high hopes, good resolutions, youthful excitement and grateful love for his parents, as shown by the touching letter that he posted at Queenstown.

Dear Father and Mother,

We arrived on board this morning after a nights rest at Southampton. We put up at an Hotel named Berrimans, the lady who owns it is a Cornish lady, we had a good supper and a good breakfast of ham and eggs, we were doing it fine. I slept with a young man named Wells a brother to the man who married Mrs Trevaskis' daughter, he came to Southampton to see [off] his sister-in-law. We had several people joined us at St Erth bound for the same place as we are going so we are a big family altogether. Well dear Mother, I suppose you are missing me but don't be down-hearted old dear, Percy will be behaved to you as a son ought to treat his Mother and Father. This going away from home will make me a better man and try and lead a good life. The *Titanic* is a marvel I can tell you, I have never seen such a sight in all my life, she is like a floating palace, everything up to date. I hope you are all well as it leaves me at present . . .

Father I shall never forget your kindness, you have done more for me than many Fathers have done for their sons. Well dear parents I don't think there is any more news I can tell you now kiss Grandma for me and tell I am sorry for all my wicked thoughts which I said to her, but never again, will I cheek her.

Give my love to all who ask for me and tell Ethel to come and see you any time. I will draw my letter to a close hoping you one and all are quite well.

I remain your loving son.[34]

Apart from the Penzance to Akron crowd, several dozen Cornish miners travelling second-class on *Titanic* were heading for the Houghton County copper belt in Michigan. Until the Guggenheims developed Bingham Canyon and Chuquicamata, Houghton County was the richest copper district in the world. It lies on the Keweenaw peninsula, a fir-covered, craggy promontory, 15 miles wide and 50 miles long, jutting into Lake Superior as Cornwall juts into the Atlantic. When men were needed in the mines, or a job was going, someone always knew a man in Cornwall who was suited for it:

'Cousin Jack'. Cornishmen formed working groups (often from the same family or village) which contracted with mine managers to find and blast copper-bearing rocks at an agreed rate. Sturdily independent and absurdly touchy, they convinced themselves that they worked for no-one but themselves: no Cornish Jack would stoop to pick up a tool from the ground in the presence of his shift boss lest it seem that he was working for a superior.[35]

Several parties heading for Houghton came from the St Ives district. William Berriman, aged twenty-five, a farm worker, and his brother-in-law William Carbines, aged nineteen, a miner, were bound for the Calumet mine in Houghton, where Carbines's brother was already settled. Stephen Jenkin, aged thirty-two, son of a Nanjivey tin miner, had become a US citizen during his nine years in the Champion copper mine at Painesdale, Houghton County. Jenkin was returning there after a long visit to his family.[36] Maud 'Maudie' Sincock hoped to celebrate her twenty-first birthday in New York on 17 April. She was travelling to join her plumber father, from Halsetown, near St Ives, who had emigrated during the previous September to Houghton, where he worked at the Quincy mine. She accompanied her mother's friend Agnes Davies, a widowed dressmaker whose first husband had been a stonemason and her second husband a miner. She was leaving St Ives with her eight-year-old son John Davies, and his nineteen-year-old half-brother Joseph Nicholls, and heading for Houghton, where her eldest son lived. She had sold all her possessions, and intended to run a lodging house for Cornish miners.

Helston was the origin of another set of Cornish second-class voyagers. A cattle market town, with tin mines outside, Helston was the birthplace of Henry Trengrouse who, after the drowning of over a hundred men in a Cornish shipwreck, had a hundred years earlier designed the first distress rockets for ships in trouble at sea. Frederick Banfield was a miner in his mid-twenties who had left a job in Nevada to spend three months with his parents at Helston. His destination was Houghton. Banfield embarked with Samuel Sobey, a quarryman in Houghton, who was returning after a visit to his family in Porthallow, a pilchard-fishing village, near the mouth of the Helford river, and with Joseph Fillbrook, an eighteen-year-old painter-decorator from Truro. In addition to Banfield and Sobey, there was an older man, William Gilbert, originally from a hamlet outside Helston, who had been apprenticed as a joiner and wheel-wright, and had steady work in a joinery shop at Butte, Montana. He had returned for three months to visit his mother and brother, and with a ticket costing 10 guineas was resuming life in Butte. William Gilbert was a man of calm, precise temperament whose hobbies were electrical tinkering and technical drawing.

Near Helston, in the south-east tip of Cornwall, lay Constantine and Porthleven. Constantine, a village atop the wooded creek that heads the Helford river, was the departure point of James Veale, a granite carver in his forties, who had returned from Barre, Vermont, to visit his family. Another established American emigrant in his forties, James Drew, also left from Constantine. Drew had emigrated in 1896 to Greenport, a harbour town on the east shore of Long Island and the terminus of a branch of the Long Island railway. There he ran a monumental marble business with his elder brother William. He and his wife were childless, and in 1911 had left on *Olympic* with their motherless seven-year-old nephew Marshall Drew for a visit to their Constantine relations. The trio was now returning to Long Island Sound.

Porthleven was a small Cornish fishing port, where the cottages were perched on rocky slopes above the granite harbour, with its 465-foot pier jutting into the sea. Two brothers, Edgar and Frederick Giles, sons of a farm worker who had left Porthleven to join their elder brother training horses at Camden, New Jersey, were transferred to *Titanic* from *Oceanic*. On the savage, wreck-strewn coast south-west of Porthleven, fields of buttercup and clover ran near to the shore with the bleak moorland of the Goonhilly Downs behind. There were touches of modernity: the golf links serving the hotel at Mullion Cove, and near the golf links the weird-looking Marconi wireless station at Poldhu. This was the earliest permanent wireless station in the world, with four scaffold towers soaring over 200 feet surrounded by a trellis of posts, wires and lower towers. It was from Poldhu that Marconi messages reached Atlantic ships, enabling first-class liners to publish daily news bulletins throughout their voyage – 'a very wonderful thing, when we remember how completely a sea voyage used to cut one away from news at home'.[37] Poldhu was soon to be humming with messages about *Titanic*.

Frank Andrew, aged thirty, lived with his wife and small child in a hamlet near Redruth, where he was respected in the Wesleyan church. The lodes were depleted in the centuries-old tin mine where he worked, and he too was bound for the Houghton copper district.[38] Other clusters of Cornishmen came from further north. Shadrach Gale, born in 1878 at Rising Sun, a hamlet of Harrowbarrow near Callington, had settled at Idaho Springs, Colorado as a miner, came to Cornwall on a family visit, and was returning to Idaho Springs accompanied by a new emigrant, his elder brother Henry. The Gale brothers were in a party with two youngsters from Gunnislake, the next village to Harrowbarrow, who were both heading for Butte.

After dinner on Sunday evening, there was impromptu music in the dining room. Douglas Norman again played the piano. Alfred Pain, a young Canadian physician returning from a study trip to King's College Hospital in London, played his flute. Mathilde Weisz, the Belgian wife of the stonemason with gold bullion hidden in his coat, sang Thomas Moore's melody, 'The Last Rose of Summer', with its haunting question, 'Oh who would inhabit this bleak world alone?' James Witter, steward in the second-class smoking room, recalled that last evening: 'It was a beautiful, clear but very cold evening, the sea was like a sheet of glass, while I, duty smoke room steward, was clearing up the 2nd class smoke room (11.40) ready for closing at midnight. All was very quiet.' About forty people sat in the room, most just talking, but for the maiden voyage the Chief Steward had suspended White Star's rule that there should be no card-playing on Sundays, and there were three tables of men intent on their cards. Usually the smoking room closed at eleven on Sunday evenings, but on this maiden voyage it was to be kept open until midnight. 'Suddenly,' Witter said, 'there was a jar, the ship shuddered slightly and then everything seemed normal.'[39] Everything seemed normal, yet within four hours, all of the Cornishmen had gone to their deaths, and only 8 per cent of men from second-class were still alive.

ELEVEN

Third-Class

An unlearned carpenter of my acquaintance once said in my hearing:
'There is very little difference between one man and another; but what
little there is, is very important.' *This distinction seems to me to go to*
the root of the matter.

William James, 'The Importance of Individuals'

Third-class accommodation on *Titanic* was dispersed over four decks.
White Star's preference for amenities rather than speed had
immeasurably benefited its poorest voyagers. Cabins were mostly
intended for two or four passengers – the provision of two-berth
rooms in third-class accommodation was a fine innovation – but in
some cabins, six, eight or ten passengers could be accommodated
together. Cabins were small, spartan but not squalid; ventilated, lit
by electricity, and equipped with wash basins. There were red and
white coverlets on the beds. Single women and families were berthed
aft, so that children with their mess and screech were not in annoying
proximity to married couples and single men berthed near the bow
of the ship. Additionally, there were open berths for 164 people on
G Deck. In the previous generation, before there were three classes
on Atlantic liners, washing by steerage passengers below deck had
been forbidden while ablutions on deck in a sea wind were unbearable. On *Titanic*, however, no-one needed to stew in their own dirt,
for there were showers and baths. Steerage had been a massacre of
privacies: in third-class it was possible to preserve self-respect. One
room no longer had to serve as ladies' room, dining room, children's

playroom, smoking room. *Titanic*'s third-class general room was panelled in whitewashed pine, and furnished in teak with fixed sofas and movable chairs. There was also a smoking room and bar. The third-class dining saloon, lying amidships, consisted of two interconnecting saloons, extending from one side of the ship to the other, with an airy, capacious look and comfortable, sturdy furniture.

Some third-class passengers found the throbbing of the engines and pulse of the ship were soothing, but others – Neshan Krekorian from Armenia, for example – felt confined and restive beneath decks. Lillian Asplund remembered disliking the smell of fresh paint. Overall, though, *Titanic* represented the highest third-class standards reached before 1914. *Aquitania* carried twice as many third-class passengers in more confined space.

Four hundred and ninety-seven third-class passengers embarked at Southampton, 102 third-class passengers embarked at Cherbourg, and 113 third-class passengers embarked at Queenstown. They amounted to 712 passengers (70 per cent of capacity: another indication that there were too many competing Atlantic liners with duplicated facilities). Reliable estimates are 118 British third-class passengers, 113 Irish, 104 Swedes, 79 Lebanese, 55 Finns, 43 Americans, 33 Bulgarians, 25 Norwegians, 22 Belgians, 12 Armenians, 8 Chinese, 7 Danes, 5 Frenchmen, 4 Italians, 4 Greeks, 4 Germans, 4 Swiss, and 3 Portuguese. The estimate of forty-four Austro-Hungarians includes about twenty Croatians. The figure of eighteen Russians includes people from Poland and the Baltic states, but excludes Finns, who were also subject to Czarist autocracy. Over sixty Finns had steamed from Hanko, a little port on the southerly tip of Finland, across the Baltic and North seas to Hull, from whence they entrained for Southampton. About fifty-five of these were third-class passengers: many had bookings for other liners, but the coal shortage forced their transfer to *Titanic*, which, as a maiden voyage ship, had a commanding priority for coal supplies. At Cherbourg the embarking third-class passengers were mainly Christians from Armenia and the Lebanon seeking to escape Turkish-Muslim persecution and privation. The Turkish authorities created many obstacles for voyaging

Armenians, who had the choice of leaving by the Black Sea ports of Trebizond and Batoum. Trebizond was nearer to Armenia, but under Turk control; Batoum was over the Russian border, but it was easier to evade controls there. Either way, baksheesh had to be paid. Armenians then crossed to Bulgaria, and made their way via Marseille to Cherbourg, and thence to New York. The Lebanese difficulties in leaving Syria via Beirut were formidable, too.

The largest category of foreigners in third-class, outnumbering the British, was Scandinavians. There were few voyagers from *Mitteleuropa* (the exceptions included the four labourers from Batic in Bosnia: Kerim Balkic, Redjo Delalic, Tido Kekic and Husein Sivic, seeking work in the Bethlehem Steel plant at Harrisburg, Pennsylvania). White Star discouraged Eastern Europeans from their Southampton service, just as Cunard diverted their embarkation from Liverpool to Fiume, because it was believed that 'their untidiness, rudeness, and other marks of semi-civilization' made them objectionable travelling companions.[1] Arthur Rostron noted that when he was Chief Officer on *Pannonia*, a Cunarder running Italian, Croat, Hungarian, Austrian, Greek, Bulgarian and Romanian emigrants from Trieste to New York, most passengers were of 'pathetic docility', but a few wild men needed watching. 'Hot tempers sometimes flared out and words would lead to the flash of a knife and an oozing wound. We had to treat these offenders with severity. That usually consisted of making them spend the night down the forepeak where, with rats for company, to the accompaniment of the pounding seas against the hull, added to the fact that it was pitch-black, they soon saw the reasonableness of better behaviour.'[2]

The segregation of *Mitteleuropeans* – Czechs, Slovaks and Poles, or 'Hunkies' as they were contemptuously called – was generally applauded. 'There is a great improvement in the class of persons who travel third-class,' a publicist of the floating hotels averred in 1913. 'Most British lines will not carry emigrants from Central Europe because of their dirty habits. This may seem unkind, but if you were to see the disgusting condition of some men and women who come from that part of the Continent, you would not wonder at the restriction.'[3] Conditions were degrading on those steamships that would carry them, as an investigator for the US Immigration Commission, disguised as a Czech peasant, had lately discovered. She reported that only low partitions separated the two-tier iron berths, with straw mattresses but no pillows. The wooden decks were neither washed nor disinfected during twelve days, although sand was lightly scattered to cover vomit. Washrooms were used by both sexes. There were no soap or towels, and the tap water was cold and salty. Women's lavatories were arranged over an open trough. They were filthy for much of the voyage, but were cleaned and disinfected shortly before American inspection. Doubtless it was felt that no better was needed for voyagers coming from hovels that were inferior to a hunting millionaire's kennels, from villages of filthy mud, churned by hoofs and wheels, defiled by horses and cows (though it is worth recalling that until 1915 there were few paved streets in Los Angeles, where streetcars bore a sign forbidding the shooting of rabbits from the platform). The open deck was cluttered with machinery, bespattered with cinders from the funnel, and a swagger-ground for the crew, who subjected passengers to oaths, insults, and crude gestures.[4]

Titanic third-class passengers included farmers, farm labourers, foresters and farriers; miners, machinists and print-compositors; engineers, stone masons, bricklayers, plumbers, carpenters, a miller's lad, potters, tinsmiths, locksmiths, blacksmiths, wire makers, a fur cutter, a leather worker, a picture framer, boxers, chemists, jewellers, bakers, tailors, dressmakers, servants, shop salesmen, door-to-door pedlars, seamstresses, a laundress, cooks, barmen, grooms, waiters.

Some of these people, notably the servants and farm workers, had never before had a week's uninterrupted holiday. Third-class amenities endowed many passengers with an unprecedented emancipation from their hackneyed round of incessant toil: the voyage seemed like a succession of saint's festival days in which they had no burdensome task but every chance to enjoy themselves. There was skipping on deck, cards in the smoking room, singing and dancing in the evenings, gossiping in the lounges, flirting in the corridors. The lounge on

227

C Deck contained a piano, card tables and games tables. In the evenings, the musicians among them brought out their instruments, and played in the saloon. It is doubtful if there had ever been as many days free of work for Erna Andersson, a servant girl of seventeen from Kulla Bay, Strömfors, Finland, since she had embarked at Hanko on *Polaris* for Hull, and then travelled across England to Southampton. As Willa Cather noted at this time, Swedish farmers' daughters on the American prairies no longer lowered themselves by entering domestic service, so farmers' wives recruited girls from Sweden and paid their fares. It was doubtless similar with Finns. Girls stayed with the farm wives until they married, when they were replaced by sisters or cousins from the old country.[5]

The third-class dining saloon on F Deck could seat 394. It had chairs rather than benches; there were two bars on D Deck, and one on C Deck by the third-class smoking room. Its diners had to master the Esperanto of transatlantic food, which was often very different from their usual diet. For breakfast on the final Sunday, third-class passengers were offered Quaker Oats with milk, smoked herrings and jacket potatoes, boiled eggs, bread and butter, marmalade with Swedish bread, tea or coffee. For (the final) Sunday dinner there was served: vegetable soup, roast pork with sage and onions, green peas, boiled potatoes, cabin biscuits, bread, plum pudding with sweet sauce; and for tea, ragout of beef, potatoes and pickles, apricots, bread and butter, currant buns.

Many of *Titanic*'s third-class passengers had never seen an ocean-going vessel before. A German called Müller (about whom little is known) had signed on as a crewman at a monthly wage of £4 10s as the interpreter-steward charged with helping third-class passengers without common languages to communicate. He doubtless supported the stewards in driving third-class passengers to retire to their little white cabins, and perhaps go to bed, by ten in the evening.

The eight young Chinese firemen working for the Donaldson steamship line, who embarked as third-class passengers at Southampton, were old hands at ocean life. Other third-class voyagers were seasoned Atlantic travellers and familiar with American ways.

They were part of the steady traffic of sojourners who traversed the Atlantic, doubled back, and later returned. Forty-year-old Carl Asplund had divided his adult life between Alseda, Småland, and Worcester, Massachusetts, the birthplace of American barbed wire and of Valentine's Day cards. Thirty years earlier a Swede had opened a factory in Worcester to make grinding wheels, and had recruited hundreds of workers from his native district, Småland. More Swedes, Carl Asplund among them, had gone to work in Worcester's famous Washburn & Moen barbed wire factory: Swedes were preferred by employers there because unlike the Irish they did not get either fighting drunk or unionized. Asplund left the Swedish community in Worcester in 1907, after his father's death, to settle family affairs, but was returning to Worcester with his wife Selma Asplund and their five children: Filip aged thirteen, Gustaf aged nine, five-year-old twins Carl and Lillian, and Felix aged three. Only Selma, Lillian and Felix survived.

Franz Karun was another sojourner. He had been born near Milje, in the upper Carniola region of Slovenia evoked in Louis Adamic's immigrant memoir *Laughing in the Jungle*. He was married with five children, and had some earnings as a padrone in Galesburg, Illinois – the railroad town through which the Chicago, Burlington & Quincy and Atchison, Topeka & Santa Fé railroads both passed, which is so memorably anatomized in Carl Sandburg's *Always the Young Strangers*. Karun also ran a boarding house or hotel on Galesburg's Depot Street, where inmates were railway workers. He and his infant daughter Manca had returned to the old country, where he had sold some parcels of land said to be worth over $700. They boarded at Cherbourg in company with his brother-in-law, heading back to Galesburg. On the first anniversary of *Titanic* hitting the iceberg, his hotel collapsed, the walls of his bedroom falling into rubble around him; and this reverse, coupled with the loss at sea of his money from the Carniola land sales, forced him to return to Milje shortly afterwards.

Stephen Graham, as a third-class passenger on an Atlantic Cunarder, regarded some of his fellow English passengers as shady or dissolute. 'Some young fellow turns out to be wilder than the rest of his family; he won't settle down to the sober, righteous, and godly life that has been the destiny of others,' Graham surmised, 'so parents or friends give him his passage-money and . . . send him away across the sea.' There were young forgers or petty embezzlers, whose thefts had been discovered, for whom Atlantic crossings were merely new escapades. There were rovers with wanderlust, men who chafed at dull jobs, harum-scarum types, as well as prudent men who were persuaded to emigrate by plausible shipping company agents.[6]

Many voyagers were convinced to emigrate by relations rather than shipping agents. Frank Goldsmith was an aspiring, self-respecting Methodist, aged thirty-three, from Strood, across the River Medway from Rochester in Kent. He worked for Aveling & Porter, tractor and steam-roller manufacturers, as a machinist. Goldsmith was travelling with his wife Emily, and their small son Frankie, in response to urgings from his father-in-law, who had moved to Detroit, and thought they would make a success of life there. They needed a clean start, for their younger son had died of diphtheria in December 1911. Goldsmith was reluctant to put his family through the ordeal of travelling third-class, but the pre-launch publicity for *Titanic* had overcome his doubts. The Goldsmiths' luggage included a new set of tools, handmade as a parting gift by his mates in Strood, including callipers and scribing blocks used in tool-making. Emily Goldsmith packed her Singer sewing machine in a packing case, and her son, who had recently swopped his whipping-top for a cap pistol, dropped the toy beside the sewing machine.

For months the nine-year-old had been elated about going to America, a land which he had been imagining from years of letters sent by an aunt in Michigan. His mother bought Eno's Fruit Salts and Gibson's Fruit Tablets as preventives of seasickness. Though the boy was not unwell on the trip, he guzzled the delicious patent remedies. It was thrilling on board. 'Not only were we going to America, we were going to another land, France! Then bonus wise, we would also be going to Ireland next, two "fairytale" places that tripled the joy in the eyes of a nine-year-old boy.' On the afternoon of their second day at sea, he stood with his mother near the stern rail, watching Ireland recede from view: 'with a thumping heart I cried, "Mummy! At last we are on the 'lantic".'[7]

In Detroit, Emily Goldsmith's father had an English neighbour who, hearing that the Goldsmiths were coming out, sent the cost of the fare to his kid brother Alfred Rush and arranged for him to travel with them. The party also included Thomas Theobald, a friend from Strood. Sunday 15 April was Alfred Rush's sixteenth birthday, which he celebrated by donning his first pair of long trousers. To his delight, he was refunded sixpence by the purser who had overcharged for his baggage. 'Look, Mrs Goldsmith! I've got a birthday present!' he exclaimed in delight. Rush was small for his age, and might have passed for a child when the lifeboats were being filled. Instead, proud of his birthday, he declared, 'I am staying here with the MEN!' and hung back with Mr Goldsmith.[8]

John and Annie Sage were travelling with their nine children to Jacksonville, Florida, where he had paid a deposit on a citrus farm. He had been born in Hackney in 1867: his early work as a corn grinder and barman had led him to become a pub landlord in Norfolk and the proprietor of a baker's shop in Peterborough. Then he had gone with his eldest son to Canada, where they are said to have worked as dining-car attendants on Charles Hays' Canadian Pacific Railway; and was returning to America with his extensive family to begin a new life. Similarly, Frederick Goodwin was a forty-year-old electrical engineer from Fulham, whose brother had previously settled at Niagara Falls, and encouraged him to obtain a job at the power station there. Goodwin booked a third-class passage for the entire family – his wife Augusta and their six children – on a cheap steamer out of Southampton; but its sailing was cancelled because of the coal strike, and they were transferred to *Titanic*. All eleven of the Sages and all eight of the Goodwins perished at sea. Bertram Dean, a twenty-five-year-old London publican, was moving to Wichita, Kansas, where he had relations who had written encouragingly of the life there. He intended to open a tobacconist's shop. He was travelling with his wife, their two-year-old son, and two-month-old daughter called Millvina:

she had been born in February, was the youngest passenger on board, the smallest of the babies with their hunger, squalls and smells; and when she died in 2009 was the last survivor of *Titanic*. The Deans, too, had transferred to the maiden voyage because of the coal strike.

The Sages, Goodwins and Deans were making their first Atlantic crossings, but another large family party were Swedish sojourners: William Skoog, aged forty, a mining labourer from Hällekis, Västergötland, had lived for some years with his wife Anna at Iron Mountain, Michigan, where he laboured in the Pewabic mine. They left Iron Mountain in 1911, but soon regretted their decision, and reached *Titanic* via Stockholm, Gothenburg and Hull with their four small children. The Skoogs were related to two young women who had long debated going to America together, but hesitated until they seized the chance of accompanying the Skoogs to Iron Mountain. Both they and all six of the Skoogs perished: large, adhesive families, who would not be separated, had no chance of entering a lifeboat together.

A few third-class passengers acted as couriers for inexperienced groups of immigrants. Olaus ('Ole') Abelseth, aged twenty-five, from Ørskog, a Norwegian fishing village east of Ålsund, had first gone to America at the age of sixteen or seventeen and had worked as a farm labourer at Hatton, North Dakota, an agricultural community on the Red River flowing towards Lake Winnipeg. He then started his own livestock farm in Perkins County, South Dakota: a remote, backward area where the little townships had names like Antelope, Bison, Horse Creek, Lone Tree, Rainbow and White Butte. Abelseth had revisited Norway in the winter of 1911–12, and was leading a group from Ålsund to Bergen, Newcastle and Southampton comprising his cousin Karen Abelseth, aged sixteen, also from Ørskog, another cousin, Peter Søholt, together with his brother-in-law Sigurd Moen (a carpenter-joiner of twenty-five from Bergen), Anna Salkjelsvik (twenty-one, from Skodje, near Ålsund, heading for Proctor, Minnesota), and Adolf Humblen (forty-two, a farmer from Ålsund).

Another guide to a Swedish travelling party was Oskar Hedman, who originated from Umva, and had emigrated to the US at the age of twenty-one in 1905. Initially, he worked at a hotel in Bowman, North Dakota, and as a motor-car driver for local businesses in Bowman, and saved enough money to buy land outside the town. By 1912 he was working for a realtor (based in St Paul Minnesota) recruiting immigrants and chaperoning them on their journeys from Scandinavia. On *Titanic* he was accompanying a group of about seventeen Swedes, few of whom had more than a few words of English. One of those who could speak English in Hedman's group was Edvard Larsson-Ronsberg, a cook in the logging town of Missoula, Montana. Aged twenty-two, a farmer's son from Ransbysäter, Lysvik, Värmland, he had returned to collect his fiancée, Berta Nilsson, aged eighteen, from Ransbysäter.

Several Lebanese women were returning to America after visiting their home villages: Mary Abrahim, or Abraham, aged eighteen, of Greensburg, Pennsylvania, had been to see her parents; and Catherine Joseph, whose husband pushed a pedlar's cart collecting scrap iron and junk in Detroit, had taken their two children to visit the old country. Most is known about a thirty-eight-year-old Lebanese originally called Shawnee or Shawneene Abi Saab. She had married George Whabee, but they used the surname of George after moving to the US, where she adopted the nickname Jenny when consorting with Americans. The couple had hoped to amass enough money to buy land in Lebanon, but he died in 1908. She went door-to-door doing laundry and housework with her rough, capable hands, and brought over her three sons and two daughters to live with her at Youngstown, Ohio. Her teenage son Thomas became dangerously ill in 1910, was recommended mountain air, and helped back to the Lebanon by another son. She rushed to the Lebanon in 1911 when his condition deteriorated, but arrived after the funeral. For several months she grieved in Lebanon before embarking at Cherbourg on a 4-guinea ticket. It was as a bereft mother that she was returning to America, where her future work lay in a steel mill in Sharon, Pennsylvania and later in an ice-cream cone factory started by her children.

Other wives were bringing out their children to join husbands

who were already settled in the United States. The Lebanese Latifa
Baclini, aged twenty-three, was joining her husband in New York
together with her three daughters, aged five, three and nine months:
she was also chaperoning a fifteen-year-old girl on her way to New
York to marry. Alma Pålsson, aged twenty-nine, was wife of Nils
Pålsson, originally a miner at Gruvan, Skåne, Sweden. After a mining
strike had disillusioned him with life in Sweden, he had gone in
1910 to Chicago, where he worked as a tram conductor and saved
money to bring over his family. Two of Alma Pålsson's brothers
worked there too. She was travelling with two sons aged six and
two, and two daughters aged eight and three, to join her husband.
Her body was recovered wearing a brown skirt with a green cardigan
and boots but no stockings, for she had dressed in frightened haste.
Her effects included 65 kroner and a mouth organ.

A glimpse of third-class shipboard life is provided by that mouth
organ. A good number of passengers wandered the decks with accor-
dions, mouth organs, even fiddles in their hands or pockets. The
sound of cheerful, amateurish music was often heard in third-class
corridors or decks. After crossing from New York to Southampton
after the war, scrutinizing every move and attitude of his fellow first-
class passengers, Sinclair Lewis depicted an old man, taking the sea
air on the promenade deck, 'commenting on the inferiority of the
steerage passengers who, on the deck below, altogether innocent of
being condescendingly observed by the gentry-by-right-of-passage-
money, jigged beside a tarpaulin-covered hatch to the pumping music
of an accordion'.[9]

Arnold Bennett, crossing the Atlantic in 1911, found the starboard
deck crowded with third-class passengers after breakfast. It was a
playground studded with 'entrances to paradises forbidden to them'.
He noticed a 'natural brazenness' about some young women, 'girls
who would not give and take to me in passing'.[10] The deck was
certainly a playground for carefree gangs of boys. Frankie Goldsmith,
then aged nine, explored the ship with half a dozen other boys,
improvised games on deck, clambering over bollards and ventilators.
After leaving Ireland, the children chose Goldsmith to try a trick.

He climbed a baggage crane, clutched the cable under its arm, and then hoisted himself hand over hand to the end of the arm, before dropping down onto the deck. The cable proved to be coated with grease to protect it from corrosion, and a gaggle of nearby sailors roared with laughter as he struggled to keep hold of the cable. His mother subjected him to robust scrubbing before she was satisfied that he was clean.

Stephen Graham's estimate of the third-class Englishwomen was mixed: 'There are the women who are going out to their sweethearts to be married, and the wives who are going to the husbands who have "made good"; there are the girls who have got into trouble at home and have slid away to America to hide their shame; there are girls going to be domestic servants and girls doomed to walk the streets.'[11] There were also wives whose marriages had collapsed. Margaret Ford was a Scotswoman of forty-eight whose husband had left her after the birth of their fifth child in 1904. She reared chickens to keep her family: the two eldest daughters became domestic servants, her son of eighteen was a blacksmith, and her boy of sixteen was a messenger. The eldest daughter was working in a household on Long Island, and Margaret Ford had decided to join her in America. She travelled with her four children, a servant girl whom her daughter knew, her sister-in-law and the latter's husband, a Scottish-born plumber from Croydon, with their son of eight and daughter of seven. All ten of Margaret Ford's party died.

Rhoda Abbott was another mother making her way in life after the collapse of her marriage. She had been brought up in the southern English market towns of Aylesbury and St Albans. She had left for Providence, Rhode Island, in 1893, and two years later married a middleweight boxing champion, Stanton Abbott. They had two sons, Rossmore, born in 1896, and Eugene, born in 1899; but she had separated from her husband by 1911, when she and her two sons had crossed on *Olympic* to test life in St Albans with her widowed mother. There she supported herself by sewing or as a seamstress, while Rossmore Abbott is said to have worked as a boot maker or for a jeweller, and Eugene attended Priory Park School. After six months in St Albans, the two American boys were homesick, and Rhoda Abbott determined to return to Rhode Island. After buying three tickets, the Abbotts were transferred to *Titanic* because of the coal strike. It is believed that she and her sons – by then aged sixteen and thirteen – were Salvation Army workers. Once embarked, she befriended Amy Stanley, Emily Goldsmith and May Howard, who all had cabins near her. Her sons roamed the ship, and doubtless gorged themselves like hungry boys at meal times when confronted by a breakfast menu of oatmeal porridge with milk; liver and bacon, Irish stew, bread and butter, marmalade with Swedish bread, tea or coffee followed by a main meal of vegetable soup, boiled mutton with capers, green peas, boiled potatoes, cabin biscuits, plum pudding.

Few third-class steerage were negligent of their clothes, though none, of course, dressed like Lady Duff Gordon's mannequins. Bridget McDermott from Addergoole in Ireland had lately been into the market town of Crossmolina to buy clothes for her journey, and others no doubt had spent money to look their best. The Croatian labourer Josip Drazenovic wore a striped green-grey suit, brown striped shirt, black boots – carrying his pipe and a set of rosary beads. His fellow Croatian Ignjac Hendekovic wore a white shirt with an embroidered front above his blue striped trousers and leather sandals. We know about the clothes only of those whose possessions were methodically noted when their bodies were recovered from the ocean. The inventory makes poignant reading. A Jewish Russian, Sinai Kantor, carried a pocket telescope in his grey and green suit. Mansour Hanna from the Lebanon had dressed in a hurry, and went into the freezing water wearing only grey flannel drawers and singlet, clutching amber beads. Sixteen-year-old Rossmore Abbott wore whatever he could swiftly lay his hands on: grey trousers, green cardigan, blue jersey, black boots, and a brown overcoat containing an empty wallet and two little knives. Mary Mangan from Addergoole dressed methodically in black skirt, blouse, coat and boots, with a red cardigan and green waterproof, and all her treasures – rosary beads, medallion, gold bracelet, locket, watch and brooch, and her diamond solitaire ring. Will Sage, aged fourteen, was found in grey knickerbockers. Shortly before his death, Sidney Goodwin, aged nineteen months, had been lovingly coddled in a grey coat with fur on its collar and cuffs, a brown serge frock, petticoat, a pink woollen singlet, brown booties and stockings. These are the clothes of the poor and striving. One unidentified corpse is described thus: 'four feet, six inches, about fourteen-years old, golden brown hair, very dark skin, refined features. Lace-trimmed red-and-black overdress, black underdress, green striped undershirt, black woollen shawl and felt slippers. Probably third-class.'[12]

As with the voyagers from Cornwall and Guernsey in the second-class cabins, there were clusters of third-class passengers from the same vicinities – ill-starred as their destinies proved. There were twenty passengers from the village of Hardin in Lebanon, and another twelve from Kfar Mishki; fourteen passengers from Addergoole in Ireland; eight passengers from Gumoshtnik in Bulgaria; and others from Keghi in Armenia.

Hardin was an isolated upland village, reached by a single road, inland from the coastal town of Batroun. It stood 1,110 metres above sea level surrounded by thick woodland, mountainside terraces and bleak snowy cliffs containing caverns, on a high rock platform. There was a temple to the god Mercury, supposedly erected in the time of the Emperor Hadrian, and a ruined medieval Christian chapel. Hardin's inhabitants were persecuted Maronite Christians, who began leaving for the USA – many of them to Wilkes-Barre, Pennsylvania. Often they were sojourners, intending to spend years in the *Mahjar*, or host society, but intent on returning periodically, and perhaps permanently, when they were old, to their homeland, *al-watan*.

A few years earlier Gertrude Bell had travelled south of Hardin to visit the ruins at Balbec. There she lodged with a woman named Kurunfuleh – meaning 'Carnation Flower' – whose husband was 'seeking his fortune in America', where she wished to join him. Bell spent several hours talking with her, her son and daughter, and friendly relations who called to play their lutes. The Islamic majority of the Balbec population, called the Metāwileh, were renowned for 'fanaticism and ignorance', Bell reported: when they heard of the Japanese victories over Russia in the war of 1905, they shook their fists at their Christian neighbours, saying, 'The Christians are suffering defeat! See, now, we too will shortly drive you out and seize your goods.' Bell asked why she did not return to her own village, where she would be protected. 'Oh lady,' Kurunfuleh replied, 'I could not endure it. There no-one has any business but to watch his neighbour, and if you put on a new skirt the village will whisper together and mock at you.' Life pinched so tightly in the Lebanon, Bell reported, that all upland Christians who could scrape together their passage money were leaving for the United States: 'it is next to impossible to find labour to cultivate the corn, the mulberry and the vine . . . The Lebanon province is a cul de sac, without a port of its own and without commerce.'[13]

Almost all of the twenty voyagers from Hardin were heading for Wilkes-Barre, encircled by collieries producing anthracite coal, and misleadingly nicknamed 'Diamond City'. We know their names, but little more of them. All embarked at Cherbourg, having travelled via Beirut and Marseille: almost all, except for the shoemaker Gerios Youssef heading for Youngstown, were listed as farm hands or labourers. Borak Hannah, aged twenty-seven (also known as Hannah Assi Borah), was a farm labourer with relations in Wilkes-Barre, but was heading for the home of a man named Hassey in Port Huron, Michigan. A few months later, in July, he married the man's daughter, became a factory worker, then ran fruit stores in Marlette and Port Huron, and ended his days as a tavern keeper in Port Huron.

From Kfar Mishki – a Christian settlement in Lebanon's lower Bekaa valley – came a dozen third-class voyagers mostly aiming at Ottawa. Boulos Hanna, an eighteen-year-old labourer, seeking work in the steel mills of Youngstown, was an exception. Mariona Assaf, aged forty-five, who had gone to work in Ottawa some five years earlier, first as a pedlar and then as a greengrocer, had returned to Kfar Mishki to see the two sons she had left behind. She was now heading back from the Lebanon, via Cherbourg, to Ottawa with a young cousin and nephew. The travellers from Kfar Mishki spent three days on horseback to reach Beirut, with some of their kin walking with them for the first hours: not for them the railway journey between Beirut and the uplands. 'There is no sense of any man having a private right in his own affairs,' reported an English clergyman who had lately made the trip and found many of his fellow travellers could speak in broken French. 'The gentleman on your left is a merchant, and before he has done with you, he will have ascertained the exact price you paid for your Kodak, your aneroid, watch, chain, hat and boots. The elderly and somewhat raw-boned person opposite, on whom his black velvet vest with great buttons sits badly, is consumed with the desire to know your name, and your friend's name, and your country, and your religion . . . he volunteers the one fact – certainly a remarkable one – that he has himself been in Manchester, and found it "*très joli*".'[14]

The Metāwileh who celebrated Japan's victory at Port Arthur, the Kodak in the Bekaa valley, the nosey old Syrian who enjoyed the bright lights of Manchester – they are all evidence of the globalization of news and rumour, of gimcrack novelties and shallow curiosity that characterized the *Titanic* world of 1912. In broken language, with gestures and smiles and scowls, some at least of the third-class passengers will have explored common ground, shown off their knowledge, and asked questions. Friendly, suspicious, over-inquisitive, muddled: they were on the way to becoming Americans.

Addergoole lies above the shores of Lough Conn – the Lake of the Hound – and beneath the bleak slopes of Nephin Mór in County Mayo. Mayo is a county in the west of Ireland, its wild shores hammered by Atlantic winds and rain, with few shelter belts of trees, although Addergoole lies on the protected inland side of Nephin Mór. The soil is as barren as the weather is bleak. Nearby at Erris is the largest bog in Ireland. Potatoes were the chief crop: pigs, sheep, cattle and poultry were the other staples of Mayo's subsistence farming. There had been turbulent relations between Protestant landlords and Catholic tenants in the recent past: Addergoole was not far from the localities where Lord Leitrim, Lord Mountmorres and the bailiff of Lord Ardilaun had been assassinated. White Star's local agent, Thomas Durcan of Castlebar, one of a family known as the Fighting Durcans, had sold tickets to ten of the fourteen Addergoole voyagers.

Every place name in Ireland sounds like a tune, Marianne Moore thought. The hamlets and farms dispersed about the parish of Addergoole – from which fourteen of the *Titanic* voyagers came – made a medley of tunes: Carrowskeheen, Cuilmullagh, Cuilnakillew, Cum, Derrymartin, Knockfarnaught, Terryduff, Tonacrick. From Cuilmallagh came Annie Kelly, who was going to join women cousins in Chicago and destined to become a nun in Adrian, Michigan. She was a cousin of two young men, James Flynn, from Cuilnakillew, who was joining his brother in New York, and of Pat Canavan, from Knockmaria, who was heading for Philadelphia.

A fortnight later, a Chicago journalist spoke to Annie Kelly and Annie McGowan, the sole survivors of the Addergoole voyagers. Several of the party were 'Yanks', 'Irish lads and lassies who have been to America and come back to Ireland for a look at the old place and the blessing of the old father and mother, before they go back to America to stay for good and all.' The Yanks included Kate Bourke, formerly M'Hugh, and Kate McGowan, who had both left Mayo for Chicago when they were young girls. Kate M'Hugh had returned to Addergoole, where she married John Bourke, who had never thought of going to America. However, when her old Yank friend Kate McGowan came for a short visit to Terryduff, her family's corner of Addergoole, the Bourkes decided to sell his farm at Carrowskeheen and accompany her back to Chicago. The Bourkes were accompanied by his sister Mary: also travelling with them were Honora ('Nora') Fleming, in her early twenties, and Mary Mangan, who had lived for some years with a sister in the States and, having got engaged to an Irishman there, had returned for a visit to Ireland before her marriage. The Bourkes' friend, Kate McGowan, left Terryduff for the last time with her young teenage niece Annie McGowan, who had relations already settled at Scranton, New Jersey. On board *Titanic*, John and Kate Bourke 'sat apart most of the day by themselves, talking and talking. There was no end of their talking about . . . what he would do in America with all the money he was taking with him from selling the farm. He was for taking a long time what to do with it, but Kate would be always telling him that America was not Ireland, and that a man must decide quickly what to do, for money would run just as fast away from you in America as toward you, if a man was not looking out.' John Bourke thought of buying horses, and becoming a teamster. For the rest of the Addergoole voyagers the voyage was like a picnic outing. 'The fun they had coming out, the games and quadrilles, the story-telling and the fortune-telling! It was grand.' There were Addergoole girls going to America for the first time: from Cum, Bridget Donahue, aged twenty-one; from Derrymartin, Delia Mahon, aged twenty; from Knockfarnaught, Bridget Delia McDermott, who was heading for cousins in St Louis, Missouri; and another cousin of Annie Kelly's, Mary Canavan, aged twenty-two, from Tonacrick. 'The young girls would talk about what they would do in America before they were married. That is, they would talk about it when they were not scurrying around the deck laughing and making friends here and there with everybody, and it's a God's mercy that Annie Kelly did joke with one of the stewards and he take notice of the girl, or she would not have been alive this moment.'[15]

Addergoole with its boggy fields, wide lake and wet winds was very different from the terrain of ravines and echoing gorges where the luckless Bulgarians originated. Gumoshtnik was a small, huddled village, reached by one road and several mountain tracks, five miles from Troyan, a small town standing on a mountain torrent, the Balabanska. It was different, too, from the boom-towns, clanging with streetcars and ear-splitting factory whistles, crowded with grim and angry industrial workers, where they were heading. A party of eight voyagers from Gumoshtnik boarded at Southampton. They were all labourers or potters: Marin Markov and Peju Colchev in their mid-thirties were the oldest; at nineteen, Nedialco Petrov and Ilia Stoytchev were the youngest. As backwoodsmen, some perhaps wore the *kalpak*, a lambskin cap; wide breeches (*poturi*); red sash (*poyas*); shoes with long laces (*opinak*). Revealingly, the Bulgarian word *patilo*, meaning 'misfortune', was also a synonym for *experience*. 'All classes practice thrift bordering on parsimony and resent any display of wealth,' reported an English visitor. 'The peasants are industrious, provident, peaceable, and orderly; they are high-spirited without being bad-tempered, the vendetta and the use of the knife in quarrels being unknown.'[16]

The spaciousness of *Titanic* may have seemed wondrous or disorientating to the party of Armenians who embarked at Cherbourg. Many of them, such as Ortin and Mapriedereder Zakarian, were hardy men in their early twenties from the Keghi district, with its soaring mountains and sweeping gorges, a region of danger and violence, where small farmers eked out a bare existence while fending off Kurdish brigands, avaricious semi-feudal Moslem landowners and extortionate Turkish officials. Previously the voyagers from Keghi had only known traditional households (*tuns*) where father, mother, bachelor and married sons with their families, unmarried daughters, single or elderly relations lived together. Each *tun* was attached to or above a stable. Its occupants lived in one room, in which they ate, sat, and slept, rolling out their mattresses at night around the fireplace. Fifteen people might live in a space that was 12 feet by 25. Some households had a cubby hole with a brick-lined cone-shaped bread oven dug into the floor. Usually kin lived in labyrinthine warrens of buildings in which they could hide with their valuables during attacks (there was a history of extortion, pillage, rape and abduction, forced conversions to Islam, forced quartering of unruly troops, land confiscation). For the Keghetsis, *Titanic*, with its public corridors, communal rooms, private sleeping cabins, invisible kitchens, must have been eye-opening: seeming more opulent, even, than the houses of the *beys* (Turkish feudal chiefs) who extorted and oppressed them.[17]

The influx of Armenians into America served as a thermometer measuring their misfortunes under Turkish rule. In 1909, 30,000 Armenians had been massacred, and in 1911–12 the ultra-nationalists among the Young Turks who had deposed the Sultan were promulgating a ruthless campaign of Turkification of Armenians. Young men left in droves: the Keghetsi on *Titanic* were all in their twenties; all but one was married, for parents customarily arranged for their sons to marry before departing abroad, as a way of ensuring that they would one day return. Few survived to leave accounts of their thoughts and activities, and the survivors have left only exiguous hints, but we know that for Armenians going to the United States (9,350 arrived in 1912 alone), New York, Illinois and Michigan were the chief destination states.[18] Some 2,000 Armenians entered Canada in the quarter century before 1914, primarily settling in the industrial towns of southern Ontario, Brantford and Hamilton. The Keghetsis Neshan Krikorian, David Vartanian and Orsen Sirayanian were all heading for Hamilton, and Sarkis Mardirosian for Brantford. Neshan Krekorian gave both Hamilton and Brantford as his destination, and ended up in St Catherine's, Ontario, working on a General Motors automobile assembly line. Several Armenians gave a Brantford factory address: the Cockshutt Plow Works or the Pratt & Letchworth Malleable Iron foundry – the 'Mybil' Armenians called it – rather than a private residence as their destination on their embarkation papers. Others gave the name and address in Hamilton of John Bertram, the demotic name of the Canada Tool Works.[19] David Vartanian, aged twenty-two when he embarked at Cherbourg, had left his new bride behind – probably as a token to his parents that he would return. She survived the horrors of 1915, when 1.5 million Armenians were massacred in the first genocide of the twentieth century, but it was over a decade before (after frightening difficulties and formidable planning) the couple were reunited, and had a grateful, fulfilled life together in Meadeville, Pennyslvania and Detroit.

Other third-class voyagers were on *Titanic* for political reasons. August Wennerström, aged twenty-seven, a socialist and a typesetter from Malmö, had earlier been prosecuted for insulting King Oscar II of Sweden. After his acquittal, he decided to shift to the USA with a fellow socialist, Carl Jansson, aged twenty-one, a handsome, strapping, blond carpenter from Örebo. Jansson and Wennerström evaded the formalities required by the Swedish government by going to Denmark, acquiring tickets and documentation in Copenhagen, and leaving from Esbjerg, Denmark's new North Sea port on the coast of Jutland, on a Wilson line steamship to Hull, and proceeding by train to Southampton. (Jansson was destined to become a carpenter in Wahoo, Nebraska; Wennerström became a gardener in Culver, Indiana.) They shared their cabin with Gunnar Tenglin, aged twenty-five, who had left Stockholm for the USA around 1903, aged about sixteen, and settled at Burlington, Iowa, where he learnt English while toiling as a labourer. He had promised his mother to return to Sweden after five years, and did so in 1908. He married in Sweden and fathered a son, but in 1912 he resolved to return to Burlington, bought tickets in Copenhagen, and made the journey from Esbjerg to Hull, and thence to Southampton. His future jobs in Burlington were in the local gas works and railway yard.

Most Jewish third-class passengers who embarked on *Titanic* at Southampton originated from the Pale of Settlement in Eastern Europe where conditions were hostile if not murderous. David Livshin was travelling under the name of Abraham Harmer, possibly the name of someone who had sold him an unwanted ticket. Livshin, who was twenty-five years old, had originated in an ill-destined sea port in Latvia which was variously known as Libau, Libava and Liepāja. This ice-free Baltic harbour had fallen under Russian dominion after the last partition of Poland. A fortress and coastal defences against German attack had been erected, a military base and naval installation had been built in the early twentieth century, and a port for seaplanes in 1912. The port was served by a good railway line: by 1906 an estimated 40,000 emigrants left Russia each year for the US with Liepāja as their port of embarkation. It was a place with a terrible past and a worse future. Stalin inflicted two mass deportations from the city, and in 1941 all but thirty of the 7,000 Jews remaining there were massacred in nearby sand dunes by German troops. We know a little of Livshin's personal history: he had come to England in 1911, had worked in Manchester as a jeweller and had married there a young woman from Lithuania who made *sheitels* (the Yiddish word for the wigs worn by orthodox Jewish women to cover their hair according to religious law). She was now pregnant. We know nothing of Livshin's life on board *Titanic*: he did not have a future.

Another Jewish passenger – they were all supplied with kosher food – was Eliezer ('Leslie') Gilinski, a locksmith aged twenty-two from Ignalina, a town in Lithuania which had been expanding since a station on the Warsaw–St Petersburg railway line was built there. Doubtless he had left Lithuania to avoid military service under the Russians, and racial prejudice. He had been staying with his brother, who was a shopkeeper at Abercynon, a mining village in the Rhondda valley, where there had been anti-Jewish riots during the previous summer; but moved on to try his luck in Chicago. He was remembered in the Rhondda as an amiable young man. Berk Trembisky had been born in Warsaw thirty-two years earlier; a leather worker and bag maker, he lived in France, where he assumed a Gallic surname, Picard, before briefly working in London. Leah Aks, who had been born in Warsaw about 1894, had left Poland for East London; there she married a tailor, and was travelling to join him in Norfolk, Virginia with their ten-month-old son Frank Philip Aks ('Filly'). Beila Moor, aged twenty-seven, a widowed Russian garment maker, was travelling with her son Meier, aged seven, who accosted passengers and with winning pertinacity asked for the cowboy and Indian picture cards that came with their cigarette packets.

Lebanese and Armenian Christians, Russian Jews, Swedish socialists – all were refugees seeking safety, liberty and prosperity in North America. They were, too, draft dodgers. Nikola Lulic, aged twenty-ninc, had been born in a Croatian village, but some ten years earlier had settled in Chisholm, Minnesota, a raw mining settlement in the Mesabai hills iron range – some years from being connected to the Duluth, Missabe & Northern Railway. Lulic worked in the Alpena iron mine, and lived in the so-called 'Balkan' district of Chisholm. In the autumn of 1911, Lulic returned to Croatia for a long visit to his wife and children, who had remained behind. It was settled that when he re-traversed the Atlantic he would act as unofficial companion to other emigrants who like him had got their tickets from the ubiquitous Swiss agent, Büchel (Lulic's cost 170 Swiss francs, equivalent to £8 13s 3d). Lulic interpreted for fellow Croatians, acted as their courier to Southampton, advised them on shipboard customs, doubtless coached his charges on their demeanour and replies when undergoing Ellis Island interrogation: if their hopes of work were too explicit they might be judged in violation of the contract labour ban; but if they were too indefinite, seeming to have no contacts or idea where to get jobs, they might be excluded as likely to become public charges. Lulic was a lifelong sojourner: in the 1920s he farmed a plot in Croatia, while often visiting France as a seasonal worker.

The destinations of the Croat farm workers being shepherded by Lulic were as varied as their starting points. Peter and Jovo Calik, twins aged seventeen, from Brezik, embarked at Southampton on tickets supplied by Büchel for Sault Ste Marie in Michigan; Ivan Stankovic, aged thirty-three, from Galgova, was going to New York City; Vagovina's Milan Karajic and Bratma's Stefan Turcin were docketed for Youngstown with its foundries and steelworks; Ludovic Cor from Kricina for St Louis, Missouri; Mirka Dika from Podgori for Vancouver; Jovan Dimic, from Ostrovca, was heading for the coal mines of Red Lodge, the county seat of Carbon County, Montana; Jeso Culumovic, aged seventeen, from Lipova Glavica, for Hammond, Indiana; Jakob Pasic, twenty-one, farmer, from Streklijevac, for the iron mines of Aurora, Minnesota, outside Duluth in the Mesabai range; and both the labourer Ivan Jalševic and the hotelier Franz Karun were journeying to Galesburg, Illinois. Many of them began their journey with an entrenched fear of slipping back into the abyss of poverty. 'My father,' wrote the son of another immigrant to Galesburg, 'had a fear of want, a dread in his blood and brain, that the "rainy day" might come and in fair weather he hadn't prepared for it.'[20] It was, on *Titanic*, the wrong fear.

TWELVE

Officers and Crew

Successive nights, like rolling waves,
Convey them quickly, who are bound for death.

George Herbert, 'Mortification'

Following trials in Belfast Lough, *Titanic* had steamed to Southampton with everyone on board at a high pitch of proud expectation. It took Herbert Lightoller, the Second Officer, a fortnight, and the Sixth Officer, James Moody, fresh from nautical school, a week to master the layout of decks and passages after joining at Belfast. Able Seaman William Lucas was still 'groping about' trying to find his way about the ship's stairwells and companionways on the night it sank.[1] Lucas and other seamen slipped ashore in Southampton for last drinks in a pub while Captain Maurice Clarke, the Board of Trade surveyor, tested the lowering of two lifeboats, and approved life-saving equipment, distress rockets, and much else. The lowering of two lifeboats, by trained seamen from a stationary ship in dock, subsequently seemed inadequate; but Lightoller stressed that Clarke, confronted with a new ship which was the biggest in the world, was extra-conscientious, and reinforced his reputation as the strictest of the Board of Trade's surveyors. 'He must see everything, and himself check every item that concerned the survey. He would not accept anyone's word as sufficient – and got heartily cursed in consequence.'[2]

Titanic surpassed *Olympic*, officers and crew agreed. 'She is an improvement on *Olympic* . . . and is a wonderful ship, the latest thing in shipbuilding,' Henry Wilde, who had been transferred from Chief

Officer of *Olympic* to the same post on *Titanic*, told his nieces in Liverpool.[3] 'This ship is going to be a good deal better than the *Olympic* at least I think so, steadier and everything,' a bedroom steward named Richard Geddes wrote during the first night at sea.[4] 'Bai jove what a fine ship this is,' declared the Captain's steward, 'much better than the *Olympic* as far as passengers are concerned, but my little room is nothing near so nice, no daylight, electric light on all day, but I suppose it's no use grumbling.'[5] A saloon steward carped about the serving of meals: 'we have to scramble for [it] like a lot of mad men but that won't last for long when things get straightened out,' he wrote after his first dinner at sea.[6]

The crew was considered as top notch as the ship's amenities. 'Having fitted out this magnificent vessel, the *Titanic*, we proceeded to man her with all that was best in the White Star organisation,' said Harold Sanderson, who had been general manager of Lord Nunburnholme's Wilson Line in Hull until recruited by Bruce Ismay to be his company's general manager in Liverpool.[7] Because *Olympic* was detained by the coal strike, Ismay and Sanderson determined that Wilde should serve on *Titanic*'s maiden voyage. William Murdoch was consequently demoted from Chief Officer to First Officer, and Lightoller from First Officer to Second on the day before sailing. This sudden reshuffling threw them both off their stride, and caused confusion. David Blair, who had been Second Officer on *Titanic*'s delivery voyage from Belfast, was assigned to another ship, while subordinate officers remained in their posts. Blair's departure had one inadvertent by-product. He took with him the key to the locker containing binoculars for the ship's look-outs to use when they were perched high in the crow's nest. Binoculars were therefore unavailable to the look-outs. Their utility in the conditions prevailing when the liner scraped the iceberg is arguable; but some commentators were indignant at their irretrievability.

The ship was under the command of Captain Edward Smith. Beneath him, there were seven deck officers. Crews of Atlantic liners were divided into three departments: Deck, Engine and Victualling (the latter was also called the Stewards' Department). The deck crew amounted to seventy-three, including the seven ship's officers, the surgeon for first-class passengers, an assistant surgeon for the rest, seven quartermasters, five look-outs, two mess stewards, two masters-of-arms, two carpenter-joiners, two window cleaners, a boatswain, a lamp trimmer, a storekeeper, plus twenty-nine able seamen.

There were 494 in the Stewards' Department, including one strong-minded, self-reliant matron, two Marconi operators and five postal clerks. There were 290 stewards and stewardesses as well as a window cleaner, linen-keeper, stenographer, masseuse, fish cook, assistant soup cook, iceman, bakers, plate washers, and nine 'Boots' to polish shoes. All 120 of the catering crew from the delivery voyage from Belfast signed on again at Southampton. Over 300 were added to their number at Southampton, so that the full complement on sailing was 431 – far more than the deck or engine crew; 231 individuals were classified as first-class victualling crew, seventy-six as second-class and 121 as third-class. The ship's musicians travelled as second-class passengers, and were not part of the Stewards' Department. Although the Marconi men, postal clerks and sixty-eight à la carte restaurant staff had signed the ship's articles, they were not White Star employees, but paid by the Marconi Company, the General Post Office and the Italian, Gaspare ('Luigi') Gatti, who held the catering contract.

Of the 892 crew, 699 had Southampton addresses. About 40 per cent of these were Hampshire men, but many had moved south when White Star transferred its operations from Liverpool in 1907 and originated from Merseyside. Over a hundred catering crew and nearly forty engineers had signed on in Belfast, and continued on the Atlantic voyage, although not all of them were from Ulster. A few crewmen were Londoners: Able Seaman Joseph Scarrott was the sort of cockney who used rhyming slang: his monthly wages of £5 he called 'bees and honey'. Most were simple patriots, like Quartermaster Bright who referred to England as 'Albion'; and some were bad husbands and fathers, like John Poingdestre, whose family in Southampton were faint with hunger when he embarked: the children were later put into care in Jersey, and his descendants repudiate his memory.

The stores needed by an Olympic-class floating hotel were reckoned at 75,000 pounds of fresh meat; 11,000 pounds of fresh fish; 8,000 head of poultry and game; 6,000 pounds of bacon and ham; 2,500 pounds of sausages; 35,000 eggs; 40 tons of potatoes; 7,000 heads of lettuce; 1¼ tons of peas; 2¾ tons of tomatoes; 10,000 pounds of sugar; 6,000 pounds of butter; 36,000 oranges; 16,000 lemons; 180 box of apples; 180 boxes of oranges; 1,000 pounds of grapes; 50 boxes of grapefruit; 800 bundles of asparagus; 3,500 onions; 1,500 gallons of milk; 1,750 quarts of ice cream; 2,200 pounds of coffee; 800 pounds of tea; 15,000 bottles of beer and stout; 1,500 bottles of wine; 850 bottles of spirit; 8,000 cigars. All these perishables were taken on board *Titanic* in the day or so before departure from Southampton. Officers worked night and day, receiving stores, allotting duties, testing instruments and contraptions, signing chits and certificates. Other indispensable items, which did not need to be fresh or refrigerated, had been loaded earlier in Belfast. Linen included 45,000 table napkins, 25,000 towels, 15,000 bed sheets and pillowcases, 7,500 bath towels, 6,000 tablecloths, 4,000 aprons. Crockery included 12,000 dinner plates, 4,500 soup plates, 3,000 tea cups, 3,000 beef tea cups, 1,500 coffee cups, 1,500 soufflé dishes, 1,000 cream jugs. Cutlery included 8,000 dinner forks, 1,500 fish forks, 1,000 oyster forks, 400 sugar tongs, 400 asparagus tongs, 300 nutcrackers, 100 grape scissors. There were 8,000 tumblers, 2,000 wine glasses, 1,500 champagne flutes, 1,200 small liqueur glasses or brandy balloons, and 300 claret jugs. Cleaning and maintenance equipment included 12 mops, 12 squeegees, 58 paint brushes and 72 brooms.

There is no king as great as a sea captain on his ship, Darwin said. Captain Edward Smith was absolute lord of these men, women and provisions. He had been born in 1850 in the Staffordshire pottery town of Hanley, and attended a Methodist school until at the age of twelve he went to work at the Etruria Forge. At eighteen he left for Liverpool, and enlisted on a clipper ship. His first command at the early age of twenty-six was a 1,000-ton three-master on the South America run. In 1888 he received his first White Star command as captain of *Baltic*. He captained a total of seventeen ships from *Baltic* to *Titanic*, and is estimated to have sailed 2 million miles for White Star. Latterly, he commanded their newest liners, and was commodore of their fleet. He had experienced gales and fogs, but had never been in an accident worth mentioning, he told a reporter in 1907 after *Adriatic*'s maiden voyage: 'I never saw a wreck, and I have never been wrecked, nor have I been in any predicament that threatened to end in disaster.'[8]

Smith was paid £1,250 a year, with a bonus of £1,000 if he brought his ships to port in good order. He had married in 1887, and fathered a daughter in 1902. On land, he enjoyed the comforting banality of an evening at home in his villa in Westwood Park, a Southampton suburb. With his sea-salt's beard and avuncular tubbiness, he looked solid, unflappable and reassuring. He had a reputation as a safe seaman, a hospitable hotelier and a good talker. Captains were often praised as raconteurs, for they had a fresh audience every week, and could vary their repertoire according to need. Smith kept to the rule that large men should be jolly and lovers of life. 'In the little tea parties in his private state room we learned to know the genial warm-hearted family man; his face would light as he recounted the little intimacies of his life ashore, as he told of his wife and the troubles she had with the dogs he loved, of his little girl and her delight with the presents he bought her,' recorded a first-class voyager who crossed the Atlantic with him on several ships. 'He read widely, but men more than books. He was a good listener . . . although he liked to get in a yarn himself now and again, but he had scant patience with bores or people who "gushed". I have seen him quell both.'[9]

Titanic was to be Smith's last post before retirement. When the ship left Southampton, with flags flying high, he might have fancied that the cheers of all the captains of the world were ringing in his ears. He belonged to the greatest seafaring nation ever known; he was captain of the greatest ship that ever sailed; and his last voyage was to be the apex of his career – the maiden voyage of *Titanic*. As the liner crossed from Southampton to Cherbourg, he conducted manoeuvres to test his ship, which performed well. Next day, *Titanic* steamed into the Atlantic from Queenstown on the extreme southern route for west-bound ships that was used by liners between mid-January and mid-August each year. With an average speed of 22 knots, it made 386 miles on 11 April, 519 on 12 April and 546 on 13 April. Smith continued to monitor the ship and its crew during the first two days of the voyage, and ate in his cabin until Friday evening. Smith spent much of Sunday on the bridge, although at 10.30 he led a Christian service lasting forty-five minutes in the first-class dining saloon. Officers and seamen liked to sail under Smith's command, and admired his seamanship. 'It was an education to see him con his own ship up through the intricate channels entering New York at full speed,' Lightoller recalled. 'One particularly bad corner, known as the South-West Spit, used to make us fairly flush with pride as he swung her round, judging his distances to a nicety; she heeling over to the helm with only a matter of feet to spare between each end of the ship and the banks.'[10]

White Star liners were supposed to hold a lifeboat drill each Sunday morning, but it was cancelled because of a robust breeze, which stopped blowing soon afterwards – the Sunday, overall, was unusually windless. English regulations did not require a lifeboat drill; and Charles Andrews, a nineteen-year-old assistant saloon steward from Liverpool who had been four years at sea, had been mustered only for boat drills in New York harbour, and on Sundays crossing back to Europe.[11] George Cavell, who had been a trimmer on White Star's *Adriatic*, *Oceanic* and *Olympic* before *Titanic*, testified that he had never been mustered for a lifeboat drill at sea: 'the only boat drill as I ever had' had been on Sunday mornings, in New York harbour, when there were no passengers about.[12]

If first-class on *Titanic* was a Waldorf-Astoria, and second-class a Lyons Corner House, the bunkers and furnaces where Cavell burned were an inferno. Few of the engine crew of firemen, greasers and trimmers who had delivered the ship from Belfast signed on again for the maiden voyage. The 280 men in *Titanic*'s Engine Department included 13 leading firemen, 162 firemen, 72 trimmers and 33 greasers (charged with cleaning and lubricating the moving parts of the engines). In 1911, Arnold Bennett was shown the innards of an Atlantic liner by the Chief Officer. He was taken up and down steel ladders, climbed over the moving chain of the steering gear, ducked past jets of steam, stepped along greasy floors beside ramparts of machinery guarded by steel rails, with pressure dials everywhere. There were 190 furnaces with roaring, red-hot jaws. The vast, terrible stokehold seemed to stretch for an infinite distance. It was like hell superimposed on a coal mine: upstairs, on higher decks, Bennett reflected, confectioners were making petits fours while first-class passengers soared in lifts.[13]

Firemen and trimmers on an Edwardian liner often came on board careening drunk. They went to work immediately, raising steam before the ship put to sea. Every day at sea, they laboured in two stints lasting four hours each. Coal was spaded from the bunkers into barrows, which were hurtled to the furnaces by trimmers running at full tilt. Gathering momentum, the trimmers dared not abate their pace, for their mates were running hard at their heels with more heavy barrows. This furious clattering convoy swerved through the ship as trimmers dodged the blistering steam pipes and furnace casings, especially when the liner rolled or pitched. Firemen in their way had to jump aside or be hurt. The leading firemen, known as 'pushers', had been promoted from the ranks of ordinary firemen. They monitored steam pressure, kept the coal at maximum heat, struck the stokehold floor with a shovel to signal when a furnace needed to be fired or stoked, and yelled at slackers among the firemen. The firemen spent seven minutes shovelling coal into the scorching furnaces, seven minutes clearing white-hot clinkers with long slicers, and another seven raking over the ashes. Every twenty-one minutes, after these three seven-minute bursts of work, the firemen rested and recuperated briefly until a gong signalled the beginning of another twenty-one minutes of strenuous exertion. This was the fireman's cycle of work for four hours on end, twice a day, for the duration of the voyage. They wore grey flannel singlets, which they would pull off to wring out when they were drenched in sweat, and then put back on. They also wrapped a sweat-rag around their neck, clenching its moist end between their teeth, to stop their urge to gulp water, which caused cramp and stomach ache. Little wonder that after this frenetic, dangerous, overheated work, they got drunk as soon as they went ashore, and often stayed sodden until they had to re-embark.[14]

'No men have ever had such hard and brutalizing work as the firemen and the trimmers in the big coal-burning steamers in the early years of the twentieth century,' wrote the Cunard officer James Bisset. 'I felt pity for them as I saw them coming off watch and trudging wearily to their quarters, utterly done in, sweat squelching in their boots. Their faces, blackened with coal dust, and streaked with sweat, had a dulled animal-like look, and they seldom smiled. It was killing work.'[15] Sixty-four firemen slept in one room lined by two-tier bunks, with just enough space for men to bend to tie their boot laces. Their sweating was so profuse that most of them were lean, and complained that they were underfed. A meal called 'oodle' was their preference: large joints of beef, with diced carrots and onions, were put in water-filled buckets, and simmered for hours until it could be ladled into plates for the twelve-to-four watch when they finished their night's toil. Few firemen or trimmers ate their midday meals, which were slopped down the swill shute. 'Men dared not risk a heavy meal prior to going down the stokehold to manoeuvre slice bars, wrestle molten clinkers out, inhale sulphur fumes and sweat non-stop,' recalled George Garrett, a fireman on *Mauretania*. 'The afternoon watch was relieved at 4 p.m. By the time all had queued their turn in the wash house, peeled off soaking clothes, swilled and tidied up, five o'clock was near. The ship's tea, hash, made them long for their "oodle" at 4 a.m. Those with pals in the four-to-eight room headed there at eight-thirty to bum some gubbins off the Black Pan. These black oblong trays placed on the floor were jumbled up with food remainders from the saloon tables. Chicken frames, scraps of meat, ham, chops, and assorted cakes, no longer presentable to passengers, were a colourful change from hash.'[16] No wonder that under such conditions there was a receptive audience on board ship for a so-called 'sea-lawyer', defined as a sailor combining 'a discontented disposition with a passion for grumbling, an uncanny knack of finding something to grumble at, the gift of the gab, and an elementary knowledge of a few of the legal points which may arise under the articles'.[17]

The crew of *Titanic* was overwhelmingly British. The chief exception was the restaurant staff, many of whom were Italian: White Star's great maiden voyage of 1912 was to provide a dark moment in the history of the Anglo-Italian community; over forty Italian restaurant staff perished. They had been recruited by Gatti, the à la carte restaurant manager, who ran two London restaurants named Gatti's in the Strand and nearby Adelphi, hard by White Star's Cockspur Street office. Gatti was the surname of the man who first imported ice from Norway to London, and thus established the Italian dominance in the English ice-cream trade. White Star's Luigi Gatti came from Montalto Pavese, south of Milan: after he had been awarded the catering contract for *Olympic* and *Titanic*, he took a house – which he named Montalto – in suburban Southampton for his family, and drew staff from his London restaurants to work on the liners. The original 'Little Italy' in England was centred on the Clerkenwell district of London, and comprised organ grinders and street-hawkers with braziers selling hot chestnuts, potatoes and peas and playing mouth organs to attract attention. In the 1890s a new Italian community – composed of people like Gatti from the northern provinces of Piedmont and Lombardy – settled in Soho. They became kitchen hands, porters, cooks and waiters in the hotels, restaurants and gentlemen's clubs of central London. It took many years' patience for an Italian boy of twelve or thirteen arriving in Edwardian London to rise from the back kitchens to serve in the salons and dining rooms; but the climb could be accomplished. Many good hotels preferred to employ Italians (although London was full of German waiters until 1914), and those like Gatti who climbed high in the hierarchy liked to employ compatriots.[18]

Although three of *Titanic*'s five postal clerks were American, few if any of the crew were. Americans were reputed to be unsatisfactory as liner stewards. 'Our boasted democracy,' Theodore Dreiser reflected after crossing the Atlantic in 1912, 'has resulted in little more than the privilege every living, breathing American has of being rude and brutal to every other, but it is not beyond possibility that sometime as a nation we will sober down into something approximating human civility.' When he travelled by Cunard to Liverpool, he appreciated the English stewards. 'They did not look at one so brutally and criti-cally as does the American menial; their eyes did not seem to say, "I am your equal or better", and their motions did not indicate that they were doing anything unwillingly.' In his experience American hotel staff were grudging in their service, and American stewards were despots who treated him as an interloper to be repulsed; but the crew on his English ship proved conspicuously civil. 'They did not stare me out of countenance; they did not gruffly order me about . . . I didn't catch them making audible remarks behind my back . . . in the dining saloon, in the bath, on deck, everywhere, with "yes, sirs", and "thank you, sirs", and two fingers raised to cap visors occasionally for good measure. Were they acting? Was this a fiercely suppressed class? I could scarcely believe it. They looked too comfort-able.'[19] Dreiser's low opinion of his fellow Americans is endorsed by a historian of Atlantic liners who judged that the ships of the United States Line lacked panache. '"Standards maintained by the United States Line," said one of that line's brochures, "are American stand-ards." That was always the trouble.' The service manual compiled for United States Line stewards had to specify that stewards must not be unshaven, reek of alcohol or tobacco, wear scruffy shoes, pick their teeth, snap their fingers or hiss to attract attention, solicit tips, or count tips in front of passengers. Waiters taking orders must never, the manual stressed, lean their arm on the chair or passenger.[20]

That English stewards were less contented than Dreiser imagined is clear from *Titanic* stewardess Violet Jessop, who compiled informative memoirs which were edited with sympathy by John Maxtone-Graham. Jessop, who was aged twenty-four in 1912, had been born in the Argentine pampas, the first child of Irish emigrants. After the death of her sheep-farmer father, the family returned to

England, where her mother took work as a Royal Mail Packet Line stewardess. When her mother's health failed, Jessop left convent school to become a Royal Mail stewardess on the routes to Rio de Janeiro and Buenos Aires. When she switched to White Star's *Majestic*, working seventeen hours a day for monthly pay of £2 10s, she was shaken by the battering of North Atlantic storms, and needed all her willpower to remain at work. Conditions for stewards were hard, she recalled. 'Men worked sixteen hours a day, every day of the week, scrubbed and cleaned from morn till night, moved mountains of baggage, carved and served food, cleaned a host of apparently useless metalwork until their very souls seemed permeated with metal polish, and kept long watches into the night, all for hasty meals standing up in a steamy pantry where decks were awash with the droppings of the last meal.'[21] Jessop felt White Star's managers were remiss. 'Had employers consciously set themselves to kill the spirit of their men, they could not have succeeded more effectively . . . because there was too much regimentation and too little consideration for the dignity of the individual. Any initiative was usually quashed.' Although stewards at sea had to be strenuous, resilient, forbearing and flexible, they were shunned when they applied for jobs ashore. This gave them 'an inferiority complex', she said, which they sheltered behind a false exterior of bravado: they were 'the kind of man who, on the slightest provocation, gets up and shouts, "Rule Britannia, Britannia rules the waves!" and then flops back into apathy.' The liners' officers, 'often mediocre themselves', regarded stewards with 'undisguised contempt'.[22]

'Even the worst kind of ship has some advantages over the best kind of hotel,' Evelyn Waugh wrote after a trip on a Mediterranean liner in 1930. 'As far as I can see, a really up-to-date ship has every advantage over a hotel except stability and fresh meat.'[23] The avarice was less obtrusive in shipboard culture than in a hotel. White Star did not count the number of hot baths and cups of tea taken during a voyage, and add them to the bill, as hotel managers did. Having paid for their tickets, passengers were not caught by cunning additional expenses. Hotel employees were always soliciting tips, even when their attention had been as brief as swinging open doors or summoning taxis. But at sea, there was one grand reckoning for tips at the end of the voyage. The avidity of servants was less dispersed and harassing, for individual stewards had more direct personal responsibility for passenger comfort than hotel staff, and everyone knew that dues would be paid in the hours before docking.

With monthly pay of only £3 15s, stewards depended on their tips, and were quick to appraise the passengers' worth and likely generosity. 'Sweetheart,' a young *Titanic* bedroom steward named Richard Geddes wrote to his wife in a letter sent from Queenstown, 'there won't be much made on the outward journey but it wont matter so long as we get something good on the homeward one.'[24] Jack Stagg, a saloon steward, was also preoccupied with tips when he wrote to his wife as the liner approached Ireland. 'What a day we have had of it, it's been nothing but work all day long, but I can tell you nothing as regards what people I have for nothing will be settled until we leave Queenstown . . . we have only 317 first, and if I should be lucky enough to get a table at all it won't possibly be more than two that I shall have, still one must not grumble for there will be plenty.' In a postscript he added, 'I made sixpence today. What luck.'[25] The violinist-bandleader Wallace Hartley was also thinking of tips when we wrote home before Queenstown: 'this is a fine ship and there ought to be plenty of money around'.[26] Ten years after the *Titanic* maiden voyage, Emily Post's handbook of etiquette guided first-class passengers on tips. Separate tips of 10 shillings ($2.50) each were recommended for the room steward or stewardess, the deck steward and the lounge steward. It was unnecessary to tip the head steward unless he had performed a special service. Passengers who took their meals in their cabin were enjoined to give at least 20 shillings ($5) to the steward or stewardess. Any steward who had exerted himself to please should be rewarded with careful words of thanks as well as a generous tip before disembarking.

Stewards' thoughts were obsessed by the jingling of coins, Jessop thought, because they felt so hopeless and futile. 'One rarely heard them complain that they found their work – years of bell-answering, slop-emptying, floor-washing, bed-making, tea-carrying or the trundling of baggage – monotonous or distasteful. They never realized that the very monotony had eaten like a canker into their souls, killing ambition and leaving them content to get along without exerting their minds, their bodies racked with fatigue.' On *Titanic* there was a telephone in every first-class cabin, and passengers could telephone, from the seclusion of bed if they wished, to order breakfast, to book a bench in the Turkish bath or a barber's shave, to arrange card games. Passengers wanted extraordinary things at odd moments, and complained if their whims were not satisfied. She saw colleagues 'snarl and snap without provocation at someone who wanted to help them, simply because they dared not do so to the one who really hurt them, those who held out the almighty tip'.[27]

Though Thomas Andrews of Harland & Wolff tried to improve liner accommodation for stewards, standards remained low. On Titanic's E Deck an eight-berth cabin was shared by the bathroom steward, saloon steward, lounge steward, deck steward, smoking-room steward, second bedroom steward and linen keeper. Such quarters were known as 'glory-holes'. 'No place can be so utterly devoid of "glory", of comfort and privacy and so wretched a human habitation as the usual ship's glory-hole,' Jessop recalled. They were foul, bug-infested places where 'all that was low in men seemed to gain the upper hand'.[28]

The Stewards' Department acutely felt the contrasts between their working lives and passengers' recreations. Occasionally their envy was poignant. *Titanic*'s liftboy was aged not more than sixteen, 'a bright-eyed, handsome boy, with a love for the sea and the games on deck and the view over the ocean – and he did not get any of them', a passenger recalled. 'As he put me out of my lift and saw through the vestibule windows a game of deck quoits in progress, he said, in a wistful tone, "My! I wish I could go out there sometimes".'[29] Jessop used to stroll on *Titanic*'s deck for fresh air before retiring each night: 'If the sun did fail to shine so brightly on the fourth day out, and if the little cold nip crept into the air as evening set in,' she wrote of the final Sunday, 'it only served to emphasize the warmth and luxuriousness within.'[30]

In addition to the internal telephones, there was – decisively for the denouement of *Titanic*'s history – an external Marconi communication system. In 1851 a submarine cable had joined England and France, and a cable was laid under the Atlantic in 1865. In 1894, when he was twenty, Guglielmo Marconi devised an apparatus which sent messages on the radio waves generated by the discharge of electric sparks. The first merchant vessel to carry Marconi's wireless apparatus was *Kaiser Wilhelm der Grosse* in 1900. Next his company built high-powered radio stations to transmit marine and international messages: the Atlantic was covered by his outposts at Poldhu in Cornwall, Clifden in Ireland, and along the east coast of the USA and Canada – notably at Cape Cod and Cape Race, on the eastern tip of Newfoundland. These transmission stations made it possible for transatlantic liners to maintain contact with the land. Passengers in mid-ocean knew within two hours of Londoners when King Edward VII died in 1910. Each morning, on White Star ships, shortly before the breakfast bugle-call was sounded, stewards distributed that morning's copy of the *Atlantic Daily Bulletin*. This was an attractive magazine, the outer pages of which had been printed ashore before sailing: these included advertisements, social and theatrical gossip, articles about cultural trends and scientific advances. The centre sheets were printed daily, and contained news summaries, Stock Exchange prices in New York, London and Paris, racing results – as well as the coming day's menus.

The Edwardians coined three new words as a result of Marconi's invention: 'wireless', 'aerial' and 'Marconigram'. In 1909 – the year he shared the Nobel prize for physics – Marconi met Godfrey Isaacs, a suitably sparky character whose history as a speculator included a Welsh gold mine, a company that tried to mine zinc in Tipperary, a weekly paper specializing in society gossip and another that dealt in mining share tips, and the syndicate that introduced motor taxi cabs to London. Marconi was impressed by Isaacs's hustling, and appointed him as managing director. Isaacs then applied to the British government for licences to operate a network of wireless stations linking the British Empire across the world. In March 1912 the British government signed a preliminary agreement to pay £60,000 each for a chain of Marconi stations in England, Egypt, Africa and Singapore. Marconi shares stood at £2 8s 9d each in August 1911, £6 15s 0d in March 1912 and peaked at £9 each in April. Godfrey Isaacs owned a large holding of American Marconi shares, some of which he offered to sell to his brothers Harry and Rufus before the London Stock Exchange started trading them on 19 April. On 17 April, the day that the *Titanic* sinking was confirmed in London newspapers with the aid of Marconigrams, Sir Rufus Isaacs (who was Attorney General, with a seat in the Cabinet) bought 10,000 shares at £2 each. His subsequent dealings in the shares were soon decried as corrupt, and caused a sensational political scandal.

The jobbery of high finance was a world away from Marconi's wireless station situated abaft *Titanic*'s officers' quarters on the boat deck. There were three cabins: the first contained the receiver, operating table and control gear; the second, the transmission apparatus; and the third, bunks. Two Marconi men, Jack Phillips and Harold Bride, worked in alternating six-hour stretches. John Phillips had been born in 1887 in Farncombe, Surrey. His parents ran a drapery. He became a telegraphist in Godalming Post Office, and after three years, in 1906, enrolled at the Marconi training school in Liverpool. There he spent six months learning about electricity, magnetism, telegraphy, theoretical and practical information on wireless apparatus, the regulations of the Radiotelegraphy Convention and repair skills. Then he set to work on *Lusitania* and *Mauretania*. In 1908 he went to the Marconi station handling transatlantic wireless traffic at Clifden. He joined the White Star liner *Adriatic* in 1911, and was promoted to be senior wireless operator on *Titanic* in 1912. Although aged only twenty-five, he was one of the world's most experienced wireless operators. His set on *Titanic* was one of the most powerful available. His deputy, Harold Bride, aged twenty-two, hailed from Bromley in Kent. Like Phillips, he had begun his career as a Post Office telegraphist and attended the Marconi training school.

Phillips and Bride were employed by Marconi, not White Star, and made their employers' profits by sending passengers' messages (costing 12½ shillings or $3 for ten words: and 9 pence or 35 cents per word thereafter) rather than navigational messages between ships. They were deluged with work. Some were business messages, as millionaires tended their interests or dealt in shares. Many were social: pride at being aboard the world's largest liner excited passengers into sending chirpy, trivial messages, boasting of their whereabouts or making appointments to be met. The apparatus failed during Friday night and Saturday morning, causing a backlog of work which both men worked at full stretch to reduce. They were exhausted by Sunday. The Marconi Company stipulated that navigational messages should have priority over private messages, but Phillips was haphazard in remitting navigational messages, including ice warnings on the final Sunday, to the bridge.

It is doubtful, though, if anything would have convinced Smith to reduce speed in the ice zone. The captains of North Atlantic liners kept to allotted times regardless of weather conditions, partly because they were carrying mail on tight schedules. They ran at full speed through both storms and ice, and used wireless warnings as spurs to vigilance rather than reasons to abate their pace. No ship's officer would dream of altering speed without his captain's authority. They trusted to experience and believed that swift reactions would avert accidents. Collisions were not regarded as inevitably fatal. The liner *Kronprinz Wilhelm* had reached port without loss of life after ramming an iceberg and crumpling its bow in 1907.

At dusk on Friday 12 April, *Titanic* received wireless notification from *La Touraine* of ice in the North Atlantic. On the Sunday morning *Titanic* received wireless warnings from the Cunarder *Caronia* and Dutch liner *Noordam* of bergs, growlers and field ice ahead. Early on Sunday afternoon came further cautions from the White Star liner *Baltic* and the German liner *Amerika*. At 5.45 p.m., Captain Smith shifted his ship's course to the south-west: the bridge officers believed that this was to avoid ice.[31] He did not reduce speed. It was not, then, a rule of good seamanship to do so. Captains and their officers – all trained under sail – assumed that the ship could out-manoeuvre any obstacle in its path. Accordingly, the ship steamed at relentless speed towards the lumbering, jagged, rock-hard shapes of ice. At 7.30 that evening a message was intercepted from the Leyland Line's *Californian* reporting three large icebergs 50 miles ahead of *Titanic*. About two hours later, at 9.40, the steamship *Mesaba* sent a wireless message warning of thick pack ice and large icebergs. Bride was trying to sleep when this message arrived, and Phillips was so busy sending passenger messages to Cape Race that he wedged the message under a paperweight on his desk. It never reached the bridge: the coordinates provided by the *Mesaba* would, if plotted on a chart, have shown the *Titanic* was inside the dangerous ice zone.

The cumulative effect of these messages would have been salutary – if they had been received and read cumulatively. Instead, there was poor coordination between the radio room and the bridge. Messages were remitted at random to the bridge, where they were treated casually or ignored. Herbert Pitman, the Third Officer who super-vised the decks and work rosters, saw a chit marked 'ice' in the chart room, but only gave it a glance. Harold Lowe, the Fifth Officer, on his first Atlantic crossing, paid little attention because he knew the ship would not reach that position during his watch. Lightoller never noticed it. Joseph Boxhall, the Fourth Officer, who was responsible for charting the ship's course and position and for displaying weather reports, remembered marking *La Touraine*'s message, but none of the others. None of the surviving officers remembered seeing the *Noordam*, *Amerika*, *Californian* or *Mesaba* messages. Smith acknow-ledged the *Noordam* message, but we do not know how he acted on it. He was handed the *Baltic*'s warning as he was going for luncheon, and meeting Ismay on the promenade deck, gave him the slip of paper. Ismay read it, folded it in his pocket and later showed it to Marian Thayer and Emily Ryerson. When Smith next saw Ismay – in the early evening – he said that he wanted to post the message for his officers to read, and Ismay returned the paper; but Smith then went to dine with the Wideners, and there is no evidence that he gave the *Baltic* sighting to the bridge.

At ten in the evening there was a change of the officers' watches, as Lightoller recalled years later. 'The Senior Officer, coming on Watch, hunts up his man in the pitch darkness, and just yarns for a few minutes, whilst getting his eyesight after being in the light; when he can see all right he lets the other chap know, and officially "takes over". Murdoch and I were old shipmates, and for a few minutes – as was our custom – we stood there looking ahead, and yarning over times and incidents part and present. We both remarked on the ship's steadiness, absence of vibration, and how comfortably she was slipping along. Then we passed on to more serious subjects, such as the chances of sighting ice, reports of ice that had been sighted, and the positions.' *Titanic* was making 22 knots: 'it was pitch dark and dead cold', recalled Lightoller, 'not a cloud in the sky, and the sea like glass'.[32] In fifteen years he had never seen such conditions.

In clear weather, icebergs are visible by moonlight half a mile ahead, but this was a moonless night. Wind and waves usually whip up white surf at the base of an iceberg, but on this night the sea was as flat as a doorstep. There was no swell, and therefore no breaking waves around any iceberg for the look-out, Frederick Fleet, to detect. Fleet was one of six look-outs on the ship, sharing his watch with Reginald Lee. If he seemed a morose and isolated individual, it was with good reason, for he never knew his father's name and had been abandoned as a baby by his mother. Reared in a Dr Barnado's orphanage, which he left at the age of twelve for a training ship, he started work as a deck boy a few years later. By 1912 he was sufficiently trusted to be used as a special look-out. Up in the crow's nest, late on the Sunday evening, Frederick Fleet hunched his shoulders against the cold.

PART THREE

Life & Death

In a solitude of the sea
Deep from human vanity,
And the Pride of Life that planned her, stilly couches she.

Steel chambers, late the pyres
Of her salamandrine fires,
Cold currents thrid, and turn to rhythmic tidal lyres.

Over the mirrors meant
To glass the opulent
The sea-worm crawls – grotesque, slimed, dumb, indifferent.

Jewels in joy designed
To ravish the sensuous mind
Lie lightless, all their sparkles bleared and black and blind.

Dim moon-eyed fishes near
Gaze at the gilded gear
And query: 'What does this vaingloriousness down here?'

Well: while was fashioning
This creature of cleaving wing,
The Immanent Will that stirs and urges everything

Prepared a sinister mate
For her – so gaily great –
A Shape of Ice, for the time far and dissociate.

And as the smart ship grew
In stature, grace, and hue,
In shadowy silent distance grew the Iceberg too.

Alien they seemed to be;
No mortal eye could see
The intimate welding of their later history,

Or sign that they were bent
By paths coincident
On being anon twin halves of one august event,

Till the Spinner of the Years
Said 'Now!' And each one hears,
And consummation comes, and jars two hemispheres.

Thomas Hardy, 'The Convergence of the Twain,
(Lines on the loss of the *Titanic*)'

THIRTEEN

Collision

The weight of twenty Atlantics was upon me ... Then came sudden alarms; hurrying to and fro; trepidation of innumerable fugitives ... darkness and lights, tempest and human faces; and at last, with a sense that all was lost, female forms; and the features that were all the world to me, and but a moment allowed – and clasped hands; with heartbreaking partings, and everlasting farewells!

Thomas de Quincey, *Confessions of an Opium Eater*

The fifth night of the maiden voyage was moonless: a flat sea, an unclouded sky, with stars gleaming in the frosty air. 'Grand weather,' said John Poingdestre, a member of the deck crew, but 'terribly cold.'[1] After 5.30 on Sunday evening, the sharp fall in temperature drove all but the hardiest passengers indoors. It was so chill that smart women in flimsy dresses retreated to their cabins early. Eloise Smith, for example, who had dined with her husband in the Café Parisien, left him at 10.30 and went to bed. Elizabeth Shutes, the American governess of the Graham family, wrote afterwards: 'Such a biting cold air poured into my state room that I could not sleep, and the air had so strange an odour, as if it came from a clammy cave. I had noticed the same odour in the ice cave on the Eiger glacier.' She lay in her berth shivering until she switched on her electric stove, which threw a cheerful red glow.[2] The Waldorf-Astoria resident Ella White remembered telling Marie Young, the musician with whom she was sharing her cabin, 'We must be very near icebergs to have such cold weather.' Her state room, too, was chilly. 'Everybody knew we were

267

in the vicinity of icebergs,' she said after she reached New York. The ship's navigation, she added with a mixture of anger and despondency, 'was a careless, reckless thing. It seems almost useless to speak of it.'[3]

Captain Smith was sufficiently concerned about ice to leave the Wideners' dinner early at 9.00 and return to the bridge. Murdoch, who replaced Lightoller as Officer on Watch an hour later, had no authority from Smith to reduce speed, although it was clear that the ship had entered an ice zone. The look-outs were told 'to keep a sharp look-out for all ice',[4] but no extra look-outs were posted. Fleet and Lee, the look-outs in the crow's-nest, knew the risks, and were straining to see. At 11.40 Fleet glimpsed a dark object in the ship's path, rang the crow's-nest bell three times (the warning for 'object dead ahead') and telephoned the bridge: 'Iceberg right ahead'.

Murdoch ordered Quartermaster Hichens to turn hard-a-starboard: then he ordered the engine room to reverse engines. He was trying to swing the ship's bow to port so that it would miss the iceberg, and then to swing the stern back to starboard so that it too would miss. But the ship was travelling at 22½ knots, covering 38 feet per second, and the iceberg was about 500 yards away. For more than twenty seconds the bow continued to plough straight ahead. Murdoch should have left the engines full ahead – not reverse – to make a sharp turn. Moreover, all officers on Atlantic liners knew that ramming an iceberg was preferable to sideswiping it: a ship with its bows buckled by a collision could remain afloat and reach port under its own steam. If Murdoch had steered the ship head-first into the iceberg, the prow would have held, and the vulnerable side of the ship been protected. Yet Murdoch's impulse was to slow the ship and turn it away just as a man has an instinct to flinch and turn his head aside before being punched. It was a fatal impulse.

To Fleet it seemed that a collision had been averted. The liner had swung starboard at the last moment, and seemed to clear. Four saloon stewards were sitting in the first-class dining room discussing their passengers when they heard a grinding sound. James Johnson thought the ship had lost a propeller blade: 'another Belfast trip', said someone, thinking of the repairs, but a man who went down to the engines returned looking worried: 'It is a bit hot'.[5] Third Officer Herbert Pitman was woken by a sound resembling 'the ship coming to anchor – the chain running out over a windlass'.[6] He lay in his bunk for a few minutes wondering why the ship was anchoring, and lit his pipe meditatively. Look-out George Symons had gone to his bunk after being relieved by Fleet and Lee. 'What awakened me was a grinding sound on her bottom. I thought at first she had lost her anchor and chain, and it was running along her bottom.'[7] Another off-duty look-out, William Lucas, had been in the mess room playing nap (a simple card game in which whoever bids the highest number of tricks chooses trumps), but stopped just before the collision 'because I was broke'. As he left the mess room he felt 'a hard shock' which 'very nearly sent me off my feet'. There was a grating sound, he added, 'like a ship running up on gravel, a crushing noise'.[8] Down below in a stokehold, fireman George Beauchamp heard a sound like 'the roar of thunder'.[9] Coal slid in one bunker and briefly trapped trimmer George Cavell.[10]

Murdoch was unsure if the ship had been damaged, but using an automatic switch, shut the doors between the sixteen watertight compartments. Firemen and stokers near Boiler-room 6, where there had been a loud bang when the starboard side of the ship broke, scrambled through the watertight doors as they shut, or scurried up escape ladders to a higher deck. Smith appeared on the bridge, ordered the engines to stop, and sent his Fourth Officer, Boxhall, to inspect the damage. Many passengers noticed when the ship stopped: Renée Harris said that her dresses on their hangers in the wardrobe stopped swaying. Emily Ryerson felt the stilling of the engines, and questioned her bedroom steward, Walter Bishop. 'There's talk of an iceberg, ma'am,' he replied, 'and they have stopped, not to run over it.'[11]

Boxhall soon reported that the mail room on F Deck was awash: everyone knew that this meant the ship was badly holed. Ismay arrived in carpet slippers with pyjamas peeping from underneath his trousers, and was told his liner had hit an iceberg. The ship's designer Thomas Andrews accompanied Smith on a tour of inspection. They were aghast to find that six forward watertight compartments had been breached as the iceberg bumped past. Three cargo holds and two boiler-rooms as well as the forepeak had been ripped into below the waterline. Andrews and Smith recognized that with six holed compartments, the bow would be sunk by the weight of sea water pouring in, and that the ocean would pour over the top of each successive bulkhead in turn. The closure of the watertight doors was futile. Andrews estimated that the ship would survive for at best two hours before sinking.

Smith visited the Marconi cabin before leaving on his inspection. The ship had struck an iceberg, he told Phillips and Bride. They should prepare to transmit messages summoning help, but not send them until he had checked the damage. Ten minutes later he returned and told Phillips to transmit CQD, the international call for help. At 12.15 on 15 April, half an hour after the accident, the first distress call was sent. CQ was Marconi code for 'all stations', and 'D' indicated an emergency call: CQD was known in slang as 'Come Quick, Danger'. 'SOS' had been introduced in 1908 as an international distress call because it was easier to transmit in Morse code than CQD. It was supposed to denote 'Save Our Souls'. At 12.30 a steamer loaded with steerage passengers making for Canada, *Mount Temple*, received the CQD, and went to the coordinates given by *Titanic*, but these were inaccurate and the ship played no part in the rescue. The wireless man on the nearest ship, the freighter *Californian*, had switched off his Marconi apparatus forty-five minutes before Phillips sent his first message. The *Californian* captain, Stanley Lord, has been heavily condemned for ignoring the distress rockets that his crewmen later saw fired on Smith's orders. At 12.45 Phillips finally heard from the small liner, *Carpathia*, 58 miles away: at full speed it would take four hours to reach the *Titanic*'s calculated position.

At Smith's order, issued after he had returned from his inspection with Andrews, the boatswain piped, 'all hands up and get the lifeboats ready'.[12] It is often said that this order was issued at 12.25 and that Smith's vacillation was culpable; but is reasonable to surmise that the order was made after he told the Marconi men to begin sending distress calls around 12.15. Smith was however so anxious to avert panic, and shaken by his knowledge that there were insufficient lifeboats, that he did not instil enough urgency into their loading. Initially, passengers doubted the gravity of their danger, so that many refused to alight in lifeboats, which left half-empty. Four hundred more people might have survived if the lifeboats had been filled efficiently.

Passengers before the collision had disported in delusive security. Lady Duff Gordon, with a cabin on A Deck costing £58 18s, pictured the first-class decks: 'A great liner stealing through the vast loneliness of the Atlantic, the sky jewelled with myriads of stars overhead, and a thin little wind blowing cold and even colder straight from the frozen ice fields, tapping its warning of approaching danger on the cosily shuttered portholes of the cabins, causing the look-out man to strain his eyes anxiously into the gloom. Inside this floating palace warmth, lights and music, the flutter of cards, the hum of voices, the gay lilt of a German waltz – the unheeding sounds of a small world bent on pleasure. Then disaster, swift and overwhelming, turning all into darkness and chaos, the laughing voices changed into shuddering wails of despair – a story of horror unparalleled in the annals of the sea.'[13]

Eloise Smith had left her husband Lucien playing bridge in the Café Parisien with three Frenchmen, the sculptor Paul Chevré, the aviator Pierre Marechal and Fernand Omont, a cotton broker. They were not gamblers without nerves, playing for small stakes, like the look-out man Lucas, with his game of nap in the mess room, but trenchant men who redoubled bids, trumped aces and, as they soon proved, appraised their chances well. A mass of ice crunched up against the portholes. The Frenchmen hastened on deck. 'Do not be afraid,' an officer said. 'We are merely cutting a whale in two.'[14] In the first-class smoking room, Henry Blank, William Greenfield and Alfred Nourney, the bogus Baron von Drachstedt, made up another card game. Archie Butt sat with Harry Widener, Clarence Moore, and William Carter nearby. Spencer Silverthorne, buyer for a department store in St Louis, was reading a novel about Wyoming cattle-ranchers lynching rustlers. The lupine money men, Hugh Woolner and Mauritz Håkan Björnström-Steffansson, were using it as their lair too. 'We felt a rip that gave a sort of twist to the whole room,' Woolner reported. 'Everybody stood up and a number of men walked out rapidly through the swinging doors on the port side, and ran along . . . guessing what it might be, and one man called out, "an iceberg has passed astern".'[15]

Lower down the ship, on Sunday night, the chief second-class steward, John Hardy, had closed the public rooms and extinguished most lights at 11 p.m. In a second-class berth on D Deck costing £13, Lawrence Beesley felt a change in the movement of the ship. 'As I read in the quietness of the night, broken only by the muffled sound that came to me through the ventilators of stewards talking and moving along the corridors, when nearly all the passengers were in their cabins, some asleep in bed, others undressing, and others only just down from the smoking-room and still discussing many things, there came what seemed to me nothing more than an extra heave of the engines and a more than usually obvious dancing motion of the mattress on which I sat. Nothing more than that.'[16]

Most third-class passengers were already in their berths, for their saloons were closed after ten. Victor Sunderland was a teenage Londoner who had paid £8 1s for a berth on G Deck. He was travelling to join an uncle in Cleveland, Ohio: later he became a plumber. He and his cabin mates were smoking in their bunks near the bow. He still wore his trousers, though his jacket hung on a rack. After hearing the jar of the collision, which he likened to the sound of coal falling on an iron plate, he and some others made for the main deck to investigate. A steward sent them back, saying that nothing was amiss. Sunderland smoked more cigarettes in his bunk until water began seeping under the cabin door.[17]

Passengers drew different analogies to describe the sound and feel of the collision. In second-class, the missionary's wife Sylvia Caldwell imagined a large dog shaking a young kitten in its mouth. The impact sounded to Emma Bucknell in first-class like a 'terrific peal of thunder mixed in with many violent explosions'.[18] Ella White was sitting on her bed, stretching to turn off her bedside light, at the moment of the collision: 'It was just as though we went over about a thousand marbles. There was nothing terrifying about it at all.'[19] George Harder, a young Brooklyn manufacturer honeymooning with his wife, felt the ship shake, then a 'rumbling, scraping noise'. Harder went to investigate on deck, where he met Dick Bishop and Jack Astor. People said reassuringly, 'Oh, it will be only a few hours before we are on our way again.'[20] In his first-class state room, Norman Chambers heard a sound like 'jangling chains whipping along the side of the ship', and was sent by his wife to investigate. At the top of a stairway leading to the mail sorting-room, he found two clerks, 'wet to their knees, who had just come up from below, bringing their registered mailbags'.[21]

Titanic had been steaming at 22½ knots: 'the instant the engines were stopped the steam started roaring off at all eight exhausts, kicking up a row that would have dwarfed the row of a thousand railway engines thundering through a culvert', Lightoller recalled.[22] The crew responded immediately to the call for 'All hands on deck', but it was impossible to give verbal orders: hand gestures set the crew swinging lifeboats out, hauling tight the falls, coiling them on deck and ready for lowering. As passengers emerged on deck, the cacophony increased their alarm. When later the deafening din of venting steam stopped, the silence seemed sinister.

Officers and crew deceived the passengers in order to avoid panic – and perhaps to protect themselves from full realization of their predicament. Passengers kept asking if the situation was serious. 'I tried to cheer them up,' wrote Lightoller, 'by telling them "No", but that it was a matter of precaution to get the boats in the water, ready for any emergency. That in any case they were perfectly safe, as there was a ship not more than a few miles away, and I pointed out the lights on the port bow which they could see as well as I could.'[23] The ship was probably the *Californian*, at whose dozy, heedless master, Lord, Lightoller flung recriminatory barbs for forty years. 'Wrap up warmly, for you may have a little trip for an hour or so in one of our lifeboats,' Lady Duff Gordon's steward told her comfortingly. 'If it had not been for this ill-advised reticence hundreds more lives would have been saved,' she felt. 'The appalling danger we were in was concealed from us all until it was too late and in the ensuing panic many of the boats were lowered half-filled because there was no time to fill them.'[24] Yet it was the stewards' duty to assuage worries and deter panic. Many of them did not recognize the danger, or realize that the ship must sink, until long after the first lifeboats were primed.

By no means all passengers were duped or assuaged. Olaus Abelseth, returning third-class to his South Dakota homestead and chaperoning a party of fellow Norwegians, later gave the best of only three third-class accounts of the sinking submitted to the official enquiries that followed: it is touching because Abelseth did not know English nautical words and described the ship as if it was one of his livestock. He shared a two-berth cabin with Adolf Humblen, also from Ålsund. The two men were stirred awake around a quarter to midnight. They donned their clothes and went to investigate. 'There was quite a lot of ice on the starboard part of the ship. They wanted us to go down again, and I saw one of the officers, and I said to him: "Is there any danger?" He said, "No". I was not satisfied with that, however.' He told his brother-in-law Sigurd Moen and cousin Peter Søholt, who were sharing a cabin, to get up and dress. They walked 'to the hind part of the ship', and roused two Norwegian girls, his cousin Karen Abelseth and Anna Salkjelsvik, who were travelling under his protection and Humblen's. They traipsed on deck, and gazing over the port side of the ship, saw a light. An officer told them a rescue ship was coming, though he did not say when. Abelseth and Søholt collected lifebelts for their group. Third-class passengers were by then crawling along the arm of a crane on their deck as their nearest way to the boat deck.[25]

Rich men were more resistant than poor to believing that life could go smash. Arthur Peuchen, a Canadian chemical manufacturer, took Charles Hays of Canada's Grand Trunk Pacific Railway to inspect the ice on deck. He felt the liner's situation was grave, and told Hays,

'Why, she is listing; she should not do that, the water is perfectly calm, and the boat has stopped.' Hays, whose delusions of invincibility were driving his railway towards ruin, replied confidently, 'You cannot sink this boat. No matter what we have struck, she is good for eight or ten hours.'[26]

In first-class the New Jersey manufacturer Henry Stengel had been moaning in his sleep. His wife had just roused him from his dream when they heard a slight crash, but he felt no concern until the throbbing engines ceased. Then, with his wife in her kimono, they went to investigate. They saw Smith returning from inspecting the damage with a grave expression, and George Widener follow the captain upstairs – doubtless with the intention of quizzing him. Worried by Smith's look, the Stengels fetched their lifejackets from their state room, and hastened on deck. Even after the lifeboat loading began, White Star officers were assuring them, 'There is no danger: this is simply a matter of precaution.'[27]

Martha Stephenson – also in first-class – 'was awakened by a terrible jar with ripping and cutting noises'. The steward told her, 'Go to bed, it's nothing', but she saw a man in an opposite cabin retrieve his shoes, which he had left in the corridor for the Boots to polish overnight, and resolved to dress. The door of another cabin had jammed, and the passenger inside was calling for help. Richard Williams, a sporting young American on his way to Harvard, rammed his shoulders to the panel and broke it in. An indignant steward threatened to have him arrested. Mrs Stephenson and her sister Elizabeth Eustis 'dressed as if for breakfast, putting on our burglar pockets containing our letters of credit and money. I determined also to do my hair and put on a lincd waistcoat and old winter suit as it was so cold. While Elizabeth was doing her hair, the ship suddenly settled, frightening me very much.' Thayer senior came to collect them as Miss Eustis was hooking her waist. It was the methodical details that they remembered afterwards. 'I put on my fur coat over everything and Elizabeth said she would wear her watch, which reminded me that mine was hanging by the bureau and I quickly put it on. I took my glasses and small change purse, also a clean handkerchief.' As the sisters left with

Thayer, they were told to don lifejackets. They realized the situation must be serious, and were 'frightened though very quiet'.

Another first-class woman was the redoubtable widow Emma Bucknell: seventy years later her great-granddaughter was to marry Jack Thayer's grandson. At the age of fifty-nine she exuded mature vigour and resolve, shone with confidence in her person, position and way of life. 'Exceedingly intellectual and much travelled,' was the description of her by Margaret Brown, who had a good brain and had circumnavigated the world.[28] Her calm, clear head impressed many in the next hours and days. Awakened by the crash, she made a foray along the corridor outside her cabin. There she found lumps of ice which had crashed through an open porthole when the iceberg struck. A steward came along the corridor denying any danger, 'but while his voice was calm and he delivered his message easily, his face belied the confidence of his words'. Emma Bucknell dressed as warmly as she could. 'I anticipated that there would come greater difficulties, and I intended to be prepared. I told my maid to dress also. About this time another man came through the hallways crying out that everyone should dress immediately and go on deck. I called to my maid to fasten my gown, and only tarried long enough to get a heavy fur coat.' Back in the corridor a woman was declaring that it was impossible for the liner to have hit an iceberg. Mrs Bucknell picked up some ice from the floor, and displaying it in the palm of her hand, said with scornful emphasis, 'Here is ice! It is an iceberg!' Her maid Albina Bazzani pleaded with her not to go up on deck: 'she cried out that we would surely be lost if we did not stay in the safety of our room, but I told her the only thing to do under the circumstances was to obey orders.'

On deck Emma Bucknell joined the Astors and Wideners talking together. As the call came for women and children, the Astors crossed to the port side of the ship: 'he was bending over her as they walked. And it was then that I saw the Wideners for the last time. They were all together.'[29] Harry Widener had recently bought a rare 1598 edition of Bacon's essays. 'Mother,' he said on deck, 'I have placed the volume in my pocket: little "Bacon" goes with me!' (A fellow bibliophile has called this 'the most touching, most pathetic, withal the most glorious incident in the romance of book-collecting'.[30])

Jack Astor's life had been as perfectly pitched as a concert-hall piano, with nothing skewed about the keys, and nothing slack in the strings to mar the tone. Now everything went discordant and awry. On the boat deck, where he went to investigate the disturbance, he met Sir Cosmo Duff Gordon, whose wife had been alarmed by the venting of the boilers. They agreed that their wives should dress. Lady Duff Gordon donned a mauve silk kimono and a squirrel coat. Madeleine Astor dressed in a black coat with sable trim, a diamond necklace and fur muff. In the A Deck foyer the Astors met Captain Smith, whom Astor took aside and quizzed discreetly. She needed reassurance about her lifejacket. The Astors were glimpsed sitting side by side on two mechanical horses in the gymnasium while he sliced open a lifejacket with a penknife to show her its cork contents.

The second-class Cornishwoman, Agnes Davies, felt a jar, and rang for a steward, who assured her party that they could safely remain in their berths. But when Robert Phillips, the widowed fishmonger who wanted a new start in America, told his daughter to dress, the Cornishwoman followed suit. She decided to wake and dress her eight-year-old son, although their steward repeated that there was no danger. 'Had it not been for our curiosity to learn what was going on, we might have perished. We went on deck about 12.15.'[31] That second-class trouble-maker, Imanita Shelley, declared that she and Lutie Parrish were awakened by the stopping of the engines. They heard excited voices in the corridor speaking of a collision with an iceberg, but a steward who appeared after her continuous ringing insisted that nothing was amiss and that passengers should return to bed. Half an hour later, second-class passengers heard stewards running down the passages, pounding on cabin doors or bursting them open, and yelling 'Everybody on deck with life belts on, at once.'[32] Both women donned their lifebelts, and went to the boat deck. 'There was practically no excitement on the part of anyone during this time,' Mrs Shelley avowed, 'the majority seeming to think that the big boat could not sink altogether, and that it was better to stay on the steamer than trust to the lifeboats.'[33]

The Polish-born leather worker Berk Trembisky was berthed in a third-class cabin. 'We knew something was wrong, and we jumped out of bed and we dressed ourselves and went out.' Other passengers started arguing: 'one said that it was dangerous and the other said that it was not; one said white and the other said black. Instead of arguing with those people, I instantly went to the highest spot.' He decided that if the ship was going to sink, he should be at the top of it: 'That was my first idea, which was the best.' He found an open door into second-class, where he saw few people, and climbed a ladder into first-class.[34] The Irish immigrant Daniel Buckley recounted that he and three other youths were asleep in a cabin. 'I heard some terrible noise and I jumped out on the floor, and the first thing I knew my feet were getting wet; the water was just coming in slightly. I told the other fellows to get up, that there was something wrong, and that the water was coming in. They only laughed at me. One of them says: "Get back into bed. You are not in Ireland now." I got on my clothes as quick as I could.' As their cabin was tiny, he stepped out to give the three others room to dress. Two sailors came along shouting: 'All up on deck unless you want to get drowned!' He hastened to the boat deck, where he realized that he had forgotten his lifejacket in his cabin; but when he went to retrieve it, water rising up the stairs forced him back. Returning to the boat deck, he met a first-class passenger with two lifejackets: 'He gave me one, and fixed it on me.'[35]

It is worth recapitulating that there were twenty boats for escape. Two (numbered 1 on the starboard and 2 on the port) were wooden emergency boats, with a capacity of forty occupants each, built for rescuing people overboard. There were fourteen wooden lifeboats designed to carry sixty-five occupants each, with odd numbers arrayed on the starboard and even numbers on the port. There were also four Engelhardt lifeboats, named after their designer, made of clinker with collapsible canvas gunwales and a rounded bottom like a canoe. Each was capable of carrying forty-seven occupants. These were designated A, B, C and D: C was stowed underneath emergency Lifeboat 1 forward on the starboard boat deck; D was under emergency Lifeboat 2 on the port side; while A and B were lashed to the inaccessible roof of the officers' quarters.

The recent capsizing in the English Channel of a lifeboat from P&O's *Oceana*, which drowned nine people, discouraged passengers from being jerked down the tall precipitous side of a liner which was not expected to sink. They anticipated a delay in reaching New York, but nothing worse, and were reluctant to leave the warm comforts of the liner for the chill perils of a frail craft bobbing on the ocean. The P&O fatalities inhibited White Star's officers, too, from filling their lifeboats. They feared that the davits and tackle for lowering lifeboats would buckle if the boats were lowered at full capacity. Lightoller, an able seaman testified, 'was frightened of the falls'.[36] Harland & Wolff had tested one of *Olympic*'s lifeboats – raising and lowering it six times bearing the equivalent weight of sixty-five people – without buckling or strain. The shipbuilders assumed that this was known to the crew of *Titanic*, which had identical equipment, but the officers filling the lifeboats either did not know or forgot. The capacity of many lifeboats was therefore squandered. Only at the last were the lifeboats full, for by then it was clear that the ship was about to plunge 2 miles deep.

People were right to be scared. Lifeboat 13, for example, was lowered into a frightening outrush of water from the ship's side about 10 feet above the ocean. This cascade was swamping the boat until its occupants wielded an oar against the ship's side, and reached the ocean without overturning. Because of *Titanic*'s shifting tilt, Lifeboat 15, which was lowered quickly afterwards, nearly crushed 13 to the horror of the latter's shouting, screaming occupants. On reaching the ocean, they could not detach it from the falls and tackle. A stoker finally severed the ropes with his knife. The turbulent outflow then swept the lifeboat away from *Titanic* into calm waters, but its occupants had endured a terrifying ten minutes.

Murdoch, who was in charge of loading starboard lifeboats, interpreted Smith's order 'put the women and children in and lower away' to mean women and children *first*. Lightoller, his counterpart on the port side, interpreted the order to mean women and children *only*. Both men ordered the lowering of boats which were not filled to capacity, but Murdoch allowed men to board if there were no women and children about. Lightoller feared, he said, that if some men were allowed to board lifeboats, excluded men would rush and overwhelm them, yet he also testified that there was no jostling of women and children by men during the loading of the earlier boats: 'they could not have stood quieter if they had been in church'. In the belief that he was applying 'the rule of human nature' as well as a rule of the sea, Lightoller was relentless in excluding men, youths and even pubescent boys.[37] His prohibition on boys seemed deplorably callous to Samuel Rule, chief bathroom steward: 'I kept a special look-out for the lift-boys and bell-boys. Little lads they were. If I had seen any of them, I would have bundled them in the boats with the women.'[38]

When early lifeboats were loaded the boat decks seemed near empty. Seaman Lucas, who helped load port lifeboats, said they were not filled 'because there were no women knocking about'.[39] This strengthens the supposition that the launching times of early lifeboats were earlier than is generally propounded. If the empty look of the boat decks sounds improbable, it is worth noting that Frank Millet, who as an artist had a strong visual sense, was awed by the size of decks as large as a tennis court or courtyard; '500 people don't make a show on the decks'.[40]

A man of the world lives by notions: he minds the opinion of the world, is driven by fear of worldly disapproval and judges by the world's standards. It was part of the world's masculine code that gentlemen acted as squires to women travelling alone. 'Though being a gentleman sometimes gets one into scrapes it also gets one out of them,' Earl Cowper had recently written: this was to be exemplified by Hugh Woolner in the early hours of 15 April.[41] He felt responsible for Helen Churchill Candee, got her lifebelt from atop her wardrobe, tied her into it, fetched his own lifebelt and gave the spare in his cabin to a third-class passenger: perhaps Daniel Buckley. His supreme wish was to get Mrs Candee into the first port lifeboat, which he did. Other women were reluctant to board until Lightoller assured them that it was 'a matter of precaution', whereupon they came forward more freely.[42] Even so, Lifeboat 6 left with thirty-seven empty places and twenty-eight occupants.

Archie Butt was another squire. He had known Marie Young when she taught music to the Roosevelt children in the White House, and handed her into Lifeboat 8, where he tucked a blanket round her as if she was going for a blowy ride in an open motor car. Washington Roebling escorted Edith and Margaret Graham with Elizabeth Shutes into Lifeboat 3. 'We passed by the palm room, where two short hours before we had listened to a beautiful concert,' Shutes recalled, and mounted stairs that had undergone a sinister transmutation. 'No laughing throng, but on either side stand quietly, bravely, the stewards, all equipped with the white, ghostly life-preservers . . . only pale faces, each form strapped about with those white bars. So gruesome a scene. We passed on.'[43]

The emergency door from third-class into second-class was opened early on. There was a route from there up the centre of the liner, past the second-class smoking room, straight to the boat deck.[44] However, an organized call for third-class passengers to proceed to the boat deck was not made until about fifty minutes after the collision. There was no realization that, given the deficiency of lifeboats, this was fatal to the chances of most third-class passengers. The explanation was not malign Edwardian snobbery, but rather human failure: Captain Smith never gave specific instructions, and Chief Officer Wilde was too dazed to think for himself. Without crew escorts, some third-classers were baffled by the maze of corridors, and excluded by the locked gates that US immigration laws required between third-class decks and other parts of the ship, though these were unlocked by 12.30. There were claims that three young Irishwomen were excluded by a locked gate guarded by a seaman until Jim Farrell, a labourer from Aghnacliffe, County Longford, shouted 'Great God, man! Open the gate, and let the girls through!'[45]

Third-class men were held back initially, forbidden to accompany women and children being guided to the boat deck, and discouraged from going upwards in the ship where they had better chances of survival. 'Jack' Poingdestre saw a distraught mass of third-class men, some with luggage, gathered beneath a ladder to second-class, which was blocked by stewards.[46] However, 'steerage passengers', so far as Trembisky saw, 'were not prevented from getting up to the upper decks by anybody, or by closed doors, or anything else'.[47]

John Hart was a third-class steward in charge of a section of single women, wives travelling with children and nine married couples with children: a total of about fifty-eight. He testified that some refused to don lifebelts: 'They did not believe the ship was hurt in any way.'[48] Around 12.30 he received the order, 'Pass your women to the boat deck.'[49] The routes from the third-class berths to the boat deck were few and circuitous so, holding back the men, Hart guided a group of about twenty-five women and children upwards to the boat deck. As he testified, 'some were not willing to go to the boat deck and stayed behind. Some of them went to the boat deck and found it rather cold, and saw the boats being lowered away, and thought themselves more secure on the ship, and consequently returned to their cabin.' A few of his entourage declared that 'they preferred to remain on the ship than be tossed about on the water like a cockle-shell'.[50] The Finnish girls in his rescue party stayed in Lifeboat 8, but other women under his aegis jumped out, and scurried back into the liner, where it was warm. After expostulating, Hart descended to collect another twenty-five third-class passengers, including Swedish and Irish. Even at this critical stage passengers refused to leave their cabins. Some women refused to leave their husbands, and children clutched at their fathers. All the adults owned was in their luggage, which some were loath to abandon. Hart insisted on taking only women and children, despite men clamouring to join his group, and altogether saved over fifty of them. His second group reached Lifeboat 15 at about 1.15 (an hour and thirty-five minutes after the collision). He started to return for another muster of third-class passengers, but was ordered to man Lifeboat 15. As this lifeboat was prepared to leave, there was a renewed cry for women and children, but wives still would not leave their husbands.[51]

This was not a night when millionaires used their money like a heavy suitcase to clear their way through the crowd. Astor, the railway president Hays, his stockbroker son-in-law Davidson, the New Jersey millionaire Roebling, John Thayer and George Widener helped women into lifeboats, but stepped back themselves. The stories of millionaires' abnegation became world famous, although the dignified fatalism of the poor passed almost into oblivion. After the collision the young Swedish socialist August Wennerström came across Johan Lundahl, a fifty-one-year-old tailor and sojourner returning to Spokane, Washington after a spell in Småland. 'Good-bye friend, I'm too old to fight the Atlantic,' he said, and went to sit in a chair in the third-class smoking room.[52] Lundahl had learnt to lose without a struggle.

The first lifeboat to be launched was Lifeboat 7, which left from the starboard side carrying three crewmen and twenty-three passengers (all first-class): twenty-six escapees with thirty-nine vacancies. It is almost uniformly stated that the lifeboat was launched at 12.45, but it may have left as much as twenty minutes earlier. The 12.45 timing is about sixty-five minutes after the collision, and yet no-one felt there was an unconscionable delay in launching it. George Hogg, the look-out man who was in charge of Lifeboat 7, had not thought that *Titanic* would sink when he left the liner. The boat decks were not full of passengers yet. All this suggests an earlier time. The three French bridge players from the Café Parisien, Chevré, Marechal and Omont, fully charged with the desire to live, boarded Lifeboat 7. So, too, did Blank, Greenfield and Nourney, who had been gambling in the first-class smoking room. All six knew that the ship had grazed an iceberg; but few passengers yet suspected that the ship was stricken. Chevré, Omont and Marechal recalled passengers shrank from joining them in their lifeboat: everyone asking, 'What's the use?'[53]

The twenty-three passengers in Lifeboat 7 comprised twelve men and eleven women. The men included two honeymooning first-class husbands, Dickinson Bishop and John Snyder, with their young brides, so perhaps Murdoch had no wish to enforce separation on newlyweds. There was also Gilbert Tucker, who escorted three young women to the lifeboat, including Margaret Hays, for whom he had an obvious *tendresse* which may have made him seem nearly as deserving as a honeymooning husband. Two other men, Frederic Seward and William Sloper, had been playing bridge with the actress Dorothy Gibson and her mother. They took the Gibsons to the lifeboat, and were induced to alight with them – perhaps to hearten or shield them, for at this stage it seems that all women shrank from boarding lifeboats which looked more vulnerable than the big liner.

Helen Bishop feared 'there was little chance of being picked up in the lifeboats' from the vast ocean.[54] Dickinson Bishop declared, 'the officers implored people to get aboard, but they seemed to fear hanging out over the water at a height of over 75 feet, and the officers ordered the boat lowered with only a small portion of what it could carry'.[55] The seamen were desperate to get people aboard. James McGough, a buyer for a department store in Philadelphia, who had alerted Margaret Brown so promptly that she had disembarked in Lifeboat 6, explained how he ended up in Lifeboat 7. 'I had my back turned,' he testified, 'and was caught by the shoulders by one of the officers, who gave me a push, saying, "Here, you are a big fellow: get into the boat".'[56]

After launching Lifeboat 7, Murdoch moved to the next starboard lifeboat aft, 5, and called for passengers. Again women were reluctant to board, and again he let men accompany their timorous womenfolk as a way of hastening the loading. It was a good decision, which preserved lives. Amongst those standing nearby was a party of six first-class voyagers. Sallie Beckwith, originally from Columbus, Ohio, was travelling with her second (and younger) husband, Richard Beckwith, a Yale man who was vice-president of a New York real estate firm, and her nineteen-year-old daughter Helen Newsom. The girl was attended by her beau, Karl Behr: they married the following year. Behr was also a Yale man, a member of the US tennis team for the Davis Cup, currently working as a Wall Street lawyer. Attached to their group were Edwin Kimball, who owned a piano business in Boston, and his wife Gertrude. Sallie Beckwith asked if all six of them, men and women, could board, and was told, 'Of course, madam, every one of you.'

Lifeboat 5 is conventionally believed to have been launched an hour and a quarter after the collision, around 12.55 (two-thirds full with thirty-six passengers and five crewmen), but this estimate may be ten or fifteen minutes late. Both Behr and Kimball later described their escape into Lifeboat 5. 'All was perfectly calm,' said Behr. 'We waited while the first boat was being filled and lowered. We went in the second boat. At the time we supposed there were plenty of life-boats for all the passengers.'[57] Kimball stressed 'the dread of being lowered a sheer 77 feet in a frail lifeboat in mid-Atlantic at night . . . and the unshakeable confidence of many passengers and many of the vessel's crew that the *Titanic* could not sink.' He had first been alarmed by seeing a postal clerk wet to the knees – 'he seemed very serious and said it was pretty bad' – although the ship's officer who helped the party into their lifejackets assured them 'that there was no danger and that everything would be alright'. As a result of these mixed messages, and the long drop to the water, officers had difficulty in coaxing people aboard Lifeboat 5, despite assuring them that 'it would not be a long while before they would probably be back on the big boat'.[58]

The first port lifeboat to be launched was 6: the orthodox estimate is that it left seventy-five minutes after the collision, at 12.55 on Sunday morning. Quartermaster Hichens (who had been at the helm when the iceberg was struck) was in charge, with Fleet, the look-out who sounded the alarm, as his only crewman. Both men were scared, defensive and shocked. A Canadian from first-class, Arthur Peuchen, had been dragooned on board to help with the rowing, and Fahim Leeni, a young Lebanese labourer from third-class (heading for Niles, an iron foundry city near Youngstown, Ohio), probably infiltrated when Lightoller's back was turned, and took refuge in a dark corner. Twenty-four out of the twenty-eight occupants were women. They included the Canadian millionaire Hélène Baxter, Quigg Baxter's girlfriend Berthe Mayné, Margaret Brown, Helen Candee, the newlywed Eloise Smith and the English mother and daughter, Edith and Elsie Bowerman. The Bowermans are named in few accounts of Lifeboat 6: although normally outspoken, they were reticent in the boat either through shock or good sense; it seems that Elsie Bowerman neither repined over her experiences nor left any record of them.

Eloise Smith, however, described the prelude to her boarding Lifeboat 6. 'There was no commotion, no panic, and no-one seemed particularly frightened; in fact, most people seemed interested in the unusual occurrence, many having crossed 50 and 60 times.' She declined to leave without her husband, Lucien, and asked Captain Smith, who was standing nearby, if he might join her in Lifeboat 6. 'He ignored me personally, but shouted again through his mega-phone, "Women and children first." My husband said, "Never mind, Captain, about that; I will see that she gets in the boat." He then said, "I never expected to ask you to obey, but this is one time you must; it is only a matter of form to have women and children first. The boat is thoroughly equipped, and everyone on her will be saved." I asked him if that was absolutely honest, and he said, "Yes." I felt better then, because I had absolute confidence in what he said. He kissed me good-bye and placed me in the lifeboat with the assistance of an officer. As the boat was being lowered he yelled from the deck, "Keep your hands in your pockets: it is very cold weather." That was the last I saw of him, and now I remember the many husbands that turned their backs as the small boat was lowered, the women bliss-fully innocent of their husbands' peril, and said good-bye with the expectation of seeing them within the next hour or two.'[59] She would never have left had she known of the shortage of lifeboats; but it was unthinkable to her. More embittering would have been the knowledge that her husband perished because they were on the port deck. On the starboard, Murdoch's team had already let two grooms join their brides.

An hour and twenty minutes after the collision, around 1 a.m., the Fourth Officer, Boxhall, began to fire distress signals, often described as rockets, from the starboard of the bridge. Lifeboat 3 had just departed half-full with Clara Hays, her daughter Orian

Davidson, Henry Harper with his wife, dragoman and Pekinese, and the Cardeza mother and son amongst its thirty-two first-class passengers. Mortars launched the signals 800 feet into the sky, where they burst into a cascade of white stars which fell slowly downwards. The boom of the signals when they were launched, and the loud detonations in the sky, scared many passengers, although Lightoller tried to subdue alarm by assuring inquirers that Boxhall was summoning the ship whose lights could be seen some miles off.

The most controversial lifeboat launching occurred at this phase of the crisis. Starboard Lifeboat 1, an emergency cutter intended to deal with such mishaps as a man overboard, with capacity for forty occupants, was launched shortly after the distress signals started, with five passengers, seven crewmen and twenty-eight vacancies. The passengers were Sir Cosmo Duff Gordon with his wife and her secretary Laura Francatelli, who were joined by the Manhattan wholesaler Abraham Salomon and Henry Stengel. As Lady Duff Gordon would not leave without her husband, and Miss Francatelli would not go alone, Sir Cosmo had asked Murdoch if they could all enter the boat, and was told, 'Yes, I wish you would.' They got in: Murdoch called again for women and children; but none appeared. Like other women, Lady Duff Gordon was scared throughout the launching. 'I shall never forget how black and deep the water looked below us, and how I hated leaving the big, homely ship for this frail little boat . . . a man was sending off rockets, and the ear-splitting noise added to the horror of being suspended in mid-air.'[60]

Henry Stengel described finding the small lifeboat with three passengers in it. 'Jump in,' Murdoch told him. Stengel did as he was told, but leapt the guard-rail clumsily, and rolled into the lifeboat. 'That is the funniest sight I have seen tonight,' Murdoch said with a laugh. Stengel felt heartened by Murdoch's amusement: 'I thought perhaps it was not so dangerous as I imagined.' Moments later, Abraham Salomon, after seeking permission, clambered in. Murdoch was keen to get Lifeboat 1 away, as he needed its davits for larger lifeboats: having called again for women and children, he despatched it two-thirds empty. At 1.10 – ninety minutes after the collision – the ocean was lapping the portholes under the ship's name as Lifeboat 1 rowed away.

The Duff Gordons were subsequently reviled by American journalists and Washington senators for having escaped in a near-empty lifeboat, and suffered in their English reputations, too. It was suspected that they had bribed the crew to leave hurriedly, or not to rescue people freezing to death in the ocean. Tips given by Duff Gordon to the lifeboat crew were misrepresented as 'hush money'. Sir Cosmo was a clean, well-groomed Englishman, so drilled in conventional manners as to be baffled and ineffectual when he was jolted off his customary tracks. His title and demeanour were held against the couple, who were decried without respite; but the fact is that they obeyed instructions at launch-time, and were not responsible for the actions of the crewmen who put Lifeboat 1 on the water with such a shockingly low occupancy.

Lifeboat 8 on the port side was launched around the same time as Lifeboat 1 was loaded on the starboard. With capacity for sixty-five, it left with three crewmen and twenty-four women whom Lightoller divided from their men. As Ella White testified, 'there was a lot of pathos when husbands and wives kissed each other goodbye'.[61] The tension was increased by the booming and bursting of distress rockets, which made it hard to believe that, as Emma Bucknell was told when she boarded, 'it is only a matter of precaution, and there is really no danger'. Lifeboat 8 was commanded by Able Seaman Thomas Jones, supported by a sailor from Cornwall, Charles Pascoe, and a bedroom steward from London, Alfred Crawford. 'They did not seem to understand how to operate the ropes, and . . . launching the lifeboat, which should not take more than two minutes, took ten,' complained Mrs Bucknell. 'On the vessel there was beginning to be the signs of the great tragedy about to descend. Wives and husbands were separated when the women were put in our boat. A few of the men grew seemingly desperate, and Captain Smith, who was standing by, cried out: "Behave yourselves like men! Look at all of these women! See how splendid they are. Can't you behave like men?"' On Lifeboat 8, she said, all but one woman stayed calm, although they had been torn from their loved ones. The exception was Maria Peñasco y Castellana, a little Spanish bride, crying inconsolably for her husband, who had been held back by other men.[62]

Lightoller also excluded men from Lifeboat 10, which he loaded immediately afterwards with heightened urgency. The distress rockets were wracking passengers' nerves as second- and third-class passengers congregated in great numbers on the boat deck. Even so, the chief baker, Charles Joughin, testified of Lifeboat 10: 'we had difficulty finding ladies for it. They ran away from the boat, and said they were safer where they were.'[63] The second-class women and children in Lifeboat 10 included the Deans, Drews and Wests. The Wests, from Cornwall heading for Gainesville, Florida, had been asleep when the accident occurred. Arthur West put his two sleepy daughters in their lifejackets, and carried them to the boat deck – his pregnant wife Ada following with her handbag. After entrusting them to safety, he lowered a thermos of hot milk by rope to his wife in the descending lifeboat: their younger daughter was eleven months old. This was his wife's last glimpse of him. The heart-wrenching partings and everlasting farewells were never forgotten by survivors. Lillian Asplund, aged five in 1912, was (when she died in 2006) the last survivor who could remember the disaster: the others had all been babies. She recalled being handed into Lifeboat 15, and had a forlorn image of her father holding her twin brother in his arms, with her two brothers aged thirteen and nine standing on each side of him.

Clara Frauenthal was among the sixteen first-class women in Lifeboat 5, the second launched from the starboard. As it was lowered, her portly husband and brother-in-law jumped in. Henry Frauenthal's boots stunned Annie Stengel, whose indignant husband ensured that this incident was publicized when they reached New York, where doubtless it would have encouraged unpleasant stereotypes if two other episodes, featuring Ida and Isidor Straus and their kinsman Ben Guggenheim, had not captured the world's imagination.

When Woolner tried to usher Ida and Isidor Straus into starboard Lifeboat 3, saying 'nobody would object to an old gentleman like you getting in', the millionaire insisted: 'I will not go before the other men.'[64] When later the Strauses were watching the loading of Lifeboat 8, Archibald Gracie heard her being asked to step in. 'No, I will not be separated from my husband,' she replied. 'As we have lived, so will we die, together.' When it was urged that no-one would object if an old man like Straus boarded a lifeboat, he declared, 'I do not wish any distinction in my favour which is not granted to others.' A steward testified that Ida Straus got into Lifeboat 8 and then stepped out – telling her husband, 'We have been living together for many years, and where you go, I go.'[65] Ida Straus gave a fur stole to her maid Ellen Bird as the latter climbed weeping into Lifeboat 8, and the elderly pair withdrew to deckchairs to await the end. This self-sacrifice was thought exemplary. A few days later, Straus's rabbi in New York called him 'a loyal son of his people, and a loyal American', and compared his death to Abraham Lincoln's. 'Isidor Straus was a great Jew,' he continued. 'Now when we are asked, "Can a Jew die bravely?", there is an answer written in the annals of time.'[66]

Shortly after the loading of Lifeboat 8, Straus's kinsman, Ben Guggenheim, escorted his mistress Léontine Aubart and her maid Emma Sägesser onto Lifeboat 9. He did not try to board it, although in addition to forty-two women, it carried six men with eight crewmen, and therefore had about ten spare places. After Lifeboat 9 was lowered around 1.20, Guggenheim discarded his lifejacket, repaired to his state room and together with valet Victor Giglio donned evening-dress. 'We've dressed in our best, and are prepared to go down like gentlemen,' he told a steward who saw them after 1.30. 'There is grave doubt that the men will get off. I am willing to remain and play the man's game if there are not enough boats for more than the women and children. I won't die here like a beast. Tell my wife . . . I played the game out straight and to the end. No woman shall be left aboard this ship because Ben Guggenheim was a coward.'[67] Guggenheim, like Straus, wished to belie the anti-Semites.

Disorder began about an hour and forty minutes after the collision. By then the boat decks were teeming with second- and third-class passengers, who saw that there were insufficient lifeboats, felt the increasing list of the ship, and were scared by the distress rockets, which were fired until about 1.20. Panic erupted during the loading of Lifeboat 14, which finally was lowered around 1.30 with twenty-eight vacancies. Many of the thirty-seven occupants were second-class women and children: the Laroches, whose husband and father was the only black man on board, the Harts, Collyers, and the Davies and Wells families. Agnes Davies, a widow from St Ives, with her eight-year-old son, was helped into the boat by her nineteen-year-old son Joseph Nicholls, her sole support. He asked permission to join her, but was told that he would be shot if he attempted to get in, she said. She never saw him after the lifeboat was lowered, and her grief was harder to bear because his death seemed unnecessary: there was spare room, she knew, in the boat. Seaman Joseph Scarrott had loaded twenty women into Lifeboat 14 when 'some men tried to rush the boat, foreigners they were, because they could not understand the order which I gave them, and I had to use a bit of persuasion [with] the boat's tiller'. One culprit jumped in twice, and twice Scarrott ejected him.[68]

The loading of Lifeboat 14 was told by the second-class grocer's wife Charlotte Collyer: 'above the clamour of people asking questions of each other, there came the terrible cry: "Lower the boats. Women and children first!" They struck utter terror into my heart, and now they will ring in my ears until I die. They meant my own safety, but they also meant the greatest loss I have ever suffered – the life of my husband.' She hung back from the first two boats she saw loaded, and would not leave her husband. 'The third boat was about half full when a sailor caught Marjorie, my daughter, in his arms, tore her away from me and threw her into the boat. She was not even given a chance to tell her father good-bye! . . . The deck seemed to be slipping under my feet. It was leaning at a sharp angle.' As she, dressed in her nightgown, clung to her husband, one man seized her arm while another held her around the waist: she was tugged and hurled into the lifeboat. Her husband called, 'Go, Lotty! For God's sake, be brave, and go! I'll get a seat in another boat.' She stumbled to her feet, and saw Collyer's back as he walked away down the deck – looking for a seat in another boat, she assumed. 'I let myself be saved, because I believed that he, too, would escape,' she said afterwards; 'but I sometimes envy those whom no earthly power could tear from their husbands' arms. There were several such among those brave second-cabin passengers. I saw them standing by their loved ones to the last.'[69]

Fifth Officer Harold Lowe jumped into Lifeboat 14 and ordered to lower away. 'The sailors on deck had started to obey him, when a very sad thing happened,' Charlotte Collyer continued. 'A young lad' – possibly the sixteen-year-old Liverpudlian Alfred Gaskell, who was being taken to Canada in second-class by bachelor Joseph Fynney – 'almost small enough to be counted as a child, was standing close to the rail. He had made no attempt to force his way into the boat, though his eyes had been fixed piteously on the officer. Now, when he realized that he was really to be left behind, his courage failed him. With a cry, he climbed upon the rail and leaped down into the boat. He fell among us women, and crawled under a seat. I and another woman covered him up with our skirts. We wanted to give the poor lad a chance; but the officer dragged him to his feet and ordered him back upon the ship.' The stripling begged for his life, saying that he would not fill much space; but Lowe drew his revolver, and thrust it at his face. '"I give you just ten seconds to get back on that ship before I blow your brains out!" he shouted. The lad only begged the harder, and I thought I should see him shot as he stood. But the officer suddenly changed his tone. He lowered his revolver, and looked the boy squarely in the eyes. "For God's sake, be a man!" he said gently. "We've got women and children to save. We must stop at the decks lower down and take on women and children".' In truth, no lifeboat halted at a lower deck for women and children. The lad climbed back over the rail speechlessly, took a few unsteady steps, then lay face down upon the deck with his head beside a coil of rope. The women in the lifeboat were sobbing.[70]

As Lowe shouted again for the lifeboat to be lowered, a third-class passenger hurled himself into the lifeboat. Lowe seized him, and by brute strength pushed him out onto the boat deck. A dozen second-class men encircled him, and pummelled his face with their fists. Lowe was 'scared' that Lifeboat 14 would plunge as it was lowered, and fired his revolver along the side of the liner to deter last-moment jumpers. The shudder of an additional body falling into the lifeboat might jerk away the hooks, or dislodge a tie, he feared. As they descended past the open deck, he recalled seeing 'a lot of Italians, Latin people, all along the ship's rail . . . all glaring, more or less like wild beasts, ready to spring. That is why I yelled out and . . . let go, bang!'[71]

Later, at sea, Lowe discovered that there was a stowaway on board, Edward Ryan, from Ballinaveen, County Tipperary, whom he described as Italian.* Lowe treated Ryan roughly, but later the youth described his escape to his parents, in an unabashed letter reproduced in the *Cork Examiner*: 'I had a towel around my neck. I just threw this over my head and let it hang at the back. I wore my waterproof raincoat. I then walked very stiff past the officers . . . They thought I was a woman.'[72]

The disorder on the port was aggravated by Lightoller's determination to exclude men even if lifeboats had spare places. Lifeboat 13, launched on the starboard with far less aggression around the same time, 1.30, as stormy Lifeboat 14, had fifty occupants, including crewmen and male passengers. The latter were a medley of nationalities and vocations. They included the first-class physician Washington Dodge, and from second-class the school-master Lawrence Beesley, missionary Albert Caldwell, Japanese bureaucrat Masabumi Hosono and Percy Oxenham, a young mason journeying from Ponders End to New Jersey. The third-class men comprised three young Norwegians, the Irishman Daniel Buckley, a fourteen-year-old Swede named Johan Svenson, and

---

*'Italian' was the epithet applied promiscuously to any man who was thought to have lacked pluck or self-control. Charlotte Collyer described the third-class man beaten up by second-class men as Italian, although he is unlikely to have been a subject of King Victor Emmanuel III. The Italian ambassador in Washington protested about the pejorative inaccuracy with which his nationality was bandied about.

David Vartanian, from Keghi, whose twenty-second birthday was 15 April 1912.

Washington Dodge stated that when women stopped arriving for Lifeboat 13, someone shouted, 'Get in, doctor!', so he did. Masabumi Hosono, the only Japanese on *Titanic*, recorded that when he reached the boat deck from his second-class cabin, he was ordered below, away from the lifeboats, by crewmen who thought of him as a third-class Chinaman. The distress flares terrified him. He tried to compose himself for death; but longed to see his wife and children again, and stepped – unchallenged – into Lifeboat 13. Similarly, with Sylvia Caldwell and her baby aboard, her husband stepped into the bow as the boat was lowered. Lawrence Beesley said that when Lifeboat 13 came swinging level with him, the call came twice: 'Any more ladies?' No women appearing, a sensible crewman eyed him and said, 'You had better jump'. He jumped. By contrast, the young Irishman Daniel Buckley attributed his survival in Lifeboat 13 to another passenger's compassion. He had got in early, with a crowd of other men, all of whom were ordered out to let women in. He started crying, and a woman threw her shawl over him, and told him to stay still. The seamen did not realize Buckley's sex.[73]

Two lifeboats were launched around 1.35 (just under two hours after the collision). Lifeboat 15 left from starboard with forty-three occupants, including five crewmen and twenty-one other men. These included the cardsharp Harry Homer from first-class, who lived by the precept that God helps those who help themselves, and three experienced Atlantic travellers, a Belgian named Guillaume de Messemaeker, who worked a homestead between Tampico and Vandalia, near Milk River in Montana; the Slovenian Franz Karun and his four-year-old daughter Manca; and Nikola Lulic, the sojourner in Chisholm, Minnesota who was chaperoning a party of fellow Croatians for the Swiss travel agent, Büchel – and inveigled his way onto Lifeboat 15 by finding a sailor's cap, which he plumped on his head. There were also six Swedes, five Finns and two Lebanese.

Lifeboat 16 was lowered from port by Lightoller with thirty occupants – twenty-three women, five crewmen, a small Lebanese boy and an Irish youth whom no-one seemed to notice called Bernard McCoy, who had joined his two sisters. The women were mostly Irish and other third-class voyagers together with stewardess Violet Jessop. According to one report of the Addergoole party, 'they shoved Annie Kelly on the boat, in her nightgown and all as she was, and they would have taken Kate Bourke, too, and Mary, her sister-in-law, but Kate clung to her husband and said if he must die, she would die with him, and so did Mary say she would not go without her brother, and they pushed the little Flynn boy back, and out away. It was pitiful that they wouldn't let the boy on the lifeboat, and he only a child, and it not full.'[74] (The 'little Flynn boy' was a labourer aged twenty-eight.) After Olaus Abelseth had shepherded his girl cousin onto Lifeboat 16, seeing there were no more port lifeboats, he crossed to the starboard side with his brother-in-law Moen and cousin Søholt. 'Are there any sailors here?' they were asked by an officer seeking help with Lifeboat C. He had started work at sea 'when I was ten years old with my dad fishing', only stopping when he moved to the American mid-west at the age of sixteen; but he said nothing, because Moen and Søholt said in Norwegian, 'Let us stay here together.' The three kin stood in gloomy silence. For Abelseth, with his restraint and self-sacrifice, there was no frantic rush to escape.

The loading of Lifeboat 1 with the Duff Gordons and three other passengers proved to be the most contentious of the night. Vying with it was the starboard launching two hours after the collision, around 1.40, of Lifeboat C. This was a so-called collapsible, with flat, clinker-built double bottom and low wooden sides topped by canvas. It left with forty-one occupants, including many Lebanese women and children, and Emily Goldsmith with her nine-year-old son Frankie. Frank Goldsmith embraced his wife and kissed her goodbye. Reaching down, he hugged his son, and said, 'So long, Frankie: I'll see you later.' Their travel companion Tom Theobald took off his wedding ring and gave it to Emily Goldsmith saying: 'If I don't see you in New York, will you see that my wife gets this?'[75] Frank Goldsmith and Tom Theobald stood back, as did their sixteen-year-old companion Alfred Rush, although there were male passengers aboard. No-one objected to the presence of Abraham Hyman, a Manchester picture framer, or four Chinese voyagers: still less to a young Lebanese, Sahid Nakid, who was accompanying his wife and their baby. The uproar occurred because, when no more women and children arrived, and the lowering of the boat was starting, Ismay stepped in, just as its gunwale reached the level of the deck, and sat in an empty place near the bow. Until this impulsive move, he had been helping, and sometimes hindering, the loading of successive lifeboats. Billy Carter followed him: both men later insisted that no women were visible nearby, and that there was room for six more people in the boat; but in America, Ismay was to become a hate-figure because of his impulse, which tarnished his name in England too.

The patience of the women millionaires was conspicuous. Lifeboat 4 had been the first one ready on the port side, but was the last of the larger lifeboats to be launched. Captain Smith told Lightoller to fill it from the promenade deck, thinking that this would be easier and safer for women than the open boat deck. Passengers waiting on the boat deck duly filed down to the promenade deck, but Smith had forgotten that the *Titanic* promenade deck, unlike *Olympic*'s, was protected from ocean winds by glass windows known as Ismay screens. Woolner reminded him of his mistake: 'By God, you are right! Call those people back.'[76] The women and children returned to the boat deck by the inner stairs as Lifeboat 4 was lowered outside to the promenade deck. Lightoller decided it would be easier to displace a glass screen rather than haul the lifeboat back, and for a second time the women and children trooped down. Madeleine Astor, Lucile Carter, Marion Thayer and Eleanor Widener were among the troopers. Their counterparts a century later might have thrown tantrums, or insisted on their privileges, but these millionaires' wives cared about showing good manners: they had a sense of entitlement, but did not confuse an infantile, assertive temper with strength of character. They waited anxiously, patiently, proudly.

It took an hour before Lightoller's men returned to Lifeboat 4. By then it was nearly 2 a.m., and the water was within 10 feet of the promenade deck. In addition to the women millionaires, Thayer senior had escorted Martha Stephenson and her sister Elizabeth Eustis to Lifeboat 4; Emily Ryerson and her lady's maid Victorine Chaudanson escaped in it; so too did the Cornish mother and daughter from second-class, Eliza and Nellie Hocking, and a third-class Finnish woman heading for Detroit with her baby. Deckchairs were stacked to make makeshift steps which enabled passengers to climb through the Ismay screen. Lightoller stood with one foot on deck and one in the lifeboat as (helped by Astor and John Thayer) he handed the women and children on board. 'Get into the lifeboat to please me,' Astor told his reluctant wife. He then asked Lightoller if he might join his pregnant wife, whom he described as in 'a delicate condition', for the boat was only two-thirds full; but Lightoller replied, 'No, sir, no men are allowed in these boats until the women are loaded first.' Astor was displeased, but made no protest. 'The sea is calm,' he told his wife. 'You'll be all right. You're in good hands. I'll meet you in the morning.' He handed his gloves to her, stepped back from the rail, and saluted her.

Emily Ryerson, whose elder son had so recently been killed in a motoring smash, said that she was determined 'not to make a fuss and to do as we were told'. When she begged her husband to let her stay with him, he replied that she must obey orders: 'You must go when your turn comes. I'll stay with John Thayer. We will be all right.' On A Deck she waited in line with the women million-aires, and her surviving son, Jack. Lightoller halted them, saying, 'That boy can't go'; but her husband insisted: 'Of course that boy goes with his mother; he is only thirteen.' Lightoller let the child pass, but reiterated, 'No more boys.' This seemed likely to exclude William Carter, aged eleven, but Astor plonked a girl's hat on the boy's head, and lifted him into the boat just before it was lowered. Then he sauntered off to find his Airedale, Kitty. Emily Ryerson kissed her husband for the last time: as the lifeboat descended, she saw him, John Thayer and Widener standing together sombrely, and the ocean swamping through open portholes. There was such hurry in launching Lifeboat 4 that twenty-nine places were left empty: it makes the attempted exclusion of the Carter and Ryerson boys seem shameful.

Collapsible D was the final lifeboat launched, from the port side shortly after 2 a.m., two hours and twenty minutes after the collision. Lightoller recalled that when first he reached it, there were men in the boat. 'They weren't British, nor of the English-speaking race. I won't even attribute any nationality to them, beyond saying that they come under the broad category known to sailors as "dagoes". They hopped out mighty quickly, and I encouraged them verbally, also by vigorously flourishing my revolver.'[77] The ocean was lapping up the stairway to the boat deck: Collapsible D needed to be lowered only 10 feet to the ocean's surface. Even at this crisis, women would not leave their men. The novelist Jacques Futrelle forced his wife Lily May aboard: 'It's your last chance: go!' She submitted and survived, but an old woman who had been coaxed into the lifeboat changed her mind, and was helped out, because she insisted on rejoining her husband.[78] Lightoller claimed that he repeatedly called for 'more women and children', but had difficulty filling D with more than twenty-four out of a possible forty occupants. Cruelly, however, passengers longing to be rescued were excluded. Just before it was lowered, Seaman William Lucas told two women appealing to him from the deck that there was no room for them: they must wait for Collapsibles A and B which would be loaded next.[79] One of them was Edith Evans, companion of the American sisters, Appleton and Brown, who were already aboard. Lucas unwittingly condemned both women to death: A and B were never loaded.

The ship's forecastle was sliding under the ocean as D was lowered. This last lifeboat to be launched was less than a hundred yards away when its occupants saw the liner sink. In addition to Quartermaster Arthur Bright, steward John Hardy, and Seaman Lucas, there were two young Finns (whom Hardy mistook for Lebanese 'chattering the whole night in their strange language'[80]), Erna Andersson, heading for New York; and a pregnant bride, Maria Backström, whose husband and two brothers were left behind and perished. The others were the young Swedish woman Berta Nilsson, travelling out with her fiancé, who was a cook in Missoula, Montana – he was lost; two of the three Lamson sisters, Charlotte Appleton and Caroline Brown (their sister Malvina Cornell had previously escaped in Lifeboat 2); Lily Futrelle, whose husband stayed on board and died; Renée Harris, wife of the producer who was left on board and lost; Maybelle Thorne, mistress of George Rosenshine, who was left on board and lost; another first-class passenger, Jane Hoyt; Joseph Duquemin, a young mason from Guernsey heading for Albion, New York, who claimed to have been hauled from the ocean but had surely secreted himself; three Irishwomen in their early twenties, Annie Jermyn and Bridget O'Driscoll, both from Ballydehob, County Cork, and Mary Kelly, from Castlepollard, County Westmeath; and three small boys: the Navrátil brothers and a four-year-old Lebanese boy called Michael Joseph.

The foregoing boarded D at the boat deck, but three men boarded it later by more dramatic means. Jane Hoyt's husband Frederick Hoyt, a broker on Broadway, with houses in Manhattan and Connecticut, a distinguished Long Island yachtsman, dived into the ocean once the lifeboat was afloat, and climbed aboard. He sat there, wringing wet, next to Hardy, helping him to row. Two other men also joined D after it had been lowered from the boat deck – Hugh Woolner and his young shipboard acquaintance Steffansson – and their story merits analysis.

Woolner himself told the story, publicly, as a witness to the Senate enquiry on the sinking. The veneer that he put on his actions was devised to stop any surmise that his survival had been unmanly. He was a public school and Cambridge man, trying to revive his credit and reputation after his bankruptcy, and needed to show that although he had saved himself, he was as fine a gentleman as Jack Astor or Archie Butt. After consigning Helen Candee to Lifeboat 6, Woolner said that he had looked to see how else he might help. 'I did what a man could. It was a very distressing scene – the men parting from their wives.' As he and Steffansson helped to load lifeboats, they saw no jostling of women by men until Collapsible D was hitched onto the davits. 'While that boat was being loaded,' Woolner testified, 'there was a sort of scramble on the starboard side, and I looked around and I saw two flashes of a pistol.' He heard

Murdoch shouting, 'Get out of this, clear out of this,' to a crowd of men swarming around starboard Collapsible C. He and Steffansson went to help clear C of men who were climbing in, because a bunch of Lebanese women, whom he mistook for Italians, were standing at the edge of the crowd, unable to reach the boat. Supposedly he and Steffansson tugged out half a dozen men – 'probably third-class passengers' – 'by their legs and anything we could get hold of'. Once the men were ejected, they helped to hoist the Lebanese women into the lifeboat – 'they were very limp'. With this tale Woolner established his superiority over the panicky foreign men who tried to save themselves before the women. Although he had survived, unlike few if any of the ejected foreigners, he surpassed their level, because he had shown Anglo-Saxon self-mastery.

Woolner perhaps missed seeing Ismay step into C after the Lebanese women: it was certainly an incident which did not fit with the purpose of his narrative. He and Steffansson wished exceedingly to board Collapsible D, but recognized that they had small hope of doing so under Lightoller's scrutiny. They descended to A Deck, now deserted after the launching of Lifeboat 4 with its cargo of American millionairesses, but bathed in a weird light, as its electric lights glowed red before they failed. 'This is getting rather a tight corner,' Woolner said to Steffansson, as the ocean lapped their feet. They hopped onto the gunwale, preparing to jump into the water, because they were in peril of being trapped under the ceiling. 'As we looked out we saw this collapsible, the last boat on the port side, being lowered right in front of our faces . . . I said to Steffansson: "There is nobody in the bows. Let us make a jump for it. You go first." And he jumped out and tumbled in head over heels into the bow, and I jumped too, and hit the gunwale with my chest . . . and caught the gunwale with my fingers, and slipped off backwards.' Steffansson caught hold of him, and yanked him in. Then, he said, they pulled Frederick Hoyt from the sea. He sat next to Renée Harris, who had broken her elbow that afternoon after slipping on a cake. The elder Navrátil boy was crying for his doll, and Woolner fed the child biscuits.[81]

'As far as I know,' wrote Lightoller, who admitted nothing of Bernard McCoy, Joseph Duquemin and Fahim Leeni, the jump of Woolner and Steffansson into Collapsible D 'was the only instance of men getting away in boats from the port side. I don't blame them, the boat wasn't full, for the simple reason that we couldn't find sufficient women, and there was no time to wait – the water was then actually lapping round their feet on A Deck, so they jumped for it and got away. Good luck to them.'[82] This is a sensible judgement: wiser than the judgement that tried to exclude pre-pubescent boys like John Ryerson and William Carter from Lifeboat 4; or had turned away Edith Evans and bullied 'dagoes' from this same Collapsible D minutes earlier.

Astor, Clinch Smith, John Thayer and George Widener stayed together in the terrible scenes after the last lifeboat had been lowered. Archie Butt had been standing to one side on the boat deck: no-one noticed whether Frank Millet was beside him, but it is unthinkable that he was not. With the final lifeboat gone, passengers and crew began jumping from the decks into the icy ocean. On the starboard deck, seventeen-year-old Jack Thayer and his shipboard friend Clyde Milton Long had watched the crowd 'pushing and shoving wildly' around Collapsible C: 'We thought it best not to try to get in it, as we thought it would never reach the water right side up, but it did.' They stood by the davits of a boat which had left, decided that their best hope was to slide down the davit ropes into the ocean, shook hands and wished one another luck. As Thayer described in a tender letter to Long's grieving parents, 'We did not give each other any messages for home, because neither of us thought we would ever get back. Then we jumped upon the rail. Your son put his legs over the rail, while I straddled it. Hanging over the side, holding onto the rails with his hands, he looked up at me and said, "You're coming, boy, aren't you?" I replied, "Go ahead, I'll be with you in a minute." He let go and slid down the side and I never saw him again.' Having slithered down the liner's side, Long was sucked away in the torrent of water rushing into the now-submerged A Deck from which Woolner had recently escaped. Thayer was horrified, but leapt as far from the ship as he could. 'I am sending you my picture, thinking you might like to see who was with him at the end,' he wrote to Long's parents. 'I would treasure it very much if you could spare me one of his.'[83]

Collapsibles A and B were fastened to the roof of the officers' quarters above the boat deck. Each boat weighed over 2 tons, and Lightoller superintended crewmen and passengers who tried to slide them down on makeshift ramps made of oars and planking. Collapsible A reached the deck successfully and was fitted into davits, but *Titanic* suddenly plunged. A steward called Edward Brown cut the lifeboat adrift so that it floated free of the ship which might otherwise have smashed it. By doing so, he saved twenty lives, including his own; for after being washed into the ocean as the ship's bridge went under water, he got through a sea of people fighting one another in panic, and clambered onto Collapsible A.

Lightoller and another seaman freed the remaining Collapsible B atop the officers' quarters and threw it down onto the waterlogged boat deck, hoping that some of the crowd there might scramble aboard as it floated off. Collapsible B landed upside down, and was washed off the deck by a great surge of water. 'Just then the ship took a slight but definite plunge – probably a bulkhead went,' Lightoller described. 'The sea came rolling up in a wave, over the steel-fronted bridge, along the deck below us, washing the people back in a dreadful, huddled mass. Those that didn't disappear under the water right away, instinctively started to clamber up that part of the deck still out of water, and work their way towards the stern, which was rising steadily out of the water as the bow went down.'[84] The frantic struggles of those trying to climb the sloping deck, fighting to keep out of the freezing ocean, made a horrible sight. Captain Smith, who had been busy and visible during the loading of the lifeboats, probably tried to return to his bridge: whether he reached it, and went down with his ship, or slithered overboard from the tilting liner before he reached his bridge, is unknowable. The alternative fancies about his death, which journalists later concocted, are sensational trumpery.

Two hours and twenty-five minutes after the collision, around

2.15, the liner's bridge dipped under the ocean, and the forward funnel – its wires unable to support its weight as the ship tilted ever more steeply – crashed downwards, splintering the deck, hitting the sea with an enormous splash near Lifeboat B and crushing several swimmers, probably including Astor. Gravity overwhelmed all the loose fittings, which crashed downwards towards the bow. Engines and machinery broke loose from their bolts, plunged through the compartments, smashing everything beneath them. For twenty seconds the noise – 'partly a roar, partly a groan, partly a rattle, and partly a smash' – reverberated across the ocean to Lifeboat 13. To Beesley it conjured heavy furniture being thrown downstairs from the top of a house, smashing the stairs and every obstacle to bits.[85]

Lights dimmed, flared up again and then finally vanished at 2.20 – two hours and forty minutes after look-out Fleet had glimpsed the shape of ice. Ismay did not wish to see his liner plunge, and sat with his back to the spectacle. Lady Duff Gordon recalled the moment as seen from Lifeboat 1: 'I could see her dark hull towering like a giant hotel, with light streaming from every cabin porthole. As I looked, one row of these shining windows was suddenly extinguished. I guessed the reason, and turned shudderingly away. When I forced myself to look again, yet another row had disappeared.' She sat in miserable stupor until her husband cried, 'My God! She is going now!' There arose, she said, 'an indescribable clamour . . . I felt my very reason tottering'.[86]

The story of Rhoda Abbott – the only woman aboard Collapsible A – is heartbreaking. She was the seamstress separated from her abusive pugilist husband and travelling third-class with her sons Rossmore and Eugene Abbott, aged sixteen and thirteen. On deck they stayed by her side, and went into the sea with her when the ship took its final plunge. They stayed with her, grateful to the mother whose loving warmth had always shone so copiously on each of them, raised and shoved her into Collapsible A, which was swamped with a foot of freezing water because its occupants had failed to raise the canvas gunwale. She had shaped their lives by the sound of her voice and the look in her eyes: now she was too cold to speak. Young men weaken and die quickly in freezing temperatures – faster than women, faster than older men, because they have a lower percentage of body fat to act as insulation, and perhaps because their over-excitement sends them quicker into shock. With an ever-loosening grip, both boys held the edge of Collapsible A with their helpless, dazed mother looking down on them. First Eugene, then Rossmore slipped away in the water with her watching. It must have felt unbelievable. Few women can have suffered as she did.

In *Titanic*'s last moments, August Wennerström was standing near Alma Pålsson with her five children and a couple named Edvard and Elin Lindell. As the ship sank the group scrabbled up the sloping deck to escape the rising waters. The incline became too steep and, clasping hands, they slid down into the Atlantic. Wennerström gripped two Pålsson children, but lost hold. He and Edvard Lindell eventually clambered onto Collapsible A. Elin Lindell was struggling in the water, and Wennerström took her hand, but was too weak from shock and cold to pull her in. Uncertain if she was dead or alive, he relinquished his grip, and she drifted away. He turned apprehensively to Edvard Lindell only to find that he was already dead. Wennerström was frozen numb by the icy water lapping his legs. He only moved when someone died, whereupon he shoved the corpse overboard.

Olaus Abelseth provided further moving testimony. 'I asked my brother-in-law if he could swim, and he said no. I asked my cousin if he could swim, and he said no.' They could see the water rising towards them, clung to ropes suspended from a davit, for the deck was so steep that people were sliding horribly into the ocean. 'My brother-in-law said to me, "We had better jump off or the suction will take us down." I said, "No. We won't jump yet. We ain't got much show anyhow, so we might as well stay as long as we can".' They were five feet above the ocean when the three men finally jumped. Abelseth's brother-in-law held his hand as they leapt. 'I got a rope tangled around me, and I let loose of my brother-in-law's hand to get away from the rope. I thought then, "I am a goner" . . . but I came on top again, and I was trying to swim, and there was a man

– lots of them were floating around – and he got me on the neck . . . and pressed me under, trying to get on top of me.' Abelseth fought free of him, then paddled in his lifebelt – it was impossible to swim on one's stomach wearing a lifebelt – until he saw a dark object, which proved to be Collapsible A. 'They did not try to push me off and they did not do anything for me to get on. All they said when I got on there was, "Don't capsize the boat".' Men (and Rhoda Abbott) stood, sat or lay there. Some fell back into the water: those who died were cast overboard. Abelseth kept warm by swinging his arms. 'We did not talk very much, except that we would say, "One, two, three," and scream together for help.'[87]

Lightoller had dived overboard a few minutes before the liner sank. 'Striking the water was like a thousand knives being driven into one's body, and, for a few moments, I completely lost grip of myself.' He had no sooner mastered himself than suction caught him. A huge air shaft stood on the boat deck with wire grating to prevent rubbish being thrown down. Beneath it was a sheer drop to a stokehold at the bottom of the ship. Lightoller was caught by the rush of ocean pouring down this shaft, and held against this wire grating with the horrifying knowledge that he would plunge to the stokehold if the wire broke. 'Although I struggled and kicked for all I was worth, it was impossible to get away, for as fast as I pushed myself off I was irresistibly dragged back, every instant expecting the wire to go, and to find myself shot down into the bowels of the ship.' He was drowning, of course, too, until a blast of hot air came up the shaft, and blew him to the ocean's surface. Eventually he scrambled onto Collapsible B.[88]

Collapsible B had floated off around 2.20. The suffering of the thirty odd people who clambered aboard was worst of all, for it was upside down. Those whose names we know, because they survived, included Algernon Barkworth, Eugene Daly, Archibald Gracie, Charles Joughin, Lightoller, stoker Henry Senior, Victor Sunderland and Jack Thayer. No women are known to have scrambled onto it.

The London teenager from third-class, Victor Sunderland, seems to have been one of the few passengers without a lifebelt. He had tried to fetch his, but found his cabin was submerged. Fearing that the companions he had left there were drowned, he returned to the boat deck – passing Byles, the Catholic priest, leading kneeling men and women in prayer. Back on the boat deck, a steward in a lifeboat clutching three lifebelts refused to give him one. A crewman whom he accosted had no idea where they were to be found. As the starboard lifeboats had all but gone, passengers turned to seek lifeboats on the port side, but were restrained by crewmen from going there as the liner was increasingly listing to port. When the ship began to plunge, Sunderland copied firemen who were jumping overboard. In the ocean he survived the fall of the forward funnel, and reached Collapsible B. Someone recited the Lord's Prayer and Hail Mary, with the others following.[89]

Archibald Gracie had been knocked over by the surging wave described by Lightoller, and was sucked into a whirlpool, swirling down and down. Knowing that his life depended on it, he swam away with all his strength. His desperation was intensified by his fear of being scalded to death by boiling water released by exploding boilers, for he recalled that after the British battleship *Victoria* sank in a collision off the Lebanese coast, the Mediterranean resembled a bubbling cauldron of boiling milk and inflicted a scorching death on sailors in the sea.[90] Reaching the surface, Gracie clung to floating debris before striking out for Collapsible B. The men there stood upright in two rows, back to back, holding one another's shoulders. Exhausted men fell overboard; others died of exposure during their hours on the swamped boat.

Chevré, Marechal and Omont recorded that from Lifeboat 7, *Titanic* resembled a picture of fairyland glittering with lights from bow to stern, or a fantastic backdrop of stage scenery. Then the lights died, and the stern reared high in the air. A terrible clamour arose, and for an hour anguished death cries rang out with wild persistency. Sometimes the cries receded, but then the chorus of death resumed, with more piercing despair. The oarsmen on Lifeboat 7 rowed hard to escape from the heartrending cries. 'Those shrieks pursued us and haunted us as we pulled away in the night.' 'Then one by one the cries ceased and only the noise of the sea remained.'[91] The Cornish widow Agnes Davies with her young son in Lifeboat 14 watched the lights of the lower decks vanish row by row under water: 'it was awful, terrible'. Her fellow passengers tried to protect her. 'When the men in the boat learnt that one of my sons was on the steamer and would not be saved, they formed a line before me, so that I could not see the ship as she plunged beneath the waves.' She heard, though, 'the screams, cries and moaning' of the dying.[92] Frankie Goldsmith in Collapsible C was aged nine: years later, as a young milk-cart driver, he lived near the Detroit Tigers baseball stadium. The roar of the crowd when a player hit a home run never ceased to remind him of the cries of the thousand people freezing to death in the Atlantic. His mother held his head in her hands so that he would not see the horror. In Lifeboat 13 they tried to sing to keep the women from hearing the appalling cries.

A minority of the 1,500 people who had not reached the lifeboats sank with the ship. Almost all of them wore lifejackets, and few drowned. But they were floating in an icy sea; the temperature was probably two degrees below freezing point Celsius (28° Fahrenheit), cold enough to kill in thirty minutes. They cried for help as they froze to death. This was 'the worst part of the disaster' for steward Samuel Rule on Lifeboat 15: 'the groans were awful, and of course we could do nothing. I shall never forget it.'[93] Jack Thayer was traumatized by the memory of that 'continuous wailing chant, from the fifteen hundred in the water all around us. It sounded like locusts on a mid-summer night, in the woods in Pennsylvania.' This terrible cry gradually died away, as over a thousand people, tight in their white lifejackets, froze to death. People in lifeboats 400 yards away heard the cries, but did not respond. It became a lifelong question for Thayer: 'How could any human being fail to heed those cries? . . . If they had turned back several more hundred would have been saved.'[94]

Only Lifeboat 14 commanded by Harold Lowe tried to save people in the water. Lowe waited until the dying people had 'thinned out', and their cries subsided. 'It would not have been wise or safe to have gone there before, because the whole lot of us would have been swamped, and then nobody would have been saved.' Having transferred his passengers to another boat, he rowed back with some volunteers but found only four men alive among the corpses bobbing in their lifejackets, and one of those died soon after being hauled aboard. 'I made the attempt,' he insisted, 'as soon as any man could do so, and I am not scared of saying it. I did not hang back.'[95] The death cries distressed Third Officer Herbert Pitman, who ordered Lifeboat 5 to row back to rescue frozen survivors. 'I told my men to get their oars, and pull toward the wreck,' he testified. The passengers in his boat protested that this was 'a mad idea', because their lifeboat 'should be swamped with the crowd that was in the water, and it would add another forty to the list of drowned.' It lay heavily with him that his lifeboat 'simply took our oars in and lay quiet . . . doing nothing.'[96]

Despite direct instructions from Captain Smith to row for the light of the ship presumed to be Lord's *Californian*, Seaman Jones, in charge of Lifeboat 8, wanted to return to the wreck site to rescue more people, 'but the ladies were frightened'.[97] One woman endorsed his initiative, but most of the rest, including some women who had taken up oars, routed his idea. 'Ladies,' Jones said, 'if any of us are saved, remember *I* wanted to go back, I would rather drown with them than leave them.' The exception in Lifeboat 8 was Lady Rothes, wife of a penurious Scottish peer. 'I saw the way she was carrying herself, and I heard the quiet determined way she spoke to the others, and I knew she was more of a man than any we had on board,' Jones later said. He installed Lady Rothes at the tiller, and her nineteen-year-old lady's maid Roberta Maioni took an oar and helped every minute. The girl, garbed only in nightgown and kimono, with luxuriant hair streaming over her shoulders and down her back, suggested they should sing to maintain morale, starting with 'Pull for the Shore'.[98]

Emma Bucknell confirmed that Jones protested that they did not have enough people aboard, and should wait near the liner to rescue others. She was exasperated to discover that his crew, bedroom steward Crawford and Seaman Pascoe, could not row. 'It was tragic. I have known how to row for a great many years as the result of much time spent in the Adirondacks, and I slipped into the seat beside the man and showed him how to work the oar.' She found the three men muddle-headed: they told her that the liner would remain afloat until 2 o'clock on Monday afternoon, a full twelve hours distant, shortly before it sank. With eight women passengers helping to row, Lifeboat 8 pushed towards the light to which they had been directed by Captain Smith. 'The men soon learned to handle the oars,' said Bucknell, 'but even though they were used to rough work, their hands were soon enflamed and blistered.' The women rowed until they collapsed from exhaustion, whereupon another woman would gently move her aside and work in her place.[99]

The women rowers in several lifeboats were valiant in meeting a terrible challenge. George Hogg, the seaman in charge of the first lifeboat launched, 7, with its load of first-class Americans, made a point of saying: 'the women ought to have a gold medal on their breasts, God bless them! I will always raise my hat to a woman, after what I saw.'[100] Whether he was sincere, or talking ingratiating cant, there is no doubt that in other lifeboats there was class tension between first-class women and low seamen. Marion Thayer found Walter Perkis, the quartermaster in charge of Lifeboat 4, so inefficient, indecisive and disagreeable that she doubted he was a quartermaster at all. Ella White reported that when Jones, in charge of Lifeboat 8, gave an order, Crawford and Pascoe, 'who knew nothing about the handling of a boat would say, "If you don't stop talking through that hole in your face there will be one less in the boat." We were in the hands of men of that kind. I settled two or three fights between them, and quietened them down.' She resented their smoking tobacco while women rowed, and doubted that they recognized their predicament. 'They speak of the bravery of the men. I do not think there was any particular bravery, because none of the men thought it was going down. If they had thought the ship was going down, they would not have frivoled as they did.'[101]

The class and gender skirmishes were worst on Lifeboat 6. It contained two seamen, Quartermaster Hichens, and look-out Fleet, together with Arthur Peuchen, a Lebanese youth, and twenty-four women or children. Hichens (who had been steering when the ship hit the iceberg and was panic-stricken) took command, and ordered Fleet and Peuchen to row hard to escape the liner's suction when it foundered. Margaret Brown and a cashier from the à la carte restaurant, Margaret Martin, also took up oars. 'Faster! Faster!' Hichens shouted. 'If you don't make better speed with your rowing, we'll be pulled down to our deaths!' After *Titanic* sank, Margaret Brown, Helen Candee and Julia Cavendish (the Chicago-born wife of an Anglo-Irishman) urged Hichens to return to save those crying for help. He refused: 'It is our lives now, not theirs. Row, damn you! Our boat will immediately be swamped if we go back . . . there's no use going back, because there's nothing in the water but a bunch of stiffs.'[102] This was a foul remark, for Hélène Baxter, Julia Cavendish, Eloise Smith and others had left sons and husbands behind. When, to keep warm, Brown elbowed her way to the stern, took the tiller from him and threatened that if he resisted, she would knock him overboard, he lapsed into a sulky gloom: 'We're likely to drift for days. There is no water in the casks, and we have no bread, no compass and no chart. If a storm should come up, we are completely helpless! We will either drown or starve.' Brown told him to keep quiet: 'By damn, I wish you'd keep your place!' Hichens swore at her at one juncture.[103] 'Hichens was cowardly and almost crazed with fear,' Helen Candee wrote afterwards. 'When asked if *Carpathia* would come and pick us up, he replied: "No, she is not going to pick us up; she is to pick up bodies".' Again this was needlessly brutal with bereft women sitting hard by.[104]

On Collapsible A, Abelseth knew that his three friends, Humblen, Moen and Søholt, were lost. With him, though, was a shipboard acquaintance from New Jersey who was freezing to death. By dawn this man was comatose, but Abelseth strove to keep him alive. The Dakota homesteader took him by the shoulder, raised him upright from the deck, and told him, 'We can see a ship now. Brace up.' He held the dying man's hand, and shook him. 'Who are you?' asked the man. 'Let me be.' Abelseth tried to support him, but got tired, and took a piece of cork flotsam from the ocean, and laid it under his head to keep his head above water; but his companion died before rescue came.[105]

The ship that Abelseth espied was a small Cunarder, *Carpathia*. Its captain, Arthur Rostron, was the hero of the disaster – a crisp, efficient sea captain who was neither as foolhardy in the ice zone as Smith of *Titanic* nor as feckless as Lord of *Californian*. 'I had the greatest respect for him as a seaman, a disciplinarian and as a man who could take a decision quickly,' wrote another Cunard officer, Bisset. 'He was not the burly type of jolly old sea dog. Far from it, he was of thin and wiry build, with sharp features, piercing blue eyes, and rapid, agile movements. His nickname in the Cunard service was "the Electric Spark".'[106] The *Carpathia* was carrying 743 passengers, three days out of New York heading for the Mediterranean ports of Gibraltar, Genoa, Naples, Trieste and Fiume. Its twenty-year-old wireless operator, Harold Cottam, worked and slept in the wireless shack atop the superstructure aft of the funnel. He was preparing for bed, stooping to unlace his boots and wearing his earphones because he was waiting for acknowledgement of a message which he had sent earlier; and it was thus that he heard transmissions from Cape Cod intended for *Titanic*. He sent a Morse message to MGY, the *Titanic* call sign, checking if the liner had received its Cape Cod messages. MGY replied instantly, 'Come at once. We have struck an iceberg.' Cottam erupted into Rostron's cabin with the news.

Rostron ordered *Carpathia* to turn about, and his engine room to get up steam. Arc lights were festooned in the gangways. Canvas bags to haul children from the lifeboats, chair slings for the injured, restraints in case anyone had gone mad as well as blankets and warm drinks were prepared. Passengers woken by the shuddering over-charged engines were asked to keep to their cabins. Rostron and his men made the journey in three and a half hours, taking evasive action to avoid six icebergs on the way, posting an extra look-out, emitting a plume of black smoke, firing rockets from her bows to signal that rescue was approaching. When *Carpathia* found the scattered lifeboats after dawn, bright sunlight was glistening on a battery of monster icebergs. 'They were of different colors as the sun struck them,' said Woolner. 'Some looked white and some looked blue, and some sort of mauve, and others were dark gray.' He specified 'one double-toothed' iceberg, which was perhaps 100 feet high and may have been *Titanic*'s killer.[107] Seaman Scarrott and Henry Stengel both likened this berg to the Rock of Gibraltar.[108]

One quality dominated, Rostron recalled, as survivors came aboard, quietness: 'there was no noise, no hurry . . . the rescued came solemnly, dumbly, out of a shivering shadow'.[109] *Carpathia*'s English physician dealt with first-class survivors in the ship's first-class dining room. The ship's Italian physician did equivalent work in the second-class dining room; and its Hungarian physician worked in the third-class dining room. The widows Astor, Thayer and Widener were assigned cabins. Ismay was taken to the ship's doctor's cabin, given a sedative, and stayed there until *Carpathia* reached New York.

On board, some men busied themselves collating experiences, compiling memoranda, and exchanging addresses. Resilient women consoled the broken and bereft, and tried to improve their material comforts. Overall, the human cargo of this mourning boat were dazed by shock and sorrow – and angry, too, that their liner had been driven and equipped so heedlessly. It had steamed westwards as if it was invulnerable, plunging too fast into an ice zone to stop when an iceberg hove in view. There had been a woeful inadequacy of lifeboats, there had been a shambles loading them, and the crewmen who were put in charge of them often proved blundering or weak nerved. The ship's last hours had been a climax of deadly folly.

FOURTEEN

The Meaning Shows in the Defeated Thing

Over the water came the lifted song –
Blind pieces in a mighty game we swing;
Life's battle is a conquest for the strong;
The meaning shows in the defeated thing.

John Masefield, 'The Wanderer'

The steamship *Kroonland* – the first ship to send a wireless distress call at sea in 1903 – had been plying the New York–Antwerp route for IMM's Red Star subsidiary for ten years. The novelist Theodore Dreiser, who had flirted with the idea of returning to New York on *Titanic*, preferred to save money by travelling on *Kroonland*, which left Antwerp on 13 April. Three days later, when *Kroonland*'s wireless operator learnt of *Titanic*'s doom, the ship's captain ordered the news to be kept secret. But a busybody on board, Herr Salz, had been bribing the wireless operator with cigars, and to him the calamity was confided. Salz bustled off to the smoking room where Dreiser was sitting, and looking portentous, gestured to the men to come on deck where he could tell some news which the women must not overhear. Someone jested that to judge by Salz's manner, Rockefeller's Standard Oil Company had gone bust. The men's nonchalance collapsed when Salz told them his story. With one accord, they went to the rail and gazed into the blackness ahead. 'The swish of the sea could be heard and the insistent moo of the fog-horn,' Dreiser recorded. 'We all began to talk at once, but no-one listened. The terror of the sea had come swiftly home to all of us . . . To think of a ship as immense as the *Titanic*, new and bright, sinking in endless fathoms of water. And the two thousand passengers routed like rats from their berths only to float helplessly in miles of water, praying and crying!' *Kroonland*'s passengers faced several days at sea before reaching New York. Some men became austerely reticent while others could not stop nervous chatter about the disaster. The women on board pretended not to know. Inwardly, wrote Dreiser, all passengers shrank at the thought of 'the endless wastes of the sea' and 'the terror of drowning in the dark and cold'. When *Kroonland* reached New York harbour, a pilot came on board with newspapers booming the news. Passengers crowded into the saloon to get every detail. 'Some broke down and cried. Others clenched their fists and swore over the vivid and painful pen-pictures by eyewitnesses and survivors. For a while we all forgot we were nearly home.'[1]

The earliest wireless messages indicating that a catastrophe had occurred in mid-ocean reached the Marconi outpost at Cape Race in Newfoundland. A terse message was relayed to the Allan Steamship headquarters in Montreal, from its cargo vessel *Virginian*, taking 18,000 barrels of apples to Liverpool, reporting that it had received a distress message from *Titanic*. Allan gave the news to a Montreal newspaper with a reciprocal news agreement with the *New York Times*. At 2 a.m. a journalist from the *New York Times* telephoned Philip Franklin, American vice-president of IMM, at his Manhattan home seeking confirmation of reports that the liner was sinking. Franklin called IMM's Montreal representative seeking Canadian confirmation of the wireless traffic. Further bulletins flashed from Cape Race with some accurate details, but garbled transmissions resulted in reports during Monday that passengers had been rescued by *Virginian* and *Parisian* as well as *Carpathia*, and that the wounded leviathan was being towed to Halifax, Nova Scotia. 'A great deal of pain was caused to the public by the improper use of wireless,' the British consul-general in New York deplored. 'Amateurs with imperfect instruments picked up parts of messages, and piecing them together sent messages that were very far from true.'[2] Aside from recklessly decrypted transmissions, there was at least one forgery, purporting to come from Phillips, the Marconi operator, assuring his parents that all was well, and *Titanic* was proceeding to Halifax.

For much of Monday, 15 April, Franklin seemed in a state of raving confidence. He declared his absolute trust in *Titanic*, even affirmed that the liner was indestructible, despite the alarming messages that were arriving. 'During the entire day we considered the ship unsinkable,' he later said, 'and it never entered our minds that there had been anything like a serious loss of life.'[3] He was quoted by reporters as saying there were sufficient lifeboats to save all passengers, but feared that there might have been fatalities while transferring voyagers to lifeboats. His messages to the family of Charles Hays in Canada raised false hopes that the railwayman and his son-in-law Thornton Davidson had survived. Later, Franklin issued journalists with a further statement betraying class-consciousness even in crisis: 'it is customary in cases of this kind for the women to be saved first; even the women in the steerage would be taken off before the men passengers of the first and second cabin'.[4] He trusted rumours that *Virginian* was towing the wounded *Titanic* towards Halifax. He even chartered a fast train to bring its passengers south to New York. His messages to Captain Herbert Haddock on *Titanic*'s sister ship *Olympic* were initially guarded, but became increasingly urgent in requesting news. It was not until 6.16 New York time on Monday evening that Franklin received confirmation from Haddock that *Titanic* had foundered: 'About 675 souls saved, crew and passengers, latter nearly all women and children.' Franklin was dumbfounded by the news, and for some time his office reeled under the blow.

The news reached England by Atlantic telegraph cable and Marconi's outpost at Poldhu – a country walk away from the Cornish villages of Constantine and Porthleven, where the dead men Jim Veale, James Drew, and Edgar and Fred Giles had begun their fatal journeys. The London evening newspapers caught the story for their Monday night editions. 'TITANIC SINKING', reported the *Globe*. It reported a message from Cape Race that 'the liner was sinking by the head, and that the women were being taken off in lifeboats. The last signals came at 12.27 this morning, but these were blurred and ended abruptly.' The ship, it added, was 'a floating palace' equipped to provide 'the comforts of wealthy Americans'.[5] Tuesday evening's report in the *Globe* was less accurate. 'When the *Titanic* struck the iceberg at 10.25 she was running at reduced speed. Most of the passengers had retired to bed, and were awakened and terrified by a thunderous impact which crushed and twisted the towering bows of the liner and broke them in like an eggshell.' The *Globe* had interviewed a man named Parton, manager of White Star's Cockspur street office. 'What discipline must have been maintained!' Parton exclaimed. 'The fact that nearly all of those who are saved are women and children is evidence of that.'[6]

On Monday evening, encouraged by optimistic early reports, a thanksgiving service was held in St Jude's church, Whitechapel, for the survival of the Reverend Ernest Carter and his wife Lillian – a service that seemed pitifully sad in retrospect, for both had perished. The English could manage to accept that 'the unsinkable has sunk',[7] but it remained unthinkable that over a thousand had died.

Belfast felt poleaxed by the news. A Harland & Wolff worker recalled that he was carrying buckets of water drawn from the well for his horses when he met an acquaintance at the orchard gate:

'And he says, "Jack", he says, "there's shocking bad news this morning."'

'I says, "What's wrong?"'

'He says, "This big ship," he says, "the *Titanic* that sailed. She's to the bottom this morning."'

A man whose father had worked as a joiner on *Titanic* recalled this eerie interlude when sectarian politics were abeyant, and no-one argued or fought about Home Rule. 'For those of us in Belfast,' he recalled, 'this news was beyond all comprehension. My father couldn't believe it. Later he broke down and cried. He was a big shipyard man and he just cried like a child. You see, his pride was broken.'[8] Dismay, horror and grief fell on Belfast: it was a failure for Harland & Wolff, humiliation for Ulster Protestantism. 'During those awful days in April, when hope of good news at last had gone, the Yard was shrouded in gloom and rough men cried like women.'[9]

The news ricocheted round the world. Pierpont Morgan, the corsair of IMM, sent a telegram from the French spa town of Aix-les-Bains: 'Have just heard fearful rumor about *Titanic* with iceberg without any particulars. Hope for God's sake not true.' Absurd rumours sped about Aix as they did London and New York: that everyone had survived, that passengers might be saved by clinging to the wreckage, or scrambling to safety atop icebergs. On Wednesday, by which time the extent of the disaster was clear, Morgan was to celebrate his seventy-fifth birthday; but in response to subdued greetings from his New York partners, he cabled that he was 'exceedingly grieved'.[10] IMM had been a loss-maker since its inception, and now it was a life-loser, too, held up to obloquy. The news was kept from convalescent Lord Pirrie until late on Tuesday.

Paris was convulsed with anxiety and grief. Hundreds of American residents in Paris, and the thousands of American tourists in the hotels, went to sleep on Monday night assured that almost everyone had been saved. On Tuesday morning *Le Matin* appeared with a front page headline announcing stupendous news: 'LE PLUS GRAND TRANSATLANTIQUE DU MONDE FAIT NAUFRAGE POUR SA PREMIÈRE TRAVERSÉE' and warned that only 675 passengers and crew had been saved.[11] White Star's office was besieged by weeping women, several of whom had sons on board, including William Dulles's mother who left in a state of collapse. Its English manager was harrowed by the weeping women, and longed to rush away. Next day the office was deserted, for all hopes had gone. 'The consternation and grief in the American colony in Paris at the *Titanic* disaster passes description,' Reuter's telegraphed round the world. 'There is hardly a leading hotel without visitors having relatives and friends on board.'[12]

Newspapers on both sides of the Atlantic went wild at their chance. Journalists had brazen confidence that their readers would forget their lies from one day to the next, as shown by one synthesis of news agency telegrams. When *Carpathia* reached New York, hundreds of stretchers had been rushed aboard, it began. 'Many survivors lost all their clothing . . . There were scores of cases of total coma . . . First Officer Wilde, of the *Titanic*, when the vessel struck, shot himself on the bridge when he realized the accident was so serious. Many women are insane. When the *Titanic* struck the iceberg, the impact was terrific, great blocks of ice were thrown on the deck killing numbers of people . . . Many *Titanic* passengers died aboard the *Carpathia* from exposure to ice floes. Three Italians were shot while struggling for places in the boats . . . All the passengers acclaimed the seamen's heroic conduct. Men sang sea songs while lowering the boats. Mrs Jacob Astor, wife of Colonel Astor, is now dead. Five women survivors have saved their pet dogs, and another has saved a little pig.'[13]

The dead were beyond blame. Captain Smith, who had maintained full speed in a dangerous ice zone, was untouched by early critics. Stanley Lord, *Californian*'s captain, was reviled for his failure of judgement, courage and humanity; but Bruce Ismay became the chief scapegoat, with the bewildered Duff Gordons on his tail. In his cabin on *Carpathia*, dazed and overwrought, Ismay kept repeating that he should have gone down with the ship. Jack Thayer, who visited his cabin, found him 'seated, in his pyjamas, on his bunk, staring straight ahead, shaking like a leaf'. He seemed oblivious of Thayer: 'when I spoke to him . . . telling him he had a perfect right to take the last boat, he paid absolutely no attention and continued to look ahead with his fixed stare'.[14] (Ismay thereafter felt gratitude to the Thayers, and corresponded with Thayer's widowed mother for years.) Ismay cannot have anticipated the fusillade of recriminations that awaited him in America. There he was vilified because instead of sacrificing himself, he had stepped onto Collapsible C as it was being lowered, and been saved. He headed the company that had launched *Titanic* with insufficient lifeboats for its human cargo. He was suspected of cajoling Captain Smith into speeding towards the ice. His restraint under interrogation exasperated a nation that required fulsome emotional show.

Against Ismay, then, Americans pitched annihilating abuse and maledictions. Isidor Rayner, Democrat from Maryland, demanded on the floor of the Senate that Ismay be hauled before Congress like a wanted man 'to explain how he, the directing manager of the company, the superior of the Captain, and not under the Captain's orders, directed the northern route which ended so fatally and then left hundreds of passengers to die while he took not the last boat, but the very first boat that left the sinking ship'. Every phrase in Rayner's preceding accusations was untrue. 'Mr Ismay claims . . . that he took the last lifeboat,' cried Rayner. 'I do not believe it, and if he did, it was cowardly to take any lifeboat, for the Managing Director of the Line, with his board, is criminally responsible for this appalling tragedy. I have not the slightest doubt that the northern route was taken in obedience to Mr Ismay's direct orders, and that with full warning he risked the life of the entire ship to make a speedy passage.'[15]

President Taft believed initial reports that the passengers were safe and heading for Halifax. On Monday evening, he went jauntily to see Avery Hopwood's comedy, *Nobody's Widow,* but became 'frantic' when he returned from the theatre and learnt the truth.[16] The President wept when he knew that Butt was lost. He moped about the White House, feeling bereft, longing to see Butt's smile or to hear his cheery voice. He rejected suggestions that he recognize the country's sombre mood by issuing a national proclamation, but agreed to order that flags be put at half-mast. Roosevelt, however, sent telegrams and issued condolences which caught the country's excited temper. Political Washington grieved over Taft's dead aide. 'In little back offices, littered with paper and adorned principally by typewriters, in bustling news bureaus, in the press room of the White House, and in the War, State and Navy Building – wherever newspaper men foregathered – the name of Maj. "Archie" Butt, once synonymous of laughter and jest, now suddenly half understood, symbolic of heroism, was repeated last night while eyes blurred and voices became queerly strained,' reported the *Washington Herald.* 'Everywhere in this city the newspaper men sought to get word through New York of the fate of Maj. Butt. The oldest men on the Row and the youngest cub reporter, the correspondent with the classic eyeglasses, and the be-whiskered man who remembers the Civil War – on through a list of men who had met Maj. Butt while covering their stories or who had helped him to cover his own – all these remembered . . . his unfailing kindliness, his friendship to newspaper men whom he barely knew, and, above all, his paramount gentility. The older men talked of him as "Archie," the correspondent. The younger remembered gratefully how, when terrified by their first assignment to a presidential function, he had helped them out. They summed up all with this oft-repeated phrase: "He was a good, square man – too good a man to die".'[17]

Washington was distracted from the momentous news that Roosevelt had trounced Taft in the Pennsylvania primary on 13 April. 'The confusion and consternation here are startling,' wrote Henry Adams on Tuesday. 'Through the chaos I seemed to be watching the *Titanic* foundering in a shoreless ocean. By my blessed Virgin, it is awful! This Titanic blow shatters one's nerves. We can't grapple it.' The next day Adams was yet more agitated. 'We have been, and still are in gloom such as I, who am gloom itself, cannot get down to. People go about, choking . . . Honestly I am scared! Everybody seems to be off their heads.' A week later, dining with George Cabot Lodge's wife, Adams was maddened by her repeating stories of the wreck. There had not been a more 'grim and ghastly' week since the crushing defeats of Union troops in the Civil War. 'The sum and triumph of civilisation, guaranteed to be safe and perfect, our greatest achievement, sinks at a touch, and drowns us, while nature jeers at us for our folly.'[18] He had been due to travel on the return voyage of *Titanic*, transferred his passage to *Olympic* but was so worried about sailing that he suffered a disabling stroke.

The families of Philadelphians aboard the mammoth liner relied on conflicting generalities until on Monday evening the dire news hit Philadelphia with a resonant and jarring crash.[19] From early Tuesday morning until late at night, crowds thronged in front of newspaper offices scanning and re-reading the bulletins giving latest details of 'the most disastrous marine catastrophe the modern world has ever experienced . . . many expressions of sorrow and grief could be heard, and to hundreds the appalling tragedy seemed incomprehensible'.[20] Several renowned Philadelphia names were on the passenger list. William Dulles was an attorney whose family had been eminent in the city since colonial times. The banker Robert Daniel and physician Arthur Brewe were distinguished there. Most prominent of all, though, were the Carters, Cardezas, Thayers, and supremely the Wideners.

Lynnewood Hall had been built as a house of imperturbable grandeur, yet by Monday night all was distraction there. On Tuesday morning, Peter Widener shuffled along a platform in Broad Street Station and was helped aboard a New York train. Grief and anxiety were stamped on the old man's face, and his faltering steps showed the blow which had hit him – the probable loss of his elder son and golden grandson. At his elbow was his younger son, Joseph, whose concern for his father was evident as he supported him with an arm. Peter Widener was a founding director of IMM, and reaching the White Star building in New York, the Wideners were ushered past the counters manned by harassed clerks and desks with awestruck stenographers into Franklin's private sanctum, with its big shiny desk and comfortable chairs laid out like a furniture showroom. There they listened to the hum and rattle of the wireless apparatus as it received one name after another of survivors.[21] On Wednesday, after a long day of waiting, and a sleepless night of foreboding, old Widener, looking weary and dejected, was taken back to Lynnewood Hall by Joseph, who then returned to New York to meet *Carpathia*. But the millionaire, to the dismay of his family, would not rest. He spent Thursday in his office in the Land Title Building, awaiting news, and broke down several times on receipt of discouraging messages from Joseph in New York. He was not reconciled to the fact that his son and grandson were dead. Repudiating advice, he went on Thursday afternoon in a private carriage to Jersey City, from whence by private ferry to the dock where *Carpathia* was expected. His surviving grandchildren Eleanor and George junior accompanied him. He insisted on being at the dock when the survivors landed because he had not lost all hope.

Just as Taft had been duped by false reports, and Peter Widener clutched at illusory prospects, so many English newspapers were cruelly deceptive. Many of the liner's crew were Liverpudlians, whose relations were given spurious comfort by the 'Stop Press' announcement in the *Liverpool Daily Post* of 16 April quoting White Star's local manager: '*Titanic* has foundered, but . . . no lives have been lost.'[22] In Liverpool, the dreadful truth came on Tuesday. 'In street and mart, in household and hostelry, on ferry-boat and on the riverside, in tramcar and in railway train, men and women talked with bated breath of the tragic tidings to hand. It was an all-absorbing topic . . . which appealed equally to all classes – rich and poor, young and old. The public were nonplussed with the magnitude of the disaster, and many people found it impossible to grapple mentally with the intelligence that the newest and biggest vessel in the world – a floating palace, a vessel declared to be practically unsinkable . . . lay thousands of fathoms deep in the Atlantic Ocean.'[23]

Similarly, in Southampton, where most of the crew lived, the *Southern Daily Echo* offered cheating reassurance. 'For some hours, great anxiety prevailed, but fortunately more reassuring tidings reached us this afternoon, when all passengers were reported to be safe', it reported on the evening of 15 April.[24] Next day the same newspaper told a different story: 'Dismay and incredulity struggled for the mastery of the faces in the anxious crowd as, regulated by the police, they pressed forward to read the fateful bulletin.' The rumour that a tramp steamer had reached Halifax carrying survivors 'raised drooping hopes a little, but did little to dispel the forebodings that gripped every heart'.[25] In the afternoon, women arrived with babies in their arms and toddlers hanging on their skirts. The crowds increased after dusk. Street lamps shone on hundreds of wan, grey faces. The dense crowd intermittently made way for a grief-stricken relation to enter the office asking for news. Each time the answer was negative, and the supplicant returned outside with head bowed in despair: 'women sobbed aloud, while tears glistened in the eyes of rough and hardy sea-faring men'. Southampton was sunk in mourning: the haggard faces of townsfolk showed 'the dull, listless apathy of helpless misery'.[26]

Newspapers on both sides of the Atlantic extolled the heroism of Astor, Guggenheim, Straus and other first-class gallants, who stepped aside so that women and children might be saved. 'The touch of nature which makes the whole world kin levelled all classes,' editorialized the *Western Morning News*. 'Every man did his duty worthily in the supreme moment . . . All Christendom mourns. Rulers and peoples of all nations have given vent to their grief at this unparalleled calamity.'[27] Such sentiments were no solace to the bereaved families of Southampton. The majority of its 900 crew lived in the city: almost 700 of them died. At a single school, 125 children lost a father, brother or uncle. What place, in these eulogies of chevaliers beyond reproach, could be allotted to the Southampton husbands, fathers and sons who had perished by the order 'women and children first'? Their deaths seemed neither heroic nor uplifting. No misfortune of such magnitude had happened since the French sacked the town in 1338, nor was to occur again until the German bombing raids of 1940. Despite the bright April sunshine, shops put up shutters, blinds were drawn in houses; flags on hotels and public buildings were put at half-mast.

A reporter described the stricken districts of Southampton. 'I have spent the day in widows' houses, houses without food or fuel and in some cases without furniture. I have seen women fainting and heard children crying for food . . . During the coal strike many bread-winners were out of work, furniture was sold or pawned, and numerous families received notice to quit. Then came the *Titanic*, and firemen, greasers, and trimmers, who had known no work for weeks, eagerly joined the big ship to save their homes.' Haggard women in their early twenties were given emergency relief by a Catholic priest and nuns in the stricken district: one such was Jack Poingdestre's wife, believing herself a widow, who arrived there with four children, the eldest aged five, and fainted away. Women loitered outside the White Star offices to prolong their hopes: to return home would be to accept that their men were dead. 'One drooping woman was leaning on a bassinette containing two chubby babies, while a tiny mite held her hand. "What are we waiting for, Mummy? Why are we waiting such a long time?" asked the tired child. "We are waiting for news of father, dear," came the choked answer, as the mother turned away her head to hide her tears.'[28]

Newspaper readers often try to enlarge themselves by dwelling on other people's greater calamities. Calamity quickens the tempo of life. 'The terrible news about the *Titanic* reached New York about eleven o'clock last night, and the scene on Broadway was awful,' a youngster wrote to his mother describing Monday evening. 'Crowds of people were coming out of the theaters, cafés were going full tilt, when the newsboys began to cry, "Extra! Extra! *Titanic* sunk with 1800 aboard!" You can't imagine the effect of those words on the crowd. Nobody could realize what had happened, and when they did begin to understand, the excitement was almost enough to cause a panic in the theatres. Women began to faint and weep, and scores of people in evening clothes jumped into cabs and taxis, and rushed to the offices of the White Star Line, where they remained all night waiting for the news.'[29] The city had not been so traumatized since 1904, when the paddle steamer *General Slocum* caught fire on the East River, within sight of land-bound New Yorkers, incinerating or drowning over a thousand women and children on a German Lutheran church picnic outing (the highest level of New York fatalities until the attack on the Twin Towers a century later).

Caroline Astor and other members of the Four Hundred had begun manipulating the society columns in their interests thirty years earlier. Now their descendants recoiled under a relentless morbid scrutiny. Watched by eager-eyed journalists, Vincent Astor, the dead millionaire's twenty-year-old son, sped to the White Star office in a touring car that Monday evening, and begged for information. On Tuesday morning he appeared early in Marconi's New York offices, distraught with grief, and cried out that he would give all the money that could be asked if only a Marconi operator would confirm his father's safety. After a Tuesday visit to the offices on the second storey of the White Star building, young Astor left sobbing with his face in his hands.[30]

From dawn on Tuesday, White Star's offices by the waterside at Bowling Green in lower Manhattan were besieged by clamouring relations and prying onlookers. Long lines of motor cars crawled along the kerbside, and richly dressed citizens hurried into White Star's building. Robert Cornell, the Manhattan magistrate, burst through the crowd into the office, frantic for news of his wife, and collapsed on being told that nothing was known of her.[31] When Edward Frauenthal was told that *Carpathia*'s list of survivors included the names of his two brothers, he was so overcome that he could hardly lurch to the telephone. When his wife answered he broke down and sobbed, 'I tell you they are saved! Yes! Yes! They are safe!' Then the telephone receiver fell from his hand, and he sank to the floor, completely overcome.[32]

A journalist described the Tuesday scene: 'The offices of the White Star Line are the focal point of woe and despair. Since last night, multitudes of pallid men and women with swollen eyes have stood in front of the stone building at 9 Broadway . . . Those who took up their vigil last night are there tonight. Fashionably gowned women whose friends rode in the deluxe state rooms of the liner are mingling with and confiding their grief to women in shawls and shabby bonnets.' The names of third-class passengers were omitted from survivors' lists. When a new name of a survivor was posted, it was read aloud by those nearest to the bulletin board, and repeated backwards through the crowd. The streets were awash with newspapers, for new editions were issued after receipt of every new bulletin. On Broadway, the theatres were open, but the actors could not hold the small audiences, who kept rushing out to buy an 'extra' edition.[33]

The maddening blur of facts, the dreadful ravage of suspense, was evoked by Sid Blake, the manager of New York's Star hotel. He knew several *Titanic* passengers from previous crossings, and was expecting Cornishmen coming to welcome their wives and children to America. While preparing for their arrival, he heard the stunning news that *Titanic* had struck an iceberg. William Drew, a Cornishman, arrived from Long Island. Before Christmas he had sent his young only son, Marshall, with his brother and sister-in-law, the James Drews, to meet the boy's grandmother at Constantine. 'Wireless messages said that only Mrs Drew was saved. Mr Drew paced the office for 20 hours out of the 24 for three days. I thought he would go out of his mind. "My poor brother; my poor son", was all you could hear. Such suffering I hope never to see again.' Nellie Hocking's fiancé George Hambly, Sib Richards, Abednego Trevaskis, Arthur Wells and Sidney Hocking came together from Akron to meet their women from *Titanic*: they heard 'pretty cheering news that all had been saved'.[34]

All large New York hotels had a steamship agent sitting at a desk arranging transatlantic passages. These men were besieged by anxious questioners, while elsewhere in the lobbies small groups loitered to debate the tragedy. George Boldt, manager of the Waldorf-Astoria, who had over thirty reservations from *Titanic* passengers, sat at his desk in suspense between the arrival of bulletins. At the Ritz-Carlton, Lord Rothes waited patiently for tidings of his wife. William Graham of the American Tin Can Company waited at the Plaza for news of his wife and daughter. The Gotham Hotel received telegraphic inquiries from Steffansson's father. Waiting in the hotels were hundreds of shipping agents who had crossed America to attend the gaudy rejoicings that were planned on board to mark the maiden voyage.[35]

On Wednesday a weeping girl asked if the name of her brother Vivian Payne, Charles Hays' secretary, was among the list of survivors. She had come from Montreal, where her widowed mother was 'insane with grief and her life despaired of', and broke down when Payne's name was not on any list. Anderson Polk, of Dayton, Ohio, brother of Lucile Carter, swayed and nearly fell when given his good news. A plainly dressed woman with her daughter came timidly forward. A millionaire stood aside for her, and retrieved her bag when she dropped it. She asked after her brother Walter Bishop, a bedroom steward, and received a reply that made her turn away with a sob. There were hysterics who wanted to aggrandize themselves by making bogus claims for attention. Joseph Marrington of Philadelphia maintained a ceaseless vigil for two days seeking news of William Lambert of Greensboro, Pennsylvania. 'He was my closest friend on earth,' said Marrington, 'and as dear to me as a brother. He saved my life several years ago in the jungles of Ecuador while we were searching for rubber.' There was no such man on the ship: Marrington seems to have been indulging in a cheap fantasy. A young man who said he was called Long created uproar by rushing through the throng screaming that his sister was lost. 'When handed a list of survivors he scanned it hurriedly, and found the name of Long. He began laughing hysterically until it occurred to him to ask if the name was that of a steerage passenger. When he was informed that the Long was a first-cabin passenger he fairly shrieked his woes in English and Italian, and became so frenzied that it was necessary to lead him into the street.'[36] He, too, was an attention-seeking impostor.

It was not until Wednesday that Arabic newspapers in New York reported that *Titanic* had carried scores of passengers from the Turkish province of Syria. The English listings of Arabic names were so misspelt that they raised a thick haze of apprehension in communities from Canada to Texas. It took time for reliable lists of passengers and survivors to be compiled by Lebanese community newspapers. In the interval, heartbreaking fears were aroused: a delegation of a dozen men from Wilkes-Barre was in New York ten days after the accident trying to establish who from Hardin had been on the liner, who was lost and who still lived. Syrian immigrants in the USA were divided by politics and religion, but this disaster briefly united them. The Syrian-American Club of New York and the Lebanese League of Progress raised $307 for Mayor Gaynor's relief fund; a Syrian hotelier provided rooms for survivors; and Bishop Rafa'el Hawaweeny of Brooklyn conducted a dignified memorial service in the Orthodox Cathedral.[37]

On Thursday, the largest crowds of all thronged White Star's offices. Broadway was choked by cars and taxicabs discharging woeful passengers – mainly women. Weary, haggard clerks shook their heads, and despondently pointed at rosters of survivors. 'There were many pathetic scenes as the harrowed inquirer turned away from the counters and stumbled, sobbing, to a chair . . . Men and women from distant cities kept coming in even greater number, many of them hysterical and scarcely able to articulate their inquiries, some so feeble they had to be supported to the counters and then almost carried out to waiting vehicles.' Several Washington women came in a limousine to ask for Archie Butt, and swooned or wept clinging to one another when they heard there was no hope. Telegrams poured into the offices from almost every city in America, and the telephones were taxed to the limit. Family and friends of third-class passengers – Italians, Slavs, Greeks, Turks, Armenians, Transylvanians, Russians, Poles, Germans and French – 'came in a swarm to fight their way into the jammed offices and wail for information'. Without inter-preters, 'they chattered and wept and wailed in vain'.[38]

Never in the history of ships had so many lives been lost except in battle; and the *Titanic* death roll was greater than the British death roll of any battle in the South African War. The whole of England was sorrowing: London had not been so sombre since the 'Black Week' of December 1899 when news arrived of three separate military defeats of the British Army by Boer irregulars with the loss of about 2,800 lives. Then sorrowing, fearful crowds had surrounded Cumberland House, the old War Office building in Pall Mall, seeking news of the dead and wounded. White Star's head office, Oceanic House, was a short distance away in Cockspur Street, which joins Pall Mall to Trafalgar Square (the building is now the Texas Embassy steakhouse). Again, sad, fearful men and women thronged Pall Mall. The crowd outside Oceanic House, although orderly, became so big that the police had to marshal them. Early reports stated that George Vanderbilt and Lord Ashburton were on board, although denials came speedily. It became clear that 'the majority of the well-known people on board belonged to New York rather than to London'.[39]

On Tuesday, Sir Courtenay Bennett, British consul-general in New York, telegraphed a coded message to London: 'Consular uncollated hipponax moramenti lives romanized eperlano fewtrils', which was deciphered as 'No hope that any more lives will be saved except by means of fishing-smacks.'[40] In Cockspur Street, on Tuesday, there was a pathetic crowd outside the building, waiting for lists to be pinned on the bulletin board. Men wearing silk hats and frock coats came and went in motor cars. Shabby women from back-to-back terraced housing walked up with defeated steps, and left with drawn faces. A smartly attired lady who found that her husband was not listed among the survivors regained her taxicab and leant forward with her despairing face buried in her hands. When a new list was affixed to the board, there was a frantic rush to scan them, and dejection on people's faces as they turned away.[41]

Lord Winterton travelled up to London on Tuesday from Sandwich, where he had been staying with Nancy Astor, with whom he was in love. 'The news of the *Titanic* disaster, in which about 1,500 persons (including Jack Astor, Stead & others) have lost their lives is just to hand, and is too terrible to think of. Everyone talking about it in the trains.'[42] Arnold Bennett heard a newspaper vendor complaining in Brighton: 'They mucked up this *Titanic* disaster for us. They put on the bills, "*Titanic* sunk". That was no use to us. They ought to have put "Hundreds drowned." Then we should have made a bit.'[43]

In Cockspur Street, on Wednesday, the early buses brought City workers, who broke their journey in the hope of allaying their fears for loved ones. Some, who had kept vigil at the office for thirty-six hours, fell asleep where they sat. Others paced the streets, too agitated to sit still, returning to check the bulletin boards. A young wife, awaiting news of her husband, dissolved into wild tears. Another young woman, after scanning the list of third-class survivors, burst into loud crying, and was consoled by a clerk. As in New York, there were impostors claiming a part in the tragedy under false pretences, and playing their part as melodrama. A demented youth, who asserted that he had four sisters and a brother among the passengers, bit his lip until it seemed that blood must flow.[44]

'There has been an astonishing disaster at sea, the *Titanic*, the largest vessel ever built, wrecked in mid-Atlantic by collision with an iceberg,' the radical-minded, aristocratic libertine Wilfrid Scawen Blunt wrote. 'It was her first voyage, and she was carrying over a thousand passengers to New York, many of them millionaires. Most of the women and children seem to have been put in boats and picked up by a passing steamer, but the rest have perished, over 1,000 souls.' Blunt gloried in the retributive justice visited on lazy, rootless epicureans and their insatiable, dolled-up harpies. 'One thing is consoling in these great disasters, the proof given that Nature is not quite yet the slave of Man, but is able to rise even now in her wrath and destroy him. Also if any large number of human beings could be better spared than another, it would be just these American millionaires with their wealth and insolence.'[45] Other members of the English upper classes, for whom fortitude was the greatest virtue, were unmoved by the deaths of soft-living parvenus. Lady Dorothy Nevill, the aged High Tory daughter of the Earl of Orford, had once defined the art of conversation as not only saying the right thing at the right time, but leaving unsaid the wrong thing at the tempting moment. She failed her own criterion when, at a women's luncheon, she told the novelist Marie Belloc Lowndes that 'the wreck was a judgement from God on those idle rich people who want all earthly luxuries even on the water'. The artificiality of the floating Ritz was detestable. Lady Dorothy, who was a famous horticulturalist, snapped with disgust: 'I am told they even had a garden!'[46] Scawen Blunt and Lady Dorothy Nevill believed in discipline, resilience and the fulfilment of hereditary responsibilities, and doubted if American millionaires knew much about these qualities.

Everywhere it was said that the craze for speed and the vanity of breaking records were endangering shipping and life, although, of course, White Star liners were not built for speed like Cunarders or German ships. 'These big steamers,' the *Economist* judged, 'to save a mere five hours on the voyage, take a dangerous course through the ice, and a liner travelling at 20 knots through an ice region is infinitely more likely to cripple herself than an old tramp doing her 8 knots, and careless of time.'[47] Porter McCumber, Republican Senator for North Dakota, was one of the few American politicians to deplore the blackguarding of Ismay and condemn the lust for speed. 'The American people are as much to blame for this catastrophe as anyone,' he courageously told the Senate on 19 April. 'We seek and encourage people to push those vessels to the very test of endurance and speed. When the *Lusitania* was launched and made her record trip the whole country . . . clapped our hands and cheered.' Neither the equipment nor the route of *Lusitania* excelled those of *Titanic* – only the latter's luck was worse. There was too much of the competitive sportsmen's bravado about American attitudes to speed, said the Senator. Rash young aviators were incited to soar above the clouds, and ascend thousands of feet. Elated by applause for his derring-do, a pilot attempts to go yet higher, 'and the following day we bury a mass of flesh and we call for another victim to satiate our thirst for the spectacular. We demand the highest limit of speed and are always ready to take the chance.'[48]

English newspapers treated the calamity as vindication of the heroism of the world's greatest seafaring nation. The self-control of Anglo-Saxon manhood was contrasted with the sneaking cowardice of 'Italians' or 'Chinese'. The gutter press declared that 'women and children first' was not just the law of the sea, but the instinct and instilled discipline of racially superior people. This opinion was upheld in unlikely quarters. 'Had the *Titanic* been a vessel manned by Chinese sailors, I can assure you there would not have been a woman or child saved,' declared Henry Moy Foi, of the Chinese Merchants Association of America, speaking in Cleveland, Ohio. 'Whenever a Chinese vessel goes down, it is the duty of the sailors to see that the men are taken off first. The children come next, and then the women [because] the Chinese government feels that the men are the most valuable for the nation. In China it would really have been a crime to take care of the women first . . . the average woman would be destitute without her husband. Children are given second choice because childless families always can be found to take care of them.'[49]

It seems singularly English to find a pretext for racial triumphalism in a national disaster, yet this was a common solace. 'In all our minds, there has been a thrill at the heroism and self-sacrifice,' declared a Cabinet minister, Lord Beauchamp. 'They were ordinary common or garden members of the Anglo-Saxon race. It makes one proud to think that there were so many men ready to face death quietly and in a self-sacrificing spirit, making way for the women and children to be rescued. Not only does it make us proud of our race, but it makes us sure that there is a great destiny reserved in the world still for the Anglo-Saxon race.'[50] Beauchamp's Cabinet colleague, Winston Churchill, then First Lord of the Admiralty, followed the *Titanic* story with fascination. 'The story is a good one,' he wrote to his wife on Thursday. 'The strict observance of the great traditions of the sea towards women & children reflects nothing but honour upon our civilization. Even I hope it may mollify some of the young unmarried lady teachers' – he meant suffragettes – 'who are so bitter in their sex antagonism, & think men so base & vile.' He felt 'proud of our race and its traditions as proved by this event. Boat loads of women & children tossing on the sea – safe & sound – & the rest – Silence.'[51]

There was a frantic outcry, not silence, on land. All newspapers, all readers, were eager for *Carpathia* to reach New York with its shocked and sorrowing survivors. 'CARPATHIA IS PLUNGING TOWARDS PORT WITH REMNANTS OF *TITANIC*'S THOUSANDS: HUGE RESCUER WITH ITS PITIFULLY FEW SURVIVORS IS EXPECTED TO DOCK IN NEW YORK', blared the *Cleveland Plain Dealer* of 17 April. Two days later, hours before *Carpathia* docked, the same paper was proliferating the abundant rumours. 'The brief wireless despatches indicate that pneumonia was prevalent among the rescued, and showed that many had gone insane. Some of the most notable men and women on board were reported among those who had lost their minds.'[52]

Carpathia reached the quayside at 9.30 during the dark night of Thursday 18 April. As the ship approached, wind began to blow hard, rain fell in torrents with thunder and lightning breaking over the sky. The ship was harried by tugs, ferries and yachts carrying reporters shouting questions through megaphones. Photographers took flashlight pictures which (coupled with the lightning flashes) made a dazzling explosion of luminosity. About 2,500 people – mostly animated by morbid curiosity – stood in the drizzling rain. They were packed so tight in the side streets, through which the survivors would have to leave, that the way was impassable. William Gaynor, Mayor of New York City, who in 1910 had been shot in the neck while walking on the deck of *Kaiser Wilhelm der Grosse* at Hoboken, and who was to die in 1913 while sitting in a deckchair on the *Baltic* as it approached Ireland, had ordered an elaborate police operation around Cunard's pier. Mounted policemen rode back and forth so that their rearing horses would send the crowds into retreat. Lieutenant Charles Becker – a corrupt officer who months later murdered the gambler Herman Rosenthal – led a police squad targeting pickpockets. The Cunard pier was under a police cordon, with 200 officers restraining journalists, sensation-seekers and souvenir-hunters. Twenty-five horse ambulances were standing by – a few attended by a surgeon in a white uniform – their clanging bells exciting the crowd; Salvation Army workers, nurses and stretcher-bearers were gathered in small numbers, and undertakers' wagons bearing coffins. Black-veiled women were helped from cabs and limousines by the police, and taken to a reserved area on the pier. The flags on the Singer building and other skyscrapers were flying at half-mast, and lit by arc lights trained on them. A small group – including Vincent Astor and Renée Harris's brother Samuel Wallach, a clothing manufacturer – stood by the head of the gang-plank in the rain. Pierpont Morgan junior stood at the dock.

The ship's docking seemed interminable. When the gangway was put down, hundreds of people waiting on the pier took off their hats. At 9.35 p.m. disembarkation began. First-class passengers came first; then second; and finally third – immigration officers spared them the customary rough processing through Ellis Island. Dr and Mrs Frauenthal ensured that they disembarked first, and were hustled into a motor car. The three Lamson sisters, Caroline Brown, Charlotte Appleton and Malvina Cornell, hatless for the first time in their adult lives and grieving for their lost companion, Edith Evans, were met by the magistrate Robert Cornell, Malvina's husband. The pregnant widow Astor, looking faint, was propped up and hurried away by her stepson Vincent. The widowed Emily Goldsmith was wearing two wedding rings on her hand – one entrusted to her by Tom Theobald as they parted on the boat deck, with a hasty injunction to give it to his widow. Two brothers had come from Montreal to collect their eleven-month-old nephew, Trevor Allison, whose parents and toddler sister had all been lost. 'Bobo' Dodge, aged four, swathed in white wool, excited and merry at the blaze of flares as photographers took pictures, was the only spark of joy in the scene.

Whether they are wide or thin, long or squat, grieving people seemed to shrink in size. Passengers looked dulled and confused as they left the claustrophobic horror of the past days for the limitless bewilderment of the present. Their usually controlled public faces had slipped askew. Survivors looked pinched and stricken: some still scared, with a fright that would never leave them; others dazed, staring, angry; and some distraught. Few had yet clambered back inside the armour of training and manners. Most were bedraggled, although a few such as the banker Robert Daniel managed to look spruce. Many felt culpable for surviving, or ashamed at being caught in an event that was already so notorious. As the missionary's wife Nellie Becker, looking overwrought, alighted with her three children, she told her twelve-year-old daughter Ruth, 'Don't you *dare* tell anybody we were on the *Titanic*.'[53]

Inside Cunard's shed a hushed crowd stood in two lines, allowing a long, narrow passage between them for survivors. As one spectator described, 'A woman came hurrying through, refusing to be comforted by her supporting friends, wildly calling, "Where's my husband; where's my husband; where's my husband?" She passed on down the long line, her friends trying in vain to console her. A huddled and muffled figure came moaning by in a nurse's arms. Then came a stalwart, healthy man, who apparently had suffered comparatively little. He gave a handshake and a cheery salutation to a friend in the crowd: "All right, Harry?" the friend inquired. "All right," was the reply.' Probably this was the hardened cardsharp, Harry Homer. A woman came down the gangplank peering anxiously on all sides. 'She uttered a great cry of joy, burst from her friends, and fell into the arms of a man who rushed up the line to meet her. They kissed each other again and again, and uttered extravagant, delighted cries as they staggered together down the line in each other's arms.' Babies, whose mothers were lost, were carried in the arms of porters: 'one or two of them were crying; one or two were looking out with blank baby wonder'. Near the end came 'a little, poorly clad, undersized steerage passenger, with a ghastly white face, bright eyes and cheek bones almost protruding through his skin'. Two women – 'from their dress and manner they evidently belonged to the best social class in New York' – approached an official. One explained that her silent companion, who bore a 'look of heavy settled despair', wished to go aboard to seek her husband. The official inquired if his name was listed among the survivors. 'No, but she must go and see. She doesn't know whether he is alive or dead.' The official refused.[54]

Similarly, the widow and children of Thomas Myles, an Irish-born land developer long resident in Cambridge, Massachusetts, were loath to accept his death, though he was lost like almost all second-class male passengers. A daughter telegraphed his son Frederick with false assurances that their father was safe, and when Frederick discovered the trick, he went hurtling through the streets of Jersey City crazed with grief until detained by the police for disorderly conduct. Despite the absence of Thomas Myles from any survivor list, his physician son Leo Myles and two family attorneys went to the Cunard pier hoping to see the old man stamp down the gangway. The young sports writer Homer Wheaton stood with Leo Myles. 'When the last of the line had filed down the plank, and we knew the worst had come, I never will forget the look that came over his face. Hoping against hope he had kept up his courage all the way. When it was all over and he knew the worst, he turned away, and with heaving sides, but dry eyes, sobbed: "How can I tell mother?"'[55]

Another group had come uncertainly to meet the survivors of the Wick party. Colonel George Wick had been the leading businessman in Youngstown, Ohio, and son of a pioneering banker in the Mahoning valley. As a middle-aged widower he had married Mary Hitchcock, whose father's ironworks had made him Youngstown's first millionaire. Wick was active in all the iron and steel enterprises of the Mahoning valley (*Titanic*'s third-class decks had contained Croats and Lebanese on their way to work in Wick's Youngstown foundries), and had promoted a great hotel that was being built at

Youngstown in 1912. The Wicks had been touring Europe with his twenty-one-year-old daughter Natalie, but his fourteen-year-old son had been left in Youngstown. The Colonel was lost in the wreck, and until shortly before *Carpathia* docked, it had been thought that his wife had perished too. 'When the mother stepped from the gangplank, the boy's happiness that one of his parents had been spared, welling through his grief at the loss of the other, moved bystanders to tears.'[56] Mary Wick, like the Myles family, could not accept that her man was dead – she had last seen him from Lifeboat 8 standing at the rail waving goodbye – and insisted on remaining in New York for several days in the hope of better news. Only his body would convince her that he was dead. She sent someone to search for him among the recovered corpses lying at Halifax, but his body was never found.[57]

The morning after *Carpathia* docked, when definitive passenger lists were available, last desperate hopes were destroyed. The tram conductor Nils Pålsson, looking ashen and ill after four days of suspense, went on Friday to the offices of White Star's agent in Chicago. In fractured English, he asked for news of his wife and four children. The clerk scanning the list of third-class survivors found no Pålssons, and suggested that perhaps they were travelling by another steamer. Then he checked the embarkation list, and found five Pålssons. Pålsson was stupefied, helped to a chair, doused in cold water to revive him, taken home by an appalled friend who had accompanied him. Few people lost so much as Pålsson.

Eleanor Widener, who had lost a husband and son, had to be helped down the gangway, and flung herself into the arms of her brother-in-law. At the Pennsylvania railroad station three special trains waited. One was to take the Wideners to Philadelphia and another was for the surviving Thayers. Philadelphia's police chief, with a handpicked corps, escorted other Philadelphia survivors to taxicabs in which they were whirled to the station for the third special.[58] At Lynnewood, Eleanor Widener (perhaps as the result of sedation) could not at first be roused. Draped in deepest mourning, she attended a Sunday service in the chapel of the Widener Home for Crippled Children, while her father-in-law rested under medical care in his palatial home. Besides the Widener and Elkins families, the cream of Philadelphia society, and ninety-eight disabled boys and girls, were arrayed in separate groups in the flower-banked chapel.[59] Marion Thayer returned to their house at Haverford, which was guarded by Pennsylvania Railroad detectives, who barred the way to journalists. This did not prevent the *Philadelphia Inquirer* reporting that 'with a well-directed blow from an oar-lock', Mrs Thayer had knocked out a drunken sailor who had been rocking and almost capsizing her lifeboat.[60]

Sid Blake, the New York hotelier, recorded his Cornish guests' mournful journey to the docks to meet *Carpathia*. 'Everybody [was] trying to bear up. Mrs Drew was one of the first [of the Cornish] to come off the boat, and with her Mr William Drew's boy. Mr William Drew, I thought, would faint – after hearing that his boy was drowned, and to find him safe. He would hold him up and say, "Are you sure you are my boy?", but his delight was short-lived, as he suddenly thought of his brother, but Mrs Drew said he was gone. The last she had seen of him was when he assisted her and the boy into a lifeboat. He kissed her and the boy goodbye, and stepped back for more women to get into the boat and be saved.' Blake reported to the Cornish newspapers that Addie Wells with two children, Emily Richards with two children, Eliza and Nellie Hocking, and Ellen Wilks 'were all, I think, of the Penzance folk who were saved'. There were poignant tales behind the Cornish death roll, as pronounced by Sid Blake. 'Mr & Mrs John H. Chapman of St Neot were right behind Mrs Richards, and ready to step in the lifeboat, but when Mrs Chapman found that her husband could not go, she turned back and said, "Goodbye, Mrs Richards, if John can't go, I won't go either".' The Penzance men, Harry Cotterill, Percy Bailey and George Hocking, had helped their women into the boats. 'As George Hocking put his mother into the boat (she was the last of the party to go), Mrs Hocking begged him to come as well, but he said, "No, mother. These men are good enough to stand back for you, and I must stay back and let their wives and mothers go." He then kissed her, and that was the last she saw of him. For such heroism Cornwall can be proud of her sons. Mrs Hocking is in a very bad way. She is constantly calling out, "Poor George, poor George".[61]

London held a *Titanic* memorial service at St Paul's Cathedral on 19 April. Thousands were turned away. The nave, aisles, transepts and galleries were crowded with people dressed in black – the only bright colour coming from the procession of the Lord Mayor. The altar was draped in black and white, stripped of its usual ornaments, except a crucifix between two tall candlesticks. The service opened with the vast congregation singing 'Rock of Ages' in slow, subdued voices – the effect was overwhelming. After the Dean read the lesson, all rose and stood in solemn silence. Then, after a tense pause, the silence was broken by the subdued sound of drums. Almost imperceptibly, the drums grew louder, until their solemn rolling filled the church, and reverberated like thunder to its dome. Then the drums gradually diminished until they had died away. There was another silence until trumpets sounded the first notes of that stately dirge, the Dead March from Saul. Women were led out fainting; and Pirrie's brother-in-law Alexander Carlisle collapsed before the first roll of the drums was done. The simple singing by the whole congregation of 'Eternal Father, strong to save' was the final act of this intensely moving service. After the band played Beethoven's funeral march, the vast congregation silently dispersed.

A pall of gloom was cast over the nation. Asquith, the Prime Minister, and his family moved into a new house on the Thames, at Sutton Courtenay, in the week that *Titanic* sank. Three thousand pounds to buy and decorate the house had been advanced to his wife by Pierpont Morgan, who could see the advantage if they were obligated to him. Friday morning's newspapers carried reports of the *Carpathia* docking, and Asquith and his wife Margot cried together after breakfast. That evening, when the adult Asquith children gathered for a house-warming party, one son read aloud new survivors' stories from late edition newspapers: the Prime Minister was deeply moved. On Saturday morning Margot sobbed again over the *Times*. Then her daughter Elizabeth, 'white & dark-ringed round the eyes & tears rolling down her distorted face', interrupted as she was dressing.

'Oh! Mother,' Elizabeth wailed, 'those poor poor people, all the young married women having to leave their husbands, & some of the boats half-full, & that wonderful Phillips & Bride going on to the end at the wireless telegraphy, & then Phillips dying of exposure – I can't, I won't hear it".'[62] The calamity also touched Violet Asquith, the Prime Minister's other daughter. 'The man *Guggenheim*! who changed into his dress clothes to die is one of the most funny & pathetic touches. The cruelty of the separations is almost unbearable – 19 widows under 23 – & one honeymooning couple of 18 & 19 – torn from each other & the one drowned & the other saved.' She despised the American harassment of Ismay. 'I suppose he was wrong to leave the ship – but no-one has a right to arraign him for it . . . he is probably going through hell enough to atone for anything he has done.'[63]

Once *Carpathia* docked and solid facts emerged, journalists could have adjusted their coverage. It was clear that women *had* died, and first-class men *had* survived, in greater numbers than initially reported: 201 out of 324 first-class passengers survived, 118 out of 277 second-class passengers; 181 out of 708 third-class. Gender was more decisive than class in determining the survival of passengers: 74.3 per cent of female passengers survived, 52.3 per cent of children and 20 per cent of men. Women travelling third-class were 41 per cent more likely to survive than men from first-class. When interpreting the survival rates of the different classes it must be remembered that 44 per cent of first-class passengers were women, but only 23 per cent of third-class voyagers. In first-class, a third of men (57 out of 175), 97 per cent of women (140 out of 144) and all but one of the six children (little Lorraine Allison) survived. In second-class, 8 per cent of men (14 out of 168), 86 per cent of women (80 out of 93) and 100 per cent of the 24 children survived. In third-class, 16 per cent of men (75 out of 462), 47 per cent of women (76 out of 165), and from a total of 79 children 27 per cent of boys and 45 per cent of girls survived.

Twenty-four per cent of crew (212 out of 885) survived, including 65 per cent of Deck Department, 22 per cent of Engine Department and 20 per cent of stewards; 87 per cent of women crew members were saved (twenty out of twenty-three), but only 22 per cent of male crew (192 out of 885). The interpretation of these statistics has been stormily debated for a century – and always unproductively if gender is not weighed in the balance with class. One question deserves prominence, even if it cannot be answered definitively. The second-class men had easier access to the boat deck than third-class, yet only eight per cent of them survived: were they more unselfish, stoical, self-consciously well-behaved, or conformist to rules than those above or below them?

After *Carpathia* survivors began to recount their stories of confusion and fear when loading the lifeboats, newspaper editors continued to give a version of events that emphasized masculine chivalry, selflessness, duty. A century after *Titanic*, tutored by two world wars and several genocides, we are accustomed to the random causation of events and haphazard consequences; but in 1912 most people could only envisage what had happened in terms of personal codes and social rules. If American journalists, politicians and public opinion soon began to criticize the English crew for bungling, funk and self-preservation, their English equivalents adulated them for their composure, courage and sacrifice. Somehow, the English imagined the *Titanic* sinking into a counterpart of Drake's defeat of the Spanish Armada in 1588 or of Nelson's victory over the French at Trafalgar in 1805. Journalists everywhere transmuted the dead – the Captain, the bandsmen, Ida Straus, Phillips the Marconi operator – into legendary creatures. They ended up duped by their own sentimental inventions, and weepy over sob stories which they had concocted. The tales that Captain Smith had swum with a child in his arms to a lifeboat and after handing it to safety had been swept away by a wave, or that he had shouted at the last, 'Be British, boys, be British!', were absurd and vulgar. To celebrate such fantasies, sand models were sculpted on Bournemouth beach, entitled 'Britannia Mourns', 'Captain Smith and Baby', 'The Plucky Little Countess', guarded by imitation lifebelts inscribed 'Women and Children First' and 'To the Heroes of the Titanic'.[64]

The string trio playing in the Café de Paris had been led by twenty-three-year-old Georges Krin, who had been born in Paris and grew up in Liège, accompanied by twenty-year-old Roger Bricoux, who had been born in Lille and worked in Monte Carlo before going to sea. The valour of all the bandsmen was saluted in France. 'During the protracted agony of the sinking, the musicians played polkas and waltzes with redoubled brio,' opined *Le Matin*. 'Perhaps it was a poor choice of music: Beethoven would have been more sublime. Blowing hard into a cornet, flattening the keys of a piano, striving for exquisite pitch, avoiding flat notes, all the time knowing that you're going to die in the black and icy waters – this is heroism at its most stirring . . . the polkas helped to maintain calm and discipline on board during the evacuation. Often, during blazes in music halls, orchestras obey the example of their leader: their oompahs subdue panic and save life. Honour to the musicians of the *Titanic* who stayed at their music stands till the death! One can wield a clarinet as bravely as a sword.'[65]

On Sunday came the pulpit oratory. Charles Parkhurst, who claimed Straus and Stead as his friends, preached a *Titanic* sermon in the Madison Square Presbyterian church on 21 April which was reproduced across America, and publicized in Europe too. 'The picture which presents itself before my eyes is that of the glassy, glaring eyes of the victims, staring meaninglessly at the gilded furnishings of this sunken palace of the sea; dead helplessness wrapt in priceless luxury; jewels valued in seven figures becoming the strange playthings of the queer creatures that sport in the dark depths. Everything for existence, nothing for life! Grand men, charming women, beautiful babies, all becoming horrible in the midst of the glittering splendor of a $10,000,000 casket!' He upheld the disaster as 'the terrific and ghastly illustration of what things come to when men throw God out of the door and take a golden calf in at the window'. He inveighed against Ismay and his co-directors: 'the vivid drama of men leaping to their death, bidding long goodbyes to their loved ones, and all to the accompaniment of the infernal music of the orchestra, ought to give them a foretaste of the tortures of the damned'.[66]

A similar line was taken by Edward Talbot, Bishop of Winchester, preaching in Southampton on 21 April. A congregation of over 1,000 was headed by Lord Winchester, Lord Lieutenant of the county. No-one could recall 'such a plunge from ease and security to darkness and destruction', preached the bishop. 'It was a thing to darken the imagination, to turn the brain, and crush the nerves.' He believed God meant that 'the cruel and wanton waste of money, which was needed on every hand for the help of the needy', should be rebuked by such a catastrophe. It was 'a mighty lesson against our confidence and trust in the strength of machinery and money', and in the iniquity of 'hyper-luxuries . . . The *Titanic* in name will stand for a monument of warning to human presumption'.[67]

On Wednesday 17 April, William Alden Smith, Republican Senator from Michigan, had proposed a sub-committee to investigate the disaster. Three Democrat and three Republican senators were appointed alongside him. Smith consulted the Attorney General to confirm that he had powers to prevent British visitors from leaving the US, visited Taft at the White House, and went to New York on Thursday. Ten minutes after *Carpathia* docked, Smith, the Senate master-of-arms and a sheriff, hustled their way on board, and into Ismay's cabin.

Who was this new actor in the *Titanic* drama? Smith had been born in 1859 in Dowagiac, a hamlet near Lake Michigan, where in 1912 the first-class passenger Dickinson Bishop was kingpin. His poverty-stricken family moved to the furniture-making town of Grand Rapids when he was twelve. As a boy he delivered newspapers and telegrams, sold popcorn on the streets with the help of a friend who drew crowds by playing 'Camptown Races' on a banjo, became a pageboy in the state legislature, a janitor for a law firm, then an attorney, joined the Republican Party, was rewarded with a sinecure as Michigan's first game warden, married the buxom daughter of a Dutch lumberman, and served in the House for Representatives for eleven year before his election as Senator for Michigan in 1906. Smith was a populist who roused voters against big business with rhetorical alliteration, and longed to injure Pierpont Morgan's interests. He was all rush and humbug, prone to sum up situations on scant facts.

The Senator, who held his first interrogations on 19 April in the Waldorf-Astoria, issued subpoenas to the four surviving officers and to twenty-seven crewmen – all of whom were itching to return home to England. They were so affronted at being herded into a second-rate Washington boarding house that they refused to cooperate with an enquiry intended, they believed, to discredit British seamanship. Only the intervention of Lord Eustace Percy, an attaché at the British Embassy, deterred the seamen from defying the senatorial summons. The Embassy attested Lightoller's 'tact, capability and good sense in handling a trying situation'.[68]

Smith was an incoherent, unsystematic questioner, who hated the Demon Drink and hoped to elicit that Captain Smith or other officers had been drunk. He also cross-examined Henry Stengel, in Ismay's presence, to elicit if Smith, Ismay and the ship's officers had participated in the pool betting on the ship's speed and arrival time. His implication was that Smith or Ismay had ordered the ship to race into the ice zone to win a bet. The Senator's firm, mellifluous voice uttered clichés that managed to seem both incontrovertible and inflammatory. He hunted clues to Ismay's accomplices with all the salivating doggedness and random sideways lunges of a young basset hound tracking hares.

White Star's sailors resented the grating stupidity of Senator Smith asking Fifth Officer Lowe what an iceberg was composed of: 'Ice, I suppose, sir,' was Lowe's rejoinder. Third Officer Pitman was quizzed about exploding icebergs and the reliability of seals as guides to icebergs' whereabouts. Smith asked Lightoller whether crew or passengers might have sought refuge in the ship's watertight compartments. He demanded of Captain Stanley Lord whether the *Californian* had dropped anchor when it stopped overnight in mid-ocean. Smith also inquired if the great funnel crashing into an ocean full of desperate people in lifejackets had injured anyone. He persisted, too, in chivvying a reluctant, distressed Pitman into describing the cries of the people freezing to death in the ocean: an unforgivable act of cheap-thrills emotional voyeurism.

Absurd allegations were made, and left unchallenged. Imanita

Shelley swore, for example, that Hélène Baxter, the Canadian million-aire, had told her on *Carpathia* that she had sent her son Quigg Baxter for advice from Captain Smith after the ship stopped, 'that her son had found the Captain in a card game, and he had laughingly assured him that there was no danger and to advise his mother to go back to bed'.[69] Yet even the bumptious Senator was stunned into respectful silence by the bald, unadorned recital of horrific experiences by the South Dakota homesteader, Olaus Abelseth, a brave, clear-headed witness, an unexceptional man who did exceptional things, and brought discomforting authenticity to the proceedings.

In an eager young democracy, politicians want votes, and use cheap stunts and flashy catchphrases to grab headlines and excite voters. In a settled older democracy, the people with power use hallowed formulae and staid circumlocution to subdue discussion and lull the electorate. Smith's enquiry was raucous scapegoating: he wanted to attract headlines, enflame emotion, apportion blame, protect American interests and wound the English. Lord Mersey, who led the London enquiry, was a judge with nautical expertise. It was unnecessary to explain to him why a sailor was not an officer, although an officer was a sailor, or that watertight compartments were not refuges in which passengers could ensconce themselves, before the ship sank to the bottom of the Atlantic, to be rescued later. He was assisted at the enquiry by the Attorney General and Marconi speculator, Sir Rufus Isaacs, who had left school at the age of thirteen and long ago had been a headstrong ship's boy. Isaacs led questioning of witnesses with limpid, courteous clarity. Mersey buried himself in blueprints, models, and deadening technical details as he sought to mitigate criticisms of his compatriots. Whereas Smith chopped and stamped his way through the shallows of American bluster, Mersey paddled cautiously beside the fathomless depths of English equivocation. Mersey with his crisp inflexions personified the unspoken rules of England with its systematic inhibiting influ-ences. His censure was so light that it sounded like applause.

Both enquiries agreed that *Titanic* was going too fast for the conditions, the look-out was inadequate, the loading of lifeboats haphazard, and that Lord's *Californian* had seen the distress rockets and should have gone to help. No third-class passengers testified to Mersey (the Duff Gordons were the only passengers to appear before him), and only three to Smith. Both enquiries concluded that there was no discrimination against third-class passengers, although two of them testified to Smith that the crew had tried to restrain them.

Titanic sank because of poor navigation. Captain Smith neglected the ice warnings, and failed to reduce speed; but he was not trying to break records, for his liner could never match the speed of a fast Cunarder. Still less did he endanger his ship at Ismay's behest. Maintaining speed in the vicinity of ice was accepted practice: the captains of all great liners went at full tilt into storms and bad weather, and did not think that they were violating either good sense or good seamanship. They did so partly in order to adhere to scheduled mail deliveries; partly out of masculine vanity. The fact that this was common practice does not reduce the captain's culpability. It was his responsibility that the ship under his command sped into the ice. Murdoch, officer of the watch, aggravated the crisis by reversing engines and swerving the helm: if the ship had struck by the bow it probably would have stayed afloat. Smith failed to impress on his men that the ship was certainly sinking when they began launching lifeboats beneath full capacity. Mersey concluded that he could not blame Smith, whose grievous mistakes were not negligent given prevailing practices in the Atlantic. He also judged that Ismay had no obligations to die with the ship: had he not clambered into Lifeboat C, he would have achieved nothing except wasting his life.

In the sequel to the disaster, regulations were revised so that ships were obliged to carry enough lifeboats for all passengers and crew. It became mandatory to train seamen to handle them. New rules were imposed covering bulkheads and life-saving equipment. All vessels carrying more than fifty passengers had to be equipped with long-range, permanently manned Marconi sets. The International Ice Patrol was established to monitor icebergs. Shipping lanes were moved south of ice-encumbered seas.

When the disaster was confirmed in New York, White Star had chartered a cable-laying vessel called the *Mackay-Bennett* to search the area to recover bodies. It sailed on Wednesday 17 April carrying a volunteer crew and undertakers as well as tons of ice and hundreds of coffins. When *Mackay-Bennett* reached the accident scene, the bodies in their white lifejackets scattered across the ocean surface looked, from a distance, like a flock of white seagulls resting on the water. The saturated remains were hauled from heavy seas, and their appearance, clothes and possessions inventoried. Overall, *Mackay-Bennett* recovered 306 bodies. First-class corpses were put in coffins; second- and third-class sewn in canvas bags; and crew members packed in ice, and laid on the foredeck under tarpaulin. One hundred and sixteen bodies – the most bloated or disfigured – were weighted and slipped overboard into the rolling seas to sink 2 miles deep.

The *Mackay-Bennett* reached Halifax on the bright spring morning of 30 April. Every flag was at half-mast; church bells tolled mournfully; shops had photographs of the dead ship, festooned in black bunting, displayed in their windows. There was a guard of honour as the corpses were brought ashore. Twenty hearses travelled back and forth between the harbour and a curling rink which had been converted into a temporary morgue. Military patrols were on guard to prevent ghoulish photography.

White Star chartered other search vessels. *Minia* retrieved seventeen bodies, including that of the railway president, Charles Hays: its crew slept at night with filled coffins stacked around them. Another chartered Newfoundland steamer, *Algerine*, retrieved the last of the 328 bodies found in the ocean: that of a saloon steward, James McGrady. A tiny boy was buried at the expense of the *Mackay-Bennett* captain and crew. The child was believed to be Gösta Pålsson, whose Swedish mother and three siblings were lost, too. Ninety years after his death, DNA testing suggested that he was thirteen-month-old Eino Panula, whose Finnish mother and four siblings all died. In 2007 further DNA tests indicated that he was nineteen-month-old Sidney Goodwin, whose parents and five siblings perished.

On 8 May a funeral service for Charles Hays was held in a Montreal church. From the Atlantic to the Pacific coast, along thousands of miles of Grand Trunk Railway branch lines, in every Grand Trunk siding and depot, the engines ceased for five full minutes to pant and snort along their tracks. All movement ceased at each Grand Trunk crossing and station as thousands of railway staff stood with bowed heads in silent tribute. Then work resumed, the wheels turned, and within seconds the Grand Trunk Railway rattled forward without its president.

One English funeral, too, made an outstanding mark. After *Carpathia* had docked, every newspaper reader could visualize the bandsmen continuing to play in order to avert panic, sticking to their posts when all was plainly lost. Their courage was saluted as sublime: a Manchester merchant declared that their valour had surpassed that of 'the Noble Six Hundred' in the Charge of the Light Brigade, for the cavalrymen obeyed a military command whereas Hartley's band obeyed a voluntary impulse.[70] The corpse of the band leader, Wallace Hartley, was found in the ocean, in evening-dress, with his music case strapped to it; and shipped to Liverpool on White Star's *Arabic*. His face, seen through a glass panel in the coffin, seemed discoloured by a blow and embalming. A horse-drawn hearse took ten hours to carry Hartley's coffin through the night the 59 miles (through congested Lancashire factory districts) to his home-town of Colne. On 18 May the body of 'Colne's hero, Britain's hero, the world's hero', was buried in his home-town. All business stopped for the day. The *Colne and Nelson Times* estimated that 40,000 people attended the funeral, coming by train and tram from across northern England, to stand on the route to the Bethel Independent Methodist Chapel. Seven bands played the Dead March (from 'Saul') with muffled drums. Twelve young men – eight of them his cousins – bore his coffin shoulder-high through Colne. Inside the cemetery, the police, bandsmen, scouts, ambulance corps, and public mourners made an avenue for the twelve bearers who bore the coffin shoulder high to its grave. Thousands of people stood around the entrance, and the countryside was dotted with onlookers. Police and bandsmen formed a cordon round the grave, which was lined with evergreen, narcissi, marguerites, lilies-of-the-valley, and rhododendrons. As the coffin was lowered into the grave, a dozen scout buglers sounded the 'Last Post'. The notes went rolling through the valley, and came echoing back. A lark sang overhead.[71]

Claims for loss of property ranged from $177,353 (£36,567) for fourteen trunks, four bags and a jewel case from Charlotte Cardeza; $100,000 from Björnström-Steffansson for Blondel's oil painting 'La Circassienne Au Bain'; $5,000 for Billy Carter's Renault motor car; $3,000 by Emilio Portaluppi for a signed picture of Garibaldi presented to his grandfather; $750 for Robert Daniel's champion French bulldog Gamin de Pycombe; $500 from Margaret Brown for Egyptian antiquities intended for Denver Museum; $50 for Eugene Daly's bagpipes; $5 for Annie Stengel's copy of *Science and Health*; and 8s 6d for Edwina Troutt's marmalade machine. The District Court of New York received claims for damages totalling $16,804,112 – the highest was $1 million from Renée Harris, widow of the Broadway producer. No claims were received from any Astor, Guggenheim, Straus or Widener; and only a claim for Thayer luggage.

On 13 May, the White Star liner *Oceanic* found Collapsible A, which had drifted 200 miles south-east of the sinking at a rate of nearly 8 miles a day. It contained three bodies: that of Thomson Beattie, a Winnipeg land developer, lying on a bench in full evening dress; a steward; and a fireman. All three had frozen to death on the night of the sinking. For a month their corpses, bleached by sun and salt, had been pitched by the Atlantic swell under the open sky. *Oceanic*'s crewmen sewed the corpses in canvas, cast them overboard, and capsized Collapsible A.

On 20 June, Hamburg-Amerika's *Imperator* left on its maiden voyage to New York. It was 900 feet long and 52,000 tons: *Titanic* would have been superseded as the world's largest vessel very soon. *Titanic* was not however surpassed as world's worst peacetime disaster at sea until 1987, when a ferry in the Philippines sank with the loss of 4,375 passengers.

Mary Nakid, who was eighteen months old at the time of the voyage, travelling with her twenty-year-old father and nineteen-year-old mother from Lebanon to Waterbury, Connecticut, became the first survivor of the disaster to die – of meningitis on 30 July 1912. The second death, of Eugenie Baclini, aged three, also Lebanese, also from meningitis, was on 30 August. The first adult to die, in December 1912, was Archibald Gracie, who never revived his powers after hours knee-deep in icy water on a half-submerged raft. Months after the accident he was moved to tears reading and re-reading survivors' accounts. As he lay dying in a New York hotel he was heard repeating, 'We must get them into the boats, we must get them all into the boats.'[72]

In January 1913, Pierpont Morgan sailed for Egypt on board White Star's *Adriatic* with his favourite Pekinese dog. He had been agitated and anxious for months. Now, travelling down the Nile, he became deluded. He could not sleep, and would not eat. Stock exchanges slumped at the news of his indisposition. In March he shifted from Cairo to the royal suite of the Grand Hotel in Rome. Throughout his life he had suffered bouts of depression, in which he felt worthless; but in Rome, as his daughter, secretaries and physicians tried to ward off dealers clamouring to see the great collector, his fears overwhelmed him. He was sedated, grew incoherent, and finally so agitated that he was given morphine. Delirious, then comatose, he died on 31 March. Physicians certified the cause of his death as 'psychic dyspepsia', a condition unknown to medical science. Italian soldiers marched in guard of honour as his body was carried to the station in Rome; in Paris the coffin was bedecked in orchids, carnations, roses and palms; at Le Havre the French army saluted his cortège; and on the day of his funeral, the New York Stock Exchange closed in his honour until noon. Thirty thousand people lined the streets of New York that day, Monday 14 April 1913 – exactly a year after his great ship had struck the iceberg.

The disaster fractured marriages. In Lucile Carter's divorce suit of 1914, she claimed: 'When the *Titanic* struck, my husband came to our state room and said, "Get up and dress yourself and the children." I never saw him again until I arrived at the *Carpathia* at 8 o'clock the next morning, when I saw him leaning over the rail.

All he said was that he had had a jolly good breakfast, and that he never thought I would make it.' Billy Carter claimed to have put her in a lifeboat before stepping into Collapsible C with Ismay; but Lord Mersey concluded that Collapsible C left fifteen minutes before Lucile Carter and her children in Lifeboat 4.

Surviving ship's officers were treated like Vietnam veterans – shunned if not ruined. Neither Lightoller nor Pitman, Boxhall or Lowe received a White Star command. Lightoller was singular in his willingness to discuss the sinking. Other survivors were punished by mass opinion. Albert Dick was ostracized, left his Canadian hotel business and sold real estate instead. Arthur Peuchen was traduced for surviving, and suffered both social and business reverses: a rich man in 1912, he died a pauper in 1929. Masabumi Hosono was denounced in Japan for having survived when others had died. His ministry sacked him; Japanese newspapers reviled his cowardice; he was shunned and although he survived until 1939, he was a broken man. The English were more forgiving of survivors: the magistrate Algernon Barkworth was always considered by his Yorkshire neighbours as an upstanding English gentleman. The story that Ismay was forced to live as a recluse is fanciful: tales of Sir Cosmo Duff Gordon's isolation are overdone.

A year after the sinking, Lightoller jumped into a cold bath at the end of a strenuous game of tennis on a summer day. The cold water induced a sudden, overwhelming shock, the memory of his hours in the freezing Atlantic overpowered him, and he fell into a scared trance until pulled from the bath by friends. Neshan Krekorian, the young Armenian who saved himself by leaping into Lifeboat 10 as it was lowered, lived for sixty-five years in Ontario, but never boarded a ship again and was dismayed by the mere sight of lakes. After his experiences, Lawrence Beesley had a deep aversion to the sea: he only once took his family on a seaside holiday, during which he insisted upon turning his beach deckchair to face inland. When the film *A Night to Remember* was being shot, Beesley was hired as a special adviser, and asked to sit by a tape recorder in a caravan at Pinewood Studios and imitate the despairing cries of freezing people that he remembered hearing from his lifeboat. He performed this macabre task: the death-cries in *A Night to Remember* at least have an enduring resonance.

The anniversary of 15 April was sad and stressful for survivors: Frank Goldsmith lived another sixty-nine years, but was always subdued on 15 April. On the second anniversary of the sinking, and thus two years after her son George's death, Eliza Hocking was killed by a streetcar in Akron, though whether she threw herself under it, lurched under it drunk or was distracted by misery is unclear. Marion Thayer died on the thirty-second anniversary of the *Titanic* collision, in 1944. Selma Asplund, who lost her husband and three sons in the disaster, died on the fifty-second anniversary of the sinking in 1964. Meier Moor, who had been a boy of seven on *Titanic*, collecting cigarette cards from the adult passengers, died on the sixty-third anniversary of the sinking in 1975.

Potomak na Titanik, meaning heir of the *Titanic*, was the phrase by which inhabitants of the Troyan region of Bulgaria referred to descendants of the eight men from Gumoshtnik who perished. Two of them left pregnant widows, who gave birth to a girl and a boy, who later married. Their son, Petko Chakarov, who became a headmaster, was a local celebrity until his death in 2004.

Standing on the pier in New York, after *Carpathia* docked, a young woman survivor was overpowered by anguish. 'Oh! my God,' she cried, 'he did it to save me! Oh, why didn't I die? Oh, why didn't I die?'[73] Survivors asked themselves, with harsh remorse, why they still lived when so many others had perished. In many cases, their survival felt despicable. They knew that for them to live, it had been necessary for others to die; that if they had been lost, someone else would have been safe. Charlotte Collyer, who escaped on Lifeboat 14, was never reconciled to leaving her husband to die, and haunted by the memory of the adolescent boy, Gaskell, lying face down on the deck in despair after being ejected from the lifeboat. She died aged thirty-three, two years after her husband. Selma Asplund enjoined her daughter Lillian never to mention the disaster, and the latter preserved her silence until her nineties. William Carter and

John Ryerson, aged eleven and thirteen when Lightoller tried to forbid their escape in Lifeboat 4, both lived to their late eighties, but refused to discuss their experiences – feeling, perhaps, unworthy as survivors. To them and the Asplunds it seemed shameful to speak of how some had died and they had lived. It was only after 1970, when the children of 1912 reached retirement age, and found vivifying new identities as disaster survivors, that they began to talk without disgrace. This extra interest kept some of them alive for decades.

Winnie Troutt became an apricot picker in California. There in 1918 she married a man with whom she ran a bakery in Beverly Hills. She married for a third time at the age of seventy-nine, and retired to Hermosa Beach, California. Two months before his resignation as President of the USA, in 1974, Richard Nixon sent her a congratulatory letter on her ninetieth birthday. She crossed the Atlantic ten times – the last in her ninety-ninth year. She was a cherished figure at *Titanic* conventions until her late nineties, and died in Redondo Beach after celebrating her century. The disaster proved, for her, life-enhancing and life-prolonging.

Not so for others. Eliza Hocking's violent death has already been mentioned. Six months later, in October 1914, travelling as a passenger on the Leyland Line *Devonian*, Annie Robinson, a survivor from *Titanic*, where she been a stewardess, became so distressed as the steamship groped towards Boston, Massachusetts in a dense fog, sounding its baleful fog horn, that she threw herself overboard. In 1919, Washington Dodge took a revolver to the garage of his San Francisco apartment building, and shot himself in the head. In agony he then lurched into an elevator, ascended to his floor, and, with brains spilling out, staggered into his apartment to the horror of his wife. Oscar Palmquist, who had escaped the icy Atlantic waters in Lifeboat 15, drowned in obscure circumstances in a shallow pond in Beardsley Park, Bridgeport, Connecticut in 1925. Henry Frauenthal, who had saved himself by leaping into Lifeboat 5, killed himself by jumping from the seventh floor of his hospital in 1927, and his widow Clara was thereafter confined in an asylum for the last sixteen years of her life. Robert Hichens botched his attempts to shoot himself and cut his wrists in 1933, and was sentenced to five years' penal servitude for the attempted murder, during an alcoholic binge, of a man against whom he nurtured a grudge. The cardsharp George Brereton, alias Brayton, fired a shotgun into his head in Los Angeles in 1942. In 1945, Jack Thayer, by then a Philadelphia banker and treasurer of the University of Pennsylvania, depressed by the death of his younger son in action, sitting in the driver's seat of his wife's sedan, parked near the trolley loop on Parkside Avenue, Philadelphia, used a razor to cut his wrists and throat. Frederick Fleet, the look-out who glimpsed the iceberg too late, ended up a husk of a man, selling newspapers on a street corner in Southampton, and hanged himself from a washing-line post in his garden in 1965.

Ben Guggenheim's daughters Peggy and Hazel never recovered their orientation after his death. In 1928, Hazel's two sons, Terrence and Benjamin, aged four years and fourteen months, fell to their deaths from a sixteen-floor roof garden in Manhattan, with the strong suspicion that she threw them during a spasm of madness – she had just separated from their father. Throughout her life she suffered *Titanic* nightmares, and requested that at her funeral (in 1995) 'Nearer, My God, to Thee' was played. Peggy, who died in 1979, said that every day she thought of her father's foul death.

These were sudden deaths – with witnesses. A slow demise, a dwindling away, without startled bystanders, policemen taking notes, undertakers removing corpses, coroner's inquests or graveyard leave-takings, came in the Sargasso Sea, that lake in the open Atlantic, as Jules Verne called it. The Sargasso is the only sea in the world without shores. It is a gyre at the centre of the North Atlantic, where the Labrador Current from the north meets the Gulf Stream from the west, the Canary Current from the east, and the North Atlantic Equatorial Current from the south. The Sargasso's azure waters are warm, tranquil, and sometimes clear to a great depth. The surface is strewn with a brown floating seaweed called *sargassum* bearing berry-like bladders – hence the name of this uncanny, pretty place. Lower in the Sargasso Sea float millions and millions of a blue-green algae, *Prochlorococcus*, so tiny that a hundred thousand of them exist in a cubic centimetre of sea water, which absorb carbon dioxide and produce as much as 20 per cent of the world's atmospheric oxygen.

Down to the Sargasso Sea the Labrador Current carried the iceberg which Henry Stengel likened to the Rock of Gibraltar. Its glassy pinnacles pointing at the sun were dissolved by warm rays. Some icebergs develop waterfalls or ponds as they melt. While they rend and fracture, they emit loud noises, like shots from a rifle, as if hurling protests at the sun. Remnants of dead creatures and plants lay fixed in the ice, and as the iceberg dissolves, the stench of decay becomes rank over the ocean. In the Sargasso Sea, at the Labrador Current's confluence with the Gulf Stream, ridges of Greenland stone and detritus lie on the ocean floor, where they have sunk from melting icebergs. On the surface, at the confluence, sea mists make it an eerie stretch of mid-ocean.

The water is suddenly warmer in the Sargasso, and the iceberg, which had sunk *Titanic* and was already razed by the sun, melted faster. Its pinnacles had receded, the uppermost exposed shape of ice turned sloshy and dripped down into the ocean, the sub-aquatic bulk, with its deadly protuberances, invisibly dissolved into sea water. The berg dwindled until it was not big enough to sink a canoe. Soon it was a shard of ice giving no sign of its murderous history. The ice turned to water, became formless, then void, deepening the blue Sargasso Sea.

ACKNOWLEDGEMENTS

Patric Dickinson, then Norroy and Ulster King of Arms, now Clarenceux King of Arms, spent assiduous days and nights reading this book in a preliminary version, and made salutary suggestions which I have gratefully adopted. One must always think, said Henry James, of some good person as a *point de repère*. In writing *Titanic Lives* I set up David Kynaston as my landmark and reference point: indeed took his books as the model that I should try to emulate. He and Dickinson are old friends of one another, and have been generous friends to me. It is fitting that they should share the primary dedication of this book.

David John is the chief begetter of *Titanic Lives*: it would not have been written without his intervention or materials that he lent me. The welter of books and articles about *Titanic* (swelling into a tumultuous outpouring as the centenary approaches) makes it impossible to avoid overlapping sources or inadvertent plagiary; but my endnotes show my debts to previous researchers. My greatest debt is to the enthusiastic volunteers who maintain the website Encyclopaedia Titanica and ensure that its facts are both varied and unimpeachable. The texts of letters written on *Titanic* before it anchored off Queenstown, and of interviews given by survivors after *Carpathia* docked in New York, are available or duplicated in many sources: for the convenience of readers I have cited the most accessible texts, *Titanic Voices: Memories from the Fateful Voyage*, compiled by Donald Hyslop, Alastair Forsyth and Sheila Jemima (Sutton Publishing, 1997), supplemented by the material collected in Nick Barratt's *Lost Voices from the Titanic: the Definitive Oral History* (Macmillan, 2009).

Authors often display a long, showy list of names, resembling a row of scalps, of those they profess to thank. Without, I hope, being meretricious, I must express gratitude for advice or pointers to Katherine Bucknell, Selina Hastings, Ian Jack, John Jolliffe, Philip Mansel, Frederic Raphael and Frances Wilson. Susan Terner and Thomas H. Cook provided hospitality and encouragement during my visit to New York. My stalwart agent Bill Hamilton, my editors, Martin Redfern in London and Henry Ferris in New York, and my copyeditor, Kate Johnson, provided practical and effective help.

My supreme obligations, however, are to Christopher Phipps, who improved my early drafts by his raillery, gave wise advice in every phase, and has compiled a victorious and exemplary index; and to Jenny Davenport for her gentle patience and inspirational courage, and for providing merriness and discipline during low-points of sullen drudgery. David Gelber's supportive friendship has been priceless.

I thank the archivists at the Bodleian Library, Oxford (papers of Viscount Milner, the Countess of Oxford and Asquith, Earl Winterton and the Marquess of Lincolnshire), Cambridge University Library (papers of the Marquess of Crewe), Hertfordshire Archives and Local Records Office (papers of Lady Desborough), the House of Lords Record Office (papers of Earl Cadogan), the Liddell Hart Centre at King's College London (diary of Lady Hamilton), the National Archives (Board of Trade, Colonial Office and Foreign Office papers) and the Public Record Office of Northern Ireland (papers of the Marquess of Dufferin and Ava). The amenities of the London Library were indispensable to my researches.

Quotations from Lord Lincolnshire's diary are made with the permission of the Hon. Rupert Carington, on behalf of the Carington family; and the extract from Lady Oxford's diary is by courtesy of Christopher Osborn and the Bodleian Library. The extract from Louis MacNeice's poem 'Autumn Journal' is published by permission of David Higham Associates. The two extracts from John Masefield's poem 'The Wanderer' are reproduced with the consent of the Society of Authors, as the literary representative of the estate of John Masefield. Excerpts from *Chicago Poems* by Carl Sandburg, copyright 1916 by Holt, Rinehart and Winston, and renewed 1944 by Carl Sandburg, are published by permission of Haughton Mifflin Harcourt Publishing Company.

Le Meygris, Ailhon, February 2011

NOTES

Prologue

1. Sir Arthur Rostron, *Home from the Sea* (1931), p. 19.

PART ONE: EMBARKATION

One: Boarding

1. H. G. Wells, *Anticipations* (1901), pp. 79, 82–83.
2. Estelle Stead, *My Father* (1913), p. 342.
3. G. K. Chesterton, 'Our Notebook', *Illustrated London News*, 27 April 1912, p. 619.
4. Ian Jack, *The Country Formerly Known as Great Britain* (2009), p. 106.
5. Edward A. Steiner, *On the Trail of the Immigrant* (1906), pp. 40–41.
6. Michael McCaughan, *The Birth of the Titanic* (1998), pp. 1–2.
7. R. A. Williams, *The London and South Western Railway*, II (1973), p. 134.
8. '"Titanic" Insurances', *Economist*, 20 April 1912, p. 846.
9. Sarah Abrevaya Stein, *Plumes: Ostrich Feathers, Jews and a Lost World of Global Commerce* (2008).
10. 'To Reassure Mr Morgan', *New York Times*, 30 Jan 1912.
11. Rollin Hadley (ed.), *Letters of Bernard Berenson and Isabella Stewart Gardner 1887–1921* (1987), p. 388.
12. E. M. Forster, *Howards End* (1910), chapter 2.
13. Hamilton Ellis, *The South-Western Railway* (1956), p. 17.
14. Sinclair Lewis, *Dodsworth* (1929), p. 57.

15. A. W. Butt, *Taft and Roosevelt, the Intimate Letters of Archie Butt*, II (1930), p. 552.

16. Rev. T. G. Carew, 'Railway Travelling', *Western Morning News*, 7 May 1912, p. 7; Lord Teignmouth, 'Railway Travelling', *Western Morning News*, 9 May 1912; 'A Reverend Autocrat', *St Ives Times*, 10 May 1912.

17. Randolph Churchill (ed.), *Winston S. Churchill: Companion Volume II* (1969), p. 1760.

18. 'Mr Churchill at Manchester', *The Times*, 24 May 1909, 10d (speech of 22 May).

19. Edith Wharton, 'The Legend' (1910), in *Collected Stories 1891–1910* (2001), p. 803.

20. Sir James Bisset, *Tramps and Ladies* (1959), p. 259.

21. Stéphane Lauzanne, 'L'Engloutissement Du Géant Des Mers', *Le Matin*, 17 April 1912, p. 1.

22. Richard Davenport-Hines, *Dudley Docker* (1984), p. 5.

23. Chesterton, 'Our Notebook', p. 619.

Two: *Speed*

1. 'The Titanic's Departure from Southampton', *Southampton Daily Echo*, 15 April 1912.

2. Nick Barratt, *Lost Voices from the Titanic* (2009), p. 101.

3. Arthur Mee, *Hampshire* (1939), pp. 332–33.

4. Emile Zola, *La bête humaine* (1890), chapter 7.

5. 'Passenger's Impressions', *Belfast Evening Telegraph*, 15 April 1912, p. 7. This account was written by a first-class passenger who disembarked at Queenstown. By a process of elimination this may be deduced to be a passenger named Nichols about whom nothing is yet known.

6. F. S. Oliver to Lord Milner, 31 March 1911, Milner papers 13, Bodleian.

7. Marinetti, *Le Figaro*, 20 February 1909.

8. 'Pékin-Paris En Aéroplane', *Le Matin*, 16 April 1912, 1; 'Channel Flown by a Lady Aviator', *Daily Telegraph*, 17 April 1912, 9; 'Une aviatrice passe la Manche', *Le Matin*, 17 April 1912, 1; 'Un Match Tragique Entre Deux Aviateurs', *Le Matin*, 19 April 1912, 3.

9. Wells, *Anticipations*, p. 59.

10. George Harvey, *Henry Clay Frick* (1936), p. 359.

11. Butt, *Roosevelt and Taft*, II, p. 468.

12. Eric Homberger, *Mrs Astor's New York: Social Power in a Gilded Age* (2002), p. xiv.

13. R. W. B. Lewis and Nancy Lewis (eds), *Letters of Edith Wharton* (1988), p. 225.

14. Edith Wharton, *The Fruit of the Tree* (1907), p. 31.

15. Carl Sandburg, *Always the Young Strangers* (1953), p. 281.

16. Edward Alsworth Ross, *The Old World in the New* (1914), p. 113.

17. Ross, *Old World*, p. 154.

18. *Geographic Journal*, 41 (March 1913), pp. 211–12.

19. Robert Scott, *Scott's Last Expedition*, I (1913), pp. 595, 607.

20. Sir James Barrie, *Peter and Wendy* (1911), pp. 229–30.

21. Shan Bullock, *A Titanic Hero: Thomas Andrews, Shipbuilder* (1912), p. 71.

22. 'The Dreadful Fire Disaster in Paris', *Illustrated London News*, 15 May 1897, 665; 'Terrible Fire in Paris', *The Times*, 5 May 1897, 7; 'The Disaster in Paris', *The Times*, 6 May 1897, 5.

23. Walter Gibson, *The Boat* (1952), pp. 35, 41.

24. 'Irish Survivor's Experience: Tipperary Man's Escape', *Cork Examiner*, 6 May 1912, 5.

25. Lawrence Beesley, *The Loss of the SS Titanic* (1912), p. 26.

26. John B. Thayer, *The Sinking of the SS Titanic* (1940), p. 4.

27. Sir Osbert Sitwell, *Great Morning* (1948), p. 259.

28. Beesley, *Loss of Titanic*, p. 27.

Three: Shipowners

1. Denys Sutton, *Letters of Roger Fry*, I (1972), p. 226.

2. Senate enquiry, testimony of Bruce Ismay, day 1.

3. Arthur Pound and Samuel Taylor Moore (eds), *They Told Barron: Conversations of an American Pepys in Wall Street* (1930), p. 7.

4. Edwin Green and Michael Moss, *A Business of National Importance* (1982), p. 28.

5. W. T. Stead, 'Lord Pirrie', *Review of Reviews*, 45 (March 1912), p. 243.

6. Herbert Jefferson, *Viscount Pirrie of Belfast* (1948), pp. 308–09.

7. Sir Schomberg MacDonnell to Earl Cadogan, 17 June 1897, HLRO CAD/1123.

8. Marquess of Dufferin and Ava to Earl Cadogan, 15 July 1898, HLRO CAD/1372.

9. Marquess of Dufferin and Ava to Earl Cadogan, 6 May 1899, HLRO CAD/1569.

10. Sir Sidney Lee, *King Edward VII*, II (1927), pp. 451–52; Cameron Hazlehurst (ed.), *A Liberal Chronicle: Journal of Lord Gainford* (1994), p. 71.

11. Diane Urquhart, *The Ladies of Londonderry* (2007), p. 109.

12. Lord Pirrie to Lord Crewe, 17 January 1913, Crewe papers C/41.

13. Lord Colebrooke to Lord Crewe, 1 February 1913, Crewe papers C/9.

14. H. H. Asquith to Lord Crewe, 5 February 1913, Crewe papers C/40.

15. Lord Crewe to H. H. Asquith, 26 June 1913, Crewe papers C/40.

16. Pound and Moore, *They Told Barron*, pp. 167, 197.

17. 'Death of Mr T. H. Ismay', *Liverpool Daily Post*, 1 December 1899, quoted in Barratt, *Lost Voices*, p. 15.

18. H. G. Wells, *Anticipations* (1902), p. 4.

19. *Daily Sketch*, 5 June 1912, quoted in John Wilson Foster, *Titanic* (1999), p. 206.

20. Diary of Marquess of Lincolnshire, 17 August and 13 September 1894, 30 December 1905, Bodleian.

21. Diary of Marquess of Lincolnshire, 31 March 1913, Bodleian.

22. E. M. Forster, *Howards End* (1910), chapter 27.

23. Lord Vansittart, *The Mist Procession* (1958), p. 61.

24. Sutton, *Roger Fry*, I, p. 292.

25. Sir Clinton Dawkins to Sir Alfred Milner, 8 Feb 1901, Milner papers 214, Bodleian.

26. Dawkins to Milner, 13 July 1901, Milner papers 214.

27. Sutton, *Roger Fry*, I, p. 230.

28. *Dictionary of Business Biography*, II (1984), p. 258.

29. Michael Moss and John Hume, *Shipbuilders to the World* (1986), p. 106.

30. Green and Moss, *Business of National Importance*, p. 20.
31. 'The Anglo-American Shipping Combine', *Economist*, 26 April 1902, pp. 645–46.
32. 'The Troubles of the Shipping Trust', *Economist*, 23 July 1904, p. 1227.
33. 'A German View of British Shipping', *Economist*, 1 June 1907, p. 934.
34. Julia Davis and Dolores Fleming (eds), *Ambassadorial Diary of John W. Davis* (1993), p. 394.
35. Sutton, *Roger Fry*, I, p. 251.

Four: Shipbuilders

1. Standish O'Grady, *Selected Essays and Passages* (1918), p. 180.
2. Sir Robert Rhodes James, *Lord Randolph Churchill* (1969), pp. 222, 233, 234.
3. William Bulfin, *Rambles in Eirinn* (1907), pp. 127–28.
4. Quoted in John Boyle, 'Belfast Protestant Association', *Irish Historical Studies*, 13 (1962–63), p. 122.
5. Diary of the Marquess of Lincolnshire, 22 January 1912.
6. 'Text of the Speech', *The Times*, 9 February 1912.
7. Diary of the Marquess of Lincolnshire, 9 February 1912.
8. 'Lord Pirrie Pelted', *The Times*, 12 February 1912.
9. Diary of Marquess of Lincolnshire, 13 February 1912.
10. Ibid., 9 April 1912.
11. Diary of Sir Robert Sanders, later Lord Bayford, 17 April 1912, quoted in John Ramsden (ed.), *Real Old Tory Politics* (1984), p. 46.
12. Chief Secretary's Office, Intelligence Notes 1912, National Archives CO 903/17.
13. Henry Paterson, *Class Conflict and Sectarianism* (1980), p. 90.
14. Pound and Moore, *They Told Barron*, p. 34.
15. Bulfin, *Rambles*, pp. 120–21.
16. Moore, *Truth about Ulster*, p. 162.
17. Thomas Pinney, *Letters of Rudyard Kipling*, IV (1999), p. 60.
18. Robert Lynd, *Home Life in Ireland* (1909), p. 185.
19. Bulfin, *Rambles*, pp. 117–18.
20. Shan Bullock, *Thomas Andrews, Shipbuilder* (1912), pp. 23–25.

21. Ireland, *Jungle*, p. 30.
22. Bullock, *Thomas Andrews*, pp. 8, 11, 17.
23. Ibid., pp. 21–23, 43.
24. Rudyard Kipling, 'The Secret of the Machines' (1910).
25. Lewis and Lewis (eds), *Letters of Edith Wharton*, p. 125.
26. Violet Jessop, *Titanic Survivor* (1997), pp. 104–05.
27. Diary of Earl Winterton, 28, 29 September and 6 October 1912, Winterton papers 11, Bodleian.
28. Alexander Carlisle, evidence to Lord Mersey's enquiry, day 20, Q 21401.
29. Sir Alfred Chambers to Mersey enquiry, day 23, QQ 22875, 22965.
30. Alexander Carlisle, Mersey enquiry, day 20, Q 21358.
31. Captain Maurice Clarke to Mersey enquiry, day 25, QQ 24173–4.
32. Captain Arthur Rostron to Senate enquiry, day 1.
33. Frank Millet to Alfred Parsons, 11 April 1912, www.encyclopaedia-titanica.org/letter-to-his-old-friend-alfred-parsons.html (accessed 9 June 2010).
34. R. A. Fletcher, *Travelling Palaces* (1913), p. 255.
35. 'Floating Lobster Palaces', *Philadelphia Inquirer*, 21 April 1912, p. 8.

Five: Sailors

1. Sir Arthur Rostron, *Home from the Sea* (1931), pp. 8–9.
2. Charles Herbert Lightoller, *Titanic and Other Ships* (1935), pp. 91–92.
3. Sir James Bisset, *Tramps and Ladies* (1959), pp. 1–2.
4. Ibid., p. 9.
5. Rudyard Kipling, 'The "Mary Gloster"' (1896).
6. Sir Bertram Hayes, *Hull Down: Reminiscences of Wind-Jammers, Troops and Travellers* (1925), p. 28.
7. Lightoller, *Titanic*, p. 4.
8. Sir James Bisset, *Ship Ahoy! Nautical Notes for Ocean Travellers* (1924), p. 22.
9. Lightoller, *Titanic*, p. 89.
10. Rostron, *Home from Sea*, p. 15.

11. Bisset, *Ship Ahoy!*, p. 59.

12. Lightoller, *Titanic*, pp. 12–13.

13. Ibid., p. 36.

14. 'The Policing of Disaster', *Spectator*, 23 March 1912, p. 468.

15. Bisset, *Tramps*, p. 132.

16. Rudyard Kipling, 'The Deep-Sea Cables' (1893).

17. Fletcher, *Travelling Palaces*, p. 242.

18. Rostron, *Home from Sea*, pp. 32–33.

19. Lightoller, *Titanic*, pp. 206–07.

20 'The Policing of Disaster', *Spectator*, 23 March 1912, p. 468.

21. Rudyard Kipling, 'The Long Trail' (1891).

Six: American Millionaires

1. John H. Davis, *The Guggenheims* (1978), pp. 43–4.

2. Helmut Schoeck, *Envy: a theory of social behaviour* (1969), p. 62.

3. Joseph Epstein, *Snobbery* (2002), pp. 14–15.

4. Henry James, *Notebooks* (1987), p. 12.

5. Lady Decies, *King Lehr and the Gilded Age* (1935), p. 7.

6. Ibid., pp. 11–12.

7. Arthur Vanderbilt, *Fortune's Children* (1990), p. 263.

8. C. W. de Kiewiet and F. H. Underhill (eds), *Dufferin-Carnarvon Correspondence 1874–78* (1955), p. 94.

9. Sutton, *Roger Fry*, I, p. 254.

10. Epstein, *Snobbery*, pp. 20, 28–29.

11. William G. Sumner, 'The Concentration of Wealth: its Economic Justification', *Independent*, 54 (1 May 1902), 1036–40; John M. Blum, *The American Experience* (1963), p. 433.

12. Butt, *Roosevelt and Taft*, II, pp. 476–47.

13. James, *Notebooks*, p. 40.

14. Homberger, *Mrs Astor's New York*, p. xii.

15. Henry James, *The Reverberator* (1888), ch. 4, p. 598.

16. *Covington Sun*, 16 April 1908.

17. Henry James, *The Bostonians* (1886), ch. 13, p. 111.

18. On William Waldorf Astor's efforts to penetrate English society, see

the diary of the Marquess of Lincolnshire, 11 July 1895, 30 May 1896, 1 June, 4 December and 9 December 1897, Bodleian.

19. Decies, *King Lehr*, p. 208.
20. Lady Desborough to Julian Grenfell, 10 April 1899, HALRO D/ERV C1072/3.
21. Edith Wharton, 'Autres Temps' (1911), *Collected Stories 1911–1937* (2001), p. 64.
22. Davis, *Guggenheims,* pp. 234–35.
23. Arnold Bennett, *Journals,* II (1932), pp. 21, 28.
24. 'P. A. B. Widener, Capitalist, Dies', *New York Times,* 7 Nov 1915.
25. 'Mrs George D. Widener Critically Ill at Home', *Philadelphia Inquirer,* 20 April 1912, p. 2.
26. Henry Adams, *Letters,* V, pp. 198–99, 231.
27. Emily Post, *Etiquette in Society, in Business, in Politics and at Home* (1922), pp. 132–33.
28. Adams, *Letters,* VI, p. 137.
29. Hadley, *Berenson-Gardner,* pp. 427–28.
30. Edith Wharton, 'A Cup of Cold Water', *Collected Stories 1891–1910,* p. 138.

Seven: Atlantic Migrants

1. Bisset, *Tramps and Ladies,* pp. 136–37.
2. Charles Issawi, 'The Historical Background of Lebanese Emigration, 1800–1914', in Albert Hourani and Nadim Shehadi (eds), *The Lebanese in the World* (1992), p. 30.
3. Carl Sandburg, *Always the Young Strangers* (1953), p. 436.
4. Hans Normand and Harald Runblom, *Transatlantic Connections: Nordic Migration to the New World after 1800* (1988), p. 48.
5. Mary Antin, *From Plotzk to Boston* (1899), pp. 11–12.
6. Mary Antin, *The Promised Land* (1912), p. 162.
7. Louis Adamic, *Laughing in the Jungle: the Autobiography of an Immigrant in America* (1932), p. 3.
8. Ibid., pp. 4–5.
9. Ibid., pp. 13–14.

10. 'Mr Harrington's Washing', in W. Somerset Maugham, *Complete Short Stories*, II (1951), p. 854; Selina Hastings, *The Secret Lives of Somerset Maugham* (2009), pp. 238–39.

11. Israel Zangwill, *The Melting-Pot* (1914), p. 33.

12. *Thomas Mellon and His Times*, p. 349.

13. Louis Adamic, *Laughing*, p. ix.

14. Gyula Illyés, *People of the Puszta* (1979 trans. of 1936 edn), pp. 71, 90, 94.

15. Emily Balch, *Our Slavic Fellow Citizens* (1910), p. 40.

16. See Josef Barton's excellent *Peasants and Strangers: Italians, Rumanians and Slovaks in an American City, 1890–1950* (1975).

17. Illyés, *Puszta*, p. 104.

18. Theodore Saloutus, *The Greeks in the United States* (1964) is a first-rate history, which has been of great general help in writing this chapter.

19. Barton, *Peasants and Strangers*, p. 48.

20. Isabel Kaprielian-Churchill, *Like Our Mountains: A History of Armenians in Canada* (2005), pp. 29–30.

21. Prpic, *Croatian Immigrants*, pp. 89–108.

22. See generally Alixa Naff, *Becoming American: the Early Arab Immigrant Experience* (1985).

23. Alixa Naff, 'Lebanese Immigration into the United States', p. 144.

24. Engin Deniz Akarli, 'Ottoman Attitudes Towards Lebanese Emigration, 1885–1910', in Hourani and Shehadi, *Lebanese*, p. 128.

25. Joseph Roth, *The White Cities* (2004), p. 54.

26. A. L. Rowse, *The Cornish in America* (1969), p. 423.

27. Balch, *Slavic Fellow Citizens*, pp. 183–90; Prpic, *Croatian Immigrants*, p. 110.

28. Kaprielian-Churchill, *Like Our Mountains*, p. 47.

29. Paul Knaplund, *Moorings Old and New: Entries in an Immigrant's Log* (1963), pp. 131–32, 135.

30. Diary of Lord Lincolnshire, 21 August 1899.

31. Knaplund, *Moorings*, p. 136.

32. Ibid., p. 138.

33. Ibid., p. 140.

34. Antin, *Promised Land*, p. 172.

35. Antin, *Plotzk*, pp. 39–40; *Promised Land*, pp. 173–74.

36. Antin, *Plotzk*, pp. 41–42.

37. Antin, *Promised Land*, p. 177.

38. Fiorello La Guardia, *The Making of an Insurgent*, pp. 57–58.

39. Broughton Brandenburg, *Imported Americans: the story of the experiences of a disguised American and his wife studying the immigration question* (1904), pp. 161, 171.

40. Ibid., p. 173.

41. Ibid., p. 176.

42. Ibid., pp. 189–90.

43. Ibid., pp. 193–94.

44. Ibid., p. 184.

45. Ibid., p. 190.

46. Stephen Graham, *Poor Immigrants*, pp. 23–24.

47. Steiner, *Trail*, p. 36.

48. Ibid., pp. 36–37.

49. Graham, *Poor Immigrants*, p. 11.

50. Ibid., p. 23.

51. Knaplund, *Moorings*, p. 146.

52. Graham, *Poor Immigrants*, pp. 12–13.

53. Ibid., pp. 18–19.

Eight: Imported Americans

1. Henry Roth, *Call It Sleep* (1934), p. 9.

2. Rupert Brooke, *Letters from America* (1916), pp. 8–9.

3. Brandenberg, *Imported Americans*, pp. 209–10.

4. Ibid., pp. 213–14.

5. Pitkin, *Keepers of the Gate*, pp. 65, 82.

6. Graham, *Poor Immigrants*, p. 44.

7. Knaplund, *Moorings*, p. 148.

8. Edward Corsi, *In the Shadow of Liberty: the chronicle of Ellis Island* (1935), p. 70.

9. Fiorello La Guardia, *Making of an Insurgent* (1948), pp. 64, 66.

10. Butt, *Taft and Roosevelt*, II, pp. 548–49.

11. William McUllagh, Major Royal Army Medical Corps, 'Ellis Island' [November 1924], NA FO 372/2230.

12. Corsi, *Shadow*, p. 78.

13. La Guardia, *Insurgent*, p. 69.

14. Martocci, quoted in Corsi, *Shadow*, p. 72.

15. Roth, *Call it Sleep*, p. 11.

16. Brandenberg, *Imported Americans*, pp. 225–26.

17. Prpic, *Croatian Immigrants*, p. 111.

18. Brandenberg, *Imported Americans*, pp. 1–2.

19. Rowse, *Cornish in America*, p. 422.

20. 'When You Land at New York', *Cornishman*, 18 April 1912, 7.

21. Rowse, *Cornish in America*, pp. 22, 79–80, 420, 423.

22. 'Cornishmen Abroad', *Cornubian*, 18 April 1912.

23. 'Cornishmen Abroad', *Hayle Mail*, 18 April 1912, 6.

24. Newton Thomas, *The Long Winter Ends* (1941), p. 127.

25. Knaplund, *Moorings*, p. 150.

26. Thomas, *Long Winter*, p. 33.

27. Sinclair Lewis, *Main Street* (1920), ch. 3, pp. 20–22.

28. Knaplund, *Moorings*, pp. 154–55.

29. Kaprielian-Churchill, *Like Our Mountains*, pp. 29–31.

30. Thomas, *Long Winter*, p. 29.

31. Antin, *Promised Land*, p. 165.

32. Kaprielian-Churchill, *Like Our Mountains*, pp. 72–73.

33. Somerset Maugham, *A Writer's Notebook* (1949), p. 176.

34. Ewa Morawska, *For Bread with Butter: the life-worlds of East Central Europeans in Johnstown, Pennsylvania, 1890–1940* (1987), pp. 1–2.

35. Francis Couvares, *The Remaking of Pittsburgh: Class and Culture in an Industrializing City 1877–1919* (1984), pp. 88–90.

36 Ibid., pp. 87–88.

37. Steiner, *Trail*, p. 220.

38. Davis, *Guggenheims*, p. 115.

39. Prpic, *Croatian Immigrants*, p. 163.

40. Illyés, *People of Puszta*, p. 280.

41. Knaplund, *Moorings*, p. 251.

42. Ignazio Silone, *Fontamara* (translation of 1985), p. 6.

43. Prpic, *Croatian Immigrants*, p. 165.

44. Brandenberg, *Imported Americans*, p. 28.

45. Steiner, *Trail*, p. 341.

PART TWO: ON BOARD

Nine: First-Class

1. Daisy, Princess of Pless, *From My Private Diary* (1931), p. 277; Ulrik Langen, 'The Meaning of Incognito', *Court Historian*, VII (2002), pp. 145–55.

2. Washington Irving, *Astoria, or Anecdotes of an Enterprise beyond the Rocky Mountains* (1976 edn), p. 12.

3. Edith Wharton, *The Custom of the Country* (1913), ch. 45.

4. Decies, *King Lehr*, p. 167.

5. Hadley, *Berenson Gardner Letters*, pp. 450, 458.

6. Lewis, *Letters of Edith Wharton*, pp. 312–13.

7. Henry James, *The Golden Bowl* (1904), book I, ch. 7.

8. 'Panniers Reign Supreme in Paris Fashion World', *Philadelphia Inquirer*, 21 April 1912, Sunday supplement, 3.

9. Lady Duff Gordon, *Discretions and Indiscretions* (1932), p. 191.

10. Violet Jessop, *Titanic Survivor* (1997), pp. 106–07.

11. Barratt, *Lost Voices*, p. 99.

12. Steiner, *Trail*, pp. 360–62.

13. Duff Gordon, *Discretions and Indiscretions*, pp. 79–80.

14. Jessop, *Titanic Survivor*, pp. 103–04.

15. Harvey O'Connor, *The Astors* (1941), p. 277. ´

16. Diary of Jean, Lady Hamilton, 14 February 1914, Liddell Hart Centre, Kings College, London.

17. Decies, *King Lehr*, pp. 149–50.

18. Emily Post, *Etiquette* (1922), pp. 598–99.

19. Kristen Iversen, *Molly Brown* (1999), p. 107.

20. Duff Gordon, *Discretions and Indiscretions*, p. 151.

21. Barratt, *Lost Voices*, p. 99.

22. Steiner, *Trail*, p. 136.

23. '1,500 Perish When Titanic Goes to Bottom', *Cleveland Plain Dealer*, 16 April 1912, 1.

24. Hadley, *Berenson Gardner Letters*, pp. 504–05.

25. Edith Wharton, 'The Marne' (1918), *Collected Stories 1911–1937*, pp. 261–62.

26. Arthur Freeman, 'Harry Widener's Last Books', *Bookseller*, 26 (1977), pp. 174, 182; A. Edward Newton, *The Amenities of Book Collecting* (1918), pp. 353–55.

27. 'Insurance at Lloyd's: Mrs Widener's Pearls', *Daily Telegraph*, 18 April 1912, 14.

28. Frank Millet to Alfred Parsons, 11 April 1912, www.encyclopaedia-titanica.org/letter-to-his-old-friend-alfred-parsons.html (accessed 9 June 2010).

29. Leon Edel (ed.), *Henry James Letters*, IV (1984), p. 613.

30. Butt, *Taft and Roosevelt*, II, p. 848

31. 'Major Butt's Suit a Wonder', *New York Times*, 3 March 1912.

32. Butt, *Taft and Roosevelt*, II, pp. 528–29.

33. Ibid., p. 833.

34. Ibid., p. 823.

35. Ibid., p. 653.

36. Ibid., pp. 468–69.

37. Ibid., pp. 573–77, 805–07.

38. W. T. Stead, evidence to Royal Commission on Divorce, 21 December 1910, Q. 43403.

39. G. K. Chesterton, *Illustrated London News*, 27 April 1912; T. P. O'Connor, 'A Famous Journalist', *Daily Telegraph*, 17 April 1912, 13.

40. Duff Gordon, *Discretions and Indiscretions*, p. 14.

41. Ibid., p. 16.

42. Ibid., p. 59.

43. Ibid., p. 69.

44. Ibid., p. 71.

45. Ibid., pp. 44–45.

46. Ibid., pp. 124–25.

47. Ibid., p. 137.

48. Ibid., pp. 188–89.

49. Ibid., p. 78.

50. Barratt, *Lost Voices*, p. 148.

51. Diary of Earl Winterton, 2 and 3 October 1912, Winterton papers 11.

52. Washington Dodge, *The Loss of the Titanic* (1912), p. 4; John Eaton and Charles Haas, *Titanic, Triumph and Tragedy* (1995), p. 114; Geoffrey Marcus, *The Maiden Voyage* (1969), pp. 66–67.

53. Gracie, *Truth about Titanic*, p. 5.

54. www.encyclopaedia-titanica.org/letter-to-his-old-friend-alfred-parsons.html (accessed 9 June 2010).

55. Duff Gordon, *Discretions and Indiscretions*, pp. 148–49.

56. Affidavit of Mahala Douglas to Senate enquiry.

57. Ford Madox Ford, *A History of Our Own Times* (1989), p. 50.

58. 'Great Cobar Examined', *The Times*, 1 October 1909, 13d.

59. Hugh Woolner, bankruptcy statement dated 16 July 1909, NA BT 226/2749; Robert Sumner-Jones, bankruptcy examination dated 27 October 1909, NA BT 226/2844.

60. Will dated 30 January 1912, proved 4 July 1917, in Probate Registry; 'High Court of Justice', *The Times*, 2 March 1917, 2e.

61. 'Notables Crowd Decks of Titanic', *Cleveland Plain Dealer*, 16 April 1912, 2.

62. Post, *Etiquette*, pp. 601–02.

63. Dawn Powell, *A Time to be Born* (1942), in *Novels 1930–1942* (2001), pp. 774, 856.

64. 'Titanic's Sinking Comes as Shock to Philadelphia', *Philadelphia Inquirer*, 16 April 1912, 3.

65. Duff Gordon, *Discretions and Indiscretions*, pp. 148–49.

66. Post, *Etiquette*, p. 603.

67. Thayer, *Sinking of SS Titanic*, p. 334.

Ten: Second-Class

1. Theodore Dreiser, *A Traveler at Forty* (1914), pp. 80–81.

2. 'From West Country', *Western Morning News*, 18 April 1912.

3. Robert Louis Stevenson, 'The Second Cabin', *The Amateur Emigrant*, in Stevenson, *From Scotland to Silverado* (1966), p. 4.

4. Bennett, *Journals*, II, pp. 12, 14.
5. Fletcher, *Travelling Palaces*, p. 165.
6. Ibid., p. 164.
7. Senate enquiry, day 14, evidence of Berk Trembisky, alias Picard.
8. Stevenson, 'Steerage Scenes', *Amateur Emigrant*, in Stevenson, *From Scotland to Silverado*, pp. 27–28.
9. 'Mr Denzil Jarvis', *Leicester Daily Post*, 17 April 1912, p. 5; 'Leicester Men on the Titanic', *Leicester Advertiser*, 20 April 1912, p. 6.
10. Maugham, *Writer's Notebook*, pp. 177–78, 296.
11. Violet Jessop, *Titanic Survivor* (1997), pp. 90–92.
12. Senate enquiry, day 18, affidavit of Imanita Shelley.
13. Barratt, *Lost Voices*, p. 102.
14. Hayes, *Hull Down*, p. 70.
15. Donald Hyslop, Alastair Forsyth and Sheila Jemima (eds), *Titanic Voices* (1997), p. 113.
16. Ibid., pp. 114–15.
17. Ibid., p. 116.
18. Dreiser, *Traveler at Forty*, p. 520.
19. Beesley, *Loss of Titanic*, pp. 28, 32.
20. Hyslop, Forsyth and Jemima, *Titanic Voices*, pp. 132–33.
21. 'Local Titanic Passenger', *Epping Gazette*, 20 April 1912, 4.
22. Henry Walker, *East London: sketches of Christian work and workers* (1896), pp. 17–18, 24.
23. *Oxford Magazine*, 30 (2 May 1912).
24. 'The Rev. E. C. and Mrs Carter', *The Times*, 20 April 1912, 11.
25. Sarah Orne Jewett, 'A Dunnett Shepherdess', in Jewett, *Novels and Stories* (1994), p. 520.
26. Jewett, 'The Queen's Twin', *Novels and Stories*, p. 493.
27. Robert Bracken, 'Searching for Kirkland' (15 February 2006), www.encyclopaedia-titanica.org (accessed 14 June 2010).
28. Hilary Spurling, *Burying the Bones: Pearl Buck in China* (2010), p. 20.
29. 'Berks County Woman Died on the Titanic', *Philadelphia Inquirer*, 20 April 1912, 5.
30. 'A qui sont les deux bébés français sauvé du Titanic?', *Le Matin*, 24 April 1912, 1.

31. 'Liverpool Men's Fate', *Liverpool Daily Post*, 17 April 1912, 7; 'Liverpool Titanic Victim', *Liverpool Daily Post*, 4 May 1912, 9.

32. 'The Guernsey Passengers', *Guernsey Weekly Press*, 20 April 1912, 4.

33. Sid Blake, 'The Titanic Disaster', *Cornishman*, 2 May 1912, 4, duplicated in *Hayle Mail*, 2 May 1912, 5.

34. *Western Morning News*, 17 April 1912.

35. I am indebted in this section to Arthur Cecil Todd's delightful *The Cornish Miner in America* (1967).

36. 'Loss of the Titanic', *St Ives Times*, 19 April 1912, 8.

37. Arthur Salmon, *The Cornwall Coast* (1910), p. 138.

38. 'Wreck of the Titanic', *Cornubian*, 18 April 1912.

39. Barratt, *Lost Voices*, p. 145.

Eleven: Third-Class

1. Steiner, *Trail*, p. 198.

2. Rostron, *Home from Sea*, pp. 47–48.

3. Fletcher, *Floating Palaces*, p. 275.

4. 61 Congress 3 Session, Immigration Commission reports on Emigration Conditions in Europe and Steerage Conditions, Senate documents 748, 753, 758.

5. Willa Cather, *O Pioneers!* (1913), part 2, ch. 3, in *Early Novels*, p. 188.

6. Graham, *With Poor Immigrants*, p. 14.

7. Frank Goldsmith, *Echoes in the Night* (1991), pp. 37, 39. Copyright Titanic Historical Society Inc.

8. Ibid., pp. 42, 50.

9. Sinclair Lewis, *Dodsworth* (1929), p. 45.

10. Bennett, *Journals*, II, p. 13.

11. Graham, *With Poor Immigrants*, p. 15.

12. Daniel Allen Butler, *'Unsinkable' – the full story of RMS Titanic* (1998), p. 202.

13. Gertrude Bell, *The Desert and the Sown* (1907), pp. 162–63.

14. John Kelman, *From Damascus to Palmyra* (1908), pp. 28–29.

15. 'On the Ship that Never Came Home: the story of how fifteen girls and boys from the West of Ireland started for America on the *Titanic*,

and how two of them arrived', *Irish Independent*, 9 May 1912, 3.

16. Naval Intelligence Division, *A Handbook to Bulgaria* (1920), p. 80.

17. Kaprielian-Churchill, *Like Our Mountains*, pp. 3, 5–6, 21–22.

18. See Robert Mirak, *Torn between Two Lands: Armenians in America, 1890 to World War I* (1983).

19. Kaprielian-Churchill, *Like Our Mountains*, pp. 48, 58, 61.

20. Sandburg, *Always the Young Strangers*, p. 77.

Twelve: Officers and Crew

1. Mersey enquiry, day 3, evidence of William Lucas, Q 1768.

2. Lightoller, *Titanic*, p. 219.

3. Alan Scarth, *Titanic and Liverpool* (2009), p. 71.

4. Hyslop, Forsyth, Jemima, *Titanic Voices*, p. 112.

5. Ibid., p. 114.

6. Ibid., p. 115.

7. Scarth, *Titanic and Liverpool*, p. 69.

8. Butler, *Unsinkable*, p. 48.

9. Barczewski, *Titanic*, p. 164.

10. Lightoller, *Titanic*, p. 214.

11. C. Andrews, testimony to Senate enquiry, day 7.

12. George Cavell, testimony to Mersey enquiry, day 5, Q 4421.

13. Bennett, *Journals*, II, p. 16.

14. Coleman, *Liners*, p. 58; *The Collected George Garrett* (1999), pp. 172–74.

15. Bisset, *Tramps*, pp. 206–07.

16. *Collected Garrett*, pp. 170–71.

17. Fletcher, *Travelling Palaces*, p. 108.

18. Terri Colpi, *The Italian Factor* (1991), pp. 58–59.

19. Theodore Dreiser, *A Traveler at Forty* (1914), pp. 32–35, 518.

20. Terry Coleman, *The Liners* (1976), pp. 214–15.

21. Violet Jessop, *Titanic Survivor* (1997), p. 92.

22. Ibid., p. 111.

23. Evelyn Waugh, *Labels* (1930), ch. 3; *Waugh Abroad* (2003), p. 38.

24. Hyslop, Forsyth, Jemima, *Titanic Voices*, p. 112.

25. Ibid., p. 115.

26. Jack, *The Country Formerly Known as Great Britain*, p. 117.

27. Jessop, *Titanic Survivor*, p. 112.

28. Ibid., p. 117.

29. Beesley, *Loss of Titanic*, p. 37.

30. Jessop, *Titanic Survivor*, pp. 123–24.

31. Mersey enquiry, day 15, evidence of George Rowe, Q 17584.

32. Lightoller, *Titanic*, pp. 224–25.

PART THREE: LIFE AND DEATH

Thirteen: Collision

1. Mersey enquiry, day 4, evidence of John Poingdestre, QQ 2780, 2786.

2. Gracie, *Titanic*, pp. 250–51.

3. Senate enquiry, day 12, evidence of Mrs J. Stuart White.

4. Mersey enquiry, day 1, evidence of Archie Jewell, Q 18.

5. Mersey enquiry, day 4, evidence of James Johnson, QQ 3360, 3363.

6. Senate enquiry, day 4, evidence of Herbert Pitman; Mersey enquiry, day 13, evidence of Pitman, Q 14932.

7. Mersey enquiry, day 10, evidence of George Symons, Q 11347.

8. Mersey enquiry, day 3, evidence of William Lucas, QQ 1399, 1417–8, 1434–5, 1809–10.

9. Mersey enquiry, day 3, evidence of George Beauchamp, Q 662.

10. Mersey enquiry, day 5, evidence of George Cavell, Q 4201–2.

11. Senate enquiry, day 16, affidavit of Emily Ryerson.

12. Mersey enquiry, day 4, evidence of John Poingdestre, Q 2829.

13. Duff Gordon, *Discretions*, p. 147.

14. *Le Matin*, 19 April 1912; 'Heard Death Chorus for Over an Hour', *New York Times*, 20 April 1912.

15. Senate enquiry, day 10, evidence of Hugh Woolner.

16. Beesley, *Loss of Titanic*, pp. 38–39.

17. 'Sticks to Titanic Till Last Minute: Young Englishman Reaches Cleveland', *Cleveland Plain Dealer*, 26 April 1912, 1.

18. 'Mrs E. W. Bucknell says Carelessness Cost Many Lives', *Philadelphia Inquirer*, 20 April 1912, 2.

19. Senate enquiry, day 12, evidence of Mrs J. Stuart White.

20. Senate enquiry, day 13, evidence of George Harder.

21. Senate enquiry, day 13, evidence of Norman Chambers.

22. Lightoller, *Titanic*, p. 229.

23. Ibid., p. 235.

24. Duff Gordon, *Discretions*, pp. 152–53.

25. Senate enquiry, day 13, evidence of Olaus Abelseth.

26. Senate enquiry, day 4, evidence of Arthur Peuchen.

27. Senate enquiry, day 11, evidence of Henry Stengel.

28. Gracie, *Titanic*, p. 126.

29. 'Mrs E. W. Bucknell says Carelessness Cost Many Lives', *Philadelphia Inquirer*, 20 April 1912, 2.

30. A. S. W. Rosenbach, *A Catalogue of the Books and Manuscripts of Robert Louis Stevenson in the Library of the late Harry Elkins Widener* (1913), p. 9.

31. 'Wreck of the Titanic – Graphic Story of Mrs Davies', *St Ives Times*, 10 May 1912, 4.

32. Senate enquiry, day 7, evidence of John Hardy.

33. Senate enquiry, day 18, affidavit of Imanita Shelley.

34. Senate enquiry, day 14, evidence of Berk Trembisky alias Picard.

35. Senate enquiry, day 13, evidence of Daniel Buckley.

36. Mersey enquiry, day 4, evidence of John Poingdestre, Q 2960.

37. Senate enquiry, day 1, evidence of C. H. Lightoller.

38. *Cornishman*, 2 May 1912.

39. Mersey enquiry, day 3, evidence of William Lucas, QQ 1502–3.

40. www.encyclopaedia-titanica.org/letter-to-his-old-friend-alfred-parsons.html (accessed 9 June 2010).

41. Earl Cowper to Marquess of Dufferin and Ava, 25 March 1901, PRONI D1071/H/B/C/655/10.

42. Senate enquiry, day 10, evidence of Hugh Woolner.

43. Elizabeth Shutes, 'When the "Titanic" Went Down', in Gracie, *Titanic*, p. 253.

44. Mersey enquiry, day 6, evidence of Charles Joughin, QQ 5961–2, 5966.

45. Walter Lord, *A Night to Remember* (1976), p. 97.

46. Mersey enquiry, day 4, evidence of John Poingdestre, QQ 2887–2901.

47. Senate enquiry, day 14, evidence of Berk Trembisky alias Picard.

48. Mersey enquiry, day 9, evidence of John Hart, QQ 9886–7.

49. Ibid., Q 9921.

50. Ibid., QQ 9924–5.

51. Ibid., Q 10076.

52. www.encyclopaedia-titanica.org/titanic-survivor/august-wenner-strom.html (accessed 9 June 2010).

53. *Le Matin*, 19 April 1912; 'Frenchmen's Account: Passengers' Faith in the Ship', *The Times*, 20 April 1912.

54. 'Mr and Mrs Bishop Give First Authentic Interview Concerning Titanic Disaster', *Dowagiac Daily News*, 20 April 1912.

55. 'Bishops Arrive Home and Relate Many Things about Titanic', *Dowagiac Daily News*, 10 May 1912.

56. Senate enquiry, day 18, affidavit of James McGough.

57. 'Lifeboat Not Filled, Karl Behr Declares', *Newark Evening News*, 20 April 1912.

58. 'Dread of Lifeboats by Passengers Told', *Chicago Evening Post*, 23 April 1912.

59. Senate enquiry, day 18, affidavit of Eloise Smith.

60. Duff Gordon, *Discretions*, p. 155.

61. Senate enquiry, day 12, evidence of Mrs J. Stuart White.

62. 'Mrs E. W. Bucknell says Carelessness Cost Many Lives', *Philadelphia Inquirer*, 20 April 1912, 2.

63. Mersey enquiry, day 6, evidence of Charles Joughin, Q 5952.

64. Senate enquiry, day 10, evidence of Hugh Woolner.

65. John Eaton and Charles Haas, *Titanic* (1986), p. 152.

66. 'Tribute to Straus Paid in Synagogues', *New York Times*, 21 April 1912.

67. Butler, *Unsinkable*, p. 123.

68. Mersey enquiry, day 2, evidence of Joseph Scarrott, QQ383, 386.

69. Collyer in Hyslop, Forsyth, Jemima, *Titanic Voices*, p. 135.

70. Ibid., pp. 135–36.

71. Senate enquiry, day 5, evidence of Harold Lowe.

72. 'Irish Survivor's Experience', *Cork Examiner*, 6 May 1912, 5.

73. Senate enquiry, day 13, evidence of Daniel Buckley.

74. 'On the Ship that Never Came Home: the story of how fifteen girls and

boys from the West of Ireland started for America on the Titanic, and how two of them arrived', *Irish Independent*, 9 May 1912, 3.

75. Goldsmith, *Echoes*, pp. 49–50.
76. Senate enquiry, day 10, evidence of Hugh Woolner.
77. Lightoller, *Titanic*, p. 244.
78. Mersey enquiry, day 3, evidence of William Lucas, Q 1817.
79. Mersey enquiry, day 3, evidence of William Lucas, QQ 1785–7.
80. Senate enquiry, day 7, evidence of John Hardy.
81. Senate enquiry, day 10, evidence of Hugh Woolner.
82. Lightoller, *Titanic*, p. 245.
83. Davie, *Titanic*, p. 55.
84. Lightoller, *Titanic*, p. 246.
85. Beesley, *Titanic*, pp. 64–65.
86. Duff Gordon, *Discretions*, p. 156.
87. Senate enquiry, day 13, evidence of Olaus Abelseth.
88. Lightoller, *Titanic*, pp. 247–48.
89. 'Sticks to Titanic Till Last Minute, Continued', *Cleveland Plain Dealer*, 26 April 1912, 3.
90. Gracie, *Titanic*, p. 67.
91. 'Frenchmen's Account', *The Times*, 20 April 1912; 'Heard Death Chorus for over an Hour', *New York Times*, 20 April 1912.
92. 'Wreck of the Titanic – Graphic Story of Mrs Davies', *St Ives Times*, 10 May 1912, 4.
93. 'Titanic Disaster – Hayle Man's Narrative', *St Ives Times*, 3 May 1912.
94. Thayer, *Titanic*, pp. 348–49.
95. Senate enquiry, day 5, evidence of Harold Lowe.
96. Senate enquiry, day 4, evidence of Herbert Pitman.
97. Senate enquiry, day 7, evidence of Thomas Jones.
98. 'Countess Rothes Brave', *New York Times*, 20 April 1912.
99. 'Mrs E.W. Bucknell says Carelessness Cost Many Lives', *Philadelphia Inquirer*, 20 April 1912, 2.
100. Senate enquiry, day 7, evidence of George Hogg.
101. Senate enquiry, day 12, evidence of Mrs J. Stewart White.
102. Butler, *Unsinkable: the full story of the RMS Titanic*, pp. 147–48.
103. Kristen Iversen, *Molly Brown* (1999), pp. 25, 27.

104. Gracie, *Titanic*, pp. 132–34.

105. Senate enquiry, day 13, evidence of Olaus Abelseth.

106. Bisset, *Tramps*, p. 229.

107. Senate enquiry, day 10, evidence of Hugh Woolner.

108. Mersey enquiry, day 2, evidence of Joseph Scarrott, Q 361.

109. Rostron, *Home from Sea*, pp. 67–69, 74.

Fourteen: The Meaning Shows in the Defeated Thing

1. Dreiser, *Traveler at Forty*, pp. 519-23; Jerome Loving, *The Last Titan: a Life of Theodore Dreiser* (2005), pp. 215–16.

2. C. W. Bennett, consular despatch 17 of 19 April 1912, NA FO 369/522.

3. Senate enquiry, day 3, evidence of Philip Franklin.

4. 'Officer Concedes Big Loss of Life', *Cleveland Plain Dealer*, 16 April 1912, 5.

5. 'Titanic Sinking' and 'A Floating Palace', *The Globe*, 15 April 1912, 5.

6. 'Sleeping Passengers', *The Globe*, 16 April 1912, 4.

7. 'The Lost Titanic', *The Globe*, 16 April 1912, 6.

8. Stephanie Barczewski, *Titanic* (2004), p. 221.

9. Bullock, *Andrews*, p. 44.

10. Jean Strouse, *Morgan: American Financier* (1999), p. 643.

11. 'Un Désastre', *Le Matin*, 16 April 1912, 3.

12. 'Consternation in Paris', *Leicester Daily Post*, 17 April 1912, 5; 'Titanic Disaster', *Daily Telegraph*, 18 April 1912, 17.

13. 'Three Italians Shot', *Cornishman*, 25 April 1912, 3.

14. Thayer, *Sinking of Titanic*, p. 356.

15. 'Rayner Puts Blame on Bruce Ismay', *New York Times*, 20 April 1912.

16. 'President Taft Stunned', *New York Times*, 16 April 1912.

17. 'Newspaper Men All Mourn Maj. "Archie" Butt', *Washington Herald*, 19 April 1912.

18. *Letters of Henry Adams*, VI, pp. 535, 536, 538.

19. 'Titanic's Sinking Comes as Shock to Philadelphia', *Philadelphia Inquirer*, 16 April 1912, 3.

20. 'Reading Inquirer's Bulletins of Titanic's Sinking', *Philadelphia Inquirer*, 17 April 1912, 5.

21. '6 Philadelphians Unaccounted For', *Philadelphia Inquirer*, 17 April 1912, 3.

22. 'Stop Press – The Titanic Sunk', *Liverpool Daily Post*, 16 April 1912, 14.

23. 'A Shock to Liverpool', *Liverpool Daily Post*, 17 April 1912, 7.

24. 'Titanic Collides with Iceberg in Mid-Ocean', *Southern Daily Echo*, 15 April 1912, 2.

25. 'Reception of the News at Southampton', *Southern Daily Echo*, 16 April 1912, 2.

26. 'Stricken Southampton', *Southern Daily Echo*, 17 April 1912, 2; 'Southampton Mourning', *Daily Telegraph*, 17 April 1912, 14.

27. Untitled editorial, *Western Morning News*, 18 April 1912.

28. 'Homes of Despair', *Daily Mail*, 19 April 1912, 8.

29. Walter Lord, *The Night Lives On* (1986), p. 13.

30. '1,500 Perish When Titanic Goes to Bottom', *Cleveland Plain Dealer*, 16 April 1912, 1.

31. 'Amazing Scenes in New York', *Southern Daily Echo*, 16 April 1912, 3.

32. *New York Times*, 17 April 1912.

33. 'Hope Vanishes for Safety of Titanic's Missing Passengers', *Cleveland Plain Dealer*, 17 April 1912, 1.

34. Sid Blake, 'The Titanic Disaster: How Brave Cornishmen Died', *Cornishman*, 2 May 1912, 4; Sid Blake, 'The Titanic Disaster: Cornishmen who Died like Heroes', *Hayle Mail*, 2 May 1912, 5.

35. 'Painful Scenes in New York', *Daily Telegraph*, 17 April 1912, 11.

36. 'Haggard Throngs Battle for News', *Cleveland Plain Dealer*, 18 April 1912, 3.

37. Leila Salloum Elias, 'The Impact of the Sinking of the *Titanic* on the New York Syrian community of 1912', *Arab Studies Quarterly* (winter–spring 2005).

38. 'Grief Stricken Crowd Storm the Office and Beg for News', *Philadelphia Inquirer*, 19 April 1912, 9.

39. 'The Titanic Catastrophe', *Leicester Daily Post*, 17 April 1912, 5.

40. Courtenay Bennett, telegram of 16 April 1912, NA FO 369/522.

41. 'Waiting for News', *Daily Telegraph*, 17 April 1912, 12.

42. Diary of Earl Winterton, 16 April 1912, Winterton 11, Bodleian.

43. Arnold Bennett, *Journals 1911–1921* (1932), p. 48.

44. 'At the London Office a Weary Vigil', *Daily Telegraph*, 18 April 1912, 14.

45. Wilfrid Scawen Blunt, *My Diaries 1888–1914*, II (1920), p. 800.

46. Susan Lowndes, *Diaries and Letters of Marie Belloc Lowndes 1911–1947* (1971), p. 31.

47. 'The Monster Ship', *Economist*, 20 April 1912, 836.

48. Senator Porter McCumber, Congressional Record, 19 April 1912, 5306–8.

49. 'Chinese Would Save Men Before Women', *Cleveland Plain Dealer*, 17 April 1912, 5.

50. 'Earl Beauchamp on Heroism', *Worcester Daily Times*, 20 April 1912.

51. *Winston S. Churchill*, companion volume II, part 3 (1969), p. 1542.

52. 'Vessel of Mercy Arrives with Titanic Survivors', *Cleveland Plain Dealer*, 19 April 1912, 7.

53. Wyn Craig Wade, *The Titanic: End of a Dream* (1980), p. 50.

54. Henry Arthur Jones, 'Arrival Scenes on New York Pier', *Daily Telegraph*, 20 April 1912, 15.

55. Homer J. Wheaton, 'Gazette Man on Carpathia's Pier', *Worcester Evening Gazette*, 19 April 1912.

56. 'Joy and Sadness Come With News', *Cleveland Plain Dealer*, 20 April 1912, 1–2.

57. 'Remains in Hope Husband Is Saved', *Cleveland Plain Dealer*, 20 April 1912, 2.

58. 'Special Trains Wait', *Cleveland Plain Dealer*, 19 April 1912, 7.

59. 'All Churches Pay Tribute to Dead of Lost Titanic', *Philadelphia Inquirer*, 22 April 1912, 2.

60. 'Mrs Thayer Felled Sailor, Says Friend', *Philadelphia Inquirer*, 23 April 1912, 2.

61. Blake, 'The Titanic Disaster'.

62. Diary of Margot Asquith, 20 April 1912, Oxford and Asquith papers, Bodleian, Eng d 3209, ff 136–7; Colin Clifford, *The Asquiths* (2002), p. 194.

63. Lord Bonham-Carter and Mark Pottle (eds), *Lantern Slides: the diaries and letters of Violet Bonham Carter 1904–1914* (1996), pp. 312–13.

64. NA COPY/1/566/70.

65. Clément Vautel, 'Propos d'un Parisien', *Le Matin*, 20 April 1912, 1.

66. 'All Due to Greed, Says Parkhurst', *New York Times*, 22 April 1912, 4.

67. 'Southampton's Great Sorrow', *Southern Daily Echo*, 23 April 1912, 2.

68. Alfred Mitchell-Innes, despatch 128 of 1 May 1912, NA FO 369/522.

69. Senate enquiry, day 18, evidence of Imanita Shelley.

70. 'Mr Wallace Hartley', *Colne and Nelson Times*, 24 May 1912, 4.

71. 'Funeral of Mr Wallace Hartley', *Colne and Nelson Times*, 24 May 1912, 7.

72. 'Colonel Gracie Dies, Haunted by Titanic', *New York Times*, 5 December 1912; Gracie, *Titanic*, 250.

73. 'Oh! The Crime Of It!', *Philadelphia Inquirer*, 20 April 1912, 8.

INDEX

Bruce Ismay Making First Trip on Gigantic Ship That Was to Surpass All Others.

The admission that the Titanic, the biggest steamship in the world, had been sunk by an iceberg and had gone to the bottom of the Atlantic, probably carrying more than 1,400 of her passengers and crew with her, was made at the White Star Line offices, 9 Broadway, at 8:20 o'clock last night. Then P. A. S. Franklin, Vice President and General Manager of the International Mercantile Marine, conceded that probably only those passengers who were picked up by the Cunarder Carpathia had been saved. Advices received early this morning tended to increase the number of survivers by 200.

The admission followed a day in which the White Star Line officials had been optimistic in the extreme. At no time was the admission made that every one aboard the huge steamer was not safe. The ship itself, it was confidently asserted, was unsinkable, and inquirers were informed that she would reach port under her own steam probably, but surely with the help of the Allan liner Virginian, which was reported to be towing her.

As the day passed, however, with no new authentic reports from the Titanic or any of the ships which were known to have responded to her wireless call for help, it became apparent that authentic news of the disaster probably could come only from the Titanic's sister ship, the Olympic. The wireless range of the Olympic is 500 miles. That of the Carpathia, the Parisian, and the Virginian is much less, and as they neared the position of the Titanic they drew further and further out of shore range. From the Titanic's position at the time of the disaster it is doubtful if any of the ships except the Olympic could establish communication with shore.

Titanic Sank at 2:20 A. M. Monday.

In the White Star offices the hope was held out all day that the Parisian and the Virginian had taken off some of the Titanic's passengers, and efforts were made to get into communication with these liners. Until such communication was established the White Star officials refused to recognize the possibility that there were none of the Titanic's passengers aboard them.

But by nightfall came the message from Capt. Haddock of the Olympic to Cape Race, Newfoundland, telling of the foundering of the Titanic and of the rescue of 655 of her passengers by the Cunarder Carpathia, which, the wireless message said, reached the position of the Titanic at daybreak. All they found there, however, was lifeboats and wreckage. The biggest ship in the world had sunk at 2:20 o'clock yesterday morning.

Mr. Franklin admitted late last night that the Parisian and the Virginian, though they were among the first to answer the Titanic's calls for help, could not have reached the scene before 10 o'clock yesterday morning, seven and a half hours after the big Titanic buried her nose beneath the waves and pitched downward out of sight. The Carpathia, so the wireless dispatch from Capt. Haddock to Cape Race announced, reached the scene of the Titanic's foundering at daybreak, several

The Lost Titanic Being To

CAPT. E. J. SMITH,
Commander of the Titanic.

hours before the expected arrival of the Virginian and the Parisian.

1,465 Lives Lost First Report.

It is unbelievable, so White Star Line officials were compelled to concede finally, that the Carpathia should have failed to pick up every lifeboat which still floated on the waves. If they failed to pick up more than 655 passengers, it was because the others of the ship's complement had gone with her to the bottom.

But it was not until nearly nightfall that the extent of the disaster was realized. Before that the reassuring nature of the bulletins issued by the White Star line was sufficient to quiet the fears of those who had relatives or friends aboard the unfortunate ship and to prevent widespread belief in a serious disaster.

Capt. Haddock's message from the Olympic, which is printed in another column of THE TIMES, strongly indicated that none but the 655 taken from life boats by the Carpathia had been saved. This message was re-

THE PROBABLE LOSS.	
Number Aboard.	
First cabin............	325
Second cabin............	285
Steerage............	710
Crew, (estimated)............	900
Total............	2,120
Saved.	
By the Carpathia............	866
Probably drowned............	1,254

layed immediately to the White Star offices, but Mr. Franklin positively declined to make the text of the message public. He offered still the hope that passengers were aboard the Parisian and the Virginian, and even when the admission was wrung from him that there seemed little hope of the saving of any others than the 655 aboard the Carpathia, he clung to the hope that in some unexplained way there were other passengers abroad the two Allan liners.

First Reported Titanic in Tow.

Throughout the day there had been reassurances that the Titanic was being towed to port by the Virginian,

Includes Bruce

and when Capt. proved this to be mission was mad offices that the T Franklin said th message was bri say that all the c But the inference passengers had it was that man and presently M the fear that the loss of life on th

This version wireless had been Star offices:

Capt. Haddock a wireless messa offices here that sank at 2:20 A. sengers and crew life boats and th ginian. The ste